Joseph Blenkinsopp
Essays on Judaism in the Pre-Hellenistic Period

Beihefte zur Zeitschrift
für die alttestamentliche
Wissenschaft

Edited by
John Barton, Reinhard G. Kratz, Nathan MacDonald,
Carol A. Newsom and Markus Witte

Volume 495

Joseph Blenkinsopp

Essays on Judaism in the Pre-Hellenistic Period

—

DE GRUYTER

ISBN 978-3-11-047514-2
e-ISBN (PDF) 978-3-11-047687-3
e-ISBN (EPUB) 978-3-11-047529-6
ISSN 0934-2575

Library of Congress Cataloging-in-Publication Data
A CIP catalog record for this book has been applied for at the Library of Congress.

Bibliografische Information der Deutschen Nationalbibliothek
The Deutsche Nationalbibliothek lists this publication in the Deutsche Nationalbibliografie;
detailed bibliographic data are available in the Internet at http://dnb.dnb.de.

© 2017 Walter de Gruyter GmbH, Berlin/Boston
Printing and binding: CPI books GmbH, Leck
♾ Printed on acid-free paper
Printed in Germany

www.degruyter.com

Foreword

These fifteen essays, either published in different formats over the last three decades or previously unpublished, deal with the earliest phase in the history of the Jewish people from the liquidation of the Judaean state in 586 B.C.E. to the Macedonian conquest in 332 B.C.E. This was an axial period in the history of the Near East and the eastern Mediterranean world in general. It witnessed the end of the great Semitic empires, Assyrian and Babylonian; decisive advances in religion with the appeal to a creator-deity in Deutero-Isaiah, Babylonian Marduk theology, and Zoroastrianism; the rise of what can be called the first world empire with the conquests of the Iranian Cyrus II; the Pre-Socratics and the great age of Greek philosophy, art and science. For the Judaean survivors of the Babylonian conquest and the subsequent deportations living in a post-collapse society there was, as always in such a situation, the issue of continuity with the past, with different groups in the land of Judah and the diaspora claiming possession of the traditions without which no society can continue in existence. This was a situation favourable to the emergence of sectarianism the first indications of which can be traced to these two and a half centuries. With the suppression of the national dynasty and, with it, the apparatus of an independent state, the rebuilt temple became the focus and emblem of national and ethnic identity. The essays deal with different aspects of the religious, intellectual and social history of this crucial period.

It is my pleasure to acknowledge and thank those who gave permission to reprint the following essays:

The Society of Biblical Literature of Atlanta, Georgia, USA for permission to reprint

"The Theological Politics of Deutero-Isaiah" from A. Lanzi and J. Stökl (eds.), *Divination, Politics and Near Eastern Empires* (Atlanta: SBL, 2014), 129–43.

"Was the Pentateuch the constitution of the Jewish ethnos in the Persian period?" from J. W. Watts (ed.), *Persia and Torah. The Theory of Imperial Authorization of the Pentateuch* (Atlanta: SBL, 2001), 41–62.

The Catholic Biblical Association and the editor of *Catholic Biblical Quarterly* for permission to reprint: "Deutero-Isaiah and the Creator-Deity: Yahweh, Ahuramazda, Marduk" from "The Cosmological and Protological Language of Deutero-Isaiah", *Catholic Biblical Quarterly* 73 (2011), 433–510.

Eisenbrauns Publishing House, Winona Lake, Indiana, USA for the following:

"Judeans, Jews, Children of Abraham" from O. Lipschits, G. N. Knoppers and M. Oeming (eds.), *Judah and the Judeans in the Achaemenid Period* (Winona Lake, Indiana: Eisenbrauns, 2011), 461–82.

"Ideology and Utopia in 1–2 Chronicles" from E. Ben Zvi and D. V. Edelman (eds.), *What was authoritative for Chronicles?* (Winona Lake, Indiana: Eisenbrauns, 2011), 89–103.

"Jewish Sectarianism from Ezra to the Hasidim" from O. Lipschits, G. N. Knoppers, R. Albertz (eds.), *Judah and the Judeans in the fourth century B.C.E.* (Winona Lake, Indiana: Eisenbrauns, 2007), 385–404.

Sheffield Academic Press, Sheffield, UK for "Temple and Society in Achaemenid Judah" from P. R. Davies (ed.), *Second Temple Studies 1* (Sheffield: Sheffield Academic Press, 1991), 22–55.

T & T Clark International US, an imprint of Bloomsbury Publishing Inc. for "Footnotes to the Rescript of Artaxerxes in Ezra 7:11–26" from P. R. Davies and D. V. Edelman (eds.), *The Historian and the Bible. Essays in Honour of Lester L. Grabbe* (New York & London: T. & T. Clark, 2010), 150–58.

Oxford University Press for "The Nehemiah Autobiographical Memoir" from S. E. Balentine and J. Barton (eds.), *Language, Theology and the Bible. Essays in Honour of James Barr* (Oxford: Clarendon, 1994), 199–212.

The Editor of *Biblica*, Rome, Italy for "The Social Context of "the Outsider Woman" in Proverbs 1–9" from the same title in *Biblica* 72 (1991), 457–73.

The editors of *Journal for the Study of the Old Testament* for "The Social Roles of Prophets in Achaemenid Judah" from: the same title, *Journal for the Study of the Old Testament* 93 (2001), 39–58.

Koninklijke Brill NV, Leiden, Netherlands for "A Case of Benign Imperial Neglect and its Consequences: An Exercize in Virtual History" from J. Cheryl Exum (ed.), *Virtual History and the Bible* (Leiden: Brill, 2000), 129–36.

Overview

Foreword —— V

I. The Theological Politics of Deutero-Isaiah —— 1

II. Deutero-Isaiah and the Creator God: Yahweh, Ahuramazda, Marduk —— 15

III. Judaeans, Jews, Children of Abraham —— 30

IV. Bethel in the Neo-Babylonian and early Achaemenid period —— 48

V. Temple and Society in Achaemenid Judah —— 61

VI. The Intellectual World of Judaism in the Pre-Hellenistic Period —— 84

VII. Was the Pentateuch the constitution of the Jewish ethnos in the Persian period? —— 101

VIII. Footnotes to the rescript of Artaxerxes in Ezra 7:11–26 —— 119

IX. The Nehemiah Autobiographical Memoir —— 132

X. Ideology and Utopia in the book of Chronicles —— 144

XI. The social context of the "Outsider Woman" in Proverbs 1–9 —— 159

XII. Social Roles of Prophets in Early Achaemenid Judah —— 178

XIII. The sectarian element in early Judaism —— 192

XIV. Jewish Sectarianism from Ezra to the Hasidim —— 207

XV. A Case of Benign Imperial Neglect and its Consequences: An Exercize in Virtual History —— 221

Abbreviations —— 227

Bibliography —— 228

Author Index —— 247

Biblical Index —— 251

I. The Theological Politics of Deutero-Isaiah

Source: *Divination, Politics and Near Eastern Empires*, ed. by Alan Lenzi and Jonathan Stökl, 129–43. Atlanta: Society of Biblical Literature, 2014.

1 Prophecy and Politics

The critical consensus is that the term "Deutero-Isaiah" or "Second Isaiah" refers to chapters 40–55 of the book of Isaiah, which is taken to be a distinct, anonymous text which, for reasons and under circumstances not entirely clear, came to be attached to chapters 1–39 which feature a prophet called Isaiah who is referred to in it by name. This historical Isaiah was active in the eighth century BC. during the heyday of the Assyrian empire, while the anonymous author of Isaiah 40–55 lived, spoke, and perhaps also wrote two centuries later, during the last years of the Babylonian empire and the rise of the Persian (Iranian, Achaemenid) empire with the conquests of Cyrus II, who is named in Deutero-Isaiah. This would be about the middle of the sixth century BC. which, in the province of Judah, would correspond to the half-century (give or take a year or two) between the fall of Jerusalem to the Babylonians in 586 and the fall of Babylon to the Persians in 539. This period marks one of the great turning points in the history of the ancient world and also of course in the history of Israel, a period which witnessed the end of the great Semitic empires in the Middle East which will reappear only with the Islamic conquests in the seventh century of the common era.

So much for the title "Deutero-Isaiah." The term "theological politics" should not be unfamiliar, since political activity driven by theological convictions is going on around us all the time, not least in the United States. But it is important to add that politics, including international politics, was a fundamental part of the agenda of Israelite prophecy. The prophets were not primarily mystics, and they have little to say about aspects of personal morality, especially those aspects which come under the rubric of sexual ethics which so preoccupy us today. Their focus was on the condition of society and politics, especially international politics. Here, a quote from Max Weber is to the point: "It must not be forgotten that in the motivation of Israelite prophets social reforms were only means to an end. The primary concern of prophets was with foreign politics, since they constituted the theatre of their god's activity."[1] Hence the frequent intervention of prophets in international affairs. An example from the last days of

---

[1] Max Weber, *Economy and Society* (Berkeley: University of California, 1978), 443.

the kingdom of Judah: the great issue during that critical period was the decision whether to participate in rebellion against the imperial power of Babylon or accept the status quo and make the best of it; a dilemma common to small nations at all times who are confronted with the overwhelming resources and power of empires and superpowers. Combing through the biblical sources for those years prior to the final catastrophe, we can identify distinct parties opposed to and in favour of rebellion, with prophets on both sides. Jeremiah acted as the spokesman and point person for the party which opposed rebellion – the appeasement party as their opponents would have called it – and on the other side Hananiah, a Judaean prophet and opponent of Jeremiah who made a short-term (and therefore risky) prediction that the Babylonians would be finished in two years, which did not happen (Jer 28:1–4). In the Babylonian diaspora two prophets, Ahab and Zedekiah, were put to a horrible death for sedition. They would have been considered martyrs to the cause of resistance in the eyes of their supporters, but were vilified by Jeremiah (Jer 29:21–23).

This was in the years leading to the final catastrophe. The prophecies of Deutero-Isaiah were in circulation, orally, in writing, or both, about three or four decades after the fall of Jerusalem. Cyrus II, king of Anshan in western Iran, was engaged in a string of conquests beginning with the Medes and Elamites, then Parthians, Armenians, Bactrians, all of Asia Minor, the vast regions of Central Asia, and some Greek cities on the western seaboard of Asia Minor, culminating in the conquest of the city of Babylon in October 539 BC. All of these became part of the Persian empire which, in terms of extent, population and organization, can be considered the first world empire. To make the point: the entire Babylonian empire including Judah became one of the twenty-two satrapies of the Persian empire listed by Herodotus.

2 The eclipse of the Davidic dynasty

While this was going on, the survivors of the catastrophe in Judah were engaged in the task of putting their lives back together. It will be hard for those of us who have not had to live through a catastrophic situation to imagine what life was like for the survivors in Judah after the obliterating events of the autumn and winter of 586 BC. The disintegration of the Judaean state and the eclipse of the Davidic dynasty, which held everything together, had already begun with the death of Josiah, the last significant ruler, in 609 BC, and was hastened by the ineptitude or inexperience of the last rulers, three sons and one grandson of Josiah, all in their mid-twenties or teens. With the final conquest, the murder, mayhem, and systematic destruction of property, followed by the deportations,

Judah became what sociologists call a post-collapse society. In that situation, often repeated throughout history down to the very recent present, the survivors had to fall back on whatever resources were available in the household and kinship networks. Sooner or later, questions about why it happened and who was responsible would emerge, and sooner or later they would be directed towards the ancestral deity who, according to one of the psalms, watches over Israel without slumbering or sleeping (Ps 121). Especially painful was the thought that the same deity, after entering into a perpetual covenant with David, had now apparently disowned him by bringing the dynasty to an end. Another hymn makes the complaint:

> You have spurned your anointed one,
> you have rejected him and raged against him,
> you have renounced the covenant with your servant,
> defiled his crown and thrown it to the ground. (Ps 89:39)

The extinction of the dynasty, signalled by the public execution of the children of Zedekiah the last king, after which he was blinded and led shackled into exile, removed the basis, the linchpin, which controlled every aspect of social life. The range of response to the religious crisis precipitated by the extinction of the dynasty and liquidation of the state is reflected in one way or another in practically every biblical text datable to the post-disaster period. One option was to reject the "Yahweh alone" theology established by Josiah and the reform party during his reign and to fall back on "the old religion," the worship of the chthonic gods, the gods of the underworld, and the goddess to whose worship throughout the history of Israel and Judah the abundant archaeological and textual evidence attests. Chapter 44 of the book of Jeremiah has preserved a remarkably vivid cameo of a scene in Egypt to which some of the military leaders and people had fled after the assassination of the Babylonian-appointed ruler of the province, taking Jeremiah with them. Jeremiah is proclaiming once again that the disaster happened because of the people's religious infidelity. In one of the few instances in the Hebrew Bible where women get to talk about religion, some of the women present summarily rejected his explanation for the disaster:

> We are not going to listen to what you tell us. We intend to burn sacrifices to the Queen of Heaven as we used to do, we and our forefathers, our kings and leaders, in the towns of Judah and the streets of Jerusalem. Then we had food in plenty and were content. But from the time we left off burning sacrifices to the Queen of Heaven we have been in great want, and have fallen victims to sword and famine. (Jer 44:16–18)

An alternative explanation for the disaster, therefore. Others who chose to remain faithful to Yahweh and the ancestral traditions would be left with the task of justifying their choice, in the first place to themselves, then to others including those who, as one of the psalms puts it, were asking, "Where now is your God?" (Ps 42:4; 115:2). This is the situation which Deutero-Isaiah is addressing, and to which he will propose a radical alternative as a basis for future restoration.

3 Tokens of faithful love for David (Isaiah 55:1–5)

The only mention of David in Isaiah 40–66, occurs towards the conclusion of Deutero-Isaiah, at the beginning of the last chapter (55:1–5), a passage in which many of the themes which recur throughout the section are recapitulated. Since one of these themes is the future governance of Judah, this one reference to the Davidic dynasty could provide a point of departure for a discussion of the theological politics incorporated in the text.

After the invitation to accept the free gift of food that really nourishes (vv 1–2), the saying continues as follows (vv 3–5):

> Come to me and listen carefully,
> Hear me, and your spirit will revive.
> I shall make a perpetual covenant with you,
> the tokens of faithful love I showed to David
> As I appointed him a witness to peoples,
> so you will summon a nation you do not know,
> and a nation that does not know you will come in haste to you,
> for the sake of your God,
> for the Holy One of Israel who has made you glorious.

The most natural interpretation of this appeal is that God will show you, the prophet's fellow-Judaeans, the same favour he showed David in the past.[2]

---

[2] ḥasdê dāvid, only here and 2 Chr 6:42, parsed as objective genitive in keeping with the context, as Hugh Williamson, "'The Sure Mercies of David': Subjective or Objective Genitive?," *JSS* 23 (1978): 31–49, rather than referring to deeds performed by David, as André Caquot, "Les 'Grâces de David': A Propos d'Isaïe 55,3b," *Sem* 15 (1965): 45–59; Willem Beuken, "Isa. 55.3–5: The Restoration of David," *Bijdragen* 35 (1974): 49–64; Pierre Bordreuil, "Les 'Grâces de David' et I Maccabee ii 57," *VT* 31 (1981): 73–76. That David is the recipient rather than the origin of the tokens of faithful love is the view of most recent commentators, e.g., Norman Whybray, *Isaiah 40–66* (London: Oliphants, 1975), 191; Brevard Childs, *Isaiah: A Commentary* (Louisville: Westminster John Knox Press, 2001), 434–45; Joseph Blenkinsopp, *Isaiah 40–55: A New Translation with In-*

These "tokens of faithful love" imply a guarantee of perpetuity for the Davidic dynasty, as stated in Nathan's oracular pronouncement (2 Sam 7:8–17), and elsewhere (e.g. Ps 89:27–37), in effect a perpetual covenant, as is explicit in 2 Sam 23:5 and implicit in our text. But the commitment made long ago concerning the dynasty has now been reinterpreted, reformulated and transferred to the people as a whole, those addressed by the author who had survived the disaster which swept the dynasty away. The passage continues by applying this insight to international relations, always of decisive significance for small nations, then as now, whose fate was to live in the shadow of great empires. David's relations with foreign nations as overlord and source of the blessings of justice and peace are now reformulated in terms of a new relationship of the people as a whole to the outside world which will bring the author's fellow-Judaeans recognition and honour. Use of the singular, *gôy*, nation, in v 5 (twice) would, in the circumstances, hint at Persia under the rule of Cyrus, a figure overwhelmingly present throughout the first section of Deutero-Isaiah (chapters 40–48). The statement "you will summon a nation you do not know, and a nation that does not know you will come in haste to you" echoes the frequent summons addressed to Cyrus in Isaiah 40–48 (Isa 41:25; 42:6; 45:3,4), even though he does not know Israel's God (45:4–5). In Isa 55:3–5, read in the light of Deutero-Isaiah as a whole, the summons would refer to Cyrus as representative of the nation summoned to act as agent of the God of Israel on the eve of the conquest of Babylon.

The need to rethink the established dogma of the perpetuity of the Davidic dynasty arose from the intractable data of historical experience. The eclipse of the Davidic dynasty, signaled by the public slaughter of the sons of Zedekiah, last of the line, and the dragging of the blinded king into exile (2 Kgs 25:7), had happened within the lifetime of many of the prophet's audience, and perhaps also that of the prophet himself writing during the last years of Babylonian rule. Ps 89 contains one of the most poignant expressions of bewilderment and anguish at the apparently definitive annulment of the covenant by which the permanence of the national dynasty was thought to have been guaranteed. The lament in this psalm has enough in common with the theme and even the language of Isa 55:3–5 to suggest that the author of our text, and of Isaiah 40–55 as a whole, was familiar with it and had it in mind. It is clear nevertheless that the Isaian author goes well beyond the psalmist who can still plead with Yahweh to bear in mind his promises, and can still utter the age-old complaint

---

troduction and Commentary (New York: Doubleday, 2002), 370–71; John Goldingay and David Payne, *Isaiah 40–55: A Critical and Exegetical Commentary*, Vol. 2 (London: T. & T. Clark, 2006), 371–75.

"how long?" (v 47 emended text). For the Isaian author, on the contrary, the dynastic promise has undergone a fundamental reinterpretation. Hence the complete absence of allusion to David and the Davidic dynasty in Deutero-Isaiah either as a historical reality, or the object of hope for the future, or a character in eschatological scenarios, a situation unparalleled in prophetic texts dated to the exilic period.[3] But this situation, remarkable in itself, leaves unaddressed the issue of an acceptable alternative form of governance once the break with the native dynasty is accepted as inevitable. It invites us to ask whether the author of Isaiah 40–55 had his own answer to that question.

4 The historical situation: prospects and options

Any attempt to address this issue must take account of the historical context in which the author of Deutero-Isaiah[4] was active, a context which takes in the period from the end of the dynasty to the time of writing, by broad agreement the last decade of Babylonian rule (ca. 550–539 BC). The final eclipse of the Davidic dynasty occupied the quarter century following the death of Josiah during which four of his descendants, three sons and one grandson, either were helpless to

---

[3] Cf. Jer 17:24–25; 22:1–4; 23:5–6; 30:8–9; 33:14–26; Ezek 34:23–24; 37:24–28; Amos 9:11–12; Mic 5:1–4, and frequently in Isaiah 1–39 (9:1–6; 11:1–9; 16:5). Taking in this broader view makes it difficult to accept the more benign alternative that the promise to David is now to be shared with all the people rather than transferred to them, as Walter Kaiser, "The Unfailing Kindnesses Promised to David: Isaiah 55:3," *JSOT* 45 (1989): 41–98.

[4] Use of the term "author" calls for explanation. Without attempting to argue the case in detail, I am assuming a basic thematic unity throughout chapters 40–55 and must confess to some hesitation with regard to recent attempts to section the work into layers, assigning dates to each. This seems to me to be especially the case with passages which ostensibly, in the context, refer to Cyrus II and have been generally so understood, but are redated to the reign of Darius I. I have in mind the dividing up of Isa 45:1–7, the primary Cyrus text, in the redactional *tour de force* of Reinhard Kratz, *Kyros im Deuterojesaja-Buch: Redaktionsgeschichtliche Untersuchungen zu Entstehung und Theologie von Jes 40–55* (Tübingen: Mohr Siebeck, 1991), but also of the older study of Jean Vincent, *Studien zur literarischen Eigenart und zur geistigen Heimat von Jesaja Kap. 40–55* (Frankfurt am Main: Peter Lang, 1977) and, more recently, Odil Hannes Steck, "Israel und Zion: Zum Problem konzeptioneller Einheit und literarischer Schichtung in Deuterojesaja" in his collected essays *Gottesknecht und Zion: Gesammelte Aufsätze zu Deuterojesaja* (Tübingen: Mohr Siebeck, 1992), 173–207; also Ulrich Berges, *Das Buch Jesaja: Komposition und Endgestalt* (Freiburg: Herder, 1998), 322–413. On the need for a less drastic approach to *Redaktionsgeschichte* see the remarks of Hans-Jürgen Hermisson, "Einheit und Komplexität Deuterojesajas: Probleme der Redaktionsgeschichte von Jes 40–55" in *The Book of Isaiah. Le Livre d'Isaïe: Les Oracles et leurs Relectures*, ed. Jacques Vermeylen (Leuven: University Press/Peeters, 1989), 286–312.

prevent the liquidation of the Judaean state or, by their ineptitude, contributed to it. The public execution of the male children of Zedekiah, last of the four (2 Kgs 25:6–7) was a deliberate act aimed at finally extinguishing the dynasty and, with it, any hope of independence for "the rebellious city harmful to kings and provinces" (Ezra 4:15). There was, however, still one surviving representative of the dynasty, the exiled Jehoiachin. An appendix to the Deuteronomistic History records that in the first year of his reign, therefore 562/561 BC, Amel Marduk (written dysphemistically as Evil-Merodach in 2 Kgs 25:27) granted amnesty to Jehoiachin and gave him a pre-eminent position among other exiled rulers at the Babylonian court (2 Kgs 25:27–30). It looks as if Jehoiachin was being groomed to return to Jerusalem as a client ruler; a move perhaps inspired by anxiety about the expansionist operations of Pharaoh Ahmose II in the western reaches of the Babylonian empire. But if this was the plan it came to nothing, since Amel-Marduk was assassinated a few months later by his brother Neriglissar. Jehoiachin therefore died in Babylon after all, as predicted by Jeremiah (Jer 22:26). At the time of the composition of Deutero-Isaiah this was very recent history.

In retrospect, it must have seemed to many contemporaries who had survived the terrible half-century since the death of Josiah as if that tragic event marked, in effect, the end of the line for the dynasty. This would have made it easier to accept the transfer of the promises to David from the dynasty to the people as a whole. The same view is expressed in a more subtle way in the Chronicler's rewritten version of Josiah's death and obsequies (2 Chr 35:20–27). The latter concludes, uniquely, with a memorial lament which reads like a lament for the Davidic house as a whole and, with it, the passing of an entire way of life.

In surveying this half-century of turmoil we can detect the emergence of different points of view on what kind of future was possible and tolerable in the absence of the native dynasty and the overwhelming presence of imperial power represented by the Babylonians and, in prospect, the Persians. To these points of view corresponded parties with conflicting views on the fundamental issue of acquiescence in or active opposition to imperial rule in its different forms. The appointment of Gedaliah over the province sharpened the issue and raised the stakes on the conflicts about a future without the dynasty (2 Kgs 25:22–26; Jer 40:1–41:18). This would be especially the case if, as I would argue, Gedaliah was appointed as client king, since he was certainly not of Davidic descent. It would also make it easier to appreciate the reticence of the biblical accounts of his appointment, as also his assassination by a certain Ishmael who was, or claimed to be, of Davidic descent (*mizzera' hammělûkâ*, Jer 41:1).

The biblical account of the situation is obviously incomplete, but the biblical texts have much to say about Jeremiah and the Shaphanids on the one hand and, on the other, policies pursued by the last Davidic rulers and their supporters, especially their determination to participate in revolts. Prominent among these supporters were those referred to as the ʿam hāʾāres. It is accepted that this designation can mean different things in different epochs and situations. In the last decades of the Judaean monarchy it connotes a distinctly identifiable group with a nationalistic and pro-dynastic program. It was this group which put both Josiah and his successor Jehoahaz on the throne (2 Kgs 21:24; 23:30), who were among the most dedicated in support of the native dynasty and the pursuit of national independence, and who were distinctive enough for sixty of them to be picked out and executed by the Babylonians after the fall of Jerusalem (2 Kgs 25:19). Nationalistic prophets in both Judah (Jer 28:1–17) and the Babylonian diaspora (Jer 29:1–32) shared the same views. This party conflict in the last phase of the kingdom of Judah may be reflected in the final chapter of the Deuteronomistic History. It seems likely that it originally ended with the definitive statement that "Judah went into exile out of its land" (2 Kgs 25:21) rather than with the inconsequential bit of information with which it concludes in its present form (2 Kgs 25:30).[5] If this is so, two appendices must have been added. The first is the account of the appointment of Gedaliah, his assassination, and an exodus en masse to Egypt to avoid the anticipated Babylonian reprisal (2 Kgs 25:22–26). The second, which holds out a sliver of hope for a future restoration, records the rehabilitation of Jehoiachin by Amel Marduk and therefore must have been added before the assassination of the latter in 560 BC.[6] All of this is in sharp contrast to the conclusion of Chronicles where the focus is no longer on the national dynasty but on Cyrus as the divinely inspired agent of Yahweh (2 Chr 36:22–23). And with Cyrus we return to DI and its author's answer to the questions of his own day.

---

[5] Recent discussion in Thomas Römer, *La Première Histoire d'Israël: L'Ecole Deutéronomiste* (Fribourg: Labor et Fides, 2006), 152.
[6] The situation is more complex for those who argue for a Josian edition of the history concluding with the statement about the incomparability of Josiah in 2 Kgs 23:25: "Before him there was no king like him who turned to Yahweh with all his heart and soul and strength, according to all the law of Moses". After experiencing the four, or maybe five rulers who followed him, a later scribe has added: "nor did any like him arise after him," followed by a statement in which Yahweh rejects Judah, Jerusalem and its temple (23:25b–27). The general sense seems to be that the dynasty ended, in effect, with Josiah. For a summary account of the double redaction theory, together with competing views of the "Cross school" and the "Göttingen school", see Albert de Pury and Thomas Römer, *Israël Construit son Histoire: L'Historiographie Deutéronomiste la Lumière des Recherches Récentes* (Geneva: Labor et Fides, 1996), 46–58.

5 Cyrus as divinely-inspired and divinely-appointed successor to the Davidic dynasty

In chapters 40–48, the first major section of Deutero-Isaiah,[7] Cyrus is destined to be the principal agent of national rehabilitation and restoration for Judaean communities in Judah and the diaspora. Karl Budde stated this very clearly many years ago: "Cyrus stands at the very centre of the prophet's world view"[8] He is the one who will defeat Judah's enemies, Babylon in the first place,[9] impose an international order based on justice and peace (42:1–4),[10] allow, even facilitate, the repatriation of those forcibly deported (42:7; 45:13), and make possible the rebuilding of Jerusalem and its temple (44:28; 45:13). These tasks are to be discharged under the direct inspiration of Yahweh, Israel's king.[11] Such expectations would not have seemed unreasonable in view of propaganda of the kind disseminated in the Cyrus Cylinder text published within a year of the fall of Babylon. In the second half of this manifesto Cyrus, speaking in his own name, claimed to have restored the gods of subject peoples to their original sanctuaries and permitted their devotees to return to their native lands.[12] Most commentators conclude that Deutero-Isaiah, or the greater part

---

[7] On the structural and thematic distinction between chapters 40–48 and 49–55 see Joseph Blenkinsopp, *Isaiah 40–55*, 73–74.

[8] Cited in Max Haller, "Die Kyros-Lieder Deuterojesajas," in *ΕΥΧΑΡΙΣΤΗΡΙΟΝ: Studien zur Religion und Literatur des Alten und Neuen Testaments*, ed. Hans Schmidt (Göttingen: Vandenhoeck & Ruprecht, 1923), 261.

[9] Isa 41:1–5, 25–29; 43:14; 45:1–7, 13; 46:11; 48:14–16.

[10] The nature of the commission mandated in 42:1–4, that of imposing an international order based on justice (*mišpāṭ*, occurring three times in this short passage), is the function of a ruler not of a prophet or priest. It has several of the features of a royal installation ritual, cf. Ps 2, 72, 110. The identification of the 'ebed in 42:1–4 with Cyrus has often been argued or assumed, e. g., Max Haller, "Die Kyros-Lieder des Deuterojesaja", 262–63; Sydney Smith, *Isaiah Chapters XL–LV: Literary Criticism and History* (London: Humphrey Milford; Oxford: Oxford University Press, 1944), 54–57; Sigmund Mowinckel, *He That Cometh: The Messiah Concept in the Old Testament and Later Judaism* (Oxford: Blackwell, 1959), 189–91. It should be added that since the book of Isaiah has been the object of a continuous and cumulative process of reinterpretation, this first of Duhm's servant passages could have been reapplied to other figures at a later time. See Joseph Blenkinsopp *Isaiah 40–55*, 209–12.

[11] Isa 41:21; 43:15; 44:6. With the verb *hā 'îr*, "stir up", "inspire" in Isa 41:2, 25; 45:13; cf. 2 Chr 36:22; Ezra 1:1.

[12] The relevant statements correspond to lines 32–33 of the Cylinder, see the translation in *ANET* 315–16. It is acknowledged, however, that this is propaganda probably emanating from Babylonian priests hostile to Nabonidus, and that Persian policy vis-à-vis subject peoples was not significantly different from that of their imperial predecessors. See, inter alios, Robartus van der Spek, "Did Cyrus the Great Introduce a New Policy towards Subdued Nations?," *Persica*

of it, was composed before the promulgation of this text, some time between 550 and 538. However, pro-Persian propaganda would have been in circulation during the last years of the reign of Nabonidus, probably disseminated by Marduk priests offended by Nabonidus' neglect of the *akitu* festival and his other impieties, and the author or authors of Deutero-Isaiah could have become acquainted with it at that time.

On the assumption that whoever wrote Isa 40–48 had a particular form of governance in mind for the immediate future, we must go on to ask in what capacity Cyrus was to fulfil this commission assigned to him by Yahweh. I will argue that this prophet is attempting to persuade his public that Yahweh is now bringing about a new dispensation in which Cyrus, as Yahweh's agent, will take over the succession to the now defunct Davidic dynasty, warranted by an authority which transcends by far descent through the male line, namely, direct divine inspiration not only of the prophetic author but of Cyrus himself.[13] Since this solution called for abandoning beliefs long cherished together with aspirations for political autonomy, we can appreciate that many of the hearers would be predisposed to reject the message. An earlier commentator put this is even stronger terms: "If Cyrus was the anointed of YHWH, he had taken the place of the line of David, and had become the true king of Judah [...]. The consequence, equally inevitable, of this proclamation of Cyrus must have been that the prophet would seem to some of his own people a traitor, worthy of death."[14] Hence the weight attached to prophetic authority in Deutero-Isaiah, validated by the Deuteronomistic verification-falsification theory (Deut 18:21–22), in other words, the fulfillment of earlier predictions.[15] Hence also the repeated emphasis on the cosmic power of the deity who sponsors and guarantees the truth of the prophet's message.[16] These recurring themes testify to the earnestness of the prophet's claim to a hearing while at the same time betraying an implicit acknowledgment of the likelihood of rejection. One indication of the latter may

---

10 (1982): 278–83; Amélie Kuhrt, "The Cyrus Cylinder and Achaemenid Imperial Policy," *JSOT* 25 (1983): 83–97.
13 The verb (*hā ʿîr > ʿr*) can have a meaning analogous to prophetic inspiration, with reference to the Servant of the Lord (Isa 50:4), Zerubbabel and Joshua (Hag 1:14), and diaspora Jews (Ezra 1:5). I take it that this is the sense in which Cyrus is said to be inspired (Isa 41:2, 25; 45:13; also 2 Chr 36:22; Ezra 1:1).
14 Sydney Smith, *Isaiah Chapters XL–LV*, 74.
15 Isa 41:22–23, 25–29; 44:7–8, 26–28; 48:3–5, 16b.
16 Isa 40:12–14, 21, 26, 28; 42:5; 45:7, 12, 18; 48:13. See Joseph Blenkinsopp, "The Cosmological and Protological Language of Deutero-Isaiah," *CBQ* 73 (2011): 493–510.

be detected in the prophet's gradually increasing exasperation at the failure of those addressed to accept the message.[17]

That this is the author's political solution to the current crisis is supported by the complete silence of Deutero-Isaiah on David, the Davidic dynasty, and its destiny, with the exception of the passage cited at the head of this essay. It can also be deduced more directly from the titles assigned to Cyrus. These include such familiar designations as "servant" (*ʿebed*) and "shepherd" (*roʿeh*) which encapsulate the millennial Mesopotamian ideal of the just ruler and are likewise part of the Davidic titulature.[18] If the first of the four Duhmian *Ebedlieder* (42:1–4), with the following comment (42:5–9), was *at that time* referred to Cyrus, as proposed earlier, it could imply a commissioning of the Persian ruler as Yahweh's royal servant and a presentation of him in that capacity to the people. Isa 42:1–4 reads, in fact, like a solemn verbatim report of a ceremony of installation in office. The idea behind the ruler as servant is not, or at least not primarily, that he is in to serve his people, but that he is to function in the service of the deity who commissioned him and whose will he is to implement. Whereas according to the Cylinder text Cyrus is commissioned by and acts in the name of Marduk, in our text he is the servant of Yahweh. An inscription from the Abu-Habba collection in the British Museum from the reign of Nabonidus refers to Marduk who "aroused Cyrus, king of Anshan, his young servant," who then went on to defeat the Medes.[19] The metaphor of shepherding, on the other hand, tempers the image of absolute royal power with a concern for justice and care for society's losers and outcasts (Isa 40:11–12). As a metaphor for just and equitable rule, it features in royal annals throughout Mesopotamian history, for example, with reference to Hammurapi and Ashurbanipal. As shepherd, therefore, Cyrus will see to the well-being of the prophet's defeated and dispirited fellow-Judaeans, the rebuilding of Jerusalem, and the restoration of the ruined cities of Judah (Isa 44:28).

The most striking of these titles attached to the native dynast in several texts,[20] and to Cyrus in Deutero-Isaiah, is *māšîaḥ*, "anointed one":

---

[17] Isa 42:18–25; 43:22–28; 45:9–13; 46:8–13; 48:1–11.
[18] David as the servant of YHWH in 2 Sam 3:18; 1 Kgs 8:24–26; 2 Kgs 19:34; Jer 33:21–22, 26.
[19] Text in Paul-Alain Beaulieu, *The Reign of Nabonidus King of Babylon 556–539 BC* (New Haven & London: Yale University Press, 1989), 108. Several scholars have noted parallels between this text and Deutero-Isaiah.
[20] E. g. I Sam 2:10, 35; 2 Sam 19:22; 22:51; 23:1 and often in Psalms; Lam 4:20 is particularly poignant and relevant to the situation addressed by Deutero-Isaah: "YHWH's anointed, the breath of our life, was taken in their traps, although we had thought to live among the nations, secure under his shadow."

This is what Yahweh says about his anointed one, about Cyrus:

"I have grasped him by his right hand
to beat down nations before him,
depriving kings of their strength;
to open doors before him,
with no gates closed to him" (45:1)

Commentators have experienced problems with the text and syntax of this verse, quite apart from the question whether *lĕkôreš* should be elided as an interpolation.[21] There is therefore more than one way of translating the verse, but the translation offered above is defensible. Anointing is an important element in ceremonies of installation in the office of kingship, in Judah as elsewhere in the Near East, and such a ceremony may be alluded to in the passage which the statement cited above introduces (Isa 45:1–7). In this ceremony the deity addresses the king-designate directly, as here and in Ps 2:7–9, and presents him to the assembly, as in Isa 42:1–4. Other features – holding him by the hand (v 1, also 42:6), calling him by name (vv 3 and 4), giving him a title or throne name (v 4), ending, perhaps, with an allusion to investiture (v 5 verb *'zar*) – are familiar features of the practice and ideology of royalty in the ancient Near East. Several of them appear on the Cyrus Cylinder with reference to Cyrus as appointee of the imperial Babylonian deity Marduk, and all are familiar from the language of the Babylonian court.[22]

---

[21] On these issues see Karl Elliger, *Deuterojesaja 40,1–45,7* (Neukirchen-Vluyn: Neukirchener Verlag, 1978), 481–503; Claus Westermann, *Isaiah 40–66: A Commentary* (Philadelphia: Westminster, 1969), 152–55.162; Joseph Blenkinsopp, *Isaiah 40–55*, 243–45; John Goldingay and David Payne, *Isaiah 40–55: A Critical And Exegetical Commentary*, Vol. 2 (London: T. & T. Clark, 2006), 17–22. Few have followed Charles Cutler Torrey, *The Second Isaiah: A New Interpretation* (New York: Charles Scribner's Sons, 1928), 42.357 and James Smart, *History and Theology in Second Isaiah* (Philadelphia: Westminster, 1965), 115–34 who, for quite different reasons, deleted *lĕkôreš* as an interpolation. Klaus Baltzer, *Deutero-Isaiah: A Commentary* (Minneapolis: Fortress, 2001), 223, agrees that it is interpolated but adds rather mysteriously that Deutero-Isaiah was the interpolator.

[22] Discussion of parallels in Isaiah 40–55 with Babylonian *Hofstil* go back all the way to the much-cited article of Rudolph Kittel, "Cyrus und Deuterojesaja," *ZAW* 18 (1898): 149–62. Kittel argued that the close parallels, even in wording, between Marduk's relation to Cyrus in the Cylinder and YHWH's relation to the same monarch in Deutero-Isaiah cannot be explained by direct dependence either way but only by familiarity on the part of Deutero-Isaiah with the traditional and stereotypical language of the Babylonian court. In the almost equally-cited article, "II Isaiah and the Persians," *JAOS* 83 (1963): 415–21, Morton Smith, while not questioning the parallels, proposed that the DI author could have drawn on pro-Persian propaganda disseminated among Jewish expatriates in Babylon before the fall of the city.

6 The international context of the prophet's endorsement of Cyrus

The prophet's endorsement of Cyrus is rendered more intelligible by what happened in the aftermath of the fall of Babylon in 539 BC. The Cylinder text states the claim of Cyrus to be king of Babylon as legitimate successor of Nabonidus, a claim justified by sponsorship on the part of Marduk, imperial god of Babylon. Marduk was angry with Nabonidus, looked for a replacement, chose Cyrus, and commanded him to take the city and restore the traditional cult.[23] Cyrus was therefore given religious legitimation as successor to the last Babylonian king. Towards the end of the Cylinder text, Cyrus reports the discovery of an inscription of Ashurbanipal whom he describes as "a king who preceded me", that is, as king of Babylon.[24] One of the titles of Cyrus which appears on contemporary inscriptions is therefore "king of Babylon, king of the lands" (šar babili šar m tāti).[25] His succession to the discredited Nabonidus, and therefore also to the illustrious Nebuchadnezzar II, was thus accepted as legitimate, at least by the Marduk priesthood, on the theological grounds of their god's sponsorship. After the conquest, Cyrus restored the akitu spring festival in Marduk's esagila sanctuary, neglected by Nabonidus, and confirmed his claim to the throne by presiding over the festival, a circumstance which could lead to reflection on the Persian attitude to the Jerusalem temple as emblematic of and instrumental in imperial control of Judah. (One indication of the new function of the Jerusalem temple, viewed from the Persian perspective, is the requirement that prayers for the royal family in Susa be incorporated into the temple liturgy, Ezra 6:9–10). It was the rejection of this *religious* legitimation of Persian succession to the Babylonian throne which led to the dynastic revolt of Nidintu-Bel who claimed, perhaps truthfully, to be the son of Nabonidus and heir to the great Nebuchadnezzar II. A second Babylonian dynastic revolt followed shortly afterwards led by a certain Arkha, referred to as an Armenian but of obscure antecedents, who was crowned in Babylon as Nebuchadnezzar IV, and whose revolt was suppressed towards the end of 521 BC.[26]

---

23 *ANET* 315.
24 Amélie Kuhrt, "The Cyrus Cylinder and Achaemenid Imperial Policy," 88; *The Persian Empire: A Corpus of Sources from the Achaemenid Period* (London & New York: Routledge, 2007), 72.
25 Muhammad Dandamaev, *Persien unter den ersten Achämeniden* (Wiesbaden: Dr. Ludwig Reichert Verlag, 1976), 96–100; *A Political History of the Achaemenid Empire* (Leiden: Brill, 1989), 54–56.
26 The primary source is the Bisitun inscription (columns I 77 – II 5; IV 28 – 29). Cuneiform texts dated to the autumn of 521, during the brief reign of Arkha-Nebuchadnezzar IV, have come to

A similar pattern emerged after the conquest of Egypt by Cambyses in 525 BC. Cambyses assumed the throne as legitimate successor to the last of the Saitic Pharaohs, Psammeticus III or, since the latter's reign was short and insignificant, that of his predecessor Amasis (570–526 BC). As such, he was accepted as the founder of the twenty-seventh dynasty, and is addressed in those terms in the autobiographical inscription of the Egyptian notable Udjahorresnet.[27]

Jerusalem, however, was not Babylon, one of the nodal points in the Achaemenid empire, nor was it Memphis. Deutero-Isaiah's argument for legitimation was of the same kind, but it was evident that Cyrus would rule over Judah neither in his own person nor through a native appointed as a client king, but through a provincial governor who would answer to the satrap of Babylon-Transeuphrates. Perhaps the memory of the convulsive events following on the death of Josiah excluded the more accommodating option of relative autonomy under a native ruling as client king, even if a suitable candidate had been available.

A final note. The prophet's acceptance of the legitimacy of empire was not unconditional. It was contingent in the first place on Jewish communities under Persian rule being left free to worship in their own way and in their own place of worship, and to conduct undisturbed their own religious practices. In this respect it anticipates the situation described in the opening chapters of the book of Daniel in which Daniel and his companions exist for the most part peaceably in the Babylonian empire, profit by the educational opportunities available, serve at the imperial court, and can even rise to high office. They do so, however, while observing strictly the dietary laws and the customary prayers and refusing to worship other deities. Deutero-Isaiah's theological politics were radical in contemplating, for the first time, the possibility of a future without the apparatus of a nation state including a native dynasty, and in pointing the way to living in an almost inconceivably larger world, the world created by the vast Persian empire, under the providence of a God whose concerns exceeded the limits of nation and ethnic group.

---

light in southern Mesopotamia; see Amélie Kuhrt, "Babylonia from Cyrus to Xerxes," in CAH 4^2 (1988), 129–30. See also Herodotus III 150–160 who, however, is not well informed on the reign of Darius I.

27 Muhammad Dandamaev, *A Political History of the Achaemenid Empire* (Leiden: Brill, 1989), 76–78; Joseph Blenkinsopp, "The Mission of Udjahorresnet and Those of Ezra and Nehemiah," *JBL* 106 (1987): 409–21.

II. Deutero-Isaiah and the Creator God: Yahweh, Ahuramazda, Marduk

Source: "The Cosmological and Protological Language of Deutero-Isaiah." *CBQ* 73 (2011): 493–510.

1 Creation in Deutero-Isaiah

The unprecedented frequency with which Deutero-Isaiah refers to Yahweh as creator of the world and cosmic deity and, as such, incomparable, seems to call for an explanation. I use the familiar term "Deutero-Isaiah," but in fact cosmological and protological language is limited to the first of the two sections in Isaiah 40–55, namely, chapters 40–48,[1] in keeping with the distinctive character of these chapters over against chapters 49–55. Not only is the language of creation absent from 49–55, including the key verb *bārā'*, "create,"[2] but we hear no more about Cyrus and the expectations raised by his victorious campaigns, a key issue throughout 40–48. In chapters 49–55 the tone is different, the emotional and affective level much lower. If there is to be a reversal of fortune, it can no longer be expected from Cyrus or any other human agency but only from direct divine intervention. The difference between the two sections also shows up in the treatment of the servant theme. With due allowance for the wide range of opinion on this issue, it seems that in 40–48, with the exception of 42:1–4, first of the four *Ebedlieder* of Bernhard Duhm, the emphasis is on the servant status of the people, while in 49–55 the profile of an individual bearer of the servant mission is unmistakable. This does not oblige us to postulate different authors, or even different locations,[3] but there can be little doubt

---

[1] Isa 40:12–14, 21–22, 26, 28; 41:3–4; 42:5; 43:10–13; 44:24; 45:7, 9–12, 18; 48:12–13.
[2] Yahweh is named *'ĕlōhê kol-hā'āreṣ*, "God of all the earth," but not in a creation context (Isa 54:5). The call to Yahweh to take up arms once again against the forces of evil represented as malevolent monsters, denizens of the Abyss (Rahab, Tannin, Yamm), Isa 51:9–11, adopts the Canaanite combat myth but without any necessary connection with creation. The only allusion in these chapters to anything in Genesis 1–11 is the reference in 54:9 to the aftermath of the great deluge (Gen 9:8–17).
[3] The location issue is surveyed comprehensively by Hans Magnus Barstad, *The Babylonian Captivity of the Book of Isaiah: "Exilic" Judah and the Provenance of Isaiah 40–55* (Oslo: Novus Forlag, 1997). Among the early proponents of a location in Babylonia for chapters 40–48 and in Judah for 49–55 are Samuel Davidson, *An Introduction to the Old Testament: Critical*,

that we are hearing about a situation dramatically different from the one to which the previous nine chapters are responding. The picture might have to be redrawn somewhat if we were to accept the existence of multiple redactional strata in these chapters, but the arguments adduced to date in favour of this more complex scenario are not, in my view, particularly persuasive.

Confining our attention, therefore, to Isaiah 40–48, the question to be posed is the following: Why do we find this concentration of language about creation *for the first time* in the circumstances of that time and place? A preliminary indication of the situation would be the occurrence of the verb *bārā'* with reference to the creation of the world and humanity. This verb occurs forty-eight times in the Hebrew Bible. Of these, thirty-seven allude to the origins of the world or of humanity: eleven in the P source in Genesis 1–11, fourteen in Isaiah 40–48, and in the rest of Isaiah only three, all in the passage which predicts the creation of new heavens, new earth, and new Jerusalem, and therefore looks to the future rather than the past (Isa 65:17–18). Of the remaining nine, four are in psalms which cannot be dated with assurance (Ps 89:13,48; 104:30; 148:5), but in any case only one of the four (Ps 148) has any cosmic resonance. Two occur in the poem about the king of Tyre in Eden, a special case which relates to Gen 2:4b–3:24 but with no cosmic overtones (Ezek 28:13,15), and one in the first of the three doxological hymn stanzas in Amos. The date of these three passages (4:13, 5:8–9, 9:5–6) is disputed but there are serious grounds for considering all of them to be interpolations. Another instance, Mal 2:10, is clearly later than Deutero-Isaiah, and the remaining example, Deut 4:32, occurs in a homily or discourse of Moses (4:1–40) which is either exilic or post-exilic.

It is accepted that questions of this kind cannot be decided on the basis of the incidence of one term, however significant. Creator deities are attested in the Near East and Levant long before the Neo-Babylonian period. On the basis of Ugaritic titulary it has been argued that Yahweh, assimilated to the Canaanite-Jebusite deity El Elyon, is designated a creator-deity in Gen 14:18–24, the encounter of Abraham with Melchizedek, by means of the epithet *qōnēh šāmayim wā'āres*, "creator of heaven and earth" (Gen 14:19,22).[4] The translation of the verb is, however, quite uncertain. A glance at a concordance will show that its

---

Historical and Theological, Vol. 3 (London: Williams & Norgate, 1863), 57–59 and Carl Heinrich Cornill, *Einleitung in das Alte Testament* (Freiburg im Breisgau, 1892), 150–54.
4 On the Ugaritic provenance of the title see Frank Moore Cross, *Canaanite Myth and Hebrew Epic: Essays in the History of the Religion of Israel* (Cambridge/Mass: Harvard University Press, 1973), 15–16, 50–51, n. 20 and 25, and Claus Westermann, *Genesis 12–36* (Neukirchen-Vluyn: Neukirchener Verlag, 1981), 193 = *Genesis 12–36: A Commentary,* Transl. John Scullion (Minneapolis: Augsburg Fortress, 1985), 205–6.

normal meaning is "to acquire," by purchase or other means. With Yahweh as subject it retains this meaning elsewhere: acquisition by ransom: Exod 15:16, Isa 11:11 and Ps 74:2, or by conquest: Ps 78:54, with reference to David's conquest of Jerusalem. However it is translated, the only occurrence of the verb with any protological implications is the opening statement of the much-debated self-description of Wisdom in Prov 8:22, "Yahweh established me (*qānānî*) as the beginning of his work").[5]

Practically the only other affirmation of Yahweh as creator deity occurs in the account of one of Jeremiah's symbolic actions performed in the first year of the reign of Zedekiah, last king of Judah, according to which the necessity of submission to Nebuchadnezzar is reinforced by Yahweh's affirmation that "with my great power and outstretched arm I made the earth, with the people and animals on it, and (therefore) I give it to whomsoever I please" (Jer 27:5). Commentators have not been slow to notice the parallelism between Nebuchadnezzar, described in the same passage as Yahweh's servant (27:6), and Cyrus, Yahweh's anointed one (Isa 45:1), and the political purpose which the affirmation is made to serve. There is a serious probability, therefore, that the reference to creation in Deut 27:5 derives from the same milieu as Isaiah 40–48.

2 Isaiah 40–48 and Genesis 1

What in any case is unprecedented in Isaiah 40–48 is the centrality of the creation theme and the cosmic scope of action assigned to Yahweh over and above his relations with Israel. Repeatedly throughout these chapters the creative activity of Israel's God is celebrated. He created the vault of the sky spread out like a tent or curtain, the heavenly bodies, the circle of the earth rising out of the cosmic waters and resting on piles driven down through the waters, and its inhabitants animated and sustained by the breath of life. These features inevitably raise the question of the relation of Isaiah 40–48 to the Priestly (P) creation narrative in Gen 1:1–2:3a. From early days mainline critical opinion has placed the P history in the post-disaster period, in the sixth or fifth century BC, allowing therefore for a broad margin of error.[6] In recent decades the tendency has

---

[5] Hence Edward Lipiński, "קנה" in *TDOT* 13 (2004), 62–63 is justified in rejecting the meaning "creator" in Gen 14:19,22 in favor of "proprietor" or "lord" of heaven and earth which, as he points out, has the support of Targum Onkelos and1QapGen as against LXX *ektisen*.

[6] To cite only some of the standard works: Otto Eissfeldt, *Einleitung in das Alte Testament* (2nd ed., Tübingen: Mohr Siebeck, 1956), 246–47 = *The Old Testament: An Introduction*, Transl. Peter Ackroyd (Oxford: Blackwell, 1956), 207; Georg Fohrer, *Einleitung in das Alte Testament* (Heidel-

been to argue for a later rather than earlier point in this broad span of time, in the early decades of Persian rule.⁷ This seems to me to be correct. The sanctuary is thematic at key junctures in the P history beginning with cosmos as temple, the subtext of the P creation narrative, then the detailed account of the construction of the wilderness sanctuary (Exod 25 – 27, 35 – 40), and, finally, its establishment after the arrival of the Israelites in Canaan (Josh 18:1). This structural and thematic feature seems to insinuate a connection with the second temple, either before or after its construction, therefore a date in the early Achaemenid period.⁸

In support of this later date I would also cite the P version of Abraham's journey from Mesopotamia to Canaan and the account of his relations with the indigenous peoples, especially in the matter of land ownership. The delicacy and prudent care displayed in his relations with the indigenous population suggest that he is being presented as a model for those who were planning to return, or actually did return, to Judah during the same period.⁹ A further indication can be found in the stories about Israel's ancestors in which the prediction that kings will arise among the descendants of Abraham and Jacob is found only in the P narrative strand (Gen 17:6, 16; 35:11). It is difficult, though perhaps not impossible, to conclude that such hopes could be entertained after the disappearance from the record of Zerubbabel, a scion of the royal line, in the early years of the reign of Darius I. In Isaiah 40 – 48 aspirations focus on return from the diaspora (43:5 etc), the restoration of Jerusalem and the other Judaean cities (44:26; 45:13), and the rebuilding of the Jerusalem temple (44:28). Nothing is said about the possible restoration of the native dynasty; on the contrary, the designation of Cyrus as Yahweh's anointed one at Isa 45:1 suggests an acceptance of the Persian

---

berg: Quelle & Meyer, 1965), 201 – 2 = *Introduction to the Old Testament*, Transl. David Green (Nashville, New York: Abingdon, 1968), 185 – 86; Jan Alberto Soggin, *Introduction to the Old Testament from its Origins to the Closing of the Alexandrian Canon* (Philadelphia: Westminster, 1976), 138 – 44; Walther Zimmerli, *1 Moses 12 – 25: Abraham* (Zürich: Theologischer Verlag, 1976), 138 – 44.

7 Jacobus Gerhardus Vink, "The Date and Origin of the Priestly Code in the Old Testament," *OTS* 15 (1969): 1 – 144; Norbert Lohfink, "Die Priesterschrift in der Geschichte," *VTSup* 29 (1978): 189 – 225, locates the P History is the late exilic period (201). According to Erhard Blum, *Studien zur Komposition des Pentateuch* (Berlin: Walter de Gruyter, 1990), the P complex belongs after rather than before the rebuilding of the temple in the early years of the reign of Darius I (see especially 257, 305, 360).

8 See Joseph Blenkinsopp "The Structure of P," *CBQ* 38 (1976): 275 – 92.

9 See Joseph Blenkinsopp "Abraham as Paradigm in the Priestly History in Genesis," *JBL* 128.2 (2009): 225 – 41. This would correspond to the "ideologia morbida" ("soft ideology") in contrast to the "ideologia dura" ("hard ideology") represented by Ezra and Nehemiah, according to Mario Liverani, *Oltre la Bibbia: Storia Antica di Israele* (2nd ed., Roma & Bari: Editori Laterza, 2003), 283 – 87.

conqueror as legitimate successor to the Judaean dynastic monarchy in the same way as he was acknowledged as the legitimate successor to the Babylonian throne and, fourteen years later, his son Cambyses was acknowledged as successor to the Pharaonic throne.[10]

If therefore a date no earlier than the Persian conquest of Babylon is correct, the P creation account must be later than Isaiah 40–48 which clearly reflect events during the final decades of Neo-Babylonian rule. The readers of these chapters are assumed to be familiar with some traditions about cosmic creation, whether written or oral ("Do you not know? Has it not been told you from the beginning? Have you not grasped how the earth was established?") – but, if so, these would not have included the creation account of Genesis 1.

In point of fact, the similarities in creation language between Isaiah 40–48 and Genesis 1 may appear impressive at first reading but are less clearly in evidence on closer inspection. Both use the standard creation verb *bārā'* but the Isaianic text employs a considerable number of other verbs none of which appears in Genesis 1.[11] The *těhôm* (abyss) of Genesis 1:1 is represented by the hapax legomenon *sûlâ* in Isa 44:27. Like Job (22:14; 26:10) and Proverbs (8:27), but unlike P, the Isaianic author speaks of the earth or earth matter as a *hûg* ("circle", Isa 40:22). In Genesis the sky is formed like a metal vault or bell over the earth (*rāqîa'* "firmament", Gen 1:6–8, 14–15, 17, 20), but in Isa 40:22 it is spread out like a tent or a curtain. In other descriptive detail the Isaian text is more reminiscent of the Yahwist than the Priestly version. Thus, the creative act is by analogy to moulding with clay in Isaiah (45: 7, 9, 18) as in Gen 2: 7–8, and creatures are animated by God's breath and spirit, which compares with the "breath of life" of Gen 2:7 and 7:22 , both from the Yahwist narrative strand. The order or sequence of creation in Isaiah 40–48 is also more often than not different from Genesis 1. In one particularly interesting case (Isa 45:7), the Isaianic version also differs in a theologically significant way from that of the priest-author of Genesis 1 who emphasizes redundantly, seven times, the goodness of the created order:

---

10 Note that towards the end of the Cyrus Cylinder Cyrus reports the discovery of an inscription of Ashurbanipal, "a king who preceded me," that is, as king of Babylon. For the text see Amélie Kuhrt, *The Persian Empire: A Corpus of Sources from the Achaemenid Period*, Vol. 1 (London & New York: Routledge, 2007), 72.

11 *mādad*, measure (40:10), *tikkēn*, direct (40:12, 13), *šāqal*, weigh (40:12), *nātāh*, stretch out (40:22; 42:5; 44:24; 45:12), *mātāh*, spread out? (hapax, 40:22), *rāqā'* spread out (42:5; 44:24), *yāsar*, form, mould (45:7, 9, 18).

> I form light and create darkness,
> I bring about well-being and create woe;
> it is I, Yahweh, who do all these things (Isa 45:7)

In the P creation account God separates light from darkness but creates only light.[12]

3 Yahweh and Ahuramazda as creator deities

A line of enquiry which has a long history looks for an explanation of this new situation to Zoroastrian beliefs about the creation of the world and humanity by a god, Ahuramazda ("Lord of Wisdom"), who is supreme though accompanied by lesser deities, the Amesha Spentas ("holy immortals"), and whose worship is aniconic, as Herodotus also attests.[13]

Ahuramazda is invoked as greatest of the gods in inscriptions of the early Achaemenids Ariaramnes and Arsames, respectively the great-grandfather and grandfather of Darius I, but the authenticity of these inscriptions is seriously in doubt.[14] As often happens with statements of a religious nature, Zoroastrian belief in a creator deity came to serve as reinforcement for a political agenda. We find this for the first time in royal inscriptions from the time of Darius I where Ahuramazda is presented explicitly as cosmic creator. The principal variant runs as follows:

---

[12] It is not impossible that Isa 45:7 is directed against Zoroastrian dualism, though the evidence for the official adoption of Zoroastrianism as early as Cyrus II is disputed. Besides, the idea of the *opus alienum* of God was already known; see, for example Amos 3:6. Tina Dykesteen Nilsen, "The Creation of Darkness and Evil (Isaiah 45:6C–7)," *RB* 115 (2008): 5–25, maintained that the statement is directed against Babylonian not Zoroastrian dualism.

[13] "It is not their custom (i.e. the Persians) to make and set up statues, temples and altars, and those who make such they deem foolish" (*Hist.* 1:131).

[14] For the texts and translations see Roland Kent, *Old Persian: Grammar, Texts, Lexicon* (2nd ed., New Haven: American Oriental Society, 1953), 116, and for discussion his "The Oldest Old Persian Inscriptions," *JAOS* 66 (1946): 306–12. Pierre Briant, *Histoire de l'Empire Perse de Cyrus à Alexandre*, Vol. 1 (Leiden: Nederlands Instituut voor het Nabije Oosten, 1996), 27, declares them to be "rien moins que sur", and they are dismissed as outright forgeries by, inter alios, Martin Schwartz, "The Religion of Achaemenian Iran," in *The Cambridge History of Iran*, Vol. 2, *The Median and Achaemenian Periods*, ed. Ilya Gershevitch (Cambridge: Cambridge University Press, 1985), 664–97 (684), and by Muhammad Dandamaev and Vladimir Lukonin, *The Culture and Social Institutions of Ancient Iran* (Cambridge: Cambridge University Press, 1989), 278.

> A great god is Ahuramazda, who created this earth, who created yonder sky, who created man, who created happiness for man, who made Darius king, one king of many, one lord of many.[15]

The wording invites comparison with similar credal statements in Isaiah 40–48. Thus, Yahweh is introduced as the God who

> created the sky and laid it out, who spread out the earth and its issue, who gives breath to the peoples on it, the spirit of life to those who tread upon it. (42:5)

A similar formulation appears later where Yahweh is described as

> the One who created the sky, the One who is God, who gave the earth form and substance, who firmly established it. He did not create it an empty void, but formed it to be inhabited. (45:18)

In the Bisitun (Behistun) trilingual rock carving, by far the longest of Achaemenid inscriptions, Darius acknowledges receiving the kingship from Ahuramazda and invokes the favour of this deity at each phase of his suppression of revolts during his *annus mirabilis* (522–521 BC). He declares himself to be a worshipper of Ahuramazda and the restorer of his sanctuaries destroyed by Gaumata the magus. He denounces rebellion as the Lie (Avestan *druj*, Old Persian *drauga*,) in keeping with the Zoroastrian idea of life as struggle between the Lie, the essence of evil, and Righteousness (Avestan *asha*, Old Persian *arta*), the embodiment of cosmic and moral order; this last a concept similar to Sanskrit *rta* and Egyptian *maat*.[16] Darius was not, however, a monotheist. In the Behistun inscription he attributes his success to Ahuramazda and "the other gods that are" (column 4 line 61), and in an inscription on the south wall of the palace at Persepolis he invokes the assistance of the gods of the royal household in addition to Ahuramazda.[17]

It would be natural to assume that Cyrus (559–530), contemporary with the author of Isaiah 40–48, was also a devotee of Ahuramazda since only eight years separates his death in battle from the accession of Darius in 522 BC. Unfortunately, however, we have no Persian inscriptions from his reign, and what we can learn from the famous Cyrus cylinder, together with the few relevant

---

15 Roland Kent, *Old Persian*, 137–38. From the tomb inscription of Darius I at Naqši-Rustam near Persepolis.
16 For the text of the inscription see Roland Kent, *Old Persian*, 116–35, and for a detailed study of the text and the events of that year Muhammad Dandamaev, *Persien unter den ersten Achämeniden* (Wiesbaden: Dr. Ludwig Reichert Verlag, 1976).
17 Roland Kent, *Old Persian*, 136.

bits of information from Greek authors,[18] aligns him with, respectively, the Babylonian Marduk cult and the polytheistic Indo-Aryan beliefs and practices of the Mede and Persian population as a whole rather than with Ahuramazda.

This silence of the record notwithstanding, there has been a steady stream of Iranian and biblical specialists who have argued that Cyrus was an adherent of the religion of Zarathustra, and that it is entirely credible that Zoroastrian religious ideas could have influenced Judaean communities at that time and therefore also the author or authors of Isaiah 40–48.[19] The possibility, even probability, of Zoroastrian influence on Judaism at this early stage was, in fact, entertained as early as the late eighteenth century. Lessing wrote about the effect of "the pure Persian doctrine" on the Jewish understanding of Jehovah. Cyrus, he claimed, would have been sympathetic to the Jewish people purely on the grounds of religious affinity.[20] Similar sentiments were expressed about a century later in Ernest Renan's *Vie de Jésus* (1835): the victory of Cyrus seemed to have realized all that the Jews had hoped for; the disciples of the Avesta and the Yahweh-worshippers saw themselves as brothers; the prophetic tone of the Iranian

---

18 Xenophon, *Cyropaedia* has him praying to ancestral Hestia, goddess of the fireplace (Anahita? Zoroastrian Ātar, "sacred fire"?), Zeus (Ahuramazda?), and the rest of the gods (I vi 1), and sacrificing to Zeus and other gods (III iii 21). In the same work Xenophon also locates magi, religious specialists, at the court of Cyrus and Cambyses (IV v 14), in agreement with Herodotus (1:132) on the magi as sacrificing adepts.
19 Mary Boyce, *Zoroastrians: Their Religious Beliefs and Practices* (2nd ed., London & New York: Routledge, 2001), 48–77, a summary of her *A History of Zoroastrianism*, Vol. 2, *Under the Achaemenians* (Leiden: Brill, 1982), argues on the basis of archaeological data (stone plinths for worship and fire towers) and onomastics (Atossa, the name of Cyrus' daughter, which she derives from Hutaosa, the name of the wife of Vishtaspa, Zoroaster's patron) that Cyrus was Zoroastrian; see also her essay "The Religion of Cyrus the Great," in *Achaemenid History*, Vol. 3, *Method and Theory*, ed. Amélie Kuhrt and Heleen Sancisi-Weerdenburg (Leiden: Nederlands Instituut voor het Nabije Oosten, 1988), 5–21. At the present time this is a minority opinion. Earlier defenders of this opinion include James Moulton, *Early Zoroastrianism: The Origins, the Prophet, the Magi* (Amsterdam: Philo Press, 1972 [1913]); George William Carter, *Zoroastrianism and Judaism* (New York: AMS Press, 1918); David Winston, "The Iranian Component in the Bible, Apocrypha, and Qumran: A Review of the Evidence," *HR* 5 (1966): 187–89; Claude Herrenschmidt, "La Religion des Achéménides: État de la Question," *Studia Iranica* 9/2 (1980): 324–39.
20 See *The Education of the Human Race* (1780), §§ 38–39, in *Lessing's Theological Writings*, Transl. Henry Chadwick (London: Adam and Charles Black, 1956), 89. The same point was made, though in an overtly prejudicial manner, a few years later by Georg Lorenz Bauer, *The Theology of the Old Testament: A Biblical Sketch of the Religious Opinions of the Ancient Hebrews from the Earliest Times to the Commencement of the Christian Era* (London: Charles Fox, 1838 [1796]), who held that the more elevated sentiments evinced by post-exilic prophecy were due to the purifying influence of Persian religious ideas.

teachings could be compared with the books of Hosea and Isaiah.[21] In spite of, or because of, the relative lack of contemporary data, combined with the lack of consensus about such basic matters as the date of Zarathustra and the interpretation of the old Avesta and the Gathas, the issue has continued to be debated.

An interesting approach to these textual affinities was taken by Morton Smith in a brief paper published in 1963.[22] Smith argued along two lines which eventually converged. The first took its cue from an 1898 article of Rudolph Kittel in which he pointed out similarities between elements in Deutero Isaiah and the clay cylinder inscription dealing with the capture of Babylon by Cyrus.[23] Kittel's point was that Marduk's benevolent attitude to Cyrus in the cylinder text is identical, at times even in wording, with Yahweh's benevolence towards the same ruler in Isaiah 40–48.[24] He concluded that, since the Babylonian priests responsible for the pro-Persian propaganda in the cylinder text evidently did not depend on Deutero Isaiah, and since Deutero-Isaiah predates the publication of the cylinder text in the year after the fall of Babylon, therefore in 538 BC, the parallels can only be explained by appeal to the stereotypical language of the Babylonian court. Smith accepted the parallels, which he went on to itemize, but rejected the explanation on the grounds that it does not cover all the parallels. His own proposal was that the kind of pro-Persian propaganda represented by the Cyrus Cylinder was already being disseminated by Persian agents in Babylon before the fall of the city. It could therefore very easily have come to the attention of the author of Isaiah 40–48, resident in the Babylonian diaspora at that time, who then reproduced it in his book.

Having thus established the plausibility of sympathetic relations between Persians and Judaeans on the political level, Smith moved on to his second line of argument about the possibility of religious parallels between Zoroastrian and Isaian concepts of cosmic creation. He claimed to find evidence in an often-

---

21 Ernest Renan, *Vie de Jésus* (13th ed., Paris: Calmann-Lévy, 1862), 52–53 = *The Life of Jesus*, Transl. unknown (London: Watts & Co., 1935), 50.
22 Morton Smith, "II Isaiah and the Persians," *JAOS* 83 (1963): 415–21.
23 Rudolph Kittel, "Cyrus und Deuterojesaja," *ZAW* 18 (1898): 149–62. For the inscription see *ANET* 315–16.
24 For example: Marduk in the cylinder text and Yahweh in Isaiah 40–48 both treat Cyrus as a friend (Isa 44:28), who is called by name (45:3) and taken by the hand (45:1), who is summoned to go up against Babylon (42:6; 43:14), and who will exercize justice (42:1). There is the same theological topos about the anger of the deity against his own people and its disastrous consequences. In the case of Babylon, the anger is directed against Nabonidus for his neglect of Marduk's rituals; in the case of Judah, the anger is redirected against the Babylonians who, as agents of divine punishment on Judah, went beyond their mandate.

cited Zoroastrian text, Yasna 44.[25] The speaker addresses questions to Ahuramazda in the form, "This I ask you, tell me truly, Ahura". One example must suffice:

> This I ask you, tell me truly, Ahura.
> Who upheld the earth beneath and the firmament from falling?
> Who (set in place) the waters and the plants?
> Who yoked swiftness to winds and clouds?
> Who, O Mazda, is the creator of good thought? (Yasna 44:4)

In this and other stanzas of Yasna 44 the speaker, presumed to be Zarathustra himself, seeks to know who controls the movements of sun, moon and stars, upholds the earth and the firmament, puts in place waters, winds, and clouds, makes light and darkness, morning, noon, and night, and what is the source and origin of righteousness (*aša*). Smith maintained that for all of these queries about protology and cosmology there can be found parallels in Isaiah 40–48 but not in chapters 49–55, sometimes also in the form of questions (Isa 40:12–14, 21, 26), though rhetorical rather than addressed to the deity.

We can agree that Persian agents may have been disseminating anti-Babylonian propaganda prior to Cyrus' campaign against the city; that they may have done so among expatriate Judeans; and that the author of Isaiah 40–48, assumed by Morton Smith to have been one of these expatriates, may have come in contact with Zoroastrian ideas about creation in connection with these activities. But these speculations must be set over against the lack of evidence for Zoroastrian influence on the Persian court prior to Darius I, together with the plurality of deities, cults and religious practices during this early period for which there is evidence.[26] There would also have been a language problem.

---

25 The Yasna is a liturgical compilation of texts comprising 72 chapters. Chapter 44 is part of one of the 17 Gathas, considered to be of great antiquity and probably composed by the shamanistic prophet Zarathustra himself. For a survey of Zoroastrian textual sources see Mary Boyce, *Textual Sources for the Study of Zoroastrianism* (Chicago: Chicago University Press, 1984). Some verses from Yasna 44 can be found on p.34 of that work. The translation in Morton Smith's article may, in addition, be compared with those of James Moulton, *Early Zoroastrianism*, 367 and Helmut Humbach, *The Gāthās of Zarathushtra and the other Old Avestan Texts*, Vol. 1 (Heidelberg: Carl Winter/Universitätsverlag, 1991), 156–163.

26 In addition to the evidence from the royal inscriptions (see above) and the Greek authors, the Persepolis fortification tablets and seal impressions contain the names of several deities including Elamite Humban and Semitic Adad. See Richard Hallock, *Persepolis Fortification Tablets* (Chicago: Chicago University Press, 1948) and "The Evidence of the Persepolis Tablets," in *CHI* 2, 588–609; Mark Garrison and Margaret Cool Root, *Seals on the Persepolis Fortification Tablets*, Vol. 1, *Images of Heroic Encounter* (Chicago: Chicago University Press); Heleen Sancisi-Weerdenburg, "Darius I and the Persian Empire," in *Civilizations of the Ancient Near East*, Vol. 2, ed.

The Gathas are sacred texts chanted only in the original Avestan, a notoriously difficult language. We need not be surprised, therefore, if the majority of specialists in ancient Iranian history and religion are sceptical of claims of significant interaction between Zoroastrians and Judaeans during the early Achaemenid period.[27]

4 Yahweh and Marduk as Creator deities

An alternative explanation of the language of creation in Isaiah 40–48 might run as follows: The exaltation in Isaiah 40–48 of the God of Israel as supreme and incomparable, cosmic creator, and controller of the course of history including the career of Cyrus, can be construed as a kind of mirror-image of the ideology expressed in dramatic form in the *akitu* New Year festival, and in literary form in *enuma elish*, the myth recited and perhaps enacted on the fourth day of this ritual of renewal.[28] By the time of writing, Cyrus' conquests – Ecbatana,

---

Jack Sasson (New York: Charles Scribner's Sons, 1995), 1044–46. By the reign of Artaxerxes II the Indo-Aryan deities Mithra and Anahita, certainly familiar earlier, were being invoked in royal inscriptions.
27 Among them Martin Schwartz, "The Religion of Achaemenian Iran," in *CHI* 2, 664–97; Muhammad Dandamaev and Vladimir Lukonin, *The Culture and Social Institutions of Ancient Iran* (Cambridge: Cambridge University Press, 1989), 320–66; Richard Nelson Frye, *The Heritage of Persia* (Costa Mesa/California: Mazda Publications, 1993), 101, reminds us that "there was no organized Church with dogmas under the early Achaemenids"; Michael Stausberg, *Die Religion Zarathushtras. Geschichte – Gegenwart – Rituale*, Vol. 1 (Stuttgart: Kohlhammer, 2002), 157–86. For a sobering account of the difficulties besetting the issue of religion under the Achaemenids see Josef Wiesehöfer, *Ancient Persia from 550 BC to 650 AD* (London & New York: I. B. Tauris, 1996), 94–101. After a thorough review of the specialist writings on the subject, James Barr concluded as follows: "Iranian religious influence, if it did come in, came in through the admixture of Oriental ideas in the Hellenistic world". See his article "The Question of Religious Influence: The Case of Zoroastrianism, Judaism, and Christianity," *JAAR* 53/2 (1985): 201–235 (229). See also the equally negative judgement of Edwin Yamauchi, *Persia and the Bible* (Grand Rapids: Baker Book House, 1990), 458–66.
28 There is an extensive bibliography on the *akitu* festival. Among more recent contributions (the last half-century or so) the following may be noted: Wilfred Lambert, "The Great Battle of the Mesopotamian Religious Year: The Conflict in the Akitu House," *Iraq* 25 (1963): 189–90; Paul-Richard Berger, "Das Neujahrsfest nach den Königsinschriften des ausgehenden babylonischen Reiches," in *Actes de la XVIIe Rencontre Assyriologique Internationale*, ed. André Finet (Brussels: Université Libre de Bruxelles, 1970), 155–59; Jeremy Black, "The New Year Ceremonies in Ancient Babylon," *Religion* 11 (1981): 39–59; Karel van der Toorn, "The Babylonian New Year Festival," *VTSup* 43 (1991): 333–44; Jacob Klein, "Akitu," in *ABD* 1, 138–40; Beate Pongratz-Leisten, *Ina šulmi īrub: Die Kulttopographie und ideologische Programmatic der akītu-Prozession in*

Sardis, the Greek-speaking cities of the Ionian seaboard, Susa – were already far advanced, leaving little doubt about the imminent fate of Babylon.[29] The claims advanced on behalf of their god and in favour of Cyrus by the Marduk priesthood and their supporters, as stated in the Cyrus Cylinder and the Verse Account of Nabonidus,[30] were directed against the perceived impiety and heterodoxy of Nabonidus, last in a long line of Babylonian kings. He is accused of using untraditional and inappropriate rituals, replacing Marduk with the moon god Sîn, and neglecting to celebrate the *akitu* New Year festival. The devotees of Marduk anticipated that this situation would be reversed after the arrival of the Persians and the disappearance from the scene of the "heretic king," and so it happened. After the conquest Nabonidus was deposed, Marduk was reinstated as supreme deity, and the celebration of the *akitu* was resumed, if only briefly, under foreign auspices.[31]

The purpose of the festival was therefore to celebrate the supremacy of Marduk among the gods ("Marduk is king!", *enuma elish* IV 28), and his cosmic role as creator and sustainer of the world, while at the same time providing religious legitimation for Babylonian imperial rule. It will not be possible to *prove* that the author of Isaiah 40–48 had witnessed the eleven-day spring festival or had read a version of *enuma elish*. It may, however, be possible to demonstrate a degree of familiarity on the author's part at least as striking as was demonstrated by Morton Smith with regard to the formulations in the Cyrus Cylinder mentioned earlier.

Let us therefore assume, for the sake of the argument, that the author of Isaiah 40–48 set out to counter the ideology of the Babylonian priesthood in-

---

Babylonien und Assyrien im 1. Jahrtausend v. Chr. (Mainz: Phillip von Zabern Verlag, 1994), 110–36; Benjamin Sommer, "The Babylonian Akitu Festival: Rectifying the King or Renewing the Cosmos?," *JANES* 27 (2000): 81–95.

29 The author refers to victories over kings and nations (Isa 41:1–5; 45:1), the anticipated conquest of Babylon and Egypt (43:3,14; 45:2–3; 45:1; 48:14–16) and, in general, repeated emphasis on the impermanence of nations and kings (40:15–17, 23; 41:1–5, 25; 45:1).

30 See Paul-Alain Beaulieu, *The Reign of Nabonidus King of Babylon 556–539 BC* (New Haven: Yale University Press, 1989), 43–65. For the text of the Cyrus Cylinder see *ANET* 2nd. ed., 315–16 and for the Verse Account see *ANET* 2nd ed, 312–15. An updated version of both texts with notes in Amélie Kuhrt, *The Persian Empire*, 70–80.

31 Cambyses, son of Cyrus, was appointed king of Babylon (*šar babili*). Since his legitimacy was acknowledged by the Marduk priesthood, he would in that capacity have taken the lead role in the *akitu*. However, his royal status lasted only a year and shortly thereafter Babylon was governed by the satrap Gubāru and we hear no more about the *akitu*. See the detailed discussion in Muhammad Dandamaev, *Persien unter den ersten Achämeniden*, 100–102 and Pierre Briant, *L'Histoire de l'Empire Perse de Cyrus à Alexandre*, 82–83 = *From Cyrus to Alexander: A History of the Persian Empire* (Winona Lake, Indiana: Eisenbrauns, 2002), 71.

scribed in the *akitu* ritual and its related theogonic and cosmogonic myth, while presenting Yahweh rather than Marduk as the one sponsoring the victorious career of Cyrus and his conquest of Babylon. While there is a great deal of polemic against iconic representations of deities in Isaiah 40–48, the only deities who are named are Bēl (Marduk) and Nebo (Nabû), the principals in the *akitu*, and the stage of the celebrations at which they would have been most visible to the public was the joyful procession of priests and people to the extramural *akitu* house on the ninth day of the festival:

> Bel crouches low, Nebo cowers,
> their images are loaded on to animals, beasts of burden.
> These things you once bore aloft
> are a load for weary animals. (Isa 46:1)[32]

This reads like a deliberate deformation of this high point of the *akitu* ritual, the procession to the *bīt akitu*, and the Isaian author goes on to contrast the Babylonian gods who must be transported in this way with the God of Israel who is the bearer and sustainer of his people from birth (46:1–7). Processions featuring the statues of the gods are dismissed elsewhere in Isaiah 40–48 as empty rituals without effect:

> Those who carry around their wooden idols know nothing;
> they make their petitions to a god that cannot save. (45:20).

There may also be an allusion to the high point of the festival in the threat that the shouts of triumph of the Babylonians will be turned into lamentations (Isa 43:14). According to Babylonian priestly theology Marduk, victor over the threat of cosmic and social chaos in *enuma elish*, is the saviour god *par excellence*. Here, too, in Isaiah 40–48, this claim is negated by appeal to the efficacious salvation offered only by the God of Israel:

> There is no god apart from me,
> a god who overcomes and saves;
> there is none but me. (45:21)

In the context, the salvation in question is primarily political. The prophetic word announces a salvation more powerful and effective than the religious resources available to the Babylonians can deliver – their omens, incantations,

---

[32] All translations of Isaian texts are from Joseph Blenkinsopp, *Isaiah 40–55: A New Translation with Introduction and Commentary* (New York: Doubleday, 2002).

and astrological calculations (Isa 47:13) – as they faced the end of their independent existence.

Enuma elish is generally described as a creation myth, but the creation of the visible world and humanity described in it is incidental to events in the world of the gods.[33] The creation of *lullu*, a kind of lowly, servile creature, was undertaken to release the lesser gods, the Igigi, from their service to the high gods, while providing the latter with their domains or spheres of influence (VI 1–44). It is a kind of *Heilsgeschichte* for gods. It is not surprising that a Judaean prophet would reject the sometimes complicated theogonies in myths like *enuma elish* (four generations of gods in II-20), and that is what we find:

> Before me no god was formed,
> and there will be none after me. (43:10)

This is the first and most fundamental reaction to Babylonian theogony: the rejection of the idea that humanity emerges on the scene as involuntarily part of a narrative already in progress, one which it neither owns nor controls. Following the same line of thought, the author insists that Yahweh as creator needed no assistance or counsel:

> Who has taken the measure of Yahweh's spirit
> or advised him as his counselor?
> With whom did he consult to be enlightened? [...]
> Who imparted knowledge to him
> or showed him the way of discernment? (40:13–14)

In *enuma elish* the situation is different: the wise Ea (Nudimmud), lord of the underworld and counselor to the gods (II 58), assists Marduk as cosmic creator (VI 38), and elsewhere is described as himself creating humanity according to a plan devised by Marduk (VI 35–38, cf. VII 29,32).

Both the myth and the ritual in which it is enacted and given dramatic expression focus on the supremacy of Marduk as world ruler, demanding absolute obedience, wielding power over life and death, whose creative and destructive power is reinforced by the symbolic act of tearing a garment and putting it

---

[33] Translations of the text in Alexander Heidel, *The Babylonian Genesis: The Story of Creation* (2nd ed., Chicago: Chicago University Press, 1951); *ANET* (2nd ed., 1955), 60–72 (transl. by Ephraim Avigdor Speiser); *The Standard Babylonian Creation Myth Enûma Eliš*, ed. Philippe Talon (Helsinki: Helsinki University Press, 2005). On the world view reflected in the myth see Thorkild Jacobsen, "Mesopotamia," in *Before Philosophy: The Intellectual Adventure of Ancient Man*, ed. Henri Frankfort et al. (Baltimore: Penguin Books, 1949), 125–222, especially 182–99.

back together (*enuma elish* IV 22–26). Both creation and destruction happen at Marduk's command (VI 131), as also at the word of Yahweh:

> I form light and create darkness,
> I bring about well-being and create woe;
> It is I, Yahweh, who do all these things. (45:7)

To repeat a point made earlier: the incomparability of Yahweh, one of the great themes of Isaiah 40–48, is equally thematic with respect to Marduk in *enuma elish*, reaching a climax in the final acclamation of the deity and the invocation of his fifty names by the assembly of gods: he is the one who has no equal among the gods (VII 14, 88) and whose divine kingship is highly exalted (VII 96).

This mirror-imaging approach to the language of Isaiah 40–48 is reinforced by a consideration of the dethronement and humiliation of Queen Babylon, "mistress of kingdoms," in Isaiah 47. It is not just another instance of the city-woman metaphor (e.g. Nineveh, Nah 3:4–7; Sidon, Isa 23:12). The description of the female persona Zion-Jerusalem in the following section of Isaiah is a mirror-image, a reversal therefore, of the presentation of the dishonoured "maiden Babylon" in Isaiah 47. The latter must descend from her throne and sit in the dust (47:1), while Zion is told to get up and shake off the dust (52:2); Babylon is stripped and exposed to view (47:2–3), while Zion is clothed in fine garments (49:18; 52:1); Babylon is shamed (47:3), but there will be no more shame for Zion (54:4). The most interesting of these reverse images is the prospect of widowhood for the woman Babylon (47:8–9). In other words, Marduk, city god and her "husband," will prove unable to protect her and will therefore be as good as dead, while the woman Zion will no longer be abandoned, but will have numerous children (49:20–21; 54:1). Read in this way, Isaiah 40–48 pioneers a new way of confronting overwhelming political power – first Babylonian, then Achaemenid – expressed and projected through its religious symbols. In doing so, it represents one of the great turning points in religious history in antiquity.

III. Judaeans, Jews, Children of Abraham

Source: *Judah and the Judeans in the Achaemenid Period*, ed. Oded Lipschits, Gary Neil Knoppers and Manfred Oeming, 461–82. Winona Lake/Indiana: Eisebrauns, 2011).

1 The continuity/discontinuity issue

Questions about the formation of group identity in Judah and the diaspora in the aftermath of the destruction of Jerusalem and its temple and the liquidation of the Judaean state lead directly into disputed issues about the origins of Judaism, the broad theme expressed by Wellhausen in the formula "aus Israel wird das Judentum." Identifying the origins of an ethnic, national or religious group seems to be an easy task when either a charismatic individual (e. g. Mohammed, Luther) or a defining historical moment is involved (e. g. the Declaration of Independence of the United States of America, July 4th 1776 or the declaration establishing the State of Israel, May 14th 1948). But we could hardly claim to grasp the identity of either the United States of America or the State of Israel were we to take these events as marking absolute beginnings. In our case there is such a defining moment, the fall of Jerusalem to the Babylonians in August 586 BC and the subsequent deportations, but these events at once raise complex issues of continuity and discontinuity. In the modern period, biblical scholarship has tended to view this "aus Israel wird das Judentum" theme refracted through ideological and theological prisms of different kinds. Since this bit of intellectual history is well-known, it will suffice to mention one or two examples by way of illustration. In Wilhelm Vatke's *Biblische Theologie*, inspired by a Hegelian view of historical development, Judaism served as the passage between the nature religion of early Israel and the absolute religion embodied in Christianity.[1] Julius Wellhausen's reconstruction of the development of religious ideas and practice throughout the history of Israel in his *Prolegomena zur Geschichte Israels* eventuated in Chronicles and the ritualism and legalism of the Priestly work in the Pentateuch, prod-

---

[1] On Wilhelm Vatke's *Die Religion des Alten Testament nach den kanonischen Büchern* (Berlin: Verlag von G. Bethge, 1885) see Hans-Joachim Kraus, *Geschichte der historisch-kritischen Erforschung des Alten Testaments* (Neukirchen: Verlag der Buchhandlung des Erziehungsvereins, 1956), 179–82 and John Rogerson, *Old Testament Criticism in the Nineteenth Century: England and Germany* (London: SPCK, 1984), 69–78.

ucts of the earliest phase of Judaism.[2] The *Heilsgeschichte* of Lutheran Pietists in the eighteenth and conservative Protestant biblicists in the nineteenth century represented a more explicitly Christian theological approach. An echo of this biblical theology can be heard in Gerhard von Rad's *Theologie des Alten Testaments* which states that the prophets proclaimed the death of Israel, and that the history of interactivity between God and Israel came to an end once the law became "an absolute entity" (*eine absolute Größe*).[3] To these we may add, at the other end of the spectrum, Yehezkel Kaufmann, the anti-Wellhausen, who, while agreeing that the history of Judaism as a religious community begins with the fall of Jerusalem, contended that all the essentials were in place from the beginning of Israel's history: monotheism, freedom from myth and magic, and a law revealed to Moses.[4]

Leaving these heavily-freighted ideologies aside, I want to focus in these pages on specific issues bearing on the process of the formation of social identities in the wake of the disasters of the early sixth century BC Since I am not a sociologist I will be saying little about theories of ethnicity, but since it is considered mandatory in these matters to cite Max Weber I may at least refer to his definition of an ethnic group, enunciated in typically apodictic fashion:

> We shall call "ethnic groups" those human groups that entertain a subjective belief in their common descent because of similarities of physical type or of customs or both, or because of memories of colonization and migration; this belief must be important for the propagation of group formation; conversely, it does not matter whether or not an objective blood relationship exists.[5]

According to a more recent descriptive account, which I take to be fairly representative, an ethnic group will exhibit some or all of the following markers or diacritics: an expressive name, a myth of common ancestry, a shared history, and elements of a shared culture which normally but not necessarily would in-

---

[2] The quotation ("aus Israel wird das Judentum") is actually from Wellhausen's article on "Israel," *Encyclopedia Brittanica* 13 (9th ed., 1881): 396–431, reprinted in William Robertson Smith's translation of the *Prolegomena* into English.
[3] Gerhard von Rad, *Theologie des Alten Testaments*, Vol. 1 (München: Kaiser, 1957) = *Old Testament Theology*, Vol.1, Transl. David Muir Gibson Stalker (New York: Harper & Row, 1962), 85–92.
[4] An English translation and abridgement of volumes 1–7 of Kaufmann's eight-volume work is available in Moshe Greenberg, *Yehezkel Kaufmann: The Religion of Israel from its Beginnings to the Babylonian Exile* (New York: Schocken Books, 1960) and parts of volume 8 in Yehezkel Kaufmann, *History of the Religion of Israel*, Vol. 4, *The Babylonian Captivity and Deutero-Isaiah*, Transl. Clarence Efroymson (New York: Union of American Hebrew Congregations, 1970).
[5] Max Weber, *Economy and Society: An Outline of Interpretive Sociology* (Berkeley & Los Angeles: California, 1978), 389.

clude language and religion.⁶ The Judaeans, who in 589–586 paid a heavy price for the rash actions of their rulers, certainly formed an identifiable ethnic and political unit. The Babylonian punitive expedition concluded with a series of acts designed to obliterate that identity: the elimination of the dynasty emblematic of the nation as a whole; the destruction of the temple which provided religious legitimation for the revolt and served as the depository of the nation's written traditions and laws;⁷ and the execution or deportation of the literate and educated classes, here as elsewhere the bearers and transmitters of the traditions essential for the survival of group identity. It will not be difficult to think of parallels in our contemporary world to this deliberate and systematic attempt to eradicate national and ethnic identity. If the Babylonians had followed the example of the Assyrians in the practice of cross-deportation the story would probably have ended there; but they did not, and so the story continued. Hence the task is to investigate the process by which new identities were formed and sustained on the other side of disaster.

On this issue of continuity/discontinuity, we begin with the observation that the tendency in biblical scholarship has been to emphasize continuity rather than discontinuity, restoration rather than reformulation, a tendency summed up in the title of Peter Ackroyd's well-known monograph *Exile and Restoration*.⁸ In this respect scholarship has followed the lead of the biblical texts. In Chronicles (2 Chr 36:20–21) the exile is presented as a hiatus lasting a limited and relatively brief period of time rather than as a tragic event with far-reaching consequences. As Sara Japhet put it, on this view "when the prescribed date arrives, everything will return to normal".⁹ In the continuation of the history in Ezra-Nehemiah, the list of the first immigrants from the Babylonian diaspora is rounded out with the information that, on arrival, they all dispersed to their respective towns, rather like returning home after a holiday abroad (Ezra 2:70). The idea of a restoration or a return is encapsulated in the expressions šûb šĕbût or šîbat ṣiyyôn, the latter borrowed from the textually disputed first verse of

---

6 John Hutchinson and Anthony Smith (eds.), *Ethnicity* (Oxford: Oxford University Press, 1996), 6–7.
7 The removal of the sacred vessels as especially emblematic of the temple is particularly significant (2 Kgs 25:13–17). Note the extraordinary importance attached in Ezra-Nehemiah to the sacred vessels of the temple as symbolic of continuity (Ezra 1:7–11; 5:14–15; 6:5; 7:19; 8:24–30.33–34); on which see Peter Ackroyd, "The Temple Vessels: A Continuity Theme," *VTSup* 23 (1972): 166–81.
8 Peter Ackroyd, *Exile and Restoration: A Study of Hebrew Thought of the Sixth Century BC* (Philadelphia: Westminster, 1968).
9 Sara Japhet, *I & II Chronicles: A Commentary* (Louisville: Westminster John Knox Press, 1993), 1075.

Psalm 126. But in fact there was no restoration of the kind of precarious national autonomy which existed prior to 586. The principal institutions were, of course, the monarchy and the priesthood, royal court and temple. Aspirations for and predictions of the restoration of the dynasty in prophetic texts (for example, Jer 23:1–8; Ezek 34:23–24; Amos 9:11–12) and in the P history in the Pentateuch (Gen 17:6.16; 35:11),[10] remained unfulfilled in spite of several attempts at realizing them.[11] The temple was razed to the ground and the site remained empty for seven decades – for some scholars even longer – and when a smaller version replaced Solomon's temple it served not as an adjunct of the native dynasty but as an instrument of imperial control, symbolized by the requirement that prayers and sacrifices for the royal family in Susa be incorporated into the temple liturgy (Ezra 6:10).

The liquidation of the state with its apparatus of control would also have deprived prophets of their patronage in court and temple. Optimist prophets who survived the disaster – and we know of several who did not – would presumably have lost their prophetic credentials. Prophets of doom, if not also discredited for contributing to the disaster, would have been left searching for a new message. The reaction of male and female deportees to Jeremiah's post-disaster preaching in Egypt is particularly instructive, since it presents an alternative explanation for the disaster. They claimed that the disaster happened because they had been persuaded or coerced to abandon their traditional religion, the worship of the "Queen of Heaven" in particular, which "we, our ancestors, our kings and officials practised in the towns of Judah and the public places of Jerusalem" (Jer 44:15–19). (This is also, incidentally, one of the few places in the Hebrew Bible where women get to speak about religion). Prophetic terminology and

---

10 The prediction that kings would be among Abraham's descendants provides a little-noticed clue to the date of the Priestly history in the Neo-Babylonian period or, at any rate, not later than the suppression of revolts in the first two years of the reign of Darius I and the disappearance of Zerubbalel from the scene.

11 The anti-Babylonian alliance of western states including Judah in 595 (Jer 27:3) coincided with the accession of Psammeticus II and an internal rebellion which confronted Nebuchadnezzar in the same year, see Donald Wiseman, *Chronicles of Chaldean Kings* (London: The British Museum, 1961), 36–37.72–73. The suppression of this revolt was followed by another incursion into Hatti land. Resistance to Babylon was encouraged by prophets in Judah (Jer 28:1–17) and Babylon (Jer 29:15–23.29–32). The assassination of the Babylonian-appointed viceroy (or puppet king) Gedaliah by Ishmael, a Davidite, probably in 582 (2 Kgs 25:25–26; Jer 41:1–3), only made a bad situation worse. The liberation of Jehoiachin from captivity in 562 at the accession of Amel-Marduk may indicate that this ruler intended to reinstate the Judaean monarchy, but if so it came to nothing after the assassination of Amel-Marduk. Realistic expectations were finally extinguished after the suppression of revolts all over the Persian empire by Darius I (521–519).

some of the literary conventions continued in use after 586, but the phenomenon of prophecy was different. In brief, the prophetic role became increasingly assimilated to the functions of scribe, homilist, and exegete of earlier prophecy.

The history of priestly houses in the Neo-Babylonian and early Persian periods, much discussed in recent years, also calls for attention in this connection. In the Introduction to his edition of the Elephantine papyri published in 1923, Arthur Cowley commented on the fact that none of the priests who played a leading role in the affairs of the colony are identified either as "sons of Aaron" or "sons of Zadok" and that, with the exception of the Priestly matter in the Pentateuch or Hexateuch and Chronicles, and one or two other allusions of uncertain origin and date, the record both pre-exilic and post-exilic is silent on Aaron *qua* priest and Aaronite priests.[12] What I have called "the mystery of the missing sons of Aaron" has been noted, and solutions have been proposed, since the late nineteenth century if not earlier, but the matter still remains *sub iudice*.[13] It seems to me that we should entertain the possibility that both Aaronites and Zadokites are products of the early Second Temple period, and that they emerged out of the struggle for control of the cult between the destruction of the first and the construction of the second Jerusalem temple. At any rate, the relations between the houses of Aaron and Zadok would, if known, have an important bearing on the religious history of the province of Judah and the Samaria region during the Neo-Babylonian and Persian periods, as well as relations between Judah and the eastern diaspora.

One of the few instances of directly attested continuity is the role of the Shaphanid family in political and religious affairs both before and after the fall of Jerusalem. Shaphan, *sôfēr* (Secretary of State?) to Josiah, was of Benjaminite descent.[14] He, his three sons (Ahikam, Elasah, Gemariah), and two grandsons (Gedaliah son of Ahikam, Micaiah son of Gemariah), took the lead in opposing the faction at the court favouring rebellion, thus sparing Benjaminite territory the effects of the Babylonian punitive campaign which devastated Judah. The Shapha-

---

12 Abraham Cowley, *Aramaic Papyri of the Fifth Century BC* (Osnabrück: Otto Zeller, 1967 [1923]), xxii–xxiii.
13 Joseph Blenkinsopp, "The Judaean Priesthood during the Neo-Babylonian and Achaemenid Periods: A Hypothetical Reconstruction," *CBQ* 60 (1998): 25–43; "The Mystery of the Missing 'Sons of Aaron'," in *Exile and Restoration Revisited*, ed. Gary Knoppers and Lester Grabbe (London & New York: T. & T. Clark, 2009), 65–77.
14 His grandfather Meshullam has a name common among Benjaminites (2 Kgs 22:3; see 1 Chr 8:17; 9:7–8; Neh 11:7). His grandson Gedaliah, appointed viceroy of the region by the Babylonians, was established at Mizpah (tell en-nasbeh) in Benjamin (2 Kgs 25:22; Jer 40:7–12), and members of the family protected Jeremiah, himself a Benjaminite, who chose to stay with Gedaliah at Mizpah "among his own people" (Jer 39:14; 40:5–6).

nids were therefore if not pro-Babylonian, then certainly in favour of maintaining the status quo. After his installation at Benjaminite Mizpah as governor or, perhaps, as puppet king, Gedaliah, Shaphan's grandson, issued an invitation to those dispersed by the Babylonian punitive campaign to submit to Babylon and accept his protection (Jer 40:9–10), an accommodating attitude paralleled by Jeremiah's letter to the deportees to seek the well-being of the places where they had been settled (Jer 29:1–28). This was no doubt seen as appeasement by their enemies, but what for some is appeasement for others is political realism and pragmatism.

It is clear from the account of Shaphan's activities under Josiah that he had oversight of the temple and its personnel (2 Kgs 22:3–10), and his descendants continued to have close links with the temple priesthood (2 Kgs 22:12; Jer 29:3; 36:10). It would be natural to conclude further that he was involved in the cleansing of the temple and reform of the temple cult which followed the reading of the newly-discovered law book (2 Kgs 23:1–14), to the extent that this account can be considered historically reliable. In more general terms, it seems that the Shaphanids played a leading role in promoting a reformed religion based on a written law attributed to Moses which emphasized the cult of Yahweh alone. If so, their contribution to national and ethnic survival should not be overlooked.

2 Judaeans or Jews?

One way of addressing the continuity/discontinuity issue would be at the most basic linguistic level by asking once again an apparently straightforward question: When is it appropriate to begin translating the gentilic *yĕhûd* as "Jew" ("Jude", "Juif" etc) rather than "Judaean"? The relevant data are readily available. To go back to the beginnings: the designation would have applied to a tribal group of the southern wilderness and the Negev before the formation of the state, comparable therefore to Kenites, Kenizzites, and Jerahmeelites (Josh 1:16; 11:21; 1 Sam 27:10).[15] In biblical texts from the time of the kingdoms, as well as in Assyrian inscriptions,[16] the term signifies ascriptive identity, membership in a nation though not restricted to those actually resident in Judah. There are, for example, *yĕhûdîm* living in Egypt (Jer 43:9; 44:1) and in the Jewish outpost

---

15 Joseph Blenkinsopp, "The Midianite-Kenite Hypothesis and the Origins of Judah," *JSOT* 33 (2008): 131–53.
16 E.g. ha-za-qi-a-ú ia-ú-da-ai, "Hezekiah the Judaean", in Sennacherib's account of the punitive expedition of 701 BC on the Taylor Prism and the Chicago Oriental Institute Prism (*ANET* 287–88).

at Elephantine.[17] In this context, therefore, "Judaean" belongs to the same category as "Edomite", "Ammonite", "Syrian", etc.

The question then arises as to when, and under what circumstances, the primary association with place was left behind or, to restate it, when did the ethnic-local-national give way to the ethnic-cultural-religious connotation? The situation is by no means clear-cut. In the first Aramaic section of Ezra (4:8 – 6:18) the designation *yĕhûdāyē'* occurs in, or in association with, cited documents of Persian officials, and the allusion is therefore to one of many ethnic groups forming a distinct unit in the Persian empire[18] Much the same usage is attested with reference to the Jewish garrison in Upper Egypt in the Elephantine papyri. This last is of particular interest since, as far as we know, none of these people had ever set foot in Judah. Usage in Nehemiah is more complex, since in addition to designating inhabitants of Yehud in general (Neh 2:16; 5:1,17), the term identifies a distinctive upper-echelon social class in the province, probably belonging to the Judaeo-Babylonian element. On the other hand, the *'îš yĕhûdî* of Zech 8:23, of uncertain date but probably late Persian period, occurs in an explicitly religious context, which is clearly the case even if the hem of the garment grasped by ten men of different nationality is not a reference to the tassels prescribed in Num 15:38. Likewise in Esther 8:17, the first and only appearance of the verb *hityāhēd* ("to become Jewish") testifies to the possibility of proselytism at the time of writing. This is so even if, in the context, the verb is interpreted as pretending to be Jewish in order to escape the furious reaction of this diasporic Jewish community.

There is, finally, the statement of Josephus, made in connection with Nehemiah's repair of the city wall (Neh 3:34), that the expression *ioudaioi* was first used with reference to those who went up from Babylon:

> The name by which they have been called from the time when they went up from Babylon is derived from the tribe of Judah; as this tribe was the first to come to those parts, both the people themselves and the country have taken their name from it (*Ant.* 11,173).

In summary: usage seems to point to the first century of Persian rule for the emergence of the ethnic-religious connotation of *yĕhûdîm*, justifying the appellative "Jew" rather than "Judaean".[19] If so, this identity marker could be regarded

---

17 Abraham Cowley, *Aramaic Papyri*, 20:2 – 3; 21:3.11; 22:1, etc.
18 Ezra 4:12, 23; 5:1,5,14; 6:7 – 8,14.
19 Needless to say, other scholars have reached different conclusions. Shaye Cohen, for example, proposes that only as late as the latter part of the second century BC is the original meaning "Judaean" supplemented by a religious and cultural meaning justifying use of the term "Jew".

as one aspect of a changing situation in the larger culture, if one of relatively low visibility on the stage of world events. For this century, which can be described as an axial period, witnessed a large-scale reshaping of the Eastern Mediterranean region and the Near East. It marked the end of the great Semitic empires which had dominated and shaped that world for millennia, and which would re-emerge only with the rise of Islam in the seventh century AD. It was the high point of Athenian culture in the Periclean age which witnessed the explosion of Greek intellectual and artistic achievement, an achievement which continues to amaze us today. This was an age which witnessed the formation of national and ethnic identities, especially in the Greek cities and Egypt, over against the dominant hegemonic power of the day. These movements are reflected in new forms of literary expression: the practice of citing sources precisely transcribed, heavily edited, or invented as the case may be; the writing of personal memoirs (Herodotus, Ion of Chios, Ezra, Nehemiah); and the first histories: Herodotus to 479, Xenophon to 362, Ctesias to 382, and Thucydides to 404 – none of which, however, mentions either the Jewish people or Judah.[20]

3 Demographic and onomastic continuity/discontinuity

Several estimates of population density in Judah before and after the Babylonian conquest, and of variations in density during the Neo-Babylonian and early Persian periods, are on offer. It would certainly be useful and relevant to the theme of identity formation in the post-disaster period to have reliable data on the population of Judah towards the end of the monarchy, the numbers involved in the successive deportations (597, 586, 582 BC) relative to the size of the surviving population left in Judah, the population of Jerusalem shortly before and after 586 BC, and the size of the Judaeo-Babylonian element in the province during the first Persian century as a proportion of the total population. We recall that demographic estimates constituted an important element in Joel Weinberg's *Bürger-Tempel Gemeinde* hypothesis which, however, also served to illustrate the

---

See his *The Beginnings of Jewishness: Boundaries, Varieties, Uncertainties* (Berkeley & Los Angeles: University of California, 1999). At the other chronological extreme, Marc Zvi Brettler, "Judaism in the Hebrew Bible? The Transition from Ancient Israelite Religion to Judaism," *CBQ* 61 (1999): 429–47 argues that we may speak of "Jews" from the beginnings of Israelite history. See further Steve Mason, "Jews, Judaeans, Judaizing, Judaism: Problems of Categorization in Ancient History," *JSJ* 38 (2007): 457–512.
20 Arnaldo Momigliano, "Fattori Orientali della Storiografia Ebraica Post-Esilica e della Storiografia Greca," *Accademia Nazionale dei Lincei* 76 (1966): 137–46.

problems besetting such calculations.²¹ Unfortunately, the biblical texts give us little help with the task of assembling the data required for even approximate estimates. These include the carrying capacity of the location in question, floor space especially covered floor space, availability of essential resources for survival, and the average size of families.²² Many attempts have been made over the past two or three decades,²³ and continue to be made, but so many variables enter into play, and estimates have to allow for such a large margin of error, that it is difficult to accept any of them with confidence.²⁴

Also relevant, but no less in need of caution, is the use of onomastic and prosopographical studies bearing on ethnic origins and religious affiliation in Judah and diasporic centers, the nature of successive immigrations into the province of Judah, and the changing character of its population. We don't need to labor the point that prosopography is not an infallible guide to social, political and religious realities. Names can change over time, the same person can have more than one name (e.g. a nickname, a *nom de guerre*), and people are not always logical and consistent in naming their children. The Murašu archive, for example, lists parents with Babylonian names whose children carry Yahweh-theophoric names, e.g., Nathaniah son of Beluballit.²⁵ Names retain nevertheless some memory of ethnic and religious origins, and therefore should not be ignored. The available data have been assembled and catalogued comprehensively by Ran Zadok who has given us a veritable telephone directory (minus the digits) of Jewish names from the Neo-Babylonian and Persian periods.²⁶ In the Babylonian diaspora the Murašu dossier testifies to a high level of interethnicity precisely in

---

21 See Joseph Blenkinsopp "Temple and Society in Achaemenid Judah" in this volume.
22 Martin Heicksen, "Archaeological Light on Population Problems," *Bulletin of the Near Eastern Archaeological Society* 6 (1975): 31–39.
23 Yigal Shiloh, "The Populationof Iron Age Palestine in the Light of a Sample Analysis of Urban Plans, Areas, and Population Density," *BASOR* 239 (1980): 25–35; Lawrence Stager, "The Archaeology of the Family," *BASOR* 260 (1985): 1–35; Jeffrey Zorn, "Estimating the Population Size of Ancient Settlements: Methods, Problems, Solutions, and a Case Study," *BASOR* 295 (1994): 31–48.
24 Compare, for example, the estimate of 13,350 for the early Persian period province and 20,650 for the later period of Charles Carter, *The Emergence of Yehud in the Persian Period: A Social and Demographic Study* (Sheffield: JSOT, 1999), 195–205 with 30,125 for the Persian period as a whole, based on a calculation of the number of settled dunams, from Oded Lipschits, *The Fall and Rise of Jerusalem: Judah Under Babylonian Rule* (Winona Lake/Indiana: Eisenbrauns, 2005), 270. These are, to my knowledge, the most recent and most carefully calculated estimates available.
25 Elias Bickerman, "The Babylonian Captivity," in *CHJ* 1, 356.
26 See Ran Zadok, *The Pre-Hellenistic Israelite Anthroponomy and Prosopography* (Leuven: Peeters, 1988).

the region where the Jewish deportees were settled, and where most of them would have taken Jeremiah's advice to "build houses and live in them ... take wives and have sons and daughters" (Jer 29:5–6) and, given the situation, not all the wives would have been from their own people. On the other hand, precisely this situation could have instigated a reaction contributing to the extreme form of self-segregation mandated in Ezekiel's "temple law" (Ezek 44:1–9) and enforced by Ezra and his supporters, the *hărēdîm*, "those who trembled at the word of God" (Ezra 9–10).

The lay agnatic units listed in Ezra 2:2–19, Neh 7:7–24, and I Esd. 5:7–23 are presented as belonging to those who were the first to return, but there is broad agreement that there was no one immigration of about five thousand individuals in response to the edict of Cyrus II or indeed at any other time.[27] The list must have served some other purpose and must date from later in the Persian period. Given this situation, what are we to make of the fact that of the seventeen or eighteen patronymics listed here,[28] said to be of diasporic origin, only four (if we include Zakkai and Bani as hypocoristic for Zechariah and Benaiah respectively) occur in pre-exilic texts and are Yahweh-theophoric, and the one with a Persian patronymic (Bigvai) is the third-largest? Since descendants of twelve of these founders of Babylonian-diasporic kinship units of the *bêt 'abôt* type, corresponding to the Babylonian *bit abim*, also accompanied Ezra (Ezra 8:3–14), the names in the list may be taken to indicate that, by the time the list was compiled, the links with the original deportees had become exiguous to the point of disappearance. This would hardly be surprising after the passage of at least a century and a half. While the destination of immigrants from Babylonia in the mid-Persian period was still Jerusalem, in the circumstances these immigrants could hardly be described as *returning* to Zion. On arrival in the province, with or without imperial authorization, Ezra and his supporters maintained their distinctive identity as the golah assembly. We might think of them as engaged in a kind of religiously-motivated colonization, a distant analogy to the Pilgrim Fathers in the early seventeenth century, driven by an ideological and basically sectarian agenda which they brought with them.[29] It is interesting to note in this regard that the LXX translates the Hebrew *gôlâ* with *apoikia* (*apoikesia*), the term used by Herodotus for the Greek colonies (*Hist.* 1,146; 5,124).

---

27 49,897 (Ezra 2:64), 49,942 (Neh 7:66 and 1 Esd. 5:41–42).
28 The unit containing the names of both Pahath-Moab and Joab in Ezra 2:6 = Neh7:11 is listed as two separate units which accompanied Ezra in Ezra 8:4,9. 1 Esdras 5 has twenty-one units.
29 Ezra and his support group could also be seen as the predecessors of those sectarian movements which, according to one hypothesis, originated in the eastern diaspora during the Hasmonaean period.

4 Tradition and identity: the narrative tradition about Abraham

The core issue in the negotiation of identity in the post-disaster period may be stated as follows. In biblical texts from the period in question the same traditional self-referential language is in use as previously – Israel, the seed of Israel, the holy seed, the people of God, the children of Abraham – *but it is no longer unproblematically clear to whom these terms refer*. There are now not only different population centers but different claimants to possess the past as mediated through traditions, written and oral as they may be, to shape it in their own image, and where necessary to invent it. Since the biblical texts favor the Judaeo-Babylonian claimants it is only rarely and by chance that we hear the arguments of their opponents.

A case in point is the claim attributed to the indigenous Judeans, those not deported, to be the authentic descendants of Abraham, and therefore to hold title to the land, including the estates vacated by the deportees. The claim is based on two arguments reported at different places in the prophecies of Ezekiel, certainly a hostile witness, who addresses the Babylonian diaspora community as "the entire household of Israel" (Ezek 11:14–16; 33:23–29).[30] The first claim – "They have gone far from Yahweh, the land has been given to us as an inheritance" – is not merely a statement of fact, as if to say possession is nine parts of the law. An argument is implied, to the effect that the deportees have been expelled from the cult community and have therefore forfeited title to their land. What is envisaged here can be seen by reference to the threat of loss of property directed at those members of the golah who failed to take part in the assembly to resolve the marriage crisis (Ezra 10:8). A further nuance is added by the claim that the land has been handed to them as an inheritance. Used with reference to land claims, this technical term (*môrāšâ*) appears only in Ezekiel (33:24; 36:1–5) and in Exodus 6:8, a repetition of the Abrahamic promise of land. That this was the point of the argument is apparent also in the refutation. Yahweh accepts responsibility for the deportations, but adds a strange promise, that he would become their sanctuary for a while, that is, during the time of the exile

---

[30] Ezek 11:14–16 is dated by most commentators to the last decades of the kingdom of Judah, though some doubts have been raised. Ezek 33:23–29 is generally thought to be post-586, in spite of the threat addressed to people living among the ruins in Judah to turn the whole country into a wasteland (v 28). For our purpose the issue of dating need not be settled.

(11:16).³¹ This statement corresponds to a major theme in Ezekiel symbolically expressed in the mobile sanctuary of Ezekiel's initial vision and the movement of the "Glory", the visible symbol of the invisible God, by stages from the Jerusalem temple, about to be destroyed, to the Babylonian diaspora (10:18–19; 11:22–25). It was therefore apparent that the power and presence of the God of Israel was no longer restricted to his own land and his own house in Jerusalem.

The Abrahamic promises play a more overt role in the second argument of the Judaeans who remained in the land (Ezek 33:23–29). It is stated succinctly as follows:

> Abraham was but one yet he inherited the land;
> There are lots of us; so the land is given to us as an inheritance.

This seems at first glance a crude and boastful a fortiori argument: if Abraham got possession of the land on his own, we who are many can certainly do it; in fact we have done it. But a moment's reflection shows that this makes little sense. Abraham was promised the land for his posterity, but he himself only came into possession of a small plot of land, and he did so by purchasing not by inheriting it. The meaning of "the one and the many" emerges more clearly when we take account of a similar statement about Abraham in Second Isaiah:

> When I called him he was but one,
> but I blessed him and made him many. (Isa 51:2)

The contrast has the simple purpose of restating the theme of numerous descendants to be brought about, against all the odds, by the blessing bestowed on this one man Abraham (Gen 12:2; 13:16, etc). The indigenous Judaeans were therefore claiming to be the numerous descendants promised to Abraham; and since the land promise was inseparable from the promise of descendants it followed that they held legitimate title to the land. The refutation came in the form of a reminder that the promise of land was conditional – a point often overlooked but made repeatedly in Deuteronomy. Their sinful conduct eating bloody meat, the cult of idols, murder, adultery – had invalidated their claim (33:25–26).

The conflict of interpretations underlying these two passages illustrates the importance for creating and sustaining group identity of common ancestry or, in

---

31 Some rabbinic texts found a reference here to the origins of the synagogue. The Targum reads: "I have given them synagogues second only to my holy temple because they are few in number".

Weber's terms, a subjective belief in common descent. It also illustrates how seminal at that time was the figure of Abraham for communities in both Judah and the Babylonian diaspora. The lack of narrative tradition about Abraham datable earlier than the Neo-Babylonian period has strengthened the case of those scholars who argue that we owe the rich and complex narrative about him in Genesis (11:27–25:11) not to oral tradition from before the formation of the kingdoms, much less from the Middle Bronze period, but to literary circles during the Neo-Babylonian or early Persian period. But whatever date is assigned to these traditions, they make a remarkable fit with the aspirations and the actual experience of those in the Babylonian diaspora who eventually returned to Judah. Abraham's journey is represented as beginning in southern Mesopotamia where the Judeans would later settle,[32] and was interrupted by a stay of indeterminate length in Harran on the Balikh river. Harran was a major center of the cult of the deity Sîn to which Nabonidus was much attached. The Judaean deportees would probably have known that Nabonidus had restored the temple of Sîn in Harran the destruction of which in 610 by the Medes was due, as Nabonidus tells us, to the anger of the native deity, in the same way that the destruction of Jerusalem was attributed to the anger of Yahweh.[33] Since Harran is too far north to be a logical stage on the route to Palestine, there may also be some connection with whatever remained of the Israelite-Samarian diaspora settled in the region of Gozan (*guzãnu*) on the river Khãbūr, not far from Harran.[34]

On his arrival, Abraham found the land, apparently under no central, local authority, inhabited by Canaanites (Gen 12:6b) and Hittites (*běnê-hēt*, Gen 23:3, etc). The former bring to mind the derogatory use of this gentilic with reference to the indigenous peoples in Ezra-Nehemiah, while the latter corresponds to the description of Syria-Palestine as "Hatti land" (*māt hattu*) in Neo-Babylonian royal inscriptions. Another indication of the contemporary flavor of the narrative is the description in the "covenant of the pieces" of the promised land as extending from the river of Egypt to the Euphrates (Gen 15:18), corresponding to the ex-

---

32 Canaan was the destination of Terah and his group from the beginning in Ur Kasdim (Gen 11:31). The biblical account gives no reason for Abraham's departure from Ur Kasdim, but the omission is rectified by later authors who emphasize Abraham's monotheistic faith and his rejection of Babylonian cults and astrology, including those cherished by Terah, his father. See, for example, *Jub.* 11:4–17; 12:1–8; *Ant.* 1:155; Philo, *On Abraham* 70–80.
33 Paul-Alain Beaulieu, *The Reign of Nabonidus King of Babylon* (New Haven & London: Yale, 1989), 43–65.
34 2 Kgs 17:6; 18:11; 1 Chr 5:26. On the Nimrud Prism Sargon II claims that he settled the Samarian deportees "in the midst of Assyria" (*ina qereb aššur*). See Mordechai Cogan and Hayim Tadmor, *II Kings: A New Translation with Introduction and Commentary* (New York: Doubleday, 1988), 197; Lawson Younger, "The Deportations of the Israelites," *JBL* 117 (1988): 201–27.

tent of the Transeuphrates section of the fifth satrapy (Babirush-Ebernari) before the conquest of Egypt in 525 BC.

Abraham's activities in the land, and his relations with its inhabitants, suggest that he could have served, and was probably intended to serve, as exemplary model for the first immigrants in the late Babylonian or early Persian period. In the Priestly version of the Genesis narrative Abraham lived in the land as an alien (Gen 17:8), and he himself insists that he is a resident alien living among them (23:4–6). He is therefore not an intruder, a carpetbagger coming in from outsider to exploit the local population or steal their land. Though entitled to take precedence, he gives Lot first choice where to settle (13:11–12). He resolves a dispute about property peacefully by negotiating with a local ruler in the Beersheba region (21:32). He bargains for a small plot of land for himself and purchases it for a price far in excess of the going rate (23:1–20).[35] In this incident, recounted in detail by the Priestly writer, the emphasis is on the complete legality of the proceedings, and it has been observed that these proceedings follow the pattern of Neo-Babylonian land contracts, another pointer to the contemporaneous relevance of the narrative.

The other incident recounted at length in the Priestly version of the Abraham story, the covenant of circumcision, raises another issue of relevance at the time of composition (Gen 17:1–27). There is no question that Ishmael, born to Abraham and his proxy wife Hagar (16:15–16), enters the covenant which is made with Abraham and all his descendants, and does so before Isaac, Abraham's other beloved son. . It is stated redundantly that Abraham is to be the ancestor of peoples, in the plural, and the circumcision of Ishmael "on that very day" (Gen 17: 23,26), a year before Isaac, puts the matter beyond doubt. This conclusion is only called into question after the announcement that Sarah, though ninety-nine years old, is to give birth to a child who will take precedence over Ishmael (vv 15–22). If, however, this further revelation is to be consistent with what has been said to that point, it can only mean that Ishmael and his descendants remain within the covenant, but not in the same way and to the same degree as Isaac. This could hardly fail to be of interest to a reader or hearer in Judah in the sixth or fifth century BC Kedar, "son" of Ishmael (Gen 25:13), was the leading member of a North Arabian tribal confederacy which by the fifth century BC had displaced the Edomites from much of their territory and settled a broad swathe of land from the Tranjordanian plateau to the Nile delta. They were sub-

---

35 With the 400 shekels offered by Ephron and accepted by Abraham compare the 17 shekels paid for a field by Jeremiah (Jer 32:9), 50 shekels paid by David for Arauna's threshing floor with some oxen thrown in (2 Sam 24:24), and the 6000 shekels (two talents of silver) paid by Omri for the entire area covered by the city of Samaria (1 Kgs 16:24).

dued by the Babylonians (Jer 49:28) and, a few years later, assisted Cambyses in the invasion of Egypt (Herodotus, Hist. 3:4,88). The sheik Geshem (Gashmu), head of the confederacy, belonged to Nehemiah's "axis of evil" together with Sanballat and Tobiah the Ammonite (Neh 2:19; 6:1–2,16), but in the Genesis account the attitude to Ishmael and his Arabian descendants is unreservedly positive. And in general, neither here nor elsewhere in the Abraham narrative in Genesis, do we sense hostility towards or hear denunciations of the local people and their "abominations". In fact, Abraham does not comment on their morals at all.

5 Legal interpretation and identity formation: Ezra and his supporters

Group identity no less than individual identity is formed by differentiation in an interactive social environment; both the group and the individual come to define themselves over against but not necessarily in opposition to others. If in his interaction with the indigenous peoples of Canaan Abraham can be said to represent a soft ideology, we would have to situate Ezra and his golah group (*běnê haggôlâ*) at the other extremity of the ideological band.[36] The account of their activities illustrates the important part played by law and legal interpretation in the formation of group identity and ethos. It goes without saying (but let us say it) that the claim to interpret laws translates readily into political power, the power to establish social and religious boundaries, to coerce, and to define those who interpret the laws otherwise out of the group.

One of the clearest and at the same time the most problematic instances of legal interpretation as a central element in the formation and reinforcement of group identity, one in which we see Ezra and his supporters in action, is the crisis created by the marriage of male members of the golah to native women (Ezra 9–10). The incident is cast in both first-person and third-person discourse. It is probably a composite since the narrative runs smoothly down to the point where Ezra administers the oath to priests, Levites and laity (Ezra 10:5), but then starts up again with Ezra praying, fasting and mourning over the infidelity of the golah (10:6–44). It concludes with a sentence unintelligible in MT but which in First Esdras (9:36) states simply that "they sent them (the native women) away togeth-

---

[36] The language of soft and hard ideology ("ideologia morbida, dura") is taken from Mario Liverani, *Oltre la Bibbia: Storia Antica di Israele* (2nd ed., Roma & Bari: Laterza, 2004), 283–87.

er with the children".[37] Shecaniah, perhaps a leader of "those who tremble at the words of the God of Israel (the *hărēdîm*)", insists that the dismissal of the indigenous wives of golah men together with their children be done "according to the law" (*kattôrâ*, Ezra 10:3). The law in question would have been a combination of Deut 7:1–4 (the prohibition of intermarriage with the seven indigenous peoples) and 23:4–6 (the exclusion of four ethnic categories from entering the Israelite assembly), or perhaps the latter interpreted intertextually and expansively in light of the former. Ezekiel's temple law (Ezekiel 40–48), with its exclusion of resident foreigners from entering the temple which, in effect, excluded them from membership in the community (Ezek 44:9), would also probably have played a part. But what "according to the law" really means is that this drastic solution, with its inevitably disruptive and even tragic consequences, is to be carried out according to one interpretation of the law, the one elaborated within Ezra's party, an interpretation by no means self-evident, and one certainly not shared by the other characters moving about in the background of the story, nor indeed by Jewish communities elsewhere at that time.

The solution also went against the grain of traditional custom. In traditional societies endogamous marriage, marriage within the tribal and clan network, was the preferred option, but without any overlay of ritual ethnicity. The marriages of Isaac and Jacob were of a type of forbidden in the ritual laws of consanquinity and affinity (Lev 18:11–13). Abraham married not one but two Arabian women (Gen 16:15–16; 25:1–6). Moses also appears to have married two Midianite (and therefore Arabian) women (Exod 2:21–22; Num 12:1),[38] Joseph married the daughter of an Egyptian priest (Gen 41:45), Judah married without comment a Canaanite woman (Gen 38:1–2), and neither David nor Solomon showed any great concern for the origin of the many women they had intimate relations with. But the most remarkable aspect of this coercive dissolution of marriages is that not only is nothing said about the possibility of less drastic solutions to the problem (e. g. conversion, a ritual of purification), and nothing about the laws protecting the rights of widows and orphans, but not a word is said about the legal consequences. One might object that what was at issue was not divorce but a unique intervention of Ezra in pursuit of an important so-

---

37 Peter Ackroyd suggested a combination of an Ezra and a Shecaniah account, which would be consistent with the dominant role assigned to this lay person in the story: Peter Ackroyd, "The Chronicler as Exegete," *JSOT* 2 (1977): 2–32 (16). Shecaniah tells Ezra that the situation is bad but not hopeless, he proposes a sworn covenant, tells Ezra to get up off the ground and discharge his responsibilities in the matter, and then disappears.
38 The *'iššâ kušît* (Num 12:1) was more probably from Cushan, linked with Midian in Hab 3:7, than with the region south of Egypt.

cial goal. Ezra was indeed pursuing such a goal, but we recall that Shecaniah insisted that it should be done "according to the law," and according to the law what happened was divorce. In all law collections from the Near East and the Levant marriage was a contractual arrangement, and the dissolution of marriage always entailed serious economic consequences.[39] Marriage contracts from Elephantine contain a detailed inventory of the goods which the woman brings into the marriage and which are to be returned to her, together with other significant disbursements, in the event of divorce. These contracts, especially those from the archive of the thrice-married Miphtahiah, clearly a remarkable lady, also show that marriage could be with an Aramean from Syene, or a local Egyptian, or another Jewish member of the garrison community.[40] All of this raises serious questions about the laconic ending to the episode: "So they sent them away, women and children alike."

As for the consequences of this campaign of Ezra and his supporters, and their policy of strictly-enforced ritual ethnicity in general, there can be no doubt that they enjoyed only a limited success. In the short term, the campaign concerned primarily the golah elite, lay and priestly (Ezra 9:2), which was precisely the class on which the imperial authorities relied as a force for the stability and preservation of the *pax persica*. The court at Susa would not have appreciated a local official stirring up a hornet's nest in a small but strategically significant province of the empire. This consideration may help to explain the abrupt conclusion to the Ezra story and the almost total absence of Ezra from the record during the later Second Temple period. The freedom with respect to marriage and other alliances exercised by the high priests Eliashib and Joiada (Neh 13:4–9, 28) was preserved and enlarged in the ranks of the Jerusalem priesthood after the transition to Ptolemaic rule, as is evident from our sources for that century and beyond.[41] By no means all Jews would have experienced the new Hellenic spirit abroad as incompatible with or necessarily compromising their religious commitments. Some of the most powerful writings from the late Second Temple

---

39 E.g. Hammurapi §§ 128, 137–140; Eshnunna § 59. The translated texts are conveniently available in Martha Roth, *Law Collections from Mesopotamia and Asia Minor* (Atlanta: Scholars Press, 1995).
40 Berkeley Porten and Ada Yardeni, *Textbook of Aramaic Documents from Ancient Egypt*, Vol. 2, *Contracts* (Jerusalem: Israel Academy of Sciences and Humanities, 1989), 30–33.60–63.78–83.131–40; Edward Lipiński, "Marriage and Divorce in the Judaism of the Persian Period," *Transeuph* 4 (1991): 63–71.
41 Apropos of the disputed issue of the marriage of Manasseh with Nikaso, Sanballat's daughter, Josephus reports that "many priests and Levites were involved in such marriages" (*Ant.* 11:312). He notes further than it was customary for Jerusalemites accused of sabbath violation or similar offences to relocate to Samaria (*Ant.* 11:346–347).

period (Wisdom of Solomon, Baruch, Fourth Maccabees, Aristeas) combine fidelity to the essentials of Judaism with the best in Greek philosophical and ethical thinking. If Ezra's policy of ritual ethnicity had enjoyed success then, and had continued to be successful, Ruth the Moabite would never have married Boaz, and Achior the Ammonite (Judith 14:10) would never have been accepted into the Jewish community. Above all, we would be unable to account for the great demographic increase of the Jewish ethnos between the Persian and the Roman periods. Understandings and expressions of Jewish identity different from those of Ezra remained available.

IV. Bethel in the Neo-Babylonian and early Achaemenid period

1 The early history of Bethel

For the history of Bethel in the Iron age, including its last phase, we have to depend almost exclusively on the biblical texts. Since Edward Robinson's epic horse ride through Palestine in 1838, the site has been identified with, and is to a considerable extent (all but four acres or sixteen dunams) covered by the Arab village of Beitin. It lies about 16 km north of Jerusalem and 2.5 km north-west of Ai (assuming the identification of Ai with et-Tell), on a hilltop site with springs nearby, on the main north-south route from the central hill country to the Jordan valley. It was excavated initially in 1934 by W. F. Albright assisted by Kelso, then by Kelso alone in 1954, 1957 and 1960. Unfortunately, the report of the excavation published in 1968 provides no reliable stratigraphy, follows the still familiar practice of extrapolating conclusions from the biblical data, and cannot be safely used for purposes of historical reconstruction.[1]

Bethel features in the city and boundary lists of both Ephraim (1 Chr 7:28) and Benjamin, the southern branch of Ephraim (Josh 18:22), and was situated on the southern boundary between Ephraim and Benjamin (Josh 16:1–2; 18:13), near the boundary between the kingdoms of Judah and Samaria. According to one version its former name was Luz (Gen 28:19; Judg 1:23), but in the Josephite boundary list Luz is located west of Bethel, between Bethel and Ataroth (Josh 16:1–2). In the Benjamin boundary list the corresponding points – reading east to west – are Beth-aven, Luz and Ataroth (Josh 18:12–13). The discrepancy can be explained as follows. The Bethel where Jacob's vision took place (Gen 28:10–22) was an ancient sanctuary situated not on the site of the city but to the east in the direction of Ai, as we learn from Abraham's itinerary (Gen 12:8; 13:3) and the military dispositions of Joshua's attack on Ai, near Beth-aven east of Bethel (Josh 7:2). Once it became from the point of view of Jerusalemite orthodoxy a dissident and heterodox center, Bethel acquired the dysphemism *Bêt-'āven*, a term deemed appropriate since *'āven* ("evil, mischief") can also con-

---

1 William Foxwell Albright, "The Kyle Memorial Excavations at Bethel," *BASOR* 56 (1934): 2–15. James Kelso et al., *The Excavation of Bethel* (Cambridge/Mass: ASOR, 1968); "Bethel," in *EAEHL* 1, 190–93; "Bethel," in *NEAEHL* 1, 192–94. See also the critical remarks of William Dever, "Archaeological Methods and Results: A Review of Two Recent Publications," *Orientalia* 40 (1971): 459–71; "Bethel," in *OEANE* 1, 300–1.

note an unacceptable cult object.² But like other originally derogatory designations it became in the course of time an ordinary place name (Josh 7:2; 18:12–13; 1 Sam 14:23). At some point, then, and under circumstances unknown to us, the sanctuary gave its name to the nearby "city" of Luz, as we see from the gloss identifying Luz with Bethel (Gen 35:6; Josh 18:13).

The biblical texts provide some information about Iron Age Bethel. The conquest narratives, in which Bethel is closely associated with Ai, provide two different accounts of its capture (Josh 7:2; 8:1–29; 12:9,16; cf. Judg 1:22–26), and during the Philistine wars there was a high place for sacrifice at Bethel frequented by ecstatics (nĕbî'îm, 1 Sam 10:3 cf. 2 Kgs 2:2–3,23). The name itself would suggest that it was an ancient sanctuary, though Kelso's archaeological arguments for its existence from the Middle Bronze period are not persuasive.³ Bethel came into its own when Jeroboam made it the principal sanctuary of his kingdom, situated on its southern border as Dan was at its northern extremity. (1 Kgs 12:28–33). Bethel, described as "a royal sanctuary, a temple of the kingdom" (Amos 7:13), was established deliberately as a rival to the Jerusalem temple (1 Kgs 12:27–28), with a different liturgical calendar (12:32–33), and non-Levitical priests referred to by the Historian in a derogatory fashion as kōhănê habbāmôt, "priests of the high places", 12:31–32). We shall see that the descendants of these priests had an important part to play in the religious history of emergent Judaism during the Neo-Babtylonian and early Achaemenid periods.

The animus of the Deuteronomistic Historian (hereafter the Historian *tout court*) against Jeroboam's cult center at Bethel is apparent from the prediction of its destruction by Josiah immediately following its establishment (1 Kings 13), the fulfillment of which is duly noted (2 Kgs 23:4,15–20). On the history of the site during the time of the two kingdoms we are not well informed. It may have changed hands more than once in the frequent wars between the two kingdoms – 2 Chr 13:19 mentions one occasion during the reign of Abijah – and it may have been occupied temporarily by Baasha during the following reign (1 Kgs 15:16–17). The important point is that it survived the Assyrian conquest in 722 BC. After the deportations and the arrival of foreign immigrants the Assyrians reactivated the Bethel sanctuary so that the new population might know and ob-

---

2 'āven is linked with tĕrāfîm ("idols") at 1 Sam 15:23 and Zech 10:2; see also Isa 66:3b *mazkîr lĕvōnâ mĕvārēk 'āven* ("the one who makes a memorial offering pronounces a blessing over an idol"). At Amos 5:5b *bêt-'ēl yihyeh lĕ'āven*, ("Bethel will become an evil thing" or "Bethel will come to nothing") it is uncertain whether Bethel is a place name or the name of the god associated with the site.
3 James Kelso, *The Excavation of Bethel*, 23.

serve "the law of the god of the land" (2 Kgs 17:24–28).[4] We may therefore accept that it continued in existence without interruption as a central place of worship, serving the remaining indigenous population and the mixed population brought in after the fall of Samaria and on subsequent occasions (Ezra 4:2,10 and Isa 7:8b). Josiah is reported to have desecrated the Bethel sanctuary and dismantled its cult apparatus (2 Kgs 23:4,15,20), but even granted the historical reliability of the report in 2 Kings 23, the effects of Josiah's reforming zeal may have been no more lasting at Bethel than they proved to be in Jerusalem. There is therefore no reason to doubt that Bethel continued to function down into the Neo-Babylonian period.

Another issue to be addressed is the identity of the deity worshipped at Bethel. There can be no doubt that a deity named *bêt-'ēl*, probably an abbreviation of *'ēl bêt-'ēl*, was known and worshipped in the Kingdom of Israel, the diaspora, and perhaps also in Judah. Bethel is a northwest-semitic deity first attested in the treaty imposed on king Baal of Tyre by Esarhaddon in 675 BC. It occurs as a theophoric element in personal names as late as the Neo-Babylonian and Persian periods.[5] In a saying directed against Moab, Jer 48:13 states that "Moab will be ashamed of Chemosh, as the house of Israel was ashamed of Bethel, the source of their confidence". Here Bethel is clearly a deity worshipped in the north, and an important deity since it is paired with Chemosh (Kamoš), the national deity of Moab. Other biblical references are less clear. The deity who appeared to Jacob in Mesopotamia identified himself as *hā'ēl bêt-'ēl*, Gen 31:13), where the context requires that Bethel is a place name rather than the name of a deity. On the way to his appointment as king, Saul is told that he will encounter three men *'ōlîm 'el-hā'ĕlohîm bêt-'ēl* (1 Sam 10:3). The interpretation is uncertain since this could mean that the men were going up either to the god Bethel or to the god at Bethel (with the preposition elided). Uncertainty also attends the denunciations of Bethel in Amos. The injunction in Amos 5:5 not to seek Bethel could be contrasted with the appeal to seek Yahveh in order to find life, and therefore most naturally be understood as an alien deity, or it could be juxtaposed with the prohibition of frequenting Gilgal (as in Hos 4:15), and therefore be a toponym. Likewise, the al-

---

4 According to James Kelso, *The Excavation of Bethel*, 37 Bethel was destroyed in 722, but since he offers no evidence in support of this statement apart from the absence of pottery the biblical record stands. A further problem is that Kelso overlooks the biblical texts which place the sanctuary outside of the town.

5 *ANET* 534; Michael David Coogan, *West Semitic Personal Names in the Murasu Documents* (Missoula/Montana: Society of Biblical Literature, 1976), 48–49; Edward Dalglish, "Bethel (Deity)," in *ABD* 1, 706–10; Wolfgang Röllig, "Bethel," in *DDD*[2], 173–75.

lusion to the altars of Bethel in Amos 3:14b could refer either to the place or the god.

A decisive factor, and one of interest and relevance for the period with which we are concerned, is the existence of a cult of the god Bethel in the Jewish settlement on the island of Elephantine at the first cataract of the Nile and among the Syrian-Arameans of Syene on the east bank opposite the island. There was a temple of Bethel and one for the Queen of Heaven in Syene, and among the Elephantine Jews oaths were sworn in the name of "Bethel the god" (AP 7:7) and offerings were made for the deities Anath-Bethel and Eshem-Bethel, different hypostases of the same deity (AP 22). The popularity of this deity is also reflected in the relatively high number of Elephantine personal names containing Bethel as a theophoric element.[6]

A final observation: In the second of the three "seek passages" in Amos (5:6) the threat of punishment on the house of Joseph is interpreted as directed against Bethel. The syntax of the sentence suggests strongly that lĕbêt-'ēl, "with respect to Bethel") is a gloss. We do not know when the gloss was added, but if in the early post-exilic period, when other additions were made to the book, it could refer to the Bethel sanctuary which, as will be argued, was in operation at that time.

2 Bethel during the exilic period

In common with other sites in Benjaminite territory, Bethel was not destroyed during the Babylonian punitive expedition of 588–586. The archaeological evidence for the last phase of Beitin is inconclusive, but it is at least clear that it survived the Babylonian conquest and continued in existence until at least the mid-sixth century BC. The dating of the archaeological evidence has gradually been pushed forward from the early sixth century to the last decades of that century.[7] Writing in Kelso's report on the dig, Sinclair dated it during the reign of either Nabonidus or Cyrus II, but in view of the reservations noted above it is still a case of *caveat lector*.[8] Bethel could have been destroyed by the dominant

---

[6] Bezalel Porten, *Archives from Elephantine: The Life of an Ancient Jewish Military Colony* (Berkeley & Los Angeles: University of California Press, 1968), 328–31; "The Religion of the Jews of Elephantine in Light of the Hermopolis Papyri," *JNES* 28 (1969): 116–21.
[7] William Foxwell Albright, "The Kyle Memorial Excavations at Bethel," *BASOR* 56 (1934): 2–15 (14); James Kelso, *The Excavation at Bethel*, 11, 37, 51.
[8] Lawrence Sinclair, "Bethel Pottery of the Sixth Century BC," in *The Excavation at Bethel*, 70–76 (75–76).

Judaeo-Babylonian element during a phase of internal strife, or as a result of encroachment from Samaria. It could also have happened in connection with one or other of the military crises of the mid to late sixth century affecting the province, for example, the obscure events news of which was brought to Nehemiah in Susa by Hananiah (Neh 1:1–4), or the revolt of Megabyzus, assuming this was not what Hananiah's news was about. In the absence of both reliable archaeological data and written information we can only speculate.

The decisive circumstance affecting Bethel at that time was its proximity to Mizpah (Tell en-Nasbeh), center of the Babylonian administration of the region. Bethel is about 6 km north of Mizpah on the north-south highway. The location of the old Beth-aven sanctuary is unknown, but if it was, as the relevant biblical texts suggest, between Bethel and Ai, it could have been even closer. The archaeological data attest that the territory of Benjamin escaped retribution at the hands of the Babylonians. The evidence has often been reviewed and its interpretation in this sense widely accepted.[9] The same conclusion is suggested by the census of Ezra 2:1–67 = Neh 7:6–68 according to which twelve or thirteen of the twenty or so locations in which the first Judaeo-Babylonian immigrants are said to have settled are in Benjamin and only two (Bethlehem and Netophah) lie south of Jerusalem (Ezra 2:20–35 = Neh 7:25–38). This circumstance has been explained on the hypothesis that the inhabitants of the Benjaminite region surrendered at an early stage of the campaign.[10] This is possible, but it seems to me more likely that, like Jeremiah who was arrested during the siege of Jerusalem as a deserter, and who owned real estate in Benjamin (Jer 37:11–16 cf. 32:6–15), the inhabitants of the region belonged from the beginning of the Babylonian takeover to the anti-war or appeasement party. Barely a generation after Josiah's incursion into the former Assyrian province of Samerina and his desecration of Bethel (2 Kgs 23:15–20), Benjaminite and Ephraimite resentment and antipathy towards Judah could still have been strong. Whatever the explanation, after the catastrophe of 586 the center of gravity, politically, socially and, I believe, religiously, moved decisively northward from the Judaean heartland to the region corresponding to the tribal territory of Benjamin.

For our knowledge of the Babylonian administration of the region we have to rely almost exclusively on the biblical texts. Neo-Babylonian royal inscriptions are not forthcoming on the subject of provincial organization and administra-

---

9 Oded Lipschits, "The History of the Benjamin Region under Babylonian Rule," *Tel Aviv* 26 (1999): 155–90.
10 Abraham Malamat, "The Last Wars of the Kingdom of Judah," *JNES* 9 (1950): 218–27 (227); Maxwell Miller and John Hayes, *Ancient Israel: A New History of Israelite Society* (Sheffield: Sheffield Academic Press, 1986), 178.

tion, but this does not justify the conclusion that none existed in the Cisjordanian region. The inscriptions of Nebuchadnezzar refer to kings and governors in Eber-nāri and Hatti land, and Gedaliah's appointment as a puppet king (as I will argue) would be in keeping with what the biblical historian reports about Babylonian practice (2 Kgs 24:1,17). We have even less information on provincial organization in the west after the Persian takeover, but it is safe to assume that the new overlords left the existing system in place, at least for a time. The relevant biblical texts are Jeremiah 40–41 and the much briefer account in 2 Kgs 25:22–26 which may be an abstract of the Jeremiah text. Gedaliah (Gedalyahu), member of the influential Shaphanite family associated with the anti-war party, and almost certainly a Benjaminite, was established as the Babylonian appointee in Mizpah, either as governor (*bēl pihāti*) or, more probably, as puppet king,[11] only to be assassinated by Ishmael, a member of the royal family, with Ammonite support. By mentioning only the seventh month (2 Kgs 25:25; Jer 41:1), the texts have left us in doubt as to how soon after the fall of Jerusalem this event took place. Several scholars, most recently Lipschits,[12] have argued for the shorter option, a period of no more than two months rather than several years. The best, and possibly the only argument in favor of this opinion rests on the pattern of dating from the siege of Jerusalem, concluding with a sequence of the fourth, fifth and seventh months (2 Kgs 25:3,8,25). But the problem with this argument is precisely that the year is missing only with the date of the assassination. Moreover, two months is hardly time enough to allow for the dust to settle after the destruction and mayhem of the Babylonian campaign, an administrative apparatus to be set up at Mizpah, the conspiracy to develop in Ammon (Jer 40:13–16), people to dribble back from other regions, some of them quite distant (Jer 40:7–8, 11–12), and the last harvest of the agrarian year to be gathered in (Jer 40:12). It therefore seems preferable to connect Ishmael's terrorist act with the deportation mentioned in Jer 52:30 dated to the twenty-third year of Nebuchadrezzar, therefore 582 BC.

---

11 The biblical texts state simply that the Babylonian king appointed him (2 Kgs 25:22–23; Jer 40:5,7,11; 41:2); "as governor" is added gratuitously in several modern versions. That Gedaliah was not of the Davidic line could account for the reticence of the texts and the use of the verb *hipqîd* ("appoint") rather than *himlîk* ("appoint as king") as with the appointment of Mattaniah renamed Zedekiah (2 Kgs 24:17). The conduct of Zedekiah as a Babylonian vassal would have discouraged a repetition of the experiment.

12 Oded Lipschits, "The History of the Benjaminite Region under Babylonian Rule," 162.

3 The reactivation of Bethel as an important cult center

The destruction of the Jerusalem temple, the personnel of which had provided religious backing for the revolt of the "rebellious city harmful to kings and prolvinces" (Ezra 4:15), was a deliberate and demonstrative act, and we can be sure that the Babylonian generalissimo Nebuzaradan did a thorough job of it. (For the condition of the ruins see Lam 1:4; 2:6–7,20 and perhaps also Ps 74:1–7). The leading priests were executed (2 Kgs 25:18) to discourage any further cultic activity on the site, and the altar was, in any case, corpse-contaminated and therefore rendered ritually inaccessible. Even if the Book of Lamentations was written for recital at the site of the ruined temple, which is possible but unprovable, such lamenting would no more have qualified as cultic activity than praying today at the *kōtel*. Hence the need for an alternative cult site, comparable in some respects to the situation following on the fall of Samaria in 722 (2 Kgs 17:27–28). In view of the political and social shift into the Benjaminite region after 586 it would be natural to think of a location for cult in connection with the administrative center of the region at Mizpah. And, in fact, a late narrative strand locates cultic activity, much of it characteristic of post-destruction piety, at Mizpah where the people gathered in plenary cultic assembly (*lipnê YHWH*, "in the presence of Yahveh"). These acts included intercessory prayer, a water pouring ceremony, fasting, sacrifice and preaching (Judg 20:1; 1 Sam 7:5–10; 10:17–25). Furthermore, the memory of Mizpah as a "place of prayer" (*topos proseuchēs*) was still alive centuries later (1 Macc 3:46).

In this connection, the puzzling incident recorded in Jer 41:4–8 in which eighty pilgrims from Shechem, Shiloh and Samaria found themselves in the wrong place at the wrong time calls for comment. As they approached Mizpah on the day after the assassination of Gedaliah and his courtiers, in mourning attire and bearing grain offering and incense for "the house of YHWH", Ishmael went out to meet them, accompanied them into the city, and treacherously slaughtered them there. The final phrase of Jer 41:4, (*vĕ'îš lo' yāda'*, "and no one knew"), that is, about the assassination, suggests that the reason for this further deed of blood was to gain time for Ishmael by preventing the knowledge of his terrorist act from spreading, which in its turn suggests that the destination of the northern delegation was a "house of YHWH" in or near Mizpah rather than in Jerusalem.[13] Whatever the date of the assassination of Gedaliah, whether 586 or

---

[13] The objection that Ishmael went out of Mizpah in order to intercept their further progress to Jerusalem is not cogent, since a glance at the concordance will demonstrate that the expression *liqrat + ys'* often refers to going out of a place to meet some one and escort them back to the place – an act of courtesy – feigned in this instance.

582, it is unlikely that a group of pilgrims from Shechem, Shiloh and Samaria would come with offerings to Jerusalem, and in any case incredible that they would not have known that the Jerusalem temple was inaccessible for making offerings, even without animal sacrifice.[14]

Further confirmation may be found in the fictional account of the crime of Benjaminite Gibeah and the campaign of extermination waged against the Benjaminites by a tribal coalition led by Judah which followed (Judges 19–21). Mizpah was the base camp for the pan-Israelite force where decisions were made and oaths were taken, but it was also the place where the *qāhāl* (20:2) or *'ēdâ* (20:1; 21:10,13,16) assembled "in the presence of YHWH" (20:1). For the more explicitly religious acts – inquiring of God (20:18,23,27–28), sacrifice (20:26; 21:4), fasting (20:26), communal lamenting (20:23,26; 21:2–3) – the allies gathered at Bethel where, we are told in a brief *addendum*, the ark of the covenant was located under the care of Pinhas (Phineas) grandson of Aaron (20:27b–28a). Several features of this narrative can be read as reflecting the situation in the years immediately following the fall of Jerusalem: animus against Benjaminites who are described in the story as *'anšê bĕnê bĕliyy'al*, "a perverse lot" (19:22; 20:13); liturgical praxis, especially fasting and communal lamentation characteristic of the Second Temple period; and the practice of deciding important issues in the plenary assembly of the *qāhāl* or *'ēdâ*, terms of frequent occurrence in post-destruction compositions (the Priestly History and Ezra-Nehemiah). It is noteworthy that presence at the assembly is required under pain of death (Judg 21:5), as in the Ezra narrative (Ezra 10:8) absenteeism from the *qāhāl* is punished with the social death of ostracism.

The sources at our disposal, such as they are, are no doubt patient of more than one interpretation. But it seems to me a reasonable hypothesis – and by no means a new one,[15] that following on the elimination of the Jerusalem temple the old Bethel sanctuary, having survived the Assyrian conquest and the reforming zeal of Josiah, obtained a new lease of life by virtue of the favored status of the Benjamin region and the proximity of Bethel to the administrative center at Miz-

---

14 Douglas Jones, "The Cessation of Sacrifice after the Destruction of the Temple in 586 BC," *JTS* 14 (1963): 12–31, noted that the unfortunate pilgrims did not bring animals, and speculated that animal sacrifice was discontinued between the destruction of the first temple and the building of the second, analogous to the situation at Elephantine. On the view defended here, however, no sacrifice was going on in Jerusalem during that period.
15 Different versions of the hypothesis were proposed some years ago by Theophile James Meek, "Aaronites and Zadokites," *AJSLL* 45 (1929): 149–66; Francis Sprarling North, "Aaron's Rise in Prestige," *ZAW* 66 (1954): 191–99; H. G. Judge, "Aaron, Zadok and Abiathar", *JTS* 7 (1956): 70–74.

pah; hence the juxtaposition of Mizpah and Bethel and the hostility between Judah and Benjamin in Judges 20–21. Unfortunately, we have no information on Babylonian administrative arrangements at the southern end of the Syro-Palestinian corridor. If, as seems plausible, even probable, the Babylonians took over the provincial system more or less unchanged from the Assyrians,[16] it is possible that Mizpah and the Bethel sanctuary served both Judah and part or all of the territory corresponding to the Assyrian provinces carved out of the old Kingdom of Samaria. This would fit well with a visit to Mizpah, rather than to Jerusalem, by devotees from Shechem, Shiloh and Samaria, and would also help to explain the endemic hostility of the Samaritan population to the reestablishment of a political and religious center in Jerusalem during the early Achaemenid period.

Something should now be said about the problematic reference to Bethel in Zech 7:1–7. MT may be translated as follows:

> 1 In the fourth year of King Darius, the word of Yahveh came to Zechariah on the fourth of the ninth month, in Chislev. 2 Sareser, Regemmelech and his men had sent to Bethel to placate Yahveh, 3 and to ask the priests who were attached to the house of Yahveh of the Hosts and the prophets, "Should we lament and practice abstinence on the fifth month, as we have been doing for these many years?" 4 Then the word of Yahveh of the hosts came to me: 5 "Say to all the people of the land and the priests: When you fasted and lamented in the fifth and the seventh month during these seventy years, was it for me that you fasted? 6 And when you eat and drink, do you not eat and drink for yourselves? 7 Was not this the message that Yahveh proclaimed through the former prophets when Jerusalem was still inhabited and at peace together with the cities round about it, and when the Negev and the Shephelah were still inhabited?"

Since the word of Yahveh announced in v 1 is cited only in vv 5–7, introduced by the resumptive v 4, the account of the mission to placate Yahveh appears to have been inserted in order to provide an occasion for the statement about fasting that follows. The assumption would then be that *vayyišlaḥ* is pluperfect and that the mission preceded the date of the saying, the fourth year of Darius I, i.e., 518 BC. The most natural construction of 7:2 would be to read *bêt-'ēl* as the destination and either Sareser alone (since the verb is singular) or Sareser *et alii* as subject, therefore "Sareser [Regemmelech and his men] had sent to Bethel ..." This reading has the support of LXX, the Peshitta and the Targum (Vulg., implausibly, has *ad domum dei*, "to the house of God" for Bethel). Though it is unusual, it is not

---

[16] This view, argued by Albrecht Alt, *Kleine Schriften zur Geschichte des Volkes Israel*, Vol. 1 (Munich: Beck, 1964 [1929]), 188, has been widely accepted; administrative continuity is the rule not the exception.

out of the question for the destination to precede the sender after the verb "to send". More importantly, by reading the text in this way we avoid the problem that at the time of the mission the Jerusalem temple was not yet rebuilt. This interpretation is admittedly uncertain, but it has a stronger claim than the alternative that takes "Bethel" to stand for "the people of Bethel", a construction which is without parallel except in poetic and symbolic personification of a city (e.g. Zion). A third option is to take Bethel-sareser as one personal name, corresponding to the Akkadian form *bit-ili-šar-usur* and similar personal names formed with *bêt-'ēl*. This, too, is possible, the name does exist, but the shorter form Sareser is also attested, and at closer quarters, in Judah (2 Kgs 19:37 = Isa 37:38), and we are still left with the problem of the date.

A similar request for a decision presented in the context of a prophetic saying is reported in Hag 2:10–14 and dated two years earlier. In this instance, the issues are ritual contamination and sacrifice rather than fasting, but the outcome is a similar statement of prophetic disapproval of what is offered *there* (*šām*, Hag 2:14), namely, a place other than Jerusalem where sacrifice of some kind was going on. As the reproach in Zechariah is addressed to the *'am hā'āres* and their priests who had been engaged since the fall of Jerusalem in disingenuous acts of piety, so the religious activity, including sacrifice, of "this people" (*hā'ām hazzeh*) and "this nation" (*haggoy hazzeh*) in Haggai are declared to be compromised and ritually unacceptable. The conclusion suggests itself that those addressed in both texts are to be identified with the *'am hā'āres* whom the dominant Judaeo-Babylonian faction considered to be religiously compromised, who opposed the political and religious restoration of Jerusalem in Ezra-Nehemiah, and insisted on worshipping elsewhere.[17]

The picture as a whole is still far from clear, but the three prophetic texts considered (Jer 41:4–5; Zech 7:1–7; Hag 2:10–14) have certain features in common: a mission or a question concerning cultic matters – lamentation, fasting, ritual purity and contamination, sacrifice – arising during the period from the destruction to the rebuilding of the Jerusalem temple; a negative attitude to the religious practices of the indigenous population; recourse to a place of worship other than Jerusalem. They do not constitute irrefutable evidence for an alternative cult site at Bethel, but they are consistent with a situation during the interim period 586–515 BCE when, for all or most of that time, Bethel served as the official sanctuary of Judah, Benjamin and perhaps also the central hill country.

---

17 Ezra 3:3; 4:1–4; 9:1–2; 10:2,11; Neh 10:31–32.

4 The Bethel priesthood

If this reconstruction of the cultic situation during the Babylonian interim is sustained, it would be of interest to know who were the priests who served at the Mizpah-Bethel sanctuary. A preliminary clue is the information that Pinhas (Phineas), son of Eleazar and grandson of Aaron, ministered to the ark at Bethel during the tribal war against Benjamin (Judg 20:27b–28a). This notice is generally taken to be a late addition, following in sequence on the presence of Eleazar at Shiloh (Josh 14:1; 17:4; 19:51; 21:1) and his death and burial at Gibeah (24:23),[18] but it is consistent with the association of Aaron *qua* eponym of the *běnê 'ahăron* with Bethel. That the connection can be deduced from the parallels between the episode of the Golden Calf (Exodus 32), in which Aaron plays the leading role, and the cult establishment of Jeroboam at Bethel (1 Kings 12), has long been acknowledged and by this time hardly calls for further elaboration. The episode concludes with the slaughter of the apostates, abetted by Aaron, at the hands of the *běnê lēvî* who in consequence are assured of priestly status (Exod 32:25–29). The same note of disparagement as we heard in the texts from Zechariah and Haggai can also be picked up in Deuteronomy 9:20, where Aaron is saved from death at the hands of an angry God by the intercession of Moses. A strong case can be made for the thesis that the Golden Calf episode in the Sinai-Horeb pericope (Exodus 32) was edited, and perhaps even composed, by a Deuteronomistic author as a polemical rewriting of what was originally the cult etiology of the Bethel sanctuary. The parallel etiology of the Dan sanctuary in Judg 18:27–31, consisting in the setting up of Micah's icon (*pesel*) in the newly-conquered city, gave rise to embarrassment of a different kind, since the Dan priesthood traced its origins to none other than Moses. It is not surprising therefore that the Masoretes felt obliged to disguise the association with Moses by introducing a *nun suspensum*, transforming "Moses" at the stroke of a pen into the reprobate "Manasseh" (Judg 18:30).

In neither Deuteronomy nor the associated History are priests known as "sons of Aaron" (*běnê 'ahăron*). In Deuteronomy the standard designation "Levitical priests" (hakkōhănîm halěviyyîm) would in fact appear to have a polemical edge in view of the notice that the priests appointed at Bethel by Jeroboam were non-Levitical (1 Kgs 12:31). If it is accepted that both Deuteronomy and the History date in their final form to the Neo-Babylonian period, currently the *opinio*

---

[18] George Foot Moore, *A Critical and Exegetical Commentary on Judges* (Edinburgh: T. & T. Clark, 1895), 433–34; John Gray, *Joshua, Judges and Ruth* (London: Nelson, 1967), 357, 386; Jan Alberto Soggin, *Judges: A Commentary* (Philadelphia: Westminster, 1981), 293.

communis, the much-discussed centralization of cultic activity in Jerusalem, repeated redundantly in the law section of the book (chapters 12 and 16 in particular), would be especially relevant to and consistent with the situation existing at that time as I have described it. In other words, the injunction to sacrifice and celebrate the festivals only in Jerusalem – whether the law was ever implemented or not – only makes good sense in the very limited confines of the province after the Babylonian conquest. The same could be said about the uncompromising rejection of non-Yahvistic cults and opposition to their practitioners among the indigenous inhabitants (Deut 7:1–6; 9:15–21; 12:1–4,29–31).

Further confirmation of the association of the *bĕnê 'ahărōn* with Bethel is at hand in the prophetic condemnation of the Eli priesthood at Shiloh recorded by the Historian (1 Sam 2:27–36). The ancestor of this priestly family, chosen by God to offer sacrifice and wear the ephod (v 28), can be none other than Aaron, and the "faithful priest" (*kōhēn ne'ĕmān*) who will displace the descendants of Aaron (v 35) none other than Zadok. This is not exactly what happened, since the priestly genealogies suggest a compromise by which the Zadokites were incorporated into the Aaronite line, but the incident testifies to conflict between two priestly factions preceding the final compromise. Aaronite descent is also indicated by the location of Eleazar, Aaron's son, in Shiloh during the conquest of the land (Josh 19:51; 21:1–2), followed by Phineas, his son, at Bethel (Judg 20:28).

Of special interest in this respect is the parallelism between the condemnation of the Shiloh priesthood, descended from Aaron, in 1 Sam 2:27–36, and that of the Bethel cult and its priesthood in 1 Kgs 13:1–10. Both condemnations are delivered by an anonymous "man of God" using the traditional prophetic *incipit* (1 Sam 2:27; 1 Kgs 13:1–2), both predict bad news for the priests in the distant future, and both give a verifiable sign in confirmation of the prediction (1 Sam 2:34; 1 Kgs 13:3). The Historian is making his point by placing the reprobation of the Shiloh-Bethel priesthood at important points in his History: the beginning of the prophetic movement and the beginning of the period of the kingdoms.

The "law of the temple" in Ezekiel 40–48 calls for a brief comment at this point. Whether the so-called Zadokite strand is from Ezekiel or a later scribal hand, it testifies to the priestly faction that opposed the Aaronite or proto-Aaronite priesthood in Neo-Babylonian Judah. To judge by the patronymic, Joshua ben Jehozadak (Hag 1:1,12; Zech 3:1–10; 6:8–14) was the principal representative of the Zadokite house in the early Persian period. According to the Zadokite strand in Ezekiel, all legitimate priests are Levitical, but among Levitical priests only the descendants of Zadok are legitimate.[19] Restriction of the priestly office to Za-

---

19 *mizzera' sādôq, bĕnê sādôq*, Ezek 40:45–46; 43:19; 44:15; 48:11.

dokites is justified on the grounds that they and they along remained faithful to their charge "when the Levites went astray" 48:11). Wellhausen took the "time of straying" to refer to the period prior to the abolition of the "high places,"[20] but since the author must have known that quite a bit of priestly straying took place after that point in time, the reference is more probably to the situation in Judah after the fall of Jerusalem.[21]

How tensions and conflicts between these priestly factions were resolved is beyond the scope of this inquiry. Our sources for the early Persian period, meager and uncertain of interpretation as they are, testify to conflict in Achaemenid Judah, not least between the dominant Judaeo-Babylonian element and indigenous groups both within the province and in neighboring territories. If the hypothesis presented above can be sustained, opposition to the reestablishment of Jerusalem as the cult center of the province and of the Jewish ethnos elsewhere, must have played a part. Archaeological data are notoriously subject to revision, but if the evidence for the destruction in the early fifth century BC of sites in Benjamin, including Bethel (Beitin), holds up,[22] it would not be surprising if religious factors had a significant part to play. Be that as it may, the resolution came in the form of a compromise between Aaronites and Zadokites, the final expression of which can be read off in the priestly genealogies (especially 1 Chr 5:27–41).

In these matters we are working more in the interstices of the biblical texts than with information which they explicitly provide. Much is uncertain, but the several lines of inquiry we have pursued converge on a strong probability: that during most or all of the period between the destruction of the Jerusalem temple and its rebuilding, Bethel served as the alternative, imperially sponsored sanctuary associated with the administrative center at Mizpah; and that the privileged position of Bethel put the priests claiming descent from Aaron who functioned there in serious but by no means undisputed contention for cultic supremacy after the restoration of Jerusalem in the early Persian period.

---

[20] Julius Wellhausen, *Prolegomena to the History of Ancient Judaism*, Transl. William Robertson Smith (New York: Meridian Library, 1957), 115–19.
[21] Joseph Blenkinsopp, "The Judaean Priesthood during the Neo-Babylonian and Achaemenid Periods: A Hypothetical Reconstruction," *CBQ* 60 (1998): 25–43 (41–42).
[22] Ephraim Stern, *Archaeology of the Land of the Bible*, Vol. 2 (New York: Doubleday, 2001), 576–77.

V. Temple and Society in Achaemenid Judah

Source: *Second Temple Studies*. Vol. 1, *Persian Period*, ed. by Philip Davies, 22–53. Shefflield: Sheffield Academic Press, 1991.

1 A brief look at sources

Any study of the Judaism which was emerging during the two centuries of Iranian rule (539–332 BC) calls for an acute sense of the fragile and provisional nature of our knowledge of the past in general and this segment of the past in particular. None of the Greek sources for the period so much as mentions Jews or Judaism, though Herodotus does refer to Palestine (1.105; 2.104), and his allusion to Syrians in Palestine (*Suroi hoi en tē Palaistinē*, 2.104) presumably includes Jews.[1] Other potential sources – Diodorus, Ctesias to 382, Xenophon to 362 – are no more forthcoming. Josephus draws primarily on 1 Esdras and Greek Esther which he paraphrases at inordinate length (*Ant.* 11.184–296), but otherwise he is not well informed on the period, and makes things worse by a tendency to conflate the three rulers named Darius and the four named Artaxerxes. The principal biblical source, Ezra-Nehemiah, covers only the first and last quarter of the first of the two centuries, and the information it offers is refracted through several interpretative and ideological prisms. The task of creating a three-dimensional model of Judaean society is also complicated by the one-dimensional religious interests which inform the relevant biblical sources, especially where they refer to the temple. The archaeological data allow for a somewhat broader perspective, but their interpretation is no less elusive and no less subject to revision or subversion by new interpretations or new discoveries. Unlike the situation for Mesopotamian temples in Babylonia under Persian and Seleucid rule, we have no archaeological evidence for the second Jerusalemite temple. There remains recourse to comparative data, in the present case information on the sociopolitical and economic function of temples in other parts of the Achaemenid empire, especially Asia Minor, Egypt and Mesopotamia. While use of such material calls for careful handling, it may at least facilitate the setting up and testing of different models against which the situation in the province of Judah can be assessed.

---

[1] Cf. Theophrastus, leader of the Peripatetic School following Aristotle, who speaks of "the Syrians of whom the Jews form a part." For the reference see Menahem Stern, *Greek and Latin Authors on Jews and Judaism*, Vol. 1, *From Herodotus to Plutarch* (Jerusalem: The Israel Academy of Sciences and Humanities, 1976), 10.

2 The social and economic role of temples

In Mesopotamia, Syria, Asia Minor and the Greek mainland city and temple belonged together. The point may be made by referring to the apparently artless story in Gen 11:1–9 about the building of a city and tower in the land of Shinar. Since Shinar is Babylon, and the tower stands for the ziggurat shrine, the story can be read as a satire directed against Neo-Babylonian imperial pretensions and their supportive cultic apparatus. A considerable amount of information has been available for some time on the social and economic impact of temples on the regions in which they were located. The larger temples throughout the Achaemenid empire were wealthy institutions with their own land ownings and work force, their own capital in specie and produce from which they advanced loans, serving more or less the same function as banks and credit unions today. Stimulation of regional economies by temples serving as storage and redistribution centres, to the evident advantage of the imperial exchequer, helps to explain why they were generally supported by successive Achaemenid rulers.[2]

The priesthoods serving these temples would have been answerable to imperial officials – in Mesopotamia the *paqdu* or *rēš šarri* – whose function was to ensure payment of tribute. As local representative of the central government, Nehemiah likewise took measures to control the economic resources of the Jerusalem temple (Neh 13:13). Priesthoods also served as custodians of the religious and legal traditions in the different provinces of the empire. In the absence of an imperial cult of the Assyrian or Babylonian type, the Achaemenids as impe-

---

[2] Muhammad Dandamaev has written extensively on the temple economy in ancient Mesopotamia. His studies include "Achaemenid Babylon" in *Ancient Mesopotamia: Socio-Economic History. A Collection of Studies by Soviet Scholars*, ed. Igor Diakonoff (Moscow: Nauka, 1969), 296–311; "Politische und wirtschaftliche Geschichte" in *Historia: Beiträge zur Achämenidengeschichte* (Wiesbaden: 1972), 15–58; "Babylonia in the Persian Age" in *CHJ* 1, 326–42. See also Raymond Bogaert, *Les Origines Antiques de la Banque de Dépôt* (Leiden: Brill, 1966); Nicholas Postgate, "The Role of the Temple in the Mesopotamian Secular Community," in *Man, Settlement and Urbanism*, ed. Peter Ucko, Ruth Tringham and Geoffrey Dimbleby (London: Duckworth, 1972), 811–25; Edward Lipiński (ed.), *State and Temple Economy in the Ancient Near East*, Vol. 1, *Proceedings of the International Conference Organized by the Katholieke Universiteit Leuven* (Leuven: Department of Orientalistiek, 1979); John Robertson, "The Social and Economic Organization of Mesopotamian Temples" in *Civilizations of the Ancient Near East*, Vol. 1, ed. Jack Sasson (New York: Charles Scribner's Sons, 1995), 443–54 with annotated bibliography; for the economic operation and impact of Egyptian temples see David O'Connor in the same volume, 319–29.

rial patrons tolerated and even occasionally supported local cults, a situation reflected, with obvious but understandable exaggeration, in the biblical sources.³

The significance of cult centres within the Achaemenid imperial system may best be illustrated by examples. During the reign of Cyrus, in Mesopotamia, the Enunmakh temple enclosure and the Eanna temple in Uruk (Warka) were restored, and according to a fragment of the Cyrus Cylinder similar restoration was going on in Babylon.⁴ Under Darius I the great Eanna temple at Uruk seems to have regained some of its past glory, and the same monarch is credited with building and restoring temples in Egypt which led, according to Diodorus (1.95) to his posthumous deification. In this respect he seems to have followed the example of Cambyses in restoring the temple of the goddess Neith at Sais.⁵ An inscription copied from a rescript of either Artaxerxes I therefore 426, or Artaxerxes II, therefore 365, refers to the Persian hyparch (satrap) of Lydia promoting the cult of the local Zeus by discouraging aberrant cult practices.⁶ Also from Asia Minor, probably during the reign of Artaxerxes III, the trilingual Xanthos inscription authorized the establishment of a cult to a Hecatomnid king at the sanctuary of the goddess Leto and granted an estate and tax exemption to its resident clergy. Also to be mentioned in this connection is the letter of Hananiah to a leader of the Jewish community on the island of Elephantine which mentions a decree of Darius II about the observance of a festival according to accepted Jewish usage.⁷

These examples illustrate a standard Achaemenid policy with respect to local cults, one which was followed, with the notable exception of Antiochus

---

3 It can no longer be taken for granted that Xerxes was an exception to the rule with respect to religious tolerance on the basis of the much-discussed *daivā* inscription, on which see Pierre Briant, *Histoire de l'Empire Perse de Cyrus à Alexandre*, Vol. 1 (Paris: Libraire Arthème Fayard, 1996), 567–70 = *From Cyrus to Alexander: A History of the Persian Empire*, Transl. Peter Daniels (Winona Lake, Indiana: Eisenbrauns, 2002), 550–54.
4 Leonard Woolley and Max Mallowan, *Ur Excavations IX: The Neo-Babylonian and Persian Periods* (London: British Museum; Philadelphia: University Museum, 1962), 2, 25; Christopher Walker, "A Recently Identified Fragment of the Cyrus Cylinder," *Iran* 10 (1972): 158–59; Amélie Kuhrt, "The Cyrus Cylinder and Achaemenid Imperial Policy," *JSOT* 25 (1983): 83–97.
5 The restoration by Cambyses of the great sanctuary in Sais and its "House of Life" is attested on the Udjahorresnet inscription. On Achaemenid policies towards temples in general see Elias Bickerman, "The Edict of Cyrus in Ezra 1," *JBL* 65 (1946): 249–75; Roland de Vaux, *The Bible and the Ancient Near East*, Transl. Damian McHugh (Garden City, New York: Doubleday, 1971), 63–96; Muhammad Dandamaev and Vladimir Lukonin, *The Culture and Social Institutions of Ancient Iran* (Cambridge: Cambridge University Press, 1989), 360–66.
6 Discussed in Peter Frei and Klaus Koch, *Reichsidee und Reichsorganisation im Perserreich* (2ⁿᵈ ed., Fribourg: Universitätsverlag; Göttingen: Vandenhoeck & Ruprecht, 1984), 19–21.
7 Abraham Cowley, *Aramaic Papyri of the Fifth Century BC* (Oxford: Clarendon, 1923), 60–65.

IV, by Alexander and his successors. They should therefore be borne in mind, without overstating their relevance, in assessing the historical credibility of measures in favour of the Jerusalem temple recorded in Ezra-Nehemiah. Needless to say, this policy was not motivated exclusively by sentiments of religious piety. One reason for the considerable measure of success achieved by Achaemenid imperial policy was tolerance for and, indeed, active exploitation of diverse local systems within an overarching imperial framework. The policy called for granting a fair measure of local autonomy once the central government had identified, or put in place, a dominant elite whose loyalty could be counted on. One such system, especially in evidence in Asia Minor and Mesopotamia, focussed on temples. Temples served as catalysts of economic exchange and promoters of social cohesion. In any given locality the temple could be seen as the point of convergence for the symbolic structures of the region, an "emblem of collective identity,"[8] thereby mitigating to some extent the inevitable resentment generated by subjection to a foreign power.

3 City and temple in Asia Minor

According to a theory first proposed by Soviet social historians, temples became the focus of a new type of sociopolitical organization towards the beginning of the first millennium BC, one which came into its own under the Achaemenids and continued on into the Ptolemaic and Seleucid periods and beyond. This "civic-temple community" (*graždansko-chramovaya obšina; Bürger-Tempel-Gemeinde*) resulted from the merger of temple personnel with the free, property-owning citizenry of a particular settlement. Out of this merger arose an autonomous and privileged social entity which provided its members with the means for self-management and mutual economic assistance. It is claimed that several of these sociopolitical units existed and flourished in the Persian empire.[9] According to the Latvian scholar Joel Weinberg, Achaemenid Judah presents a well-documented case history of such a temple community, though one with its own peculiar features. We will evaluate his theory in due course, but in the meantime it will be useful to survey briefly some of the case histories on the basis of which Weinberg's hypothesis is constructed.

---

8 The phrase is from Walter Burkert, "The Meaning and Function of the Temple in Classical Greece," in *Temple in Society*, ed. Michael Fox (Winona Lake/Indiana: Eisenbrauns, 1988), 44.
9 The earliest studies, by Iosif Davidovich Amusin and Gagik Sarkisian, were in Russian, but Sarkisian also dealt with the topic in "City Land in Seleucid Babylonia," in *Ancient Mesopotamia*, ed. Igor Diakonoff (Moscow: Nauka, 1969), 312–31.

In Asia Minor instances can be cited in which the city appears to have been more or less an appendage of the temple. Comana in Cappadocia, centre of the cult of the goddess Ma-Enyo, was governed by the local high priest who, as Strabo informs us (*Geog.* 12.2,3) was next in rank to the monarch. This temple possessed extensive domains the usufruct of which was controlled by the priesthood. It was also the principal catalyst for the circulation of wealth in the city and its agrarian hinterland. Citizenship appears to have been contingent on support of and participation in the temple cult and temple personnel made up a good percentage of the citizenry.[10] A similar situation obtained in the other Comana in Pontus, dedicated to the same goddess (Strabo 12.3,32). The royal sanctuary of Zela in that province, centre of the cult of the Persian goddess Anahita introduced by Artaxerxes II, also disposed of extensive domains administered by temple officials. Strabo (12.3,27) reports that "in earlier times the kings governed Zela not as a city but as a sacred precinct of the Persian gods, and the priest was the master of the whole thing." This seems to have been an example of officially sponsored syncretism, comparable to what we might suppose was the Persian attitude to Yahveh "God of Heaven" – a view which we may be sure the Jerusalem priesthood did nothing to discourage.[11]

The situation in the city of Venasa, dedicated to a local hypostasis of Zeus and home to almost 3,000 temple servants, was somewhat similar. It also had its sacred territory (*chora hiera*) bringing in an annual revenue of fifteen talents (Strabo 12.2,6). In these cases, and others from Mesopotamia to be considered shortly, the proponents of the civic temple community/*Bürger-Tempel-Gemeinde* hypothesis invite us to see a special type of social organization with its own domains and operating its own economic system. A somewhat different situation is exemplified by the sanctuary of Mylasa-Olymos in Caria. The large corpus of inscriptions dealing with this sanctuary covers such matters as prebends, support of the clergy, and who may participate in the rites.[12] Here, too, the priests of the local Zeus under their chief priest (*archiereus*) administered extensive temple holdings and played a leading role in deliberations of the city assembly (*boulē*). But since the citizens owned land in their own right and worked it themselves, this type of organization, temple domains but no temple economy, is clas-

---

10 Pauly-Wissowa, *Realencyclopädie der klassischen Altertumswissenschaft* XI 1.1127.
11 On the title "the God of Heaven" used for both Yahveh and Ahura Mazda, see D. K. Andrews, "Yahweh the God of the Heavens" in *The Seed of Wisdom: Essays in Honor of Theophile James Meek*, ed. Warren Sturgis McCullough, (Toronto: University of Toronto Press, 1964), 45–57.
12 Pauly-Wissowa, *Realencyclopädie der klassischen Altertumswissenschaft* XVI.1, 1046–64; Franciszek Sokolowski, *Lois Sacrées d'Asie Mineure* (Paris: 1955), 152–59.

sified as a distinct form of social organization. Weinberg suggested that it was this type which came to prevail in the Hellenistic period.[13]

While much of the data presented here comes from a time later than the Persian period, it can be taken to illustrate what was the normal scope of the social and economic outreach of temples under Persian rule, but to what extent it justifies creating a distinct type of temple economy is another matter. There had always existed a close symbiotic relationship between temple and city. In Greek-speaking regions temple lands, theoretically property of the resident deity, had from the earliest times been administered or monitored by city officials – *tamiai, hieropoioi, epitimētai* – answerable to the city assembly. Priests were civic officials appointed by the city, and they could also serve in municipal offices, especially as magistrates. The city treasury was often deposited in a temple, which also advanced credit and leased land.[14] Temple privileges were automatically extended to free, propertied citizens who jealously guarded their status and controlled admission to their ranks. It was normal, therefore, for temple and city to be interdependent in the economic as well as the religious sphere.

4 City and temple in Mesopotamia

The situation with respect to temples in Achaemenid Mesopotamia was similar in several respects. Here, fortunately, there is no dearth of documentation. Thousands of tablets dealing with temple economy from Babylonia of the Neo-Babylonian, Achaemenid and Seleucid periods have been published and many more await publication.[15] We therefore know much more about the social and econom-

---

13 Joel Weinberg, "Agrarverhältnisse in der Bürger-Tempel-Gemeinde der Achämenidenzeit," in *Wirtschaft und Gesellschaft im alten Vorderasien*, ed. János Harmatta and György Komoróczy (Budapest: Akadémiai Kiadó, 1976), 485.
14 Examples in John Harvey Kent, "The Temple Estates of Delos, Rheneia and Mykonos," *Hesperia* 17 (1948): 243–338.
15 For the sources to the time of publication see Riekele Borger, *Handbuch der Keilschriftliteratur*, Vol. 3 (Berlin: Walter de Gruyter, 1975) and David Weisberg, *Texts from the Time of Nebuchadnezzar* (New Haven: Yale University Press, 1980); and for a brief survey Walther Hinz and Gerold Walser (eds.), *Beiträge zur Achämenidengeschichte*, 5–14. The later period is covered by Joachim Oelsner, "Zwischen Xerxes und Alexander: Babylonische Rechtsurkunden und Wirtschaftstexte aus der späten Achämenidenzeit," *Die Welt des Orients* 8 (1976): 310–18. The Murašu archive, covering the years 454–404, is of prime importance but provides little information on temple economy. A more recent study of the archive is Matthew Stolper, *Entrepreneurs and Empire: The Murašû Archive, the Murašû Firm and Persian Rule in Babylon* (Istanbul: Nederlands Historisch-Archaeologisch Instituut te Istanbul, 1985).

ic aspects of temple administration than about Jerusalem at the other extremity of the Babili-Ebirnari satrapy. While a comprehensive study of temple economy in the later period still remains to be written, we know enough to draw some at least provisional conclusions relative to the issue under discussion.

One of the best documented case histories is the ancient temple-city of Uruk (Tell el-Warka) and its Eanna temple dedicated to the cult of the goddess Inanna. Some 1,500 legal and economic texts from the Neo-Babylonian and Persian period have been published which provide information on several aspects of the administration of this temple, and this information can be supplemented with material dating to the Seleucid period.[16] The temple area covered about 60,000 square meters and included some 150 storage facilities. It owned substantial tracts of land for cultivation and pasture as well as farms for the cultivation of the date farm. These domains of "the Lady of Uruk" were sublet to dependent farmers with specific provisions for the amount of produce owed to the temple. The entire operation was controlled by assessors answerable to the governing board of the temple and the city administration. The day-to-day operation of the temple was financed by tithes,[17] contributions (not all voluntary), and ex voto offerings of the faithful, in addition to rents. The economic tablets from the temple archives reveal the remarkable variety of professions required to operate this system. In addition to different classes of priests – under the general rubric of "temple enterer" (*ēreb bīti*) – we hear of transactions involving temple musicians, exorcists, porters, scribes, bakers, brewers, carpenters and others.[18] Also attested is a type of temple slave or oblate, known as a "child of the god" (*māru ša anu*), given to the sanctuary as a child by indigent or insolvent parents. Throughout Mesopotamia, temples were among the leading employers of slave

---

16 Albert Tobias Clay, *Neo-Babylonian Letters from Erech* (New Haven: Yale University Press, 1919); Adam Falkenstein, *Archäische Texte aus Uruk: Ausgrabungen der deutschen Forschungsgemeinschaft in Uruk-Warka II* (Berlin: Deutsche Forschungs-Gemeinschaft, 1936); "Zu den Inschriften der Grabung in Uruk-Warka 1960–1961," Baghdader Mitteilungen 2 (1963): 1–82; Denise Cocquerillat, *Palmeraies et Cultures de l'Eanna d'Uruk (559–520): Ausgrabungen der deutschen Forschungsgemeinschaft in Uruk-Warka VIII* (Berlin: Deutsche Forschungsgemeinschaft, 1968). Much information on Hellenistic Uruk is available in Gilbert McEwan, *Priest and Temple in Hellenistic Babylonia* (Wiesbaden: Franz Steiner Verlag, 1981).
17 Muhammad Dandamaev, "Der Tempelzehnte in Babylonien während des 6.–4. Jh. v.u.Z.," in *Beiträge zur Alten Geschichte und deren Nachleben: Festschrift für Franz Altheim*, ed. Ruth Stiel (Berlin: de Gruyter, 1969), 82–89.
18 On these categories of temple personnel see Mariano San Nicolò, *Beiträge zu einer Prosopographie neubabylonischer Beamten der Zivil- und Tempelverwaltung* (Munich: Bayerische Akademie der Wissenschaften, 1941).

labour, which will incidentally remind us that slaves are also listed among temple personnel in texts from Achaemenid Judah.(Ezra 2:43–58 = Neh 7:46–60).[19]

Responsibility for the maintenance of the temple and its many activities including the operation of its cult was in the hands of an assembly (*puhru, puhur uruk*), comparable to the *boulē* which administered civic and cultic affairs in the Greek-speaking areas. As was the case with the latter, membership was restricted by ethnic and property qualifications and the members of the assembly were grouped according to their ancestral house (*bīt abim*), comparable to the *bêt 'ăvôt*, the paternal household, of which we hear often in Ezra-Nehemiah. Not all inhabitants of the city, therefore, qualified for membership in the assembly. This city-temple *puhru*, presided over by a dean (*šatammu, paqdu*), dealt with a wide range of secular and religious matters, deciding issues related to marriage and property, assessing penalties, hearing petitions and grievances. One of the Murašu tablets, for examples, records the case of a Jew heard before the *puhru* of Nippur.[20]

The social and economic outreach of the Inanna temple at Uruk is remarkably well documented, but we can assume that a similar situation obtained in other less well documented Babylonian cities. The citizens of Babylon itself belonged to the assembly of one or other of the temples in the city, and lived apart from the dependent farmers who had their own subdivision.[21] In the Seleucid period we hear of Babylonian members of the *esagila* assembly under the supervision of a royal representative.[22] Like the Eanna sanctuary, the *esagila* owned lands and irrigation canals, water being a particularly valuable commodity. It also leased out plots to dependent farmers (*ikkarātu*), for the most part reserving the less cost-productive labour of slaves for the temple itself. No aspect of this form of sociopolitical and economic organization centred on temples was peculiar to the Achaemenid period or the product of Achaemenid imperial initiative,

---

19 On temple slaves see Raymond Philip Dougherty, *The Shirkûtu of Babylonian Deities* (New Haven: Yale University Press, 1923), and on the Judaean *netînîm*, apart from the commentaries, Ephraim Avigdor Speiser, "Unrecognized Dedication," *IEJ* 13 (1963): 69–73; Baruch Levine, "The Netînîm," *JBL* 82 (1963): 207–12. Muhammad Dandamaev has written extensively on the subject of slavery in ancient Mesopotamia; see *Slavery in Babylon from Nabopolassar to Alexander the Great* (De Kalb/Illinois: Illinois University Press, 1984); "Slavery and the Structure of Society," in *The Culture and Social Institutions of Ancient Iran*, ed. Muhammad Dandamaev and Vladimir Lukonin (Cambridge: Cambridge University Press, 1989), 152–77.
20 Elias Bickerman, in *CHJ* 1, 349.
21 Leo Oppenheim, *Ancient Mesopotamia: Portrait of a Dead Civilization* (Chicago: University of Chicago Press, 1964), 320–21.
22 Gilbert McEwan, *Priest and Temple*, 17–18.

but the fact remains that it was allowed to continue, and indeed flourish, during those two centuries.

5 The situation in Yehud (Judah)

Unfortunately, no comparable source material is available for reconstructing the situation in the province of Yehud (Judah). We have no temple archives comparable to those of the Eanna sanctuary, and no economic tablets comparable to the files of the Murašu and Egibi commercial firms have come down to us, and the texts we do have are not designed to provide us with the information we need. The basis for a straightforward point-by-point comparison with the situation as described above therefore simply does not exist. It would, nevertheless, be surprising if the social and economic co-ordinates of the Jerusalem temple and the social situation in general in the province were entirely sui generis. To begin with, Judah belonged to the same satrapy as Babylonia down to the reign of Xerxes, and we learn from Ezra-Nehemiah that immigrants from Babylonia were responsible for rebuilding the temple and that, once it was built, they staffed it and controlled its operations. Measures taken by Ezra and Nehemiah to control membership in the assembly of those who had returned from the diaspora, the *běnê haggôlâ*, might be compared with the roughly contemporary Periclean law of citizenship requiring Athenian ancestry on both paternal and maternal sides. The right to exclude from the assembly, the *qĕhal haggôlâ*, exercized by Ezra (Ezra 10:8) could likewise bring to mind the Athenian decree of *atimia* involving loss of civic privileges.[23] We can therefore begin our enquiry by assuming that the province was not hermetically sealed off, socially and culturally, from the rest of the western reaches of the Persian empire.

After the fall of Babylon in 539 Judah, within the Neo-Babylonian empire, passed automatically under Persian rule. Effective control of Judah and other outlying provinces must have taken some time to establish; the Cyrus Cylinder speaks only of the submission of "all the kings of the west lands living in tents" (*ANET*, 136). It is unclear how the province was administered during the two decades prior to the reorganization of the empire by Darius.[24] The territory

---
23 Hermann Bengtson, *The Greeks and the Persians: From the Sixth to the Fourth Centuries* (New York: Delacorte Press, 1968), 89–93; Gerald Blidstein, "Atimia: A Greek Parallel to Ezra X 8 and to Post-biblical Exclusion from the Community," *VT* 24 (1974): 357–60.
24 Kurt Galling, "Denkmäler zur Geschichte Syriens und Palästinas unter der Herrschaft der Perser," *PJ* 34 (1938): 59–79; *Studien zur Geschichte Israels im persischer Zeitalter* (Tübingen:

of the former Neo-Babylonian empire was governed by the satrap Gubaru (Gobryas), and the biblical sources tell of the appointment of a certain Sheshbazzar, described in Tattenai's report as governor (*pehâ*, Ezra 5:14), and in the Hebrew source as "prince of Judah" (*nāśî' lîhûdâ*, Ezra 1:8). We do not know what the writer wished to suggest by referring to him as "prince of Judah". His name suggests that he was a Babylonian, perhaps a Babylonian Jew, though there is no reason to identify him with Shenazzar, son of the exiled Jehoiachin.[25] The term translated "governor" can mean different things, and its occurrence at Ezra 5:14 need not presuppose that the region had already been divided into provinces, always assuming that the elders were filing a truthful report. Sheshbazzar's jurisdiction may have had a quite limited scope. Some administrative measures may have been taken preparatory to the invasion of Egypt, perhaps already during the reign of Cyrus who set the scene for the invasion, but it is unlikely that they would have been fully in place before Darius. And if this is so, it is also unlikely that Babylonian Jews would have made the journey to Judah in significant numbers before that time. Some may have accompanied Cambyses on his Egyptian campaign, the main staging area for which would have been Syria-Palestine. The disturbances in Babylon occasioned by the revolts of Nidintu-Bel and Arakha at the beginning of the reign of Darius may have encouraged others to emigrate, a possibility suggested by Zechariah's call to "flee from the land of the north" (Zech 2:10). At any rate, it is significant that no progress was made towards building the temple before the reign of Darius, as prophetic writings from that time explicitly attest.[26]

During this early period, Judah was therefore part of a vast satrapy coextensive with the former Neo-Babylonian empire. According to the tribute list of Herodotus (3.89–97), Phoenicia, Syria-Palestine and Cyprus formed the fifth of twenty satrapies (*archai* or *nomoi*), distinct from Babylon which is listed as ninth, but it is clear from the Behistun inscriptions and other inscriptions of Darius that the list corresponds to the situation following on the suppression of the Babylonian revolts by Xerxes, at which time Babylon was made into a separate satrapy. The administrative centre of the Transeuphrates region may have been Damascus, though other candidates have been suggested.[27] During the early

---

Mohr, 1964), 47–48; Muhammad Dandamaev, "Politische und wirtschaftliche Geschichte," 15–58; "Babylonia in the Persian Age," in *CHJ* 1, 326–42 (328–29).
25 Paul-Richard Berger, "Zu den Namen šsbsr und šn'sr," *ZAW* 83 (1971): 98–100, has demonstrated that the identification is highly improbable, but it continues to be accepted uncritically.
26 Hag 1:4,9; 2:15; cf. Zech 1:16; 6:12,15; 8:9.
27 Tripoli on the Phoenician coast according to Kurt Galling, *Studien zur Geschichte Israels im persischer Zeitalter*, 48, and Hermann Bengtson, *The Greeks and the Persians*, 404.

years of Darius' reign Ushtani was satrap, followed by another only part of whose name can be read on a recently published inscription dated to the year of the death of Darius (486).[28] During part of this time Tattenai held a subordinate position as governor of Eber Nari (the Transephrates satrapy). The territory under his jurisdiction included different kinds of polities – vassal kingdoms, tribal sheikdoms, and provinces of which Judah was one. It is therefore referred to in the biblical sources as a province (*mĕdînâ, yĕhûd mĕdîntāʾ*), though the term *mĕdînâ* could also be used of larger administrative units.[29]

The hypothesis, first proposed by Albrecht Alt, that Judah became an administrative adjunct of Samaria after the assassination of the Babylonian-appointed governor Gedaliah, and remained under Samarian jurisdiction until Nehemiah secured its independence in the mid-fifth century, has been widely accepted but is not well founded.[30] Nehemiah himself refers to governors who preceded him (Neh 5:15), and the context suggests that he is talking about governors of Judah. The Jewish petition to Darius states that Sheshbazzar had been appointed governor by Cyrus (Ezra 5:14), and in his reply Darius refers to "the governor of the Jews" (Ezra 6:7), though the phrase is missing from the Greek version. Haggai addresses his message to Zerubbabel governor of Judah and Joshua the chief priest (Hag 1:1). Several years ago Nahman Avigad reconstructed a list of four governors of Judah prior to Nehemiah with the help of bullae, seal impressions and impressions on jar handles: (1) Zerubbabel (Hag 1:1,14); (2) Elnathan, from a bulla which Avigad dates to the late sixth century; (3) Yeho'ezer, from an early fifth century jar impression; (4) Ahzai, also from a jar impression, from the same period. It should be noted, however, that the bullae and seals are unprovenanced, in at least one instance, i.e., Elnathan, the reading "governor" (*phvʾ*)

---

28 A Babylonian tablet published by Matthew Stolper, "The Governor of Across-the-River in 486 BC," *JNES* 48 (1985): 283–305 records instructions given by a satrap the first part of whose name reads *Hu -a*. One of those addressed is Gadalama (Gedalyahu?) and another Siha (cf. Ezra 2:43). On satrapal administration in general see Oscar Leuze, *Die Satrapieneinteilung in Syrien und im Zweistromlande von 520 bis 320* (Halle: Max Niemeyer Verlag, 1935), 36–42.

29 E.g. Ezra 2:1 = Neh 7:6; Ezra 5:8; 6:20; 7:16; Neh 1:3; 11:3. The term *mĕdînâ* is also used of Media (Ezra 6:2) and Babylon (Ezra 7:16). See Sean McEvenue, "The Political Structure of Judah from Cyrus to Nehemiah," *CBQ* 43 (1981): 353–64 (359–61); Frank Charles Fensham, "Mĕdînâ in Ezra and Nehemiah," *VT* 25 (1975): 795–97, proposed that the term as occurring in Ezra 2:1 refers to Babylon.

30 Albrecht Alt, "Die Rolle Samarias bei der Entstehung des Judentums," in *Kleine Schriften zur Geschichte des Volkes Israel*, Vol. 2 (Munich: Beck, 1953), 316–37; also Martin Noth, *The History of Israel* (London: A. & C. Black, 1960), 288–89; Kurt Galling, *Studien zur Geschichte Israels im persischer Zeitalter*, 92 n. 2. For a criticism of the hypothesis see Morton Smith, *Palestinian Parties and Politics that Shaped the Old Testament* (New York: Columbia University Press, 1971), 195–98.

has been disputed, and the dating remains uncertain. Avigad's list should therefore be treated with caution.[31]

The fact that a governor is not mentioned on the occasion of Tattenai's tour of inspection (Ezra 5:3–5), or following the arrival of both Ezra and Nehemiah in the province (Ezra 8:32–34; Neh 2:9), may simply mean that the office was vacant at that time, as it was at other times of political crisis. Judah may have been placed under Samarian control after whatever event precipitated the complaints recorded in Ezra 4:7–16, but that is quite a different matter.

Judah, therefore, was a distinct administrative and fiscal unit from the time of Darius if not earlier, one of the smallest in the Transeuphrates region, with its own governor and provincial administration, comparable in that respect to other provinces such as Samaria, Dor and Ashdod which go back essentially to Assyrian provincial administration. The subdivision of the province into districts (*pĕlākîm*) under administrative officials (*śarîm*) may also date to this time (Neh 3:9,12, 14–18). There is no reason to think that this system was subsequently altered, though there may have been interruptions in times of political crisis. It looks as if one such interruption occurred towards the middle of the fifth century, following which the vigorous measures of Nehemiah re-established the relative autonomy enjoyed by the province.

6 The building of the second temple

According to the biblical sources, the first stage in the creation of a viable Jewish community in Judah was the rebuilding of the Jerusalem temple and the resumption of its cult. Unfortunately, however, these sources do not give us a clear and unambiguous picture of how, when, and by whom this was accomplished. Ezra 1:2–4 presents the rescript of Cyrus as the fulfillment of prophecy in a way reminiscent of the exilic Isaiah (Isa 44:28–45:4). It is certainly not a transcript of an actual Persian period document and is contradicted in several respects by the Aramaic version of the same decree recorded in Ezra 6:1–5.[32] The enthusiastic

---

31 Nahman Avigad, *Bullae and Seals from a Post-exilic Judaean Archive* (Jerusalem: Hebrew University, 1976).
32 Elias Bickerman, "The Edict of Cyrus in Ezra 1," *JBL* 65 (1946): 249–75, argued that Cyrus issued two decrees, the first – in Ezra 1 – an oral proclamation permitting the return and rebuilding, the second – in Ezra 6 –the official rescript a copy of which would have been deposited in the state archives. The hypothesis does not, however, explain the major discrepancy that the project is to be financed from the private sector in the former and from government funds in the latter.

response to the decree leading to a mass emigration of some 50,000 Judaeo-Babylonians is equally implausible. The setting up of the altar before the work of rebuilding in order to ward off danger (Ezra 3:1–3) is modelled on the action of David who set up an altar in Jerusalem for the same reason (1 Chr 21:18–22:1). The foundations of the temple were laid by Zerubbabel within a year of his arrival according to Ezra 3:7–11, by Sheshbazzar about the same time according to Ezra 5:16, and by Zerubbabel early in the reign of Darius in Zech 4:9. The delay in getting on with the building is explained by external opposition in Ezra 4:1–5 and by the indifference of the population and the bad economic situation in the province according to Haggai 1:1–11. There is also a suggestion in Haggai and Zechariah that the impetus to build the temple came from the political crisis of the first two years of Darius when it may have seemed to Judaean nationalists that the Persian empire was about to collapse (Hag 2:20–23). Furthermore, none of these sources takes account of the fact that the administrative capital of the province was still Mizpah, north of Jerusalem, probably associated with a cult centre which had replaced Jerusalem after the destruction of the city and its temple in 586.[33]

The problems multiply when we turn from Ezra-Nehemiah to Haggai and Zechariah, dated firmly in the early years of Darius I, for here there are no royal decrees and no mention of Sheshbazzar. Zerubbabel simply laid the foundations and supervised the building project with the support of Joshua the chief priest (Hag 1:12–14; Zech 4:9; 6:12–13). Their account is silent on the role of diaspora Jews who are mentioned only obliquely and incidentally (Zech 6:9–14), and we are given the impression that nothing was accomplished prior to the reign of Darius. And, as noted a moment ago, the delay of about two decades is explained not by external opposition but by indifference, if not outright oppositionto the project within the province itself.

It hardly needs saying that any historical reconstruction based on these sources will be speculative. There is an information gap for the first years following on the fall of Babylon in 539, the period corresponding to the reigns of Cyrus and Cambyses, the latter not mentioned in any biblical source. In this period the province would probably still have been administered from Mizpah in the tribal territory of Benjamin which had survived the Babylonian conquest relatively unscathed. Writing from within the ideological world view of the author of Chroni-

---

33 See Joseph Blenkinsopp, "Bethel in the Neo-Babylonian Period," in *Judah and the Judeans in the Neo-Babylonian Period*, ed. Oded Lipschits and Joseph Blenkinsopp (Winona Lake/Indiana: Eisenbrauns, 2003), 93–107. This paper argues for the revival of the ancient sanctuary of Bethel as the imperially-designated cult centre of the province in association with the administrative centre at nearby Mizpah.

cles about two centuries later, a scribe has filled in the gap with an account of the way he believed things ought to have happened, and he has given his account an air of plausibility with the help of official or official-looking documents. The result of his labours is to be found in Ezra 1–6, and the one firm piece of information which we can derive from it, information confirmed by the prophecies of Haggai and Zechariah, is that the temple was built during the early years of the reign of Darius I. While the initial impetus for rebuilding the temple may have been the hope of restored national independence, briefly kindled during Darius' *annus mirabilis*, once built, the Jerusalem temple could have been given official sanction as part of the same monarch's programme of pacification and imperial reorganization. This, at any rate, is one possible hypothesis, reading on and occasionally between the lines of the biblical sources, the only ones we have.

About the temple itself these sources provide little information. It was constructed of stone and timber (Ezra 5:8; 6:4), and it was built on the site of its predecessor, which was normal practice (Ezra 5:15). The dimensions given in the Cyrus decree allegedly recovered from the Ecbatana archives – sixty cubits in breadth and height – are implausible, and remain no less so if we add sixty cubits for length, as was the case with the first temple (Ezra 6:3; 1 Kgs 6:2). It is never said so explicitly, but it seems to have been smaller and less impressive than its predecessor, which is also what we would expect (Ezra 3:10; Hag 2:3). Its status differed from that of Solomon's temple in that the latter was, like Bethel in the Kingdom of Samaria, "a royal sanctuary, a temple of the kingdom" (Amos 7:13); in other words, it was a royal and state facility. The land on which the first temple was built was purchased by the ruler (2 Sam 24:18–25), its construction was funded out of the royal treasury (1 Kgs 5:15–32; 7:51; 9:10–14), and the requisite endowments continued to be provided from the same source (2 Kgs 12:18). This did not exclude private donations and ex voto offerings, but it is worth noting that the public collection for the repair of the temple during the reign of Jehoash (Joash) is changed by the author of Chronicles into a temple tax imposed on the entire population.[34] The status of the second temple was quite different. We learn from Ezra-Nehemiah that both the cost of rebuilding and the temple endowment came from the imperial exchequer (Ezra 6:4,8–10, etc). The requirement that sacrifices and prayers for the royal family be incorporated into the temple liturgy (Ezra 6:10) reinforced the point that the Persian emperor had now taken the place of the native dynast, and that the temple was now part of the apparatus of imperial control. This aspect, at any rate, is consistent

---

[34] 2 Kgs 12:4–16; 2 Chr 24:6, 9–10; cf. Neh 10:33.

with what we know of Persian imperial policy and therefore historically plausible. But we are also told that substantial contributions were made by the Babylonian Jewish community represented by the heads of its "houses" (Ezra 1:4,6; 2:68–69; 7:16), and that Judaeo-Babylonian immigrants reserved to themselves the actual task of rebuilding (Ezra 4:1–5). If this additional information is correct, it would seem that the *běnê haggôlâ*, the assembly of those who returned, in effect claimed control of the Jerusalem cult under the supervision and protection of the imperial authorities. It is this circumstance of a *limited* participation in temple control and governance which confers at least some initial plausibility on the civic-temple community hypothesis mentioned earlier. It is time to take another look at this hypothesis as it was applied to Judah and its temple in Jerusalem by Joel Weinberg.

7 The civic-temple community hypothesis applied to the province of Judah

As expounded by Weinberg with reference to the Achaemenid province of Judah (Yehud), the hypothesis rests on the supposition that there existed in that province a collectivity attached to the temple which was not identical with the province either demographically or territorially.[35] Given the nature of the evidence, demographic studies of ancient societies are notoriously hit-or-miss, and the situation is no different with early Second Temple Judah. Starting out from the tribute paid by Menahem of the Kingdom of Samaria to Tiglath-pileser III (2 Kgs 15:19–20), Weinberg estimated the population of that kingdom in the eighth century BC at about 500,000 to 700,000 and the kingdom of Judah at about 220,000 to 250,000.[36] He then turned to the biblical figures for deportees from Judah between 598 and 582 and, on the basis of the high figures in the History (2 Kgs

---

35 My assessment is based on the following: Joel Weinberg, "Demographische Notizen zur Geschichte der nachexilischen Gemeinde in Juda," *Klio* 34 (1972): 45–59; "Probleme der sozialökonomischen Struktur Judäas vom 6. Jahrhundert v.u.Z. bis zum 1. Jahrhundert u.Z.: Zu einigen wirtschaftshistorischen Untersuchungen von Heinz Kreissig," *Jahrbuch für Wirtschaftsgeschichte* 1 (1973): 237–51; "Das BÊIT ĀBÔT im 6.–4. Jh. v.u.Z.," *VT* 23 (1973): 400–14; "Der *'am hā'āres* des 6.–4. Jh. v.u.Z.," *Klio* 56 (1974): 235–335; "Nᵉtînîm und 'Söhne der Sklaven Salomos im 6.–4. Jh. v.u.Z.," *ZAW* 87 (1975): 355–71; "Die Agrarverhältnisse in der Bürger-Tempel-Gemeinde der Achämenidenzeit," in *Wirtschaft und Gesellschaft im alten Vorderasien*, ed. János Harmatta and György Komoróczy, 473–86; "Bemerkungen zum Problem 'der Vorhellenismus im Vorderen Orient'," *Klio* 58 (1976): 5–20; "Zentral- und Partikulargewalt im achämenidischen Reich," *Klio* 59 (1977): 25–43.
36 Joel Weinberg, "Demographische Notizen," 45.

24:14–16; 25:11–12,26), arrived at a total of 20,000 or some ten per cent of the total population.[37] This meant that the population of the province in the early Persian period, before the arrival of immigrants from Babylon, stood at about 200,000.

A crucial plank in Weinberg's thesis is the contention that the list of repatriates in Nehemiah 7, which he takes to be the original version, is a census of the civic-temple community about the mid-fifth century shortly before the activity of Ezra and Nehemiah. This list gives a total of 42,360 exclusive of 7,337 slaves and 200 male and female singers, which he took to represent only about twenty per cent of the total population of the province at that time. On the basis of later lists, especially the census list in Neh 11:4–22, he then claimed that in the period subsequent to Nehemiah the membership of the collectivity increased to about 150,000 or about seventy per cent of the total. This trend would eventually lead to the total assimilation of the province to the temple community. Province and temple community become one.

Moving from demographics to topography, Weinberg went on to argue that these conclusions are supported by the lists of settlements occupied by the immigrants. We are told that they returned to their former settlements, each to his own *naḥălâ* (Neh 7:6,73), and we must assume that each of these settlements had its own agrarian holdings, referred to in Ezra-Nehemiah as *migrāšîm* or *ḥăsērîm*. The settlements listed in the main census list (Ezra 2:20–35 = Neh 7:25–38) are located in three regions: around Jerusalem, the coastal plain, and the Jordan valley. They therefore by no means account for the total area of the province, and even within these three regions there were settlements not occupied by immigrant families. But when we turn to the census list in Neh 11:25–36, dated later than the mid-fifth century, we note an increase from nineteen to about fifty occupation sites, the greatest concentration being in southern Judah, the part which had suffered most severely from the Babylonian punitive campaign. Archaeological evidence for new settlements in the second half of the fifth century (e. g. Arad, Engeddi, Lachish, Beersheba) seemed to provide additional support.[38] Weinberg then concluded that the topographical data agree with his demographic analysis, confirming the existence and gradual expansion of a distinctive social entity within the province centred on the temple.

---

[37] Joel Weinberg, "Demographische Notizen," 46–50; "Agrarverhältnisse", 479. Compare Heinz Kreissig, *Die Sozialökonomische Situation in Juda zur Achämenidenzeit* (Berlin: Akademie Verlag, 1973), 22–23 who arrived at a total of 15,600 deportees or one in eight of the population, leaving some 60,000 behind after 582 BC.

[38] Joel Weinberg, "Demographische Notizen," 55–57.

7 The civic-temple community hypothesis applied to the province of Judah — 77

In our assessment of the hypothesis we should bear in mind a point already made, about the difficulty of obtaining reliable demographic data on ancient societies. For Weinberg this problem is especially severe, and he compounds it by taking the biblical figures at face value. Furthermore, some of the inferences he draws from these figures are questionable. If, for example, some researcher in the distant future were to calculate the population of the United Kingdom in the early third millennium on the basis of its size relative to the United States, as Weinberg does for Judah relative to Israel, he or she would be wrong by a factor of about ten. But let us assume for the moment that his figures for the two kingdoms from the eighth to the sixth century are more or less accurate. The issue then is to calculate the number of deportees between 598/597 and 582, that is, from the first Babylonian occupation of the city and the (probable) date of the failed coup of Ishmael and the exodus which followed. The biblical historian gives the impression that only the poorest stratum of the population, the *dallat hā'āres*, was left behind, and adds that after the assassination of Gedaliah all the (remaining) people, great and small, fled to Egypt (2 Kgs 25:26). The same source provides statistics only for the first deportation in 598/597 (2 Kgs 24:14–16), but at this point of the story two parallel versions are conflated. The first (24:14) lists the population of Jerusalem, the princes, 10,000 "men of substance," and all the craftsmen and smiths. The second list (24:15–16) consists in the royal family, court officials, the chief men of the land, 7,000 "men of substance", and 1,000 craftsmen and smiths. In Jer 52:28–30 the total for all three deportations, 4,600, conveys a much clearer impression of dependence on an archival source, and this conclusion has been widely accepted. But in defiance of what this text (Jer 52:29) actually says, Weinberg maintained that the figures in 2 Kings refer to Jerusalem and those in Jeremiah to Judaeans exclusive of Jerusalemites. His total of 20,000 deportees, therefore, includes Jerusalemites (2 Kings), other Judaeans (Jeremiah), and those who left to avoid Babylonian reprisals or on account of the bad economic situation.

However this may be, Weinberg's conclusion that the province still had a population of about 200,000 – a density of ca. 230 to the square mile – after the successive deportations and emigrations, not to mention the loss of life during the conquest and occupation, must be considered wide of the mark.[39] His calculation of the size of the temple-community relative to the total population of the province is flawed by his acceptance of the grand total of 42,360 immi-

---

39 Compare William Foxwell Albright's estimate of 20,000, *The Biblical Period from Abraham to Ezra: An Historical Survey* (New York: Harper Torchbooks, 1963), 87 and n.180. About all we can say is that the correct total is somewhere between these two extremes, but closer to Albright than to Weinberg.

grants (Ezra 2:64) which does not match even approximately the sum of the subtotals in the list. As for his account of the boundary list in Neh 11:25–36: comparison with the city and boundary lists in Joshua 15–18 suggests that what we have here is a description of the *ideal* boundaries of Judah. The language about Judaeans "encamping" from Beersheba to the Valley of Hinnom (11:30) reads like one more example of the exodus-occupation typology in evidence throughout Ezra-Nehemiah. There is also the fact that several of the places mentioned are known to have been under Edomite control in the mid-fifth century, and that some remained outside of the Jewish sphere as late as the Maccabean conquests (cf. 1 Macc 5:65; 11:34).

I conclude, then, that while the civic-temple community/*Bürger-Tempel-Gemeinde* hypothesis is suggestive, the arguments supporting it are seriously flawed. Beyond the points of detail discussed there remains also, and not just for Weinberg, the major issue of the ideology inscribed in Ezra-Nehemiah, and how the ideology bears on the crucial issue of the self-segregating immigrant community (*běnê haggôlâ*) as presented in this source or complex of sources.

8 Aspects of Persian period Judaean society relative to the temple

In casting around for an alternative to Weinberg's hypothesis, we can begin by acknowledging that the relevant biblical sources, and Ezra-Nehemiah in particular, represent the point of view of the dominant Judaeo-Babylonian element in Judah under Persian rule. In attempting to say something about social conditions in the province the historian must therefore allow for a fair amount of distortion or refraction due to this dominant ideology. In the census list, which played such an important part in Weinberg's hypothesis, those listed are described as an assembly (*qāhāl*, Ezra 2:64 = Neh 7:66), a term which serves to designate the immigrants as representing and reproducing the cult community of the wilderness period, with special emphasis on defining and regulating membership in the community of those who returned from captivity. We are dealing therefore with a distinctive collectivity which defines itself over against others in the region, membership in which is regulated and authenticated by incorporation in lists and genealogies, and which has its own procedures for ensuring self-segregation. This group, the *běnê ha-gôlâ*, recruited members from successive immigrations from Babylon, but membership was not confined to Judaeo-Babylonians. The first Passover after the settlement in Judah was celebrated by "the Israelites who had returned from exile" but also by "all those who had joined them, separating themselves from the impurity of the peoples of the land to seek Yahveh, God of Israel" (Ezra 6:21).

We should also take note of the ways in which the gentilic *yĕhûdîm* is used in Ezra-Nehemiah. More often than not it applies simply to inhabitants of the province of Yehud (e. g. Ezra 6:7; Neh 1:2; 13:23), or to those of Judaean descent living outside the province (e. g. Neh 4:6; 5:8). But the shift from the basically territorial to the broader ethnic-religious connotation is already underway by the time of Nehemiah, about the middle of the fifth century. One example: several members of the Jewish settlement in Elephantine at the first cataract of the Nile with good Yahwistic-theophoric names, who had probably never set foot in Judah, are referred to as *yĕhûdîm*.[40] But there seems to be a more specialized usage in the Nehemiah memoir with reference to a privileged class among Judaeo-Babylonian repatriates (Neh 2:16; 5:1). This more limited meaning is especially clear in the allusion to the one hundred and fifty *yĕhûdîm* and officials entertained by the governor on a regular basis (Neh 5:17).

According to Weinberg, the principal unit of which the Judaean temple community was composed was the *bêt 'ăbôt* (ancestral household).[41] According to the census list there were seventeen of these agnatic units or phratries in the pre-Ezra temple community, the average size being in the order of 800 to 1,000 adult males, somewhat larger than the typical Persian phratry which numbered approximately 600. This basic unit, in which both laity and clergy were organized, was under the leadership of elders who played an important role in the affairs of the province, as they had previously in the Babylonian diaspora (cf. Jer 29:1; Ezek 8:1; 20:1). Good standing in the community was secured by descent from an eponymous founder of the phratry and inclusion in the appropriate genealogy. Each ancestral house had its own land holdings divided into plots worked by individual families, a form of social organization which probably reproduced the situation which had obtained among ethnic minorities in southern Mesopotamia.

So much for the laity. Our information on temple personnel is incomplete, to say the least; we can only speculate on what the situation would look like if we had the good fortune to retrieve the archives of Zerubbabel's temple, as archaeologists have recovered those of the Eanna temple in Uruk. Having to make a virtue of necessity, we note that, according to the census list, roughly one in ten of the male adult population were priests. Other temple personnel included Levites, liturgical musicians and gatekeepers who were at some point co-opted into the

---

40 Abraham Cowley, *Aramaic Papyri*, 6:3, 8–10; 8:2; 10:3.
41 Joel Weinberg, "Das BÊIT ĀBŌT," 400–14.

ranks of the Levites, and substantial numbers of slaves who performed the more menial tasks. Weinberg calculated the number of slaves at about eighteen per cent of the total population, though he bases this estimate on the grand total of the census list rather than on the sub-totals.⁴² Beyond this we have little to go on, but we may assume the need for other specializations – masons, carpenters, bakers, brewers etc – organized in guilds as in Mesopotamia.⁴³ Temple treasurers in charge of the storerooms are mentioned (Neh 12:44; 13:13), and the Eliashib of Neh 13:4–9, one of several clerics to incur the wrath of Nehemiah, was probably in charge of maintenance and responsible for the temple fabric. Pethahiah mentioned in Neh 11:24 seems to have functioned as overseer, and may have been an imperial appointee.

By the time of the Hasmonaeans at the latest, the Jerusalem temple served as a kind of bank or credit union which provided loans at interest and in which private funds could be deposited.⁴⁴ That something like this was the case much earlier is suggested by the measures taken by Nehemiah to control the temple's considerable resources through a panel the composition of which reflected his own interests. It consisted in one priest, two members of the lower clergy, and a fourth, a certain Zadok, probably the governor's own representative (Neh 13:13). Nehemiah seems to have adopted a policy of supporting Levites as a counter to the power of the temple priesthood. He appointed Levites to key positions on the temple treasury board (13:13), and Levites also served as city guardians (Neh 13:22) and district administrators (3:17–19). Nehemiah also took special care for their provisioning (Neh 10:39; 11:23; 13:10–12). That the temple was already serving as a storage and redistribution centre at the time of Nehemiah is suggested by the concession granted to Tobiah the Ammonite in the temple precincts. The facility provided for him had previously been used for storage, and it is difficult to see why Tobiah would be looking for accomodation in the temple if not for better access to its considerable assets (Neh 13:4–9).

---

42 Weinberg's discussion of slaves in the temple community "Raby i drugije kategorii zavisimych ljudej v palestinskoj graždansko-chramovoj obščine VI–IV vv.do n.e." (Die Sklaven und anderen Kategorien abhängiger Leute in der palästinischen Bürger-Tempel-Gemeinde des 6.–4. Jh. v.u.Z.)" appeared in *Palestinskij Sbornik* 25 (1974): 63–66 and is summarized in *ZAW* 88 (1976): 129.
43 Isaac Mendelsohn, "Guilds in Ancient Palestine," *BASOR* 80 (1940): 17–21; "Guilds in Babylon and Assyria," *JAOS* 60 (1940): 68–72; David Weisberg, *Guild Structure and Political Allegiance in Early Achaemenid Mesopotamia* (New Haven: Yale University Press, 1967).
44 Macc 3:5–6, 10–12; Josephus: *War* 6:282; *Ant.* 14:110–13.

9 Conclusions

Putting all this together, the situation may be described tentatively as follows. The Civic-Temple Community/*Bürger-Tempel-Gemeinde* hypothesis stimulated and advanced the discussion on the social situation in Judah of the Persian period, but it has now become clear that it does not hold up. The province was not subject to Samaria prior to Nehemiah. Final authority resided with a Persian-appointed governor not a temple priesthood subsidized by the imperial authorities. Nehemiah was governor of the province not the leader of a civic-temple community; on the contrary, he expended a considerable amount of energy in efforts to control the temple, its personnel and its considerable resources. The temple almost certainly had its own land holdings but did not claim ownership of all Judaean land, as the hypothesis would require, not even as a theoretical postulate; it therefore did not play a role comparable to the examples from Asia Minor discussed earlier in the essay. Weinberg's figures for the population of both the civic-temple community and the province are much too high, and the conclusion he draws from them, that the *Bürger-Tempel-Gemeinde* system and the provincial system eventually merged, leading to complete political control exercized by the temple priesthood at the beginning of the Hellenistic period, cannot be sustained.[45]

We need to emphasize, once again, how important it is to remain alert to the ideology which controls the way in which the activities of the *běnê haggôlâ* and its character as a dominant force in the province are described. This dominant group of diaspora origin was a well organized entity, claiming control of the temple and its liturgies (Ezra 4:1–5, cf. 8:35), deciding on what conditions others may belong to it (Ezra 6:19–22), and regulating the marriage of its members (Ezra 9–10). Significantly, it is featured only in the Ezra material and is absent from the Nehemiah first-person narrative which has the best claim to be contemporary with or close to the events described. While the relation between Ezra-Nehemiah and Chronicles remains in dispute, it seems likely that the dominance of the Ju-

---

[45] Among recent English-language criticisms of the theory I mention Hugh Williamson, "Judah and the Jews," in *Achaemenid History XI: Studies in Persian History, Essays in Memory of David Lewis*, ed. Maria Brosius and Amélie Kuhrt (Leiden: Nederlands Instituut voor het Nabije Oosten, 1998), 145–63; Charles Carter, *The Emergence of Yehud in the Persian Period: A Social and Demographic Study* (Sheffield: Sheffield Academic Press, 1999), 294–307; Peter Ross Bedford, *Temple Restoration in Early Achaemenid Judah* (Leiden: Brill, 2001), 207–30; My own earlier assessment, Joseph Blenkinsopp, "Temple and Society in Achaemenid Judah," in *Second Temple Studies, Vol. 1: Persian Period*, ed. Philip Davies (Shefflield: Sheffield Academic Press, 1991), 22–53, I now consider too positive.

daeo-Babylonian party and the almost total silence of the native population in Ezra-Nehemiah owes a considerable debt to the ideology of Chronicles, according to which Judah remained empty of inhabitants until Cyrus issued his edict permitting the rebuilding of the temple (2 Chr 36:21–23). It is not hypercritical to insist that we cannot read off facts and figures from the surface of the text without taking this ideological bias into account.

The ideology notwithstanding, it can be argued that some of the more prominent features of Judaean society in the Achaemenid period replicate features of life in the diaspora. The deportees were settled in the Nippur region of the alluvial plain. Ezekiel's vision took place near the Chebar canal (*nār kabari*) which looped through the city of Nippur on its way back to the Euphrates. Other sites mentioned in the biblical sources – Tel-Aviv, Ahava, Tel-Melah, Tel-Harsha, Cheruv, Addan, Immer (Ezek 3:15; Ezra 2:59; 8:15,17,21) – have not been identified but were doubtless in the same region. Some few Jewish personal names have turned up in the Murašu archive, and there were Jews living in twenty-eight out of about two hundred settlements in that area.[46] That they were not enslaved was due to pragmatic considerations rather than the result of Babylonian magnanimity. The Nippur region, recently taken over by the crown, was due for redevelopment – digging and dredging canals and working the land – for which slave labour was not cost-effective.[47] The prevalence of place names formed with the element *tel*, meaning the ruins of a former settlement, points in the same direction since it indicates a deliberate policy of settling abandoned sites. This plan of internal colonization, in which ethnic minorities were destined to play a major role, con-

---

[46] According to Guillaume Cardascia, *Les Archives des Murašû: Une Famille d'Hommes d'Affaires Babyloniens à l'Époque Perse* (Paris: Imprimerie nationale, 1951), 2 n. 2 and Elias Bickerman, "The Babylonian Captivity," in *CHJ* 1, 342–358 (344), eight per cent of the names are Jewish, but Ran Zadok, *The Jews in Babylonia during the Chaldean and Achaemenid Periods* (Haifa: The University Press, 1979), 78, finds only three per cent, as also Edwin Yamauchi, *Persia and the Bible* (Grand Rapids: Baker Book House, 1990), 243–44 with further bibliography. Names, even names with a theophoric element, do not infallibly indicate the nationality of their bearers, so some uncertainty is understandable. For the most recent texts from āl-Yāhūdu, Nashar and other locations in the same region see Laurie Pearce, "New Evidence for Judeans in Babylonia," in *Judah and the Judeans in the Persian Period*, ed. Oded Lipschits and Manfred Oeming (Winona Lake/Indiana: Eisenbrauns, 2006), 399–411, and "'Judean': A Special Status in Neo-Babylonian and Achemenid Babylonia?" in *Judah and the Judeans in the Achaemenid Period*, ed. Oded Lipschits, Gary Neil Knoppers and Manfred Oeming (Winona Lake/Indiana: Eisenbrauns, 2011), 267–77, both with up-to-date bibliographies.

[47] Muhammad Dandamaev, "Social Stratification in Babylonia (7th–4th Centuries BC)," *AcAnt* 22 (1974): 433–44 (437); Israel Eph'al, "The Western Minorities in Babylonia in the 6th–5th Centuries BC: Maintenance and Cohesion," *Orientalia* 47 (1978): 74–90; Elias Bickerman, "The Babylonian Captivity".

tributed to the considerable demographic and economic expansion of Lower Mesopotamia under Neo-Babylonian and Achaemenid rule. It is reasonable to conclude that many of the Jewish settlers shared in the ensuing economic boom.[48]

Ethnic minorities were also permitted to maintain their distinct identities, principally for administrative and fiscal rather than humanitarian reasons. Elamites, Egyptians, Lydians, Jews and others formed self-governing collectivities under imperial supervision. Their internal affairs were regulated by an assembly organized in large kinship groups (*bīt abim*) and composed of property owners (*mār banē*) together with cult personnel where a local cult existed. It is possible that the Jewish ethnic minority in Babylonia, like the Elephantine Jews, had its own temple. It has been argued that the elders came to Ezekiel to seek his support for building a temple (Ezek 20:1,32), and that a temple was actually built has been proposed on the basis of Ezra 8:15–20 which refers to "the place Casiphia" under the regency of a person called Iddo, a priest to judge by the name, where Ezra was able to recruit additional cult personnel.[49] There must at any rate have been some form of organized worship and some institutional framework for preserving the exiled community's traditions.

There are therefore grounds for thinking that some aspects of the situation in Achaemenid Judah described above may reproduce social arrangements obtaining in the Jewish ethnic minority in southern Mesopotamia. One of these was the assembly (*puhru*, *qāhāl*) organized according to ancestral houses of free, property-owning citizens and temple personnel under the leadership of tribal elders and, further afield, under imperial supervision. The Judaeo-Babylonians also succeeded in achieving the two essential goals of winning back land confiscated and redistributed after the deportations (2 Kgs 25:12; Jer 39:10; 52:16, cf. Ezek 11:14–21), and securing control of the temple. The situation which resulted is, as clearly as we can discern it, the basis on which the dominant ideology as laid out in Chronicles and Ezra-Nehemiah was constructed.

---

48 Muhammad Dandamaev, "Achaemenid Babylonia," in *Ancient Mesopotamia*, ed. Igor Diakonoff, 296–311 (297, 309); Robert McCormick Adams, *The Uruk Countryside* (Chicago: University of Chicago Press, 1972), 55–57; *Heartland of Cities: Surveys of Ancient Settlement and Land Use on the Central Floodplain of the Euphrates* (Chicago: University of Chicago Press, 1981), xiv.
49 Several scholars of a former generation argued for a Jewish temple in Babylon: see Laurence Browne, "A Jewish Sanctuary in Babylonia," *JTS* 17 (1916): 400–1; Antonin Causse, *Les Dispersés d'Israël: Les Origines De La Diaspora et Son Rôle Dans La Formation Du Judaïsme* (Paris: Alcan, 1929), 76–77; Abram Menes, "Tempel und Synagoge," *ZAW* 50 (1932): 268–76. Morton Smith, *Palestinian Parties and Politics*, 90–91, thought it more likely that one was built at the time of the rebuilding of the Jerusalem temple. Zech 5:5–11 alludes to a shrine (to Asherah?), but whether anything concrete corresponds to this notice we do not know.

VI. The Intellectual World of Judaism in the Pre-Hellenistic Period

> "When I ask a question, the response comes to me from passages in the text which come back to life through my question, whereas the reader without questions glides right through the text."
>
> Karl Jaspers

1 An unpromising intellectual landscape

The question I want to ask is one which the biblical texts may have trouble answering. A survey of texts from the pre-Hellenistic period – the period from the fall of Babylon to the Persian Cyrus II in 539 BC to the Macedonian conquest of Persia in 332 BC – gives the impression of a limited amount of intellectual activity outside of the sphere of ritual or religious practice in general. The authors of our principal historiographical sources, the books of Chronicles, Ezra, and Nehemiah, move in a world that is bounded by the temple and its liturgies, the prerogatives and duties of temple personnel, and the moral and ritual obligations incumbent on participants in temple worship. We can therefore understand, even if we do not share, the antipathy towards these texts of a liberal humanist like Julius Wellhausen who found in Chronicles what he took to be the most stultifying traits of the emergent Judaism which, in his view, this composition both embodied and helped to shape. In dealing with the Chronicler's account of David's dispositions concerning cultic and military personnel (1 Chr 22–29) he comments sardonically on the monotonous "artificial marshalling of names and numbers" and "the enumeration of mere subjects without predicates which simply stand on parade and neither signify nor do anything."[1] Wellhausen's aversion to Judaism, indeed to any form of institutional religion, is well known and need detain us no further. Many later commentators have expressed themselves with more moderation, if with less wit, but without abandoning this basically negative view of the author of Chronicles as one of the epigoni. But complaints of this kind have not been confined to Chronicles, nor to the time of its

---

[1] Julius Wellhausen, *Prolegomena to the History of Ancient Judaism*, Transl. William Robertson Smith (New York: Meridian Library, 1957), 181.

composition, probably in the late Persian-Achaemenid period. Writing about a much earlier time, Max Weber commented on what he called the "culture hostility" of Israelite prophecy, by which he meant an attitude unsympathetic to cultural expressions outside of the explicitly religious sphere.² A lack of esteem for the intellectual traditions of other nations has also been noted, one example of which is Second Isaiah's dismissive attitude to Babylonian astronomy and omen lore, important ingredients of an intellectual tradition far more ancient than that of Israel (e. g. Isa 44:25; 47:8–13). A dismissive or deterrent attitude to the more speculative and discursive kinds of intellectual activity is expressed, much later, in a cautionary note appended by a more orthodox scribe to Qoheleth's free-ranging lucubrations:

> One further warning, my son: there is no end to the writing of books, and much study is wearisome. This is the end of the matter: you have heard it all. Fear God and obey his commandments; this sums up the duty of mankind. (Qoh 12:12–13 REB)

The pious glossator is saying, in effect: fear God, keep the commandments, keep it simple; don't take these speculations too seriously. A similar disquietude may have occasioned the verse which, according to most commentators, has been added to the poem about inaccessible wisdom in Job chapter 28. This poem, one of the most powerful in the Hebrew Bible, now ends as follows:

> Behold, the fear of the Lord, that is wisdom,
> to turn aside from evil is true understanding (Job 28:28)

So wisdom can be found, and found easily, after all.

To return to Chronicles and Ezra-Nehemiah. The author of Chronicles does not polemicize against secular learning or intellectual speculation; they simply are not in the picture. The concept of wisdom is limited to conduct evaluated according to a revealed law available in writing from the very beginning of Israel's history. Public figures are judged according to a simple moral code which some modern readers will no doubt judge to be also simplistic. In short, Chronicles evinces little evidence in intellectual matters outside the spheres of law and cult. The author even omits the reference in his source to Solomon as a cataloguer of flora and fauna, a kind of botanist, an ancient forerunner of Linnaeus (1 Kgs 4:29–34).³

---

2 Max Weber, *Ancient Judaism*, Transl. Hans Gerth and Don Martindal (New York: The Free Press, 1952), 285.
3 The only exception, if indeed it is one, is the obscure allusion to members of the tribe of Issachar "skilled at determining the signs of the times in order to know what course Israel should

It will probably be pointed out at this juncture that the Chronicler is not a *litterateur* or a *savant*; his forte is the homily, one of the most distinctive literary genres of the period which can be traced back to Deuteronomy and its authors. The idea of the homily as literature, or even as the product of intellectual activity, will no doubt seem counter-intuitive to some, but this has not always been the case. To cite only English-language preaching: consider the towering rhetoric of Wesley and Wilberforce or, to go back further, the sermons of John Donne which attracted greater crowds than those frequenting the London theatres. The brief sermons or outlines of sermons in Chronicles owe a debt to the much longer homilies attributed to Moses in Deuteronomy. Several years ago, Gerhard von Rad argued that the examples in Chronicles derive from Levitical preachers who delivered them orally as they went in circuit around the country instructing the people. Typically, the Chronicler's homily contains instruction, application by means of historical examples, and final exhortation.[4] In spite of his enthusiasm for liturgical music, the Chronicler clearly regards instruction as a very important Levitical function. What we seem to be witnessing in Chronicles is the emergence of ecclesiastical literature which certainly can claim its own distinguished history. But the question can still be asked to what extent this counts as an authentic form of intellectualism, and the suspicion remains that the mind-set from which this kind of writing proceeds tends to blunt curiosity about the kinds of issues which at that time, and even earlier, had occupied minds in the Greek-speaking world.

2 The Contrast between Persian period Judah and the contemporary Greek-speaking world

Mention of the Greek-speaking world brings us to a further consideration. The reader of the few writings which have survived from Achaemenid Judah may well be impressed by the contrast with the Greek intellectualism of that time, the more striking in that Greece and Palestine shared the same ecology, typical

---

take" (1 Chr 12:33). The Targum understands this, no doubt correctly, to refer to astronomical or astrological matters, with a practical application in mind. See Roger Le Déaut and Jacques Robert, *Targum des Chroniques*, Vol. 1, *Introduction et Traduction* (Rome: Pontifical Biblical Institute, 1971), 70–71.

4 Gerhard von Rad, "Die levitische Predigt in den Büchern der Chronik," in *Gesammelte Studien zum Alten Testament* (Munich: Kaiser, 1961), 248–61 = "The Levitical Sermon in I and II Chronicles," in *The Problem of the Hexateuch and Other Essays* (Edinburgh & London: Oliver & Boyd, 1966), 267–80.

of the eastern Mediterranean rim. The period in which Ezra and Nehemiah are presented as active in Jerusalem was, in Athens, the Periclean age (461–429 BC). In cities on the Greek mainland, in Ionia, and Southern Italy the sixth and fifth centuries saw decisive advances in metaphysics, cosmology, astronomy, mathematics and medicine. This was also the age of the itinerant Sophists, of Protagoras, Hippocrates and Anaxagoras, Pericles' mentor. The philosopher Parmenides arrived in Athens from Italy about five years before Nehemiah arrived in Judah from Susa. Socrates was engaged in intellectual debate with his disciples in mid-fifth century Athens at the same time that Nehemiah was rebuilding the wall of Jerusalem. The half century from the defeat of Xerxes' expedition in 479 to the outbreak of the Peloponnesian war in 431 was the high period for the theatre, the plastic arts, and architecture in Athens. The Parthenon was completed two years before Nehemiah began to rebuild the city wall around Jerusalem. Sophocles and Euripides were both close contemporaries of Nehemiah.

How explain this remarkable contrast? One approach would start out at the level of social and economic realities. As a later Jewish writer pointed out, intellectual activity requires leisure, and leisure generally requires a degree of wealth (Sir 38:24–39:11). Both may have been in short supply in the province of Judah during the two centuries of Persian rule. In texts from that time and place we hear many complaints of economic distress, and the situation would have been exacerbated by the fiscal policies of the Persian monarchs, a burden which the mainland Greek cities were spared.[5] From the Greek side, the tribute lists of the Delian League provide one of several indication of the wealth of Athens in the years following the defeat of Xerxes. The commercial prosperity of the Greek-speaking cities of the western Asian seaboard, the spread of literacy, colonizing activity, the frequency of travel and contact with a broad range of peoples and ideas, prepared the ground for emancipation from the moral universe of the Homeric epics and the mythic world in general. Among the most representative products of the new situation which was emerging everywhere in the Greek-speaking world in the fifth century were the Sophists who disseminated the ideas of the Ionian philosophers and subjected conventional morality to critique and, not infrequently, to attack.[6] As a way of highlighting the contrast with

---

[5] See, for example, Hag 1:6,8–11; Zech 8:10; Mal 2:13–16; Isa 58:3–4; 59:6, 9–15; Neh 5:14–19.
[6] On the philosophical ideas of the Sophists, their place in the development of Greek philosophy, and their critique of Plato, see Alasdair MacIntyre, *A Short History of Ethics: A History of Moral Philosophy from the Homeric Age to the Twentieth Century* (New York: Macmillan, 1966), 14–32; John Michael Rist, *Stoic Philosophy* (Cambridge: Cambridge University Press), 54–80, 233–38; Anthony Arthur Long, *Hellenistic Philosophy: Stoics, Epicureans, Sceptics* (2nd ed., Berkeley & Los Angeles: University of California Press, 1986), 179–209.

the contemporaneous world of Palestinian Judaism, we might imagine a theological conversation between Nehemiah and his contemporary Protagoras, author of the famous saying that "man is the measure of all things."

Another factor in the emergence of this new *Weltanschauung* in Greek-speaking regions was the increasing control over religious matters exercised by the Greek polis. Cultic display was restricted by sumptuary legislation, civic officials were appointed to oversee the finances of temples, the legal and judicial authority of priesthoods was curtailed, and cultic practices were more closely integrated with the affairs of the polis and the deme. The pressure of civic control effectively nudged the development of Greek societies away from the temple-state or priest-state type, common in Mesopotamia, Asia Minor, and Syria-Palestine, into which they might otherwise have evolved, and probably would have done so, if Persian rule had spread to the Greek mainland. In his explanation of this process, the classicist J. K. Davies emphasized the disengagement of legal process and public order from its original theocentric framework and the greater involvement of the state in the direction and financing of cult and ritual. He summarized as follows: "Both (of these processes) combined to tip the balance of power between religion and state further in favour of the latter, and thereby to make the latter increasingly the main framework of religious activity and to intensify the difficulties and fragmentation of fifth-century theodicies."[7]

We also have to reckon with the limited contact and reciprocal awareness between Jews and Greeks during the two centuries of Achaemenid rule. In the so-called Table of Nations in Genesis 10 Yavan (*yāvān*) stands for the Ionians, the Greek-speaking cities of the western Asian seaboard. According to this genealogical scheme Yavan is the "son" of Yephet, and Yephet is the Hebrew equivalent of Iapetos, in Greek myth a Titan, son of Ouranos and Gaia and father of Prometheus. The "sons" of Yavan – Elishah, Tarshish, Kittim and Rodanim (Gen 10:4) – point to an association of the eastern Greeks with Cyprus, Rhodes and the Aegean region in general. According to another mythic tradition recorded by Hellanicus of Lesbos, writing probably in the fifth century BC, Deucalion, survivor of the great deluge, became the progenitor of a new humanity and the ancestor of the Dorians, Ionians and Aeolians, the three branches of Greek-speaking people. It is tempting to see these mythic-historiographical traditions as developing at roughly the same time in Greece and Judah, but the problem of dating the biblical texts continues to elude us. At any rate, the Table of the Nations cannot be earlier than the seventh century BC since several of the places named were unknown before that time, and some of them occur in Ezekiel in

---

[7] John Keyton Davies, "Religion and the State," in *CAH* 4², 388.

the following century, usually in the context of commercial relations.⁸ In any case, the Table of the Nations does not betray any great knowledge of the Greek-speaking world on the part of the learned in Judah at the time it was committed to writing.⁹ But this is not to say that Judah was hermetically sealed off from the wider world of the eastern Mediterranean. Its educated elite at the time of Ezra and Nehemiah and later would, presumably, have followed the course of events outside their borders, events in which the Athenians were playing a leading role. During the Egyptian revolt at the beginning of the reign of Artaxerxes I, a year before Ezra's arrival in Judah according to Ezra 7:8, Athens sent a formidable naval expeditionary force in support of the rebellion which contributed to the initial defeat of the Persians. Five years later, however, the Athenian fleet was trapped and destroyed at Prosopitis, a disaster comparable to the defeat of the Athenian expedition to Sicily in 431 which hastened the end of the Peloponnesian war. But knowledge of current affairs involving Greeks seems not to be reflected in any significant way in the surviving texts.

Looking at the issue from the Greek side, we see that no historian writing in Greek during the two centuries of Persian rule so much as mentions Judah or Jews, not even the indefatigably curious and gregarious Herodotus, though his allusion to "Syrians of Palestine" (*Suroi tōn Palaistinōn*) would presumably have included Jews. The only information Herodotus provides about these "Syrians of Palestine" is that, together with the Phoenicians, they picked up the practice of circumcision from the Egyptians.¹⁰

3 The contribution of archaeology

Archaeological indications of Greek presence, in the shape of Attic and eastern Greek ware, the occasional lamp, and a few coins, do not essentially contradict

---

8 Gomer (Ezek 38:6), Magog (38:2; 39:6), Yavan (27:13), Tubal and Meshech (27:13; 32:26; 38:2–3; 39:1), Elishah (27:7), Tarshish (27:12,25), Kittim (27:6).
9 On the Table and the names in it associated with Yavan see Claus Westermann, *Genesis 1–11: A Commentary*, Transl. John Scullion (Minneapolis: Augsburg Fortress, 1984), 495–530; and on the relation between the Genesis myths of origin and those of the Greeks, John van Seters, *In Search of History: Historiography in the Ancient World and the Origins of Biblical History* (New Haven: Yale University Press, 1993), 8–54.
10 *Hist.* II 104; III 5,91; IV 39; VII 89. The Jews are explicitly counted among Syrians by Theophrastus (in Porphyry's treatise *On Piety* II 26) and by Clearchus, a student of Aristotle's (in Josephus, *C. Ap.* I 179). See Elias Bickerman, *The Jews in the Greek Age* (Cambridge/Mass: Harvard University Press, 1988), 13–25.

the impression conveyed by the literary evidence just surveyed. Before considering these indications it will be well to recall the problems besetting the use of archaeological evidence from the Persian period. In the first place, the data base has been severely reduced due to the erosion of sites lying near the surface and their destruction by previous excavators anxious to get down to the real goods at the Bronze and Iron Age levels. Moreover, part of what has been excavated has remained unpublished, often years after the site in question has been excavated. There is the further difficulty of identifying what is chronologically Achaemenid as opposed to earlier Neo-Babylonian or later Hellenistic material; in which respect the still common assumption about the presence of Attic ware as a leading criterion for Achaemenid period levels involves a misleading circularity.[11] However, the presence of Attic, Eastern Greek or Cypriot ware at a site, especially an inland site, does not necessarily entail contact with Athenians, Ionians or Cypriots respectively. The material in question could have been purchased from itinerant merchants, perhaps like the (probably Phoenician) sellers of all kinds of merchandise who aroused the wrath of Nehemiah by camping out near the wall of Jerusalem (Neh 13:20).[12]

Most of the archaeological evidence for Greek contact is found, not surprisingly, in settlements along the Mediterranean coast, the Sharon plain, and Philistia. The presence of Greek ware at these sites, most of which were under Phoenician control as far south as Ashkelon, attest to commercial relations with mainland Greek cities, the eastern Greeks, Cyprus and other Aegean islands.[13] Greek presence along the coast and offshore would have been especially in evidence after the defeat of Xerxes in 480–479, the establishment of the Athenian empire, and the movement of Athenian land and sea forces in support of the frequent revolts in Egypt.

---

[11] On imported ceramic ware during the Persian period see Ephraim Stern, "The Archaeology of Persian Palestine," in *CHJ* 1, 88–114 (95–99); *Archaeology of the Land of the Bible*, Vol. 2, *The Assyrian, Babylonian, and Persian Periods* (New York: Doubleday, 2001), 518–22.
[12] John Boardman, *Persia and the West* (London: Thames & Hudson, 2000), 203, points out that the graffiti on ceramic ware of Greek origin indicate that the Phoenicians were the principal commercial middlemen.
[13] On the archaeology of these sites, including Akko, Hawam, Shiqmona, Tel Megadim, Tel Mevorach and Dor, see Ephraim Stern, *Material Culture of the Land of the Bible in the Persian Period* (Warminster: Aris & Philips, 1982), 9–29; *Archaeology of the Land of the Bible*, Vol. 2, 373–422. On the finds of Greek origin see Dominique Auscher, "Les Relations entre la Grèce et la Palestine avant la Conquête d'Alexandre," *VT* 17 (1967): 8–30; Robert Wenning, "Attische Keramik in Palästina: Ein Zwischenbericht," *Transeuphratène* 2 (1990): 157–67; Wolf-Dietrich Niemeier, "Archaic Greeks in the Orient: Textual and Archaeological Evidence," *BASOR* 322 (2001): 11–32.

The situation inland, in Judah, was rather different. Attic and Eastern Greek sherds have turned up at several sites including Ramat Rachel, Gezer, and En-Gedi, and in significant amounts in Tell en-Nasbeh (Mizpah), the administrative center of the province during the Neo-Babylonian and early Persian period. A few Athenian coins have been excavated at other locations (Tell el-Fûl, Bethany, Beth-zur), and a small fragment of an Attic lekythos was unearthed at Beitin (Bethel).[14] To the best of my knowledge, no significant archaeological evidence for Greek presence, direct or indirect, during the two centuries of Persian rule has turned up in Jerusalem, though such judgements in matters pertaining to Palestinian archaeology are notoriously subject to revision. In summary: Greek ware, greatly superior to local products, is in evidence unevenly and sparsely throughout Judah, but to what extent it indicates a knowledge of Greeks and the Greek way of life among Judaeans remains uncertain. More direct, if transient, contact would have been by way of Greek mercenaries, renowned through the Near East, especially during the frequent military campaigns in the region.

Taking all the archaeological data currently available into account, the impression remains that during these two centuries Judah, though of strategic significance, especially in view of frequent revolts in Egypt, was an economic and cultural backwater. The import and use of articles of everyday use does not necessarily amount to serious cultural impact, even less to influence at the intellectual level, and Greek-speaking lands were not the only possible source of intellectual stimulation. Elias Bickerman pointed out some years ago that although Jews in the Persian period were part of a universal Levantine civilization, they are not mentioned in classical Greek literature, and "no Greek traveler in the Orient, neither Herodotus nor Ctesias, paid any attention to Jerusalem or its Deity."[15] From the Jewish side, moreover, the surviving writings contain no Greek personal names and no Greek loan words.[16] Looking further ahead, distance from Greek

---

14 On the few Greek, mostly Athenian, coins of the fifth and fourth century from Palestine see Uriel Rappaport, "Numismatics" in *CHJ* 1, 25–29. On Persian period coinages in general see Oren Tal, "Negotiating Identity in an International Context under Achaemenid Rule: The Indigenous Coinages of Persian-Period Palestine as an Allegory," in *Judah and the Judeans in the Achaemenid Period*, ed. Oded Lipschits, Gary Neil Knoppers and Manfred Oeming (Winona Lake/Indiana: Eisenbrauns, 2011), 445–459. On the Attic lekythos discovered at Bethel see James Kelso, *The Excavation of Bethel* (Cambridge/Mass: ASOR, 1968), 80 and Plate 37.10.
15 Elias Bickerman, *The Jews in the Greek Age*, 14.
16 Al Wolters, "Sôpiyyâ (Prov 31:27) as Hymnic Participle and Play on *Sophia*," *JBL* 104 (1985): 577–87, argued that the participial form *sôpiyyâ* at Prov 31:27 was chosen to make a play on the Greek word *sophia*. The suggestion is ingenious but does not fit the context, and the pun would require initial *samek* rather than *tsade*. In any case, Wolters dates the poem to the Hellenistic period. With the possible exception of *appiryôn* ("palanquin", "sedan chair") in Cant 3:9,

culture would have been compounded for more traditional Jews as a result of the crisis of Hellenization, thus anticipating the ambiguity towards secular learning or "Greek wisdom" (*hokmâ yavanît*) in certain rabbinic texts from the Tannaitic and Amoraic periods.

4 Nomistic Wisdom

We may find a point of entry for a kind of intellectualism different from but not entirely foreign to that of the Greeks of the classical epoch in what Wellhausen described, with reference to Chronicles, as "the enumeration of mere subjects without predicates," but which we may characterize more benignly as nomistic wisdom. Just as the Deuteronomistic History, the final edition of which can be dated no earlier than the Neo-Babylonian period, served as a primary source for Chronicles, so it is primarily the Deuteronomic/Deuteronomistic law which provided the author of Chronicles with a basic legal and ethical orientation. A fundamental postulate of the legal theory of these scribes is that the law is to be for Israel the equivalent of the intellectual traditions of other peoples, whether Mesopotamian, Egyptian, Greek, or whatever. The Israelite is assured that observing this law will "manifest your wisdom and discernment to (other) peoples, so that when they hear about all these statutes they will say, 'Surely this great nation is a wise and discerning people!'" (Deut 4:6). This optimistic assessment is based on the conviction that legal wisdom is divinely revealed and is therefore attainable without the kind of speculation about "hidden things" (*nistārôt*), not limited to knowledge of the future, the pursuit of which was seen to be characteristic of foreign intellectualism (Deut 29:28). That these "hidden things" belong to God, and are therefore beyond the reach of the unaided human intellect, imposes limits on human intellectual achievements. Speaking in the persona of Moses, the preacher affirms that this wisdom, encapsulated in the divine commandment, is to be sought neither in heaven, that is, in the quest for arcane knowledge, nor overseas, that is, among foreign peoples: "The word is very near you; it is in your mouth and in your heart" (Deut 30:11–14). It is therefore readily available as an authoritative written law, a law which Moses gave to his people and in which they, in turn, must educate their children. These observations are interesting since they demonstrate some degree of knowledge, or at least awareness, of the intellectual traditions of other peoples and cultures, to-

---

which may derive from Greek *phoreion*, the earliest Greek loan words are the names of the musical instruments in Nebuchadnezzar's orchestra in Daniel 3.

gether with a consciousness that ethical practice in the form of law observance requires justification by means of a theoretical framework of some kind.

Apropos of this point, it is significant that the Deuteronomists were the first to use the term *tôrâ* for a written legal corpus, with the result that after that point it would not be possible to use the same word in the plural (*tôrôt*) for individual legal stipulations. Other terms would have to be found such as *misvôt, huqqîm* or *dibrê hattôrâ*. I take this linguistic fact to be symptomatic of a unifying and synthesizing intent, the first step in the direction of viewing law in some way as a conceptual system. One could perhaps find parallels in the development of Roman law or mediaeval canon law at the time of Gratian.

True to this perspective, the author of Chronicles regards the law, certainly including the Deuteronomic law, as having been available in writing from the beginning of the history of Israel.[17] Antiquity meant authenticity, in legal as in other matters. In the same writer's account of the charge addressed to Solomon by David, wisdom is explicitly associated with law observance, in that to observe the law is to bring into play the full exercise of discretion and understanding (1 Chr 22:12–13). Following Solomon's example (the author prudently omits the great king's involvement with foreign women, if indeed he knew of it), the truly wise rulers – Asa, Jehoshaphat, Hezekiah, Josiah – were those who "sought Yahveh" by following the guidance of a written law.[18] Movements of political and religious renewal always begin with a return to this law. In one of his many departures from 1–2 Kings, the author describes how Jehoshaphat sent a panel of lay and clerical scholars round the cities of Judah to instruct the people out of a copy of the law which they carried with them, an incident which no doubt reflects practice in the author's own day (2 Chr 17:7–9). The same ruler set up a central and regional judicial system in imitation of Moses and in keeping with a stipulation of the Deuteronomic law.[19] In this religious culture judicial activity is also a form of wisdom, and judges can therefore be listed among the sages.[20] For the author of Chronicles the custodians, teachers and interpreters of the law are the true depositories of the wisdom proper to Israel.

In Ezra-Nehemiah, this very specific form of nomistic wisdom shows up in the most unlikely place, an imperial decree issued by Artaxerxes, probably the first of that name (465–424). The close parallelism in the decree between "the

---

[17] 1 Chr. 10:13; 16:40; 22:12–13; 28:7, 19; 2 Chr 5:10.
[18] 2 Chr 14:3; 17:4; 19:3; 20:4; 22:9; 31:21; 34:3.
[19] 2 Chr 19:4–11, cf. Deut 1:16–18; 17:8–13.
[20] The statement in the so-called Covenant Law that "a bribe blinds the eyes of the clear-sighted" (Exod 23:8) is reworded in the section of Deuteronomy dealing with judges to say that "a bribe blinds the eyes of the wise" (*hăkāmîm*, Deut 16:19).

law of your God which is in your hand" (Ezra 7:14) and "the wisdom of your God which is in your hand" (7:25) – a turn of phrase which has no place in an imperial rescript – recalls the identification of law and wisdom in Deuteronomy, therefore one of several indications of the hand of a Jewish scribe in the redaction or, more likely, the composition of the edict.

Beginning with Deuteronomy, therefore, the identification of law and law observance with wisdom or, in other words, the subordination of intellectualism to ethics, became one of the defining characteristics of early Judaism. It finds lapidary expression in a saying attributed to the first century AD Galilean sage Hanina ben Dosa:

> Those whose fear of sinning has precedence over their wisdom, their wisdom will endure; those whose wisdom has precedence over their fear of sinning, their wisdom will not endure" (*m. Avot* 3:11).

Whether this moralistic approach qualifies as genuine intellectualism will still be subject to doubt since it appears to leave little space for curiosity about the specifically human, the physical world, the nature of reality, the problems of being and becoming, the entire range of questions which were being asked by the early Greek philosophers. While this is by no means a negligible proviso, it should be noted that the primacy of ethics within philosophy was not an exclusively Jewish trait. Stoic teachers dealt with the big philosophical issues – fate, death, time, and so on – but with respect to the basics they would have agreed with Qoheleth that intellectual activity is, in the first place, concerned with "what is good for human beings to do under heaven for the brief span of their lives" (Qoh 2:3). According to Stoic educational theory, ethics formed the most important branch of the trivium: logic, physics, and ethics.[21] The conviction that philosophy should not lose sight of practical goals and should provide impetus to living the good life, was in fact a basic presupposition of most if not all philosophical schools in Greek antiquity. Alastair MacIntyre has argued that the need to solve problems of personal and societal morality provided the impulse for the development of Greek philosophy in the first place:

> The suggestion that asking and answering moral questions is one thing, and asking and answering philosophical questions about morality quite another thing, may conceal from

---

21 On Stoic ethics consult John Michael Rist, *Stoic Philosophy*; Ian Kidd, "Moral Actions and Rules in Stoic Ethics," In *The Stoics*, ed. John Rist (Berkeley & Los Angeles: University of California Press, 1978), 247–58; Maximilian Forschner, *Die Stoische Ethik: Über den Zusammenhang von Natur-, Sprach- und Moralphilosophie im altstoischen System* (Stuttgart: Klett-Cotta, 1981); Anthony Arthur Long, *Hellenistic Philosophy*, 179–209.

us the fact that in asking moral questions of a certain kind with sufficient persistence we may discover that we cannot answer them until we have asked and answered certain philosophical questions. A discovery of this kind provided the initial impulse for philosophical ethics in Greek society.[22]

It is therefore not so surprising that when members of the Greek schools began eventually to come in contact with Jews they had no difficulty acknowledging that Judaism also represented a philosophy. Theophrastus, head of the Lyceum after the retirement of Aristotle, speaks of the Jews as a philosophical race (*philosophoi to genos ontes*), while another Peripatetic, Clearchus of Soli, reports a discourse of the master in which he asserts that the Jews were descended from the Indian philosophers. Aristotle goes on to describe, in a somewhat patronizing manner, how he encountered a Jew who not only spoke Greek but had the soul of a Greek. The same connection between Indian and Jewish philosophy is made by Megasthenes writing towards the beginning of the third century BC.[23]

An early stage in the emergence of a theoretical framework for life according to a law of divine origin can be found in a poem about Wisdom, first-born of creation, in Proverbs 8:22–31. The poet presents the teachings of the sages as wisdom personified, the primordial element in creation, present and co-active with the Creator God, "rejoicing at all times in his presence, rejoicing in his world, delighting to be with human kind" (vv 30–31). And since *hokmâ*, like *sophia*, is feminine, wisdom can have the attributes of a good, virtuous, and desirable woman. The poem carries no certain date. Several scholars opt for the early Hellenistic period, but a date in the late Achaemenid period is equally possible.[24] The editor who arranged the seven compilations of aphoristic material in the book placed the personification in high relief by enclosing his compilations of aphorisms within discourse about the Woman Wisdom at the beginning (Prov 1:20) and an acrostic poem in praise of an idealized feminine figure at the end (31:10–31). In the Hebrew Bible, cities and countries are frequently personified (Virgin Daughter Zion, Babylon, etc), but in contrast to Greek practice (e.g. *eris, nemesis, tuchē*) personification of abstract qualities is relatively rare.

The studied ambiguity with which the author of the poem describes how the Woman Wisdom came into existence could be due to the need to avoid the im-

---

22 Alasdair MacIntyre, *A Short History of Ethics*, 5.
23 Relevant texts in Menahem Stern, *Greek and Latin Authors on Jews and Judaism*, Vol. 1, *From Herodotus to Plutarch* (Jerusalem: Israel Academy of Sciences and Humanities, 1976), 10, 46, 50. See also Martin Hengel, *Judaism and Hellenism*, Vol. 1, *Studies in their Encounter in Palestine during the Early Hellenistic Period* (Philadelphia: Fortress Press, 1974), 255–61.
24 On the date of the passage see Michael Fox, *Proverbs 1–9: A New Translation with Introduction and Commentary* (New York: Doubleday, 2000), 48–49.

plication that *hokmâ/sophia* was the daughter of Yahweh in the same way, for example, that Maat was the daughter of Re, the Egyptian solar deity. This concern notwithstanding, the mythic biography of Maat provided a parallel to Wisdom in Prov 8:22–31. The favourite child of Re, she came down to humanity at the beginning of time as the embodiment and preserver of cosmic order and guardian of justice and the rule of law. Without her benign influence the world would collapse into chaos and ruin. The poem in Proverbs chapter 8 is sophisticated enough to suggest that its author was familiar with Egyptian mythological categories and was exploiting them with the purpose of recommending religious and moral teachings. In this respect it may be read as analogous to Platonic philosophizing or Stoic allegorizing by means of myth.

A further stage in this interpenetration of a religion based on law with philosophy in the guise of myth can be found in the "Praise of Wisdom" poem in Sir 24:1–29 in which *hokmâ/sophia*, whose self-presentation is modelled on the Isis aretalogies,[25] is identified with "the book of the covenant of the Most High God" (Sir 24:23). By adopting and indigenizing this genre, the author is claiming for the Jewish law a universal significance, and in so doing he no doubt is also concerned to answer charges of intellectual obscurantism and xenophobia directed at Jewish religious thought and practice which were in the air at that time.[26] The poem of this *savant* comes to us from the early second century BC, but its presentation of the law as the supramundane principle and source of moral order revealed to Israel had roots among priests and scribes in Judah and elsewhere centuries earlier.

5 Concluding observations

More direct parallels with contemporaneous Greek literary productions have been proposed from time to time. It has been suggested, for example, that the book of Job betrays the influence of the Greek tragedians, and it has even

---

[25] Several of these aretalogies have survived, including a brief example reported by Diodorus Siculus (I 27:3–4) and the one extracted from the *Metamorphoses* of Apuleius which concludes with the transformation of the hapless Lucius from asinine to human form (11:5). For references see Robert John Getty, "Isis," in *The Oxford Classical Dictionary,* ed. Simon Hornblower and Antony Spawforth (3rd ed., Oxford: Oxford University Press, 1999), 768–69.

[26] Hecataeus, for example, writing at the time of Alexander the Great and otherwise not obviously prejudiced against the Jewish people, states that Moses introduced an unsocial and intolerant way of life (*apanthrōpon tina kai misoxenon bion eisēgēsato*). For the text see Menahem Stern, *Greek and Latin Authors on Jews and Judaism,* 26.

been described as a Jewish version of the Prometheus myth, comparable to Aeschylus' *Prometheus Bound*.[27] Agur the sage, whose cryptic saying is recorded in Prov 30:1–6, has been interpreted as expressing a religious scepticism similar to that of Xenophanes.[28] The poem on the inaccessibility of wisdom in Job 28, probably an insertion into the book, might also bring to mind some aspects of the enigmatic views of Heraclitus, as in the saying attributed to him, that "the unexpected is not to be tracked down and no path leads to it."[29] Like the aristocratic Pindar, perhaps a contemporary, the author of Job has a strong sense of mortality and the fragility of human endeavour and is wary of attempts to explore the complexities of human existence (Job 38–41). But none of these correspondences is strong enough to suggest direct borrowing from a Greek repertoire.

Greece was not, in any case, the only source of intellectual stimulation for their Jewish contemporaries during those centuries, and Greek thought did not provide the only standard by which the literary productions of other countries could be assessed. Egyptian didacticism was held in high esteem in Judaean scribal schools, as it was among Greek litterati. One of the seven compilations which form the core of the book of Proverbs, the one containing thirty proverbial sayings (22:22–23:11), is an adapted and indigenized version of *The Instruction of Amenemope*, composed during the late New Kingdom period but copied frequently thereafter. The influence of the immemorial Mesopotamian intellectual tradition on Israelite didactic and discursive writing is also well documented, and may be exemplified by the personification of *hokmâ* in *The Sayings of Ahiqar*, a didactic work of Assyrian origin an Aramaic translation of which was dis-

---

[27] That Job was modelled on the Greek dramas was proposed in the fourth century by Theodore of Mopsuestia (*PG* lxvi. 697–98). The idea persisted into the modern period and was refuted in the commentary of Samuel Rolles Driver and George Buchanan Gray, *A Critical and Exegetical Commentary on the Book of Job* (Edinburgh: T. & T. Clark, 1921), xxi–xxiv. Comparison with the figure of Prometheus is not, however, inappropriate; on which see William Andrew Irwin, "Prometheus and Job," *Journal of Religion* 30 (1950): 90–108; Martin Hengel, *Judaism and Hellenism*, Vol. 1, 109; Vol. 2, 73.

[28] Any conclusions about this impenetrably obscure passage must be provisional, but it is possible to detect in it an ironic note in the disavowal of knowledge of God comparable to Zophar's denunciation of Job's stupidity in claiming to know "the deep things of God" (Job 11:7–12). Use of the designation *ĕlôha* (30:5), frequent in Job, and the sarcastic *kî tēdāʻ*, "surely you know!" (30:4, cf. Job 38:5), suggest the possibility of reading the saying as a response to and critique of the Job debate.

[29] Fragment 18 cf. Job 28:7–8,13. See Edward Hussey, *The Presocratics* (New York: Charles Scribner's Sons, 1972), 38–39.

covered among the Elephantine papyri.³⁰ Frequent reference to "discourses of the sages" (*dibrê hăkāmîm* (e. g. Prov 1:6; 22:17; Qoh 12:11) points to the practice of compiling the sayings of notable teachers, of which however only a few samples have come down to us. It is unlikely, for example, that Prov 30:1–6 and 31:1–9 represent all that existed of the sayings of Agur and Lemuel. The practice was certainly underway by the Achaemenid epoch and continued down into the Roman period and beyond.³¹

The agenda, themes and even the language of the sages can also be detected in the story of the patriarch Joseph (Genesis 37–50), described as not only discerning and wise (*îš nābôn věhākām*, Gen 41:33,39) but also successful (*îš maslîah*, Gen 39:2). The affinities of the Joseph story with didactic and sapiential texts from the Second Temple period and with novelistic diaspora narratives from the same late period establish its date, at least in general terms.³² Its literary character also sets it apart from the rest of the Pentateuch and gives it a more internationalist character, comparable with the Assyrian story of the sage Ahiqar at the Assyrian and Pharaonic courts and the Greek physician Democedes of Croton at the court of Darius I.³³

There are, finally, more pragmatic considerations to bear in mind in comparing the Jewish intellectual world of that time with that of Greek-speaking peoples, Jerusalem with Athens. In the first place, our assessment is necessarily based on the few writings which have physically survived from the two centuries prior to the Macedonian conquest. The preferred writing surface for texts of any length would have been papyrus, and papyrus has a hard time surviving the wet Palestinian winters; apart from the Samaria papyri from the last decades of Achaemenid rule, no papyri have survived from that time. Chronicles refers to sources some of which, assuming that they actually existed, have not survived.³⁴

---

30 James Lindenberger, *The Aramaic Proverbs of Ahiqar* (Baltimore: Johns Hopkins University Press, 1983), especially 68–69; Abraham Cowley, *Aramaic Papyri of the Fifth Century BC* (Oxford: Clarendon, 1923), 204–48.
31 For the New Testament see James Robinson, "'Logoi Sophon': On the Gattung of Q," in *Trajectories through Early Christianity*, ed. James Robinson and Helmut Koester (Philadelphia: Fortress Press, 1971), 71–113.
32 See Norman Whybray, "The Joseph Story and Pentateuchal Criticism," *VT* 18 (1968): 522–28; Donald Redford, *A Study of the Biblical Story of Joseph* (Leiden: Brill, 1970); Arndt Meinhold, "Die Gattung der Josephsgeschichte und des Estherbuches: Diasporanovellen II," *ZAW* 88 (1976): 72–93.
33 On the Book of Ahiqar see James VanderKam, "Ahiqar, Book of," in *ABD* 1, 119–20. The adventures of Democedes are narrated in Herodotus 3:129–137.
34 The putative authors of almost all of these sources are prophets: Samuel (1 Chr 29:29), Nathan (1 Chr 29:29; 2 Chr 9:29), Gad (1 Chr 29:29), Ahijah (2 Chr 9:29), Shemaiah (2 Chr 12:15), Iddo

We are also dependent on what has been allowed to survive. In a much-cited passage, Josephus contrasts the twenty-two Jewish books, eighteen of them comprising history and law, with the numerous writings of the Greeks produced without quality control (*C. Ap.* 1:37–41). The comparison is of course misleading, even absurd. He should have compared the "justly accredited" Jewish books with the canonical Homeric epics, but that would not have served his purpose. We have no direct information on the actual procedures and measures by which certain writings were included and others excluded from a canonical list, but discussion about certain borderline texts in early rabbinic and early Christian circles suggests that several writings were filtered out and lost. There is, in addition, the intractable problem of dating the texts which have survived and tracing their redactional history.

The contrast between the intellectual world of pre-Hellenistic Judaism and that of the Greek cities and their colonies, is also, as we have seen, the product of historical contingencies. The pursuit of learning and the production of literary works require patronage and some kind of institutional framework, but after the liquidation of the Judaean state, the suppression of the dynasty, and the deportations, this support structure would have been removed. Then, under Persian rule, Judah became in effect a temple community of a kind common throughout the empire.[35] There is much we do not know about the temple staff and its operations, but it would have included something like the Egyptian "House of Life" (*pr-ʿnh*) or the Mesopotamian "tablet house" (*bīt tuppi*), but on a smaller scale.[36] There would have been scribes responsible for the drafting of laws, and the leading priests would have authorized a compilation of texts, the "justly accredited books" of Josephus (*C. Ap.* 1:37–41), in other words a literary canon.[37] But the fact that the list includes Esther, Job, the Canticle, and collections of gnomic material including Proverbs and Qoheleth testifies that intellectual and literary activity was not confined to the temple. Under Persian rule the governor's palace could have provided patronage and hospitality to such activity. Nehemiah boasted that he provided accommodation for one hundred and fifty people including

---

(2 Chr 12:15; 13:22), Jehu ben Hanani (2 Chr 20:34), Isaiah (2 Chr 26:22; 32:32). The sources are described as annals (*dĕbārîm*), prophecy (*nĕbû â*), visions (*hăzôt*), and midrash (*midraš*).

35 See Joseph Blenkinsopp, "Temple and Society in Achaemenid Judah," in *Second Temple Studies*, Vol. 1, *Persian Period*, ed. Philip Davies (Sheffield: Sheffield Academic Press, 1991), 22–53.

36 Joseph Blenkinsopp, *Sage, Priest, Prophet: Religious and Intellectual Leadership in Ancient Israel* (Louisville: Westminster/John Knox, 1995), 66–114; Karel van der Toorn, *Scribal Culture and the Making of the Hebrew Bible* (Cambridge/Mass: Harvard University Press, 2008), 51–73.

37 See the section on "The Closing of the Canonical Era" in Karel van der Toorn, *Scribal Culture*, 252–64.

foreigners, and some of these may have been engaged in literary activities (Neh 5:17). A later tradition, of uncertain historical value, records that Nehemiah put together a library containing royal annals, writings of David (probably psalms), and liturgical material (2 Macc. 2:13). The patronage of aristocratic families, for example the Tobiads in Amman, may also have helped to making such literary activity possible. The fact remains that we have practically no information on the circumstances of the production and first reception of these and similar writings. The earliest reference we have to a Jerusalemite school or academy apart from the temple is ben Sira's *bêt midrāš* (*oikos paideias*, Sir 51:23) from the early second century BC. Our source material is woefully inadequate, but here as elsewhere we have to work with what we have.

VII. Was the Pentateuch the constitution of the Jewish ethnos in the Persian period?

In: *Persia and Torah: The Theory of Imperial Authorization of the Pentateuch*, ed. by James Watts, 41–62. Atlanta: Society of Biblical Literature, 2001.

1 The Persian concept and practice of law

Albert Olmstead, one of the early maximalists, argued in his *History of the Persian Empire* that following on the military successes of his *annus mirabilis*, Darius I set about drawing up a law code called "the Ordinance of Good Regulations" to be enforced throughout the empire. The compilation of this document was accomplished in record time since it was already being implemented, Olmstead claimed, in a transaction recorded in 519 BC. Such unusual expedition would compare favourably with the compilation of the Egyptian laws that was getting under way about the same time and which the Demotic Chronicle tells us lasted sixteen years. According to Olmstead, this remarkable achievement of Darius was made possible by a deliberate and systematic borrowing, in style and substance, from the ancient Mesopotamian legal tradition – the Code of Hammurapi in particular – perhaps even, he speculated, from the original stele in Susa, now in the Louvre, rather from one or other of the copies produced in the course of the sixth and fifth centuries BC.[1] Olmstead therefore enthusiastically endorsed the high opinion of Darius as lawgiver prevalent among the Greeks, including Plato, Xenophon and Diodorus Siculus.[2]

Since caution is in order when dealing with issues between maximalists and minimalists, I begin by recording the judgement of T. Cuyler Young Jr. in *The Cambridge Ancient History* that evidence for legal codification and legal reform in the early Achaemenid period remains elusive (*CAH*² 4, 94). The state was based on the foundations of law and the administration of justice, and royal inscriptions abound in such terms as *aršta* (justice), *arta* (good order, truth) and, of course, *dāta*. This Old Persian term (cf. Akkadian *dātu*) is generally translated "law" but this rendering calls for no less elaboration than the Hebrew *tôrâ*. Where it occurs in royal inscriptions it refers either to a specific decree or a gen-

---

[1] See Albert Olmstead's *A History of the Persian Empire* (Chicago: University Press, 1940), 119–34 and "Darius as Lawgiver," *AJSL* 51 (1934/1935): 247–49. The document mentions "the law of the king" (*dātu šarri*).
[2] Plato, *Ep.* 7:332b; *Leg.* 695c; Xenophon, *Oec.* 14:6; Diodorus, *Hist.* 1:94–95.

eral condition of law and order imposed by the will of the sovereign. In the Bisitun (Behistun) inscription Darius speaks of his *dāta* and adds, in lapidary fashion, "as was said to them by me, so was it done." Similar expressions occur in the funerary inscriptions at Naqsh-i-Rustam and in one of the Susa inscriptions from the reign of Darius. In a Persepolis text Xerxes enjoins on his subjects respect for the law established by Ahura Mazda.³ The firman of Xerxes, apparently the most religious of Achaemenid rulers, forbidding the worship of *daiva* (demons i.e. false gods) and enjoining the worship of Ahura Mazda and Arta, implied that the observance of *dāta* was rooted in the will of the cosmic creator-deity and expressed as the will of the ruler.⁴

Thus far, therefore, there is no evidence for Olmstead's thesis, and we know of no Persian compilation of laws prior to the collection of instructions in the *Vidēvdāt* (or *Vendidat*) ("Antidemonic Law") from the Parthian period. This is not to say that the dominant ethnic class would not have brought elements of customary law with them from their tribal and nomadic past and from Median or Elamite borrowings which could have been combined with Mesopotamian legal traditions. Those traditions were still pervasive, as we see from private and family law in the Elephantine and Daliyeh papyri.⁵ But what was lacking, on evidence currently available, was a legal code compiled for use throughout the empire.

Where cuneiform texts from the same period allude to "the law of the king" (*dātu ša šarri*), here too the reference is to a decree or royal command having the force of law.⁶ More often than not such texts deal with fiscal matters, always of great concern to the Achaemenids; we recall Darius I's nickname, "the Huckster" (*kapēlos*) as recorded by Herodotus, *Hist*. 3:89.⁷ In one of the Persepolis Fortress

---

3 For these texts see Roland Kent, *Old Persian: Grammar, Texts, Lexicon* (New Haven: American Oriental Society, 1953), 119, 138, 140–41, 152.

4 *Arta*, represented as an archangel or spirit attendant on Ahura Mazda, embodies the idea of justice and legal order and is an element in several theophoric names, for example Artaxerxes. This justice and this order is rooted in the will of the creator-deity and therefore in the cosmic order. Naqsh-i-Rustam A begins in a manner reminiscent of Deutero-Isaiah: "A great god is Ahura Mazda, who created this earth, who created yonder sky, who created humanity, who created happiness for humanity, who made Darius king, one king of many, one lord of many". Roland Kent, *Old Persian*, 138.

5 Jonas Greenfield, "The Aramaic Legal Texts from the Achaemenian Period," *Transeuph* 3 (1990): 85–92.

6 Leo Oppenheim, "The Babylonian Evidence of Achaemenian Rule in Mesopotamia," in *CHI* 2, 529–87 (547).

7 Raymond Descat, "Darius, le roi kapēlos," in *Continuity and Change: Proceedings of the last Achaemenid History Workshop April 6–8, 1990*, ed. Amélie Kuhrt, Margaret Cool Root and

Tablets *datam* (Elamite for *dāta*) refers to regulations to be followed by those in charge of storerooms.⁸ Another example of common usage is the statement in the official, Aramaic version of the Xanthus inscription line 19, that "he (the satrap Pixodarus) wrote this decree", with reference to a specific disposition of the local community.⁹

On the basis of the available evidence, therefore, the legal terminology in use in the early Achaemenid period either refers to a particular edict backed by the absolute authority of the ruler or is expressive of a broad, global concept of a legal order. All legal enactments of any kind originating in any part of the empire are therefore, theoretically, "law of the king" (Ezra 7:26). And since the king ruled by favour of the creator deity Ahura Mazda, the royal law could be said to be rooted in the cosmic order, though we have no evidence that law was the object of theoretical reflection. In any case, evidence is lacking for a compilation or code of law in force throughout the empire.¹⁰ A caveat is also in order with respect to the related term *dātabara*, lierally "law bearer," often translated more precisely than the context warrants – for example, as "judge" or "magistrate" in Dan 3:2. We must also avoid being misled by Herodotus whose occasional allusions to Persian laws (*nomoi, thesmoi*) generally refer to local customs. An example would be that Persian boys are brought up with the women for the first five years of life (*Hist.* 1:137). Herodotus' typical mix of the plausible and the implausible is illustrated by a story he tells about Cambyses who, wishing to marry his sister, enquired of the royal judges (*tous basilēious dikastas*), interpreters of the laws of the land, whether such a union was permitted. Since exegesis was apparently a more dangerous occupation then than now, the judges replied that there was no law permitting it, but there was a law according to which the king could do as he pleased (*Hist.* 3:31).

Read as potential source material, the relevant biblical texts may be said to be somewhere between the inscriptions and Herodotus. The book of Esther, the diaspora narratives in Daniel , and Ezra, in which the Persian loan word *dāt* oc-

---

Heleen Sancisi-Weerdenburg (Leiden: Nederlands Instituut voor het Nabije Oosten, 1994), 161–66.
8 Pierre Briant, *Histoire de l'Empire Perse de Cyrus à Alexandre* (Paris: Libraire Arthème Fayard, 1996), 527.
9 Peter Frei and Klaus Koch, *Reichsidee und Reichsorganisation im Perserreich* (2nd ed., Fribourg/Göttingen: Universitätsverlag/Vandenhoeck&Ruprecht, 1996), 39–47.
10 This conclusion commands a broad consensus. See, for example, Muhammad Dandamaev and Vladimir Lukonin, *The Culture and Social Institutions of Ancient Iran* (Cambridge: Cambridge University Press, 1989), 116–30; Pierre Briant, *Histoire de l'Empire Perse*, 526–28, 981–83; Richard Nelson Frye, The History of Ancient Iran (Munich: Beck, 1984), 119; Amélie Kuhrt, "Babylonia from Cyrus to Xerxes," in *CAH²* 4, 132.

curs in both Hebrew and Aramaic, show familiarity with aspects of life under Persian rule. In this respect biblical usage corroborates, or at least is not inconsistent with the non-biblical evidence. The book of Esther, which purports to describe events affecting Jewish communities during the reign of Xerxes (486–465 BC), refers quite often to the royal laws (*dātê hammelek*, 3:8), but in every instance it is a matter of ad hoc decrees, not stipulations that could be part of a law code. There is, for example, a *dāt* or edict governing the behaviour of recalcitrant queens (Esth 1:13, 15, 19), recruitment for and the day-to-day operation of the royal harem (2:8, 12), permission for Gentiles to kill Jews and for Jews to kill Gentiles (3:12–15; 4:3, 8), and for hanging the corpses of the ten sons of Haman (9:14). The only exception occurs where Haman claims, falsely in the view of the author, that the Jewish *dātîm* are incompatible with those of the king (3:8). In Daniel, likewise, *dāt* designates measures of a decidedly ad hoc nature, including a decree commanding the extermination of all the sages in the country (Dan 2:9, 13, 15). A more substantive instance is Darius' confirmation of the decree of Cyrus after it had turned up in the archives in Ecbatana, the Median capital (Ezra 6:1–12), to which we shall return. The emphasis on the immutability and irrevocability of such measures ("the laws of the Medes and the Persians which cannot be annulled", Esth 1:19; Dan 6:9) reflects, not without a subversively sardonic note, a sense of the overwhelmingly arbitrary power exercized by Persian rulers.

2 The Relation between the King's Law and Provincial Legal Systems

In the absence of a legal system imposed on the empire as a whole, a degree of legal autonomy in the many satrapies and province was inevitable and accepted, so long as local systems remained subordinate to imperial *raison d'état* and the will of the sovereign. The variety of forms of political organization in the empire included satellite kingdoms with their own dynasties (Cilicia, Caria, Sidon), city-states , some with their own dependencies (e. g. Ashkelon under the control of Tyre), hyparchies (Bactria), tribal units (Kedarite Arabs), and temple communities, of which there were many in Mesopotamia, Asia Minor and Egypt. In all probability, Judah belonged to this category. Such variety ruled out the feasibility of one centralized legal system for all. In all matters of judicial control, the first concern of the central administration was the preservation of the *pax Persica* and avoidance of insurrection. And since trouble could be expected to arise, and often did arise, from satrapal courts no less than from popular movements, the authorization and enforcement of local law and custom could serve as a counterbalance to the ambitions of provincial governors.¹¹ The other major concern was fiscal, in the first place prompt payment of taxes and tribute. In all cases of intervention on the part of the central administration, we may expect to find a fiscal issue playing a role. Apart from these basic concerns, the Persian state was relatively non-interventionist in contrast to the Hellenistic kingdoms, perhaps due in part to its tribal past. One indication of this attitude is linguistic: the language of the conquerors – Old Persian – was practically restricted to the ethnic ruling class. There are no private (non-royal) inscriptions in Old Persian, and a Semitic language, Aramaic, became the diplomatic and to some extent the cultural *lingua franca*. Something similar can be said for cultural influence: in most parts of the empire the archaeological record to date provides relatively little evidence for specifically Persian culture.¹²

The phenomenon of imperial authorization of law documented by Peter Frei is one aspect of the tensive relationship between centralism and local autonomy, between coercive power projected from the centre and provincial self-regulation.¹³ Understood as authorization for a local initiative solicited from the central administration, it was only one channel by which the latter projected its power and maintained its control, and not the most important one. Of the case histories from western Asia Minor presented by Frei perhaps only one, the Xanthos trilingual inscription, fits the pattern. These case histories deal with special situations where some essential interest of the central government, was seen to be involved. Most of them are concerned with cultic initiatives, one or two deal with territorial disputes between cities, others record grants of hospitality and citizenship (*proxenia*), or freedom from taxation or other civic burdens (*ateleia*) in favour of certain individuals. One of the more interesting of these cases is the inscription discovered in Sardis in 1972 recording the erection of a statue to a local Zeus. To this was attached a prohibition addressed to the cult personnel associated with the cult of this Zeus against taking part in the mysteries of Sabazios and other local deities. Since both the initiative and the prohibition originated with Droaphernes, hyparch of Lydia, therefore with a high-ranking Persian, it cannot count as a case of imperial authorization in the terms defined by Frei. But togeth-

---

11 In addition to appointees of the central government in residence in provincial courts, somewhat like Soviet commissars, envoys were sent on investigative missions, e. g., Udjahorresnet to Egypt, Histiaeus to Ionia (*Her.* 5:106–8), and Nehemiah to Judah (Neh 2:5–8).
12 Pierre Briant, *Histoire de l'Empire Perse*, 7–8. For Judah as a Persian province see Ephraim Stern, "The Archaeology of Persian Palestine," in *CHJ* 1, 88–114.
13 Peter Frei, "Persian Imperial Authorization: A Summary," in *Persia and Torah: The Theory of Imperial Authorization of the Pentateuch*, ed. James Watts (Atlanta: Society of Bblical Literature, 2001), 5–40.

er with the Gadatas inscription it illustrates the Persian tendency to regulate, one might almost say micromanage, local cult practice.[14] But none of the case histories from Asia Minor bears on the issue of local legal systems authorized by the central administration, much less do they provide evidence that all legal codes had to have explicit official approval.

While there is no question of reviewing Frei's case histories one by one, we might take a brief glance at the parade example: the trilingual Xanthus inscription which records the written approval by the satrap Pixodarus of a cultic initiative by the citizens of Xanthus.[15] Like the final redaction of the Egyptian laws and the imperial decrees in Ezra-Nehemiah, the official texts was in Aramaic. Leaving aside the possibility that this initiative on behalf of Carian deities actually originated with Pixodarus, himself a Carian, and that therefore the one petitioning was also the one authorizing, we would assume that what made authorization necessary were the conditions stipulated in the decree. These included tax-exempt status for the priest of the sanctuary and the withdrawal from the local property tax base of city real estate vowed to the sanctuary. If authorization was petitioned by the Xanthians and their *perioikoi* (dependents), it would have been because they were aware that essential imperial interests were involved, in this case, as in most, of a financial nature. It was therefore a matter of simple prudence to forestall future problems by getting official approval in writing. It seems exaggerated to claim, as Frei does, that the satrap's written approval of the decree was taken up into the law of the empire.[16]

The importance of obtaining official clearance for matters in which the central authority had a fiscal interest is confirmed by inscriptions from the same region in which imperial taxes (*basilika telē*) are explicitly excluded from the grant-

---

14 The evidence for Persian practice vis-à-vis local cult practices has long been available, and much of it was made available by Roland de Vaux, "The Decrees of Cyrus and Darius on the Rebuilding of the Temple," in *The Bible and the Ancient Near East* (Garden City, New York: Doubleday, 1971), 63–96. On the Sardis inscription see Louis Robert, "Une Nouvelle Inscription Grecque de Sardes: Réglement de l'Autorité Perse Relativ à un Culte de Zeus," *CRAI* (1976): 303–31; Marie-Louise Chaumont, "Un Nouveau Gouverneur de Sardes à l'Époque Achéménide d'après une Inscription Récemment Découverte," *Syria* 67 (1990): 579–608; Pierre Briant, *L'Histoire de l'Empire Perse*, 696–97. In the letter of Darius I to Gadatas, a Persian official in Ionia, the latter is threatened with punishment for levying a tax on the sacred gardeners of Apollo in Magnesia. In the letter Darius refers to his "policy about deities" (*tēn huper theōn mou diathesin*). See Russell Meiggs and David Lewis, *A Selection of Greek Historical Inscriptions to the End of the Fifth Century BCE* (Oxford: Clarendon, 1969), 20–22.
15 Peter Frei and Klaus Koch, *Reichsidee*, 12–16, 32–34, 39–47.
16 Peter Frei and Klaus, *Reichsidee*, 14–15.

ing of an *ataleia* by provincial cities.¹⁷ The steady flow of revenue into the imperial treasury could also be affected negatively by border disputes, which therefore called for intervention by the local satrap.¹⁸ Other examples adduced by Frei from western Asia are either too obscure or too incomplete to be of use.

The only case history apart from that of Judah and the Jews of potential relevance to the issue under discussion is the notice about the codification of Egyptian laws by command of Darius I about the year 518 BC. The text is written on the verso of the Demotic Chronicle (papyrus 215 of the Bibliotèque Nationale in Paris) and dates to the Ptolomaic period. It records how Darius commanded the satrap of Mudriya (Egypt) to appoint a commission of priests, sages (scribes) and warriors in order to codify Egyptian laws in force up to the forty-fourth year of Pharaoh Amasis, that is to 526 BC, shortly after the Persian conquest of Egypt by Cambyses. This stipulation falls into the category of imperial propaganda since its intent was to showcase Darius' respect for native Egyptian traditions. It would also have had the effect of repealing ordinances issued by Cambyses curtailing the revenues of Egyptian temples,¹⁹ and therefore have served as a *captatio benevolentiae* with the powerful Egyptian priesthood. The commission worked at it for sixteen years , and the result of their labours was written up in demotic Egyptian and "Assyrian", namely, Aramaic.²⁰ The authenticity of the Chronicle is widely accepted and is supported by the reputation of Darius among the Greeks as the sixth great lawgiver of the Egyptians (Diodorus Siculus, *Hist.* 1.95. 4–5).

A word of caution is, however, in order with regard to the claim that at least here we have a clear case of the compilation of traditional laws by imperial edict, resulting in a code comparable to the major law collections in the Hebrew Bible.

---

17 See the inscriptions from Labrauna and Lagina in Caria, Peter Frei and Klaus Koch, *Reichsidee*, 40–41, 99–100. Neither is a case of imperial authorization.
18 For example, the case history from Tralles in the Meander Valley; Peter Frei and Klaus Koch, *Reichsidee*, 27 n.58, 100, 96–97. For the text see Franciszek Sokolowski, *Lois Sacrées de l'Asie Mineure* (Paris: École française d'Athènes, 1955), 173–74. For another incident see Herodotus, *Hist.* 6:41–42.
19 This is stated explicitly in the Demotic Chronicle and is quite independent of the stories about Cambyses' sacrilegious disregard for Egyptian religion recorded in the Greek historians, beginning with Herodotus (*Hist.* 3:27–38).
20 In addition to Peter Frei and Klaus Koch, *Reichsidee*, 16–18, 47, see Wilhelm Spiegelberg, *Die sogenannte demotische Chronik des pap. 215 der Bibliotèque Nationale zu Paris* (Leipzig: Hinrichs, 1914), especially pp. 30–32; Nathaniel Reich, "The Codification of the Egyptian Laws by Darius and the Origin of the 'Demotic Chronicle'," *Mizraim* 1 (1933): 178–85; George Posener, *La Première Domination Perse en Egypte* (Cairo: IFAO, 1936), 175–76; Pierre Briant, *Histoire de l'Empire Perse*, 488–500.

It is possible that the Egyptian compilation was more a case of patents, endowments, privileges and immunities rather than a law code as generally understood.[21] In view of the potential for internecine conflict arising out of conflicting claims, it would have been in the interests of the central government to see these issues settled. The length of time it took to settle them testifies to the tensions within Egyptian society and, as suggested earlier, one of the aims of Darius would have been to win over the priests by restoring the revenues of the temples which Cambyses had drastically reduced. If the imperial edict was in fact a special case, dictated by the potential for unrest following on the measures put in place by Cambyses and the first of several Egyptian revolts that followed, it suggests caution in taking it as illustrative of government policy.

It is hardly coincidental that the initiative of Darius took place in the same year in which he sent the Egyptian collaborator Udjahorresnet back to Egypt from Susa on a mission. The purpose of the mission was to supervise the work of restoration after the disturbances following on the death of Cambyses. On this matter the edict is understandably vague, but there were disturbances also in the first two years of the reign of Darius, for the Bisitun (Behistun) inscription lists Egypt among the provinces in revolt at that time (522–519). The satrap Aryandes was confirmed in office and remained in office until 510 when he was executed, according to Herodotus (*Hist.* 4:166), for minting his own coinage. The mission of Udjahorresnet was therefore part of the pacification programme of Darius' early years. It also prepared for the visit to Egypt of Darius which took place in 518 BC.[22] The goal of the mission was the restoration of the status quo ante, the situation preceding the Persian conquest and the "very great turmoil" that accompanied it, according to the inscription. The achievements of the mission are also of interest in view of what was happening in Judah according to Ezra-Nehemiah. Udjahorresnet claims that already during the reign of Cambyses foreigners had been expelled from the state sanctuary at Sais, ritual impurities had been eliminated, legitimate cult personnel installed, traditional religious observances reinstated, all this with the support of the Persian exchequer (lines 19–31). But the main purpose seems to have been the restoration of

---

21 A point made by John Manuel Cook, *The Persian Empire* (London: Dent, 1983), 71. Cook provides a parallel to the Egyptian codification from 1908–1909, after the Russian occupation of Turkestan, when the governor had a collection of Islamic laws compiled from existing French codifications together with case law from British India. They were written in Russian and published in the local language. See p. 241 n.13.

22 Alan Lloyd, "The Inscription of Udjahorresnet: A Collaborator's Testament," *JEA* 68 (1982): 166–80; Joseph Blenkinsopp, "The Mission of Udjahorresnet and Those of Ezra and Nehemiah," *JBL* 106 (1987): 409–21.

the "houses of life", centres of learning attached to temples, and one of the principal activities of these institutions would have been the codification and interpretation of the laws.²³

In summary: the notice provided by the Demotic Chronicle does not oblige us to conclude that something of the sort also happened in the neighbouring province of Yehud (Judah), or indeed anywhere else in the Persian empire. On the other hand, Darius' action was part of a pacification programme following on the critical years 522–519, a crisis by no means confined to Egypt. The relevant biblical sources also attest that Judaeans were affected by the events of those years, that there were expectations of the collapse of the Persian empire established by Cyrus, and aspirations for national independence focussed on the person of Zerubbabel of the Davidic line.²⁴ Judah was important because of its proximity to Egypt where revolts were endemic throughout the two centuries of Persian rule. It is therefore at least plausible to suggest that the situation in Judah called for an intervention of some kind by the imperial administration at that time, and that it may have taken a form analogous to what the Demotic Chronicle and the Udjahorresnet inscription tell us happened in Egypt.

3 The Impact of Persian Imperial Policy on Life in Judah

The only explicitly attested case of imperial Persian interest in Jewish affairs, apart from the biblical texts, is the so-called Passover Papyrus from the Jewish colony in Elephantine written in 419 BC during the reign of Darius II.²⁵ It is a message sent by a certain Hananiah, with a good Yahwistic name, to his co-religionists in the settlement informing them that Darius had sent orders to the satrap Arsames about the due celebration of the feasts of Passover and Unleavened Bread. The papyrus is lacunous, but this much is clear. The bearer of the message is certainly a Jew. He may have been a secretary of the satrap who was tipping off his fellow-Jews about another regulation of concern to them which had arrived

---

23 See Alan Gardiner, "The House of Life," *JEA* 24 (1938): 157–79.
24 Hag 2:20–23; Zech 6:9–15. Zerubbabel may have been sent to Judah with the idea of the eventual establishment of a client kingdom similar to others in the Persian empire. We do not know what happened to Zerubbabel, but one possibility is that there were disturbances in Judah like those in Egypt which led to the recall and execution of Zerubbabel and the end to any hope of national independence.
25 AP 21 in Abraham Cowley, *Aramaic Papyri from the Fifth Century BC* (Osnabrück: Otto Zeller, 1967 [1923]), 60–65; more recently in TAD 1, 54.

on the satrap's desk.²⁶ As for the content of the message: while it is tolerably clear that it refers to the celebration of Passover, even though the festival is not named in it, Hananiah was not quoting the decree verbatim and certainly not in extenso. The decree may therefore have dealt with religious observances in general, or it may have insisted that the garrison align its religious observances with Jerusalemite praxis. In any case, it was not stipulating a new observance since we know that Passover was already being celebrated in that community, and the emphasis in the message on the precise timing of the festival may have been the one point on which they needed a reminder.

Relations with the civic and religious authorities in Judah are further illustrated by a letter written in 408 BC by Jedaniah, a leader of the garrison and probably a priest, to Bagavahya (Bagoas) governor of Judah requesting permission to rebuild the temple of Ya'u (Yahweh) destroyed in a pogrom three years earlier.²⁷ Permission was received in a brief memorandum (*zikkārôn*) dispatched jointly by Bagavahya in Jerusalem and Daliyah son of Sanballat of Samaria couched in language reminiscent of the edict of Darius in Ezra 7.²⁸ The Elephantine correspondence suggests, incidentally, that we should not dismiss the documents cited in Ezra-Nehemiah out of hand as potential source material.

Some scholars have found a similar instance of imperial supervision of local cults in the allusion to a royal disposition (*misvat hammelek*) concerning the temple musicians (Neh 11:22–23). Use of the term *'ămānâ* suggests that the decree dealt with their day-to-day obligations as temple personnel rather than their economic support, but in any case the reference is more probably to a disposition of king David who set up the guilds of temple singers and instrumentalists in the first place (1 Chronicles 25).²⁹ A note added to Neh 11:22–23 refers to a certain Pethahiah of the Zerah phratry who served as the royal counsellor "at the king's hand" (*lĕyad hammelek*) in matters concerning the people (Neh 11:24). The absence of this phratry from the lists in Ezra-Nehemiah would be consistent with the supposition that this individual held a position at the court in Susa with the task of advising the central administration on Jewish affairs in the empire. But here, too, we are in the realm of speculation.

---

26 A suggestion of Morton Smith, "Jewish Religious Life in the Persian Period," in *CHJ* 1, 230–33.
27 AP 30, with the duplicate copy AP 31 (Abraham Cowley, *Aramaic Papyri*, 108–22; *TAD* 1, 68–75). The destruction of the temple is referred to at greater length in a petition addressed to the satrap Arsames ca. 410 BC (AP 27; Abraham Cowley, *Aramaic Papyri*, 97–103).
28 AP 32 (Abraham Cowley, *Aramaic Papyri*, 122–24).
29 Cf. Neh 12:24, a *misvat dāvid* concerning Levites.

4 The decree of Artaxerxes and the mission of Ezra

This brings us to the decree of Artaxerxes mandating Ezra's mission (Ezra 7:11–26).[30] Most scholars now assume that it has been extensively edited, if not actually composed, by a Jewish scribe, perhaps a member of what we might call "the school of the Chronicler." There is the reference to "Judah and Jerusalem", the standard formulation in Chronicles, allusion to offerings freely made and people freely offering themselves for God's service (verb *hitnaddēb*) of frequent occurrence in Chronicles, the listing of the sacrificial animals, and "the wisdom of your God that is in your hand" (7:25) parallel with "the law of your God that is in your hand" (7:24), reflecting a familiar Deuteronomic topos (e. g. Deut 4:6). Our concern for the moment, however, is with Ezra's mission to make enquiry about law observance, appoint judges and magistrates to administer the law, and to instruct those unfamiliar with it. The importance of this part of his mission is indicated by its position at the beginning and end of the rescript:

> You are sent by the king and his seven counsellors to enquire about Judah and Jerusalem with respect to the law of your God with which you are entrusted. (7:14)

> You, Ezra, in keeping with the wisdom of your God which is yours, are to appoint magistrates and judges who will judge all the people in the Transeuphratene province, that is, all who are familiar with the laws of your God; and those who are not familiar with them you must instruct. Whoever will not obey the law of your God and the law of the king, let judgement be swiftly executed upon him, whether sentence of death, corporal punishment, confiscation of property, or imprisonment (7:25–26)

Some provisional observations. First: the phrase "the law of your God with which you are entrusted" or, more literally, "the law of your God which is in your hand" does not refer to a law Ezra brought with him, a new law, since it is assumed to be familiar to Jews in the Transeuphratene province. Second: It is not a case of imperial authorization as defined by Frei since it is not a response to a request from a Jewish individual or community. More than a century ago, however, Eduard Meyer suggested that the decree was written by a Jewish official with the precise purpose of submitting it for approval to the imperial authorities.[31] To take his suggestion further, the rescript may even have been the successful

---

[30] Either the first or the second of that name, therefore the mission is to be dated either 458 or 398 BC. For arguments in favour of the former see Joseph Blenkinsopp, *Ezra-Nehemia: A Commentary* (Philadelphia: Westminster, 1988), 139–44.

[31] Eduard Meyer, *Die Entstehung des Judentums: Eine historische Untersuchung* (Tübingen: Niemeyer, 1896; reprint: Hildesheim: Georg Olms, 1965), 60–68; see also Kurt Galling, *Studien zur Geschichte Israels in Persischen Zeitalter* (Tübingen: Mohr Siebeck, 1964), 165–66.

outcome of the cunning manipulation of the authorities in distant Susa in the interests of the rigorous party under Ezra's leadership. These possibilities remain open, but it is also possible that the decree was the expression of a direct imperial initiative occasioned by the critical situation in the western provinces of the empire: the recent revolt of Inaros in Egypt (460–454) which resulted in the defeat and death of the satrap Achaemenes, and a formidable Athenian fleet of some two hundred vessels in support of the revolt off the Palestinian coast. Third: Unlike the situation in Egypt under Darius I as described in the Demotic Chronicle, there is no mention here of the codification of laws. Laws already in existence, deemed to be familiar to many, are to be taught, an activity which necessarily would include interpretation. At the public reading of the law described in Nehemiah 8, for example, Levites read from the book, the law of God, with interpretation (Neh 8:8).

A further point of unclarity in the rescript is the extent of Ezra's jurisdiction during the mission, whether limited to Judah, *yĕhûd mĕdîntā'*, or extending to all Jews in the Transeuphratene province. Certainty is unattainable, but we may cite in support of the broader interpretation of Ezra's jurisdiction the request for permission to rebuild their temple addressed to Jerusalem by the Jews in Elephantine and the positive respond to the request (AP 30 and 32). The problem then arises whether the authorities in Susa would hand over to a member of the Jewish diasporic community powers usually reserved to the satrap. This is quite apart from the issue of authenticity and the possibility that a Jewish scribe belonging to the Ezra party, the *běnê haggôlâ*, has had a hand in the composition of the rescript.

In Frei's discussion of Ezra's law as a case history of imperial authorization a great deal hangs on the interpretation of the phrase "the law of your God and the law of the king" (7:26).[32] The issue to be decided is whether the reference is to two distinct laws, namely, the Jewish law sanctioned by the God of Israel and Persian law expressed in the will of the sovereign; or to Jewish law alone, distinguishing between sacral cultic law and civic law; or to Jewish law but now sanctioned by and subsumed under the supreme authority of the ruler, and therefore the official law for Jews in the satrapy. Here, too, we must introduce the complicating factor of authenticity. A putative Jewish redactor, perhaps one belonging to the school of the author of Chronicles, may have understood the expression very differently from the equally putative official who drafted it in the chancellery office where – on the hypothesis of its substantial authenticity – it originated. In the account of Jehoshaphat's reign (2 Chr 19:8–11) the Chronicler records

---

32 Peter Frei and Klaus Koch, *Reichsidee*, 51–61.

the establishment of a judicial system in which the chief priest was responsible for "the matter of Yahweh" (*děbar YHWH*) and a leading lay person was in charge of "the matter of the king" (*děbar hammelek*), closely parallel to "the law of your God and the law of the king" in Ezra 7:26. Another close parallel in the same passage is the remark that law observance has the purpose of deflecting the divine anger (*qesep*), an idea which occurs in the decree (Ezra 7:23) and in Chronicles (2 Chr 19:10). Elsewhere the same author distinguishes between different spheres of law but without having to posit two distinct jurisdiction (1 Chr 26:32).[33] But making all due allowance for such editorial elaboration, the fact that the Jewish law is the only one specified in the decree (7:14, 21, 25), and that the penalties for infraction of the law, listed in descending order of severity, are characteristic of Persian rather than Jewish penal practice, suggests the conclusion that the Jewish law Ezra was authorized to enforce is now invested with the absolute authority of the ruler, and therefore is, in effect, royal Persian law as far as Jews in the satrapy are concerned.

5 Ezra's law and the laws in the Pentateuch

The question may now be asked: What relation, if any, exists between Ezra's law and the Pentateuch, or at least the legal content of the Pentateuch? The author of Ezra 7 clearly wishes us to understand that "the law of your God" (Ezra 7:14, 26), also in the plural (7:25), , or "the law of the God of heaven" (7:12, 21) is identical with "the law of Moses" (7:6) with which, according to the preface to the decree, Ezra is said to be concerned as priest and scribe (7:10).[34] In Jewish tradition

---

[33] Similar distinctions are made in the Demotic Chronicle between the law of the Pharaoh, temple law, and the law of the people, that is, civic law. See Wilhelm Spiegelberg, *Die sogennante demotische Chronik*, 3–32.

[34] The responsibility of the priest for torah, religious instruction, is attested in Deuteronomy and is stated in lapidary fashion in Jer 18:18 and its parallel in Ezek 7:26 ("torah must not perish from the priest"). Scribes associated with priests were responsible for the drafting of laws and probably also for their interpretation, to judge by Jeremiah's denunciation of "the false pen of the scribes who have made it into a lie" (Jer 8:8). Hans Heinrich Schaeder, *Esra der Schreiber: Beiträge zur Historischen Theologie*, Vol. 5 (Tübingen: Mohr Siebeck, 1930), 39–59, who accepted the Artaxerxes rescript as essentially authentic, understood the reference to Ezra as *sōpēr* (Ezra 7:12, 21) by analogy with Akkadian *šāpirum*, in the sense of a high official at the Persian court, a kind of High Commissioner for Jewish affairs. Rolf Rendtorff, "Esra und das Gesetz," *ZAW* 96 (1984): 165–84, is chiefly concerned to deny that the public reading of the law in Nehemiah 8 deals with the law committed to Ezra in the rescript, makes too categoric a distinction between secular and religious law. It is also difficult to see how "the law of your God" in Ezra 7:14,26

Ezra's mission is understood in the sense that Ezra restored the law of Moses, the written copy of which had either been burned in the sack of Jerusalem, as in 2 Esd.14:21–48, or had fallen into desuetude and neglect, as stated in *b. Sukkah* 20a. If Moses had not preceded him, we are told, Ezra would have been worthy to bring Torah into the world (*b.Sanh. 21b*). Wellhausen stood this tradition on its head in arguing that the Pentateuch, or rather the Hexateuch, was produced in Babylon, brought to Judah by Ezra in 458 BC, and promulgated on the first day of the seventh month in 444 BC,[35] and this view of the matter, or something like it, became, for a time, the received wisdom.

A critical approach cannot, however, simply assume that the Pentateuch and its legal content were in place whole and entire at the time of Ezra's putative mission, or at the time when the account of the mission was produced. We can make some progress by noting those occasions in Ezra-Nehemiah where actions are taken according to written law. Some of these involve laws in Deuteronomy: the setting up of an altar on entering (or re-entering) the land (Ezra 3:2 cf. Deut 27:6–7), prohibition of marriage with indigenous women (Ezra 9:11–12; Neh 10:31; 13:25, cf. Deut 7:3), exclusion from the community of certain ethnic categories (Neh 13:1–2, cf. Deut 23:3–4). Others are more closely related to the Priestly legislation: the daily offering (Ezra 3:3, 5, cf. Exod 29:38–42), Passover (Ezra 6:19–22, cf. Exod 12:1–6, 19, 45; Lev 23:5–6; Num 9:3–5), duties of priests and Levites (Ezra 6:18, cf. Exod 29; Lev 8). Even stipulations widely understood to bvelong to a late stage of redaction have their counterpart in Ezra-Nehemiah and Chronicles, among them the tithe of tithes (Neh 10:38–40, cf. Num 18:25–32) and the postponed Passover (2 Chr 30:2, 15; 35:12, cf. Num 9:6–14). So it seems that the author of Ezra 7 was familiar with both Deuteronomic and Priestly legislation, including the Holiness Code.[36]

The situation becomes more complex when injunctions and decisions are justified on the basis of legal authority not drawing on Pentateuchal law. The coercive divorce of wives from outside the golah group is to be carried out "according to the law" (Ezra 10:3), but no such law can be found in the Pentateuch. The

---

could exclude religious law, especially in view of the well-documented imperial concern for religious matters. Compare Esth 3:8 and Dan 6:6 where the term *dāt* is clearly identical with *tôrâ*.
35 Julius Wellhausen, *Prolegomena to the History of Israel*, Transl. William Robertson Smith (New York: Meridian Books, 1957), 384–85, 405–7.
36 On this subject it is a question of *tot capita quot sententiae*. Ulrich Kellermann, "Erwägungen zum Esragesetz," *ZAW* 80 (1968): 373–85, may be taken to represent the view that Ezra's law draws primarily on Deuteronom(ist)ic laws, while Klaus Koch, "Ezra and the Origins of Judaism," *JSS* 19 (1974): 173–97, argued for dependence primarily on the Priestly law (P) and the Holiness Code (H).

great fast and penitential ritual takes place on the twenty-fourth day of the seventh month (Tishri) in Neh 9:1, but this is not in accord with the date for Yom Kippur in Lev 16:29, 23:27–32 and elsewhere. Perhaps the date was not yet fixed, as seems to have been the case with Passover in the Elephantine settlement. Variations in the articles of Nehemiah's covenant, perhaps from a time later in the Second Temple period, may be explained as the product of *midrash halakha*. For example: selling on Sabbath is forbidden in Amos 8:5, but both buying and selling are forbidden in Neh 10:32; 13:15–22, a step in the direction of the thirty-nine forbidden activities in *m. Sabb.* 7:2. The wood offering (Neh 10:35, cf. 13:31) is the subject of an explicit prescription only in the Mishnah.[37] Other discrepancies could be due to the need to adjust laws and regulations to changing circumstances. A small-scale example would be the temple tax which is set at one third of a shekel in Neh 10:33–34 and at half a shekel in the Pentateuch (Exod 30:11–16; 38:25–26) which remained in force down to the Roman period (Josephus, *War* 7:216–18; *Ant.* 18:312). Given the tendency of taxation to increase inexorably, this could suggest that the Pentateuchal ordinance is later than Ezra-Nehemiah. On the other hand, the minimum age for Levites is thirty in Num 4:3, 23, 30, twenty-five in Num 8:24, and twenty in Ezra 3:8 and 1 Chr 23:24–27. This might suggest that the age was progressively lowered to accommodate a broader range of Levitical activities. In both cases, however, other explanations are possible; this entire issue of dates is too complex to allow for one definitive conclusion. In summary, then, we may accept, as a plausible working hypothesis, that Ezra's law corresponds to the legal content of the Pentateuch at a mature but not final stage of development, with the further proviso that, given what we know of the aims of Ezra and his party, it represents a particular sectarian or quasi-sectarian interpretation of the laws, for example with regard to marriage and divorce and the observance of Sabbath.[38]

6 The Theory of Imperial Authorization

In authorizing the mission of Ezra, Artaxerxes and his officials would have had in mind something similar to the codification, promulgation and enforcement of

---

[37] See David Clines, "Nehemiah 10 as an example of early Jewish biblical exegesis," *JSOT* 21 (1981): 111–17; Michael Fishbane, *Biblical Interpretation in Ancient Israel* (Oxford: Clarendon, 1985), 129–34, 165–66, 213–16.
[38] Morton Smith, *Palestinian Parties and Politics that Shaped the Old Testament* (New York: Columbia University Press, 1971), 173–74, described Nehemiah's covenant as the first example of Jewish sectarianism.

Egyptian laws under Darius I. They would have looked for a compilation of laws which would represent a compromise between different classes of people and different factions in Judaean society, with a view to preserving the *pax Persica* west of the Euphrates. That something like this actually happened when the Pentateuch finally emerged as a finished product is now being increasingly accepted. While there are few detailed, concrete matters in the Pentateuch pointing unmistakeably to the Persian period,[39] several scholars adopted the "imperial authorization" explanation of the final compilation of the Pentateuch. The basis for the hypothesis is (1) the assumption that the Pentateuch in its final form is a product of the Persian period, and (2) the juxtaposition in the Pentateuch of mutually incompatible stipulations of law and mutually irreconcilable perspectives on law, for example between Deuteronom(ist)ic and Priestly legal theories. This was taken to represent the same kind of compromise as, according to the Demotic Chronicle, was imposed on Egypt by Darius I.

Credit for being the first to apply the theory of *Reichsautorisation* to Jewish law is usually assigned to Erhard Blum. He argued that the comprehensive Deuteronomistic work (his KD) and the Priestly work (his KP), with their contrasting prescriptions on such matters as priesthood, festivals, tithes and profane animal slaughter, were combined under pressure from the imperial authorities no later than Darius I.[40] Frank Crüsemann also saw pentateuchal law as a compromise between conflicting interests, but went further in attempting to probe the divergent social forces at work in the province of Judah which account for this situation. He finds indications in the legislation of a coalition between the temple priesthood and independent land owners.[41] Several other scholars have taken a similar position. Ernst Axel Knauf accepts the hypothesis in its broad lines, reading the Pentateuch as a monument to Persian policy with respect to minor-

---

39 One detail: linen trousers (*miknĕsê-bād*, Exod 28:42; 39:28) prescribed for priests, since this article of clothing is characteristically Persian and previously unattested.
40 Erhard Blum, *Studien zur Komposition des Pentateuch* (Berlin: Walter de Gruyter, 1990), 333–60. Erhard Blum and Frank Crüsemann seem to have reached the same conclusion at more or less the same time; see the latter's opinion in "Le Pentateuque, une Tora: Prolégoménes à l'Interprétation de sa Forme Finale," in *Le Pentateuque en Question*, ed. Albert de Pury (Geneva: Labor et Fides, 1989), 345–54.
41 See, in addition to the previous note, Frank Crüsemann, "Israel in der Perserzeit: Eine Skizze in Auseinandersetzung mit Max Weber," in *Max Webers Sicht des antiken Christentums: Interpretation und Kritik*, ed. Wolfgang Schluchter (Frankfurt am Main: Suhrkamp, 1985), 205–32; *The Torah:Theology and Social History of Old Testament Law*, Transl. Allan Mahnke (Minneapolis: Fortress, 1996 [German original, Munich: Kaiser, 1992], 339–45.

ities, especially in religious matters.[42] David Carr is aware of some of the problems attending the hypothesis but accepts it as set out by Blum.[43] My own view was, and with some modifications still is, similar in the main lines: quite apart from the authenticity issue, it accepts that political pressure on the province of Yehud to consolidate the laws would have been most likely to occur as part of the reorganization and restoration carried out in successive stages by Darius I and Artaxerxes I, in both instances following on a period of political and military crisis.[44] In this connection, mention should be made of Morton Smith's illuminating analysis of the social and religious tensions, alliances, and trade-offs within Jewish communities during the period in question. He does not refer to imperial authorization, but the role of the dominant political power in the emergence of the Pentateuch as a compromise document between hard liners and assimilationists is acknowledged.[45]

During the 1990s when the Imperial Authorisation hypothesis was a major focus of discussion it seemed as if it might become the received wisdom and achieve canonical status. It soon became apparent, however, that there were too many problems. First: since there is no evidence that Jewish civil or religious authorities presented the Pentateuchal laws for official approbation, this is not a case of imperial authorization as defined by Frei. The same is true of the Egyptian laws as described in the Demotic Chronicle. Second: We must be clear whether we are speaking of the Pentateuch as a complex whole or of the legal content of the Pentateuch. No one supposes that some official at the imperial court in Susa was handed a copy of the five-book Pentateuch seeking for an official *imprimatur*.

But the legal compilations in the Pentateuch, as well as individual stipulations of law are inseparable from their narrative context, not to mention narrative elements which are part of the legal statements, for example, the motivation clauses. Are we to suppose that the imperial authorities took the time and trouble to read the narrative in which the laws were embedded to check for seditious or otherwise unacceptable content? This seems inherently improbable since there is no evidence that the Persian authorities monitored the religious literatures of the numerous peoples – with their numerous languages – under their

---

[42] Ernst Axel Knauf, *Die Umwelt des Alten Testaments* (Stuttgart: Katholisches Bibelwerk, 1994), 171–75.
[43] David Carr, *Reading the Fractures of Genesis* (Louisville: Westminster/John Knox Press, 1996), 327–30.
[44] Joseph Blenkinsopp, *The Pentateuch: An Introduction to the First Five Books of the Bible* (New York: Doubleday, 1992), 239–43.
[45] Morton Smith, *Parties and Politics*, 119–25, 170–74.

control.⁴⁶ Third: We must ask whether there are not alternative and perhaps better ways of explaining the emergence of the Pentateuch, together with its laws, as a compromise document. The juxtaposition of divergent and mutually incompatible views in other parts of the Hebrew Bible, the book of Isaiah for example, obliges us in the first place to address the issue of editorial procedures in these ancient compositions and to acknowledge the common practice of neutralizing by addition rather than by deletion. Imperial authorization is an interesting hypothesis and the discussion about it has raised a number of interesting issues, but at least for the time being the verdict is not proven.

---

46 *Pace* Jean-Louis Ska, "Un nouveau Wellhausen?," *Bib* 72 (1991): 261–62, who points to texts in the Pentateuch dealing with the promise or conquest of the land which he believed the Persians would have found unacceptable. Maybe, if they had read them. For the same reason we must doubt the idea that the creation of a Pentateuch rather than a Hexateuch, thus excluding the conquest of neighbouring peoples, was due to the need not to offend Persian susceptibilities. There are plenty of references to conquest in the Pentateuch.

VIII. Footnotes to the rescript of Artaxerxes in Ezra 7:11–26

Source: *The Historian and the Bible: Essays in Honour of Lester Grabbe*, ed. by Philip Davies and Diana Edelman, 150–58. New York & London: T. T. Clark, 2010.

1 The problem with official documents cited in the book of Ezra

A major problem for using the book of Ezra as a document for the early and critical stage in the emergence of Judaism under the Persian empire is the decision on the historical value of the seven official texts – imperial decrees and correspondence – cited in it. Clearly, these texts are, potentially, of first-rate importance for understanding this crucial period; much is therefore at stake in determining their authenticity. The texts in question are the following:

1. A decree of Cyrus, inspired by Yahweh God of heaven to build his temple in Jerusalem, permitting expatriate Jews to return to fulfil this task on his behalf, and recommending (hence commanding) people in regions where exiled Jews were settled to provide material support for the return (1:2–4).

2. A letter of Rehum and other officials in Samaria to Artaxerxes lodging a complaint about repatriated Jews rebuilding Jerusalem (4:9–16).

3. The reply of Artaxerxes with a cease and desist order on the rebuilding (4:17–22).

4. A letter of Tattenai, governor of the Transeuphratene province, to Darius questioning the authorization for the rebuilding of the temple in Jerusalem, then in progress (5:6–17).

5. The decree of Cyrus recovered from the archives at Ecbatana, the Medean capital, authorizing the rebuilding with architectural and other specifications (6:2–5).

6. The reply of Darius permitting the work to continue, expenses to be disbursed from the provincial exchequer, and prayers for the royal family in Susa to be incorporated eventually in the temple liturgy (6:6–12).

7. A letter of Artaxerxes to Ezra permitting, indeed mandating, his return to Judah with lay persons, priests and Levites bringing bullion provided from the imperial treasury together with the sacred vessels for the temple. Ezra is also to be a kind of Commissioner for Jewish Affairs in the province, the one responsible for the observance of the Jewish law (7:11–26). This letter contains an enclosure for the treasurers in the Transeuphratene province who are to provide ad-

ditional support for Ezra in goods and specie; priests and other temple personnel are also to be exempt from taxation (7:21–24).

These documents are in Aramaic with the exception of the first which is in Hebrew. On the probable assumption that the Cyrus of 1 and 5 is Cyrus II, founder of the Persian empire (559–530), the Artaxerxes of 2, 3 and 7 is Artaxerxes I (465–424), and the Darius of 4 and 6 is Darius I (522–486); the list is therefore out of chronological order, and the reason is that the order is dictated by the narrative logic of the first major section of the book in chapters 1–6 rather than by straightforward chronological considerations. The narrative in these chapters relates the return en masse of close to 50,000 expatriates and the beginning of the rebuilding of the temple (Ezra 1–3), opposition from local authorities which brings the work temporarily to a halt (4–5), the final solution of the problem with the opportune rediscovery of the decree of Cyrus permitting the rebuilding, following which the work is crowned with success in the sixth year of the reign of Darius I (516/515). The last of the citations is exceptional in length and detail since it serves to introduce the story of Ezra in the second major section of the book in chapters 7–10. The many correspondences between the letter of Artaxerxes and the unfolding of the Ezra story in chapters 8–10 have often been noted.[1] The suggestion has even been made that the story functions as a kind of midrash composed by the author of Chronicles on the letter.[2] On this last point something more will be said in due course.

From this point on I propose to limit the discussion on the authenticity of these cited texts to the seventh and last, the rescript addressed to Ezra by Artaxerxes, on which there is still no consensus. As an entry into this issue we might begin with the contributions of a scholar who has given it a lot of attention over a period of several years. In his essay "Reconstructing history from the book of Ezra" published in 1991 Lester L. Grabbe was beginning to question the consensus about the basic authenticity of the rescript permitting Ezra and his supporters to "go up" to Judah with rich gifts for the temple and mandating him to investigate the practice and observance of law in the Transeuphratene satrapy.[3] In the following year, in the first volume of his *Judaism from Cyrus to Herod*, he gave more attention to problems with the authenticity thesis, including orthography typical of the Graeco-Roman period, and concluded by stating the need for a

---

1 E.g. Martin Noth, *Gesammelte Studien zum Alten Testament* (2nd ed., Munich: Kaiser, 1960) = *The Laws in the Pentateuch and Other Essays*, Transl. Norman Porteous (Edinburgh & London: Oliver & Boyd, 1968), 74–85.
2 Ulrich Kellermann, "Erwägungen zum Problem der Esradatierung," ZAW 80 (1968): 55–87.
3 Lester Grabbe, "Reconstructing History from the Book of Ezra" in *Studies in the Persian Period*, ed. Philip Davies (Sheffield: JSOT Press, 1991), 98–106.

new and thorough review of the issue.⁴ Two years further on, it was time to focus on discrepancies between the terms of the edict and the account of Ezra's actual activities as recorded in the so-called Ezra Memoir in which the edict is embedded. In this piece Grabbe also pointed out the difficulty involved in coming up with comparative material, especially given the dubious authenticity of both the Gadatas edict and the letter of Xerxes to Pausanias cited by Thucydides (I 129).⁵ His most thorough investigation to date, to my knowledge, is a paper read at a conference in July 2003 in Heidelberg on "Judah and the Judaeans in the Achaemenid Period" and published three years later. This study surveyed all seven texts listed above, presented in the book of Ezra as verbatim copies of documents from and to the imperial Achaemenid court. The objections to the claim of authenticity, perhaps no longer the majority opinion among commentators, were marshalled: standard literary Aramaic orthography characteristic of the Hellenistic period, epistulary formulary in some respects uncharacteristic of the Achaemenid period, prevalence of Jewish theological and cultic references, and general implausibilities, especially the amount of precious metal, beyond dreams of avarice, bestowed on the Jerusalem temple by the imperial and satrapal courts.⁶ He concluded notwithstanding that among the seven putative documents surveyed only 4, the letter of Tattenai to Darius (Ezra 5:7–17) had a better claim than 7, the Artaxerxes rescript to at least a substratum of authenticity, but – surprisingly – he clearly did not think any of them contributed much to our knowledge of Judaism in the mid-fifth century BC.

Grabbe's growing but always circumscribed scepticism about the authenticity of the rescript has a long and sometimes colourful history behind it which complements his own trajectory. One of the earliest sceptics was Ernest Renan author of the famous – or infamous – *Vie de Jésus*. Renan suggested that the Ezra figure was a fictitious creation of priests who wanted to counter the preponderance and prestige of the layman Nehemiah, an opinion which may have been influenced by the author's experience as a seminarian at Saint Sulpice.⁷ Three

---

4 Lester Grabbe, *Judaism from Cyrus to Herod*, Vol. 1, *The Persian and Greek Periods* (Minneapolis: Fortress Press, 1992), 32–36.
5 Lester Grabbe, "What was Ezra's mission?" in *Second Temple Studies*, Vol. 2, *Temple and Community in the Persian Period*, ed. Tamara Cohn Eskenazi and Kent Harold Richards(Sheffield: JSOT, 1994), 286–99.
6 Lester Grabbe, "The 'Persian Documents' in the Book of Ezra: Are they authentic?" in *Judah and the Judeans in the Persian Period*, ed. Oded Lipschits and Manfred Oeming (Winona Lake/ Indiana: Eisenbrauns, 2006), 531–70. Comparative material for epistulary formulas is taken from Dirk Schwiderski, *Handbuch des nordwestsemitischen Briefformulars: Ein Beitrag zur Eichtheitsfrage der aramäischen Briefe des Esrabuches* (Berlin: Walter de Gruyter, 2000).
7 Ernest Renan, *Histoire du Peuple d'Israël* (Paris: Calman-Lévy, 1893), 96–106.

years later Eduard Meyer published his *Die Entstehung des Judentums*, the principal thesis of which was that the emergence of Judaism came about as a direct effect of Persian imperial intervention.[8] Fundamental to this thesis was the conviction of the essential authenticity of the documents cited in Ezra. In the following year Wellhausen published his review of *Die Entstehung* in the scholarly journal of the University of Göttingen.[9] The quite extraordinary venom and sarcasm of Wellhausen's reaction to Meyer's monograph was no doubt due in part to his suspicion that Meyer's thesis was directed against his – Wellhausen's – tendency to ignore data external to the analysis of the biblical texts. Wellhausen didn't think much of Meyer's scholarship. He is (he noted) in the habit of proclaiming ex cathedra things he has just learned himself; we didn't need him to tell us that without Cyrus and Artaxerxes the restoration and reformation of Judaism would not have happened since we can find it for ourselves in the biblical texts; and, warming to his task, Meyer would be well advised to leave the writing of history to others. Wellhausen also hinted darkly at plagiarism of his own work in Meyer's monograph.

In his reply, added as an appendix to later printings of *Die Entstehung*, Meyer began by foreswearing polemics but continued in the same heated vein as his adversary. He reiterated the case for authenticity, including appeal to the Gadatas inscription from Lydia, now widely considered to be a Hellenistic forgery,[10] and the presence of Persian loan words in the decrees which he took to indicate Old Persian as the original language. This last point was easily, and typically, disposed of by Wellhausen who replied that, in that case, the book of Daniel must also have been written in Old Persian. It will not be necessary to comment in detail on Weber's rebuttal of Wellhausen's objections. He concluded by complaining that he was in a no-win situation. If he contradicted his opponent he was guilty of *lèse-majesté*; if he agreed with him he was a plagiarist. But he would continue to write as often as he thought fit; Wellhausen didn't have to read

---

8 Eduard Meyer, *Die Entstehung des Judentums: Eine historische Untersuchung* (Tübingen: Niemeyer, 1896; reprint: Hildesheim: Georg Olms, 1965).

9 Julius Wellhausen, Rezension zu Eduard Meyers "Die Entstehung des Judentums," in *Göttingische Gelehrte Anzeigen* 159 (1897): 89–97. Since this journal may be hard to find, a full account of the debate is provided by Reinhard Kratz (ed.), himself a Göttingen scholar, in *Das Judentum im Zeitalter des Zweiten Tempels* (Tübingen: Mohr Siebeck, 2004), 6–22.

10 The most recent case against authenticity is that of Pierre Briant, "Histoire et Archéologie d'un Texte: La Lettre de Darius Gadatas entre Perses, Grecs et Romains," in *Licia e Lidia Prima dell'Ellenizzazione: Atti del Convegno Internazionale, Roma 11–12 Ottobre 1999*, ed. Mauro Giorgieri et al. (Roma: Consiglio Nazionale delle Ricerche, 2003), 107–44. Briant thus reversed the opinion he expressed in his *Histoire de l'Empire Perse de Cyrus à Alexandre*, Vol. 1 (Paris: Libraire Arthème Fayard, 1996), 507–9.

any of it. This clash of titans thus ended without having contributed much to the debate apart from confirming the importance of the rescript and the other putative documents in Ezra for understanding the origins of Judaism.

A more persuasive, or at least a more influential case for inauthenticity was made by two Harvard scholars a generation apart, Charles Cutler Torrey and Robert H. Pfeiffer. Torrey, who wrote with a wit and grace unusual both then and now in biblical scholarship, carried the already well-established idea of the Ezra narrative, including the rescript, the work of the author of Chronicles, a step further by arguing that the Ezra story, unlike the Nehemiah Memoir, is a pure fiction. This was in keeping with his view of the Chronicler as "by taste and gift a novelist".[11] About three decades later Pfeiffer commented on the Jewish terminology in the rescript which, he maintained, cannot be explained as a revision by a Jewish scribe, or on the assumption that Ezra or another co-religionist had a hand in its composition or, much less (this against Meyer), as reproducing the language of Ezra's petition (Ezra 7:6). The powers given to Ezra, surpassing by far those given Nehemiah as governor, are simply incredible, especially since they gave him jurisdiction over the entire satrapy not just its Jewish population (Ezra 7:25). Equally incredible is the profligate generosity of the Persian authorities towards the Jerusalem temple and its personnel. Pfeiffer concluded by stating that, if the rescript is a Jewish forgery, it casts serious doubt on the entire first-person Ezra narrative of which it is an integral part.[12]

It would be tedious to take the reader through the later history of the debate which, in any case, has been competently covered in recent years by historians of the period, including Professor Grabbe. One variant, which stands the most familiar approach to the issue on its head, nevertheless deserves mention. In the course of strenuously promoting the chronological priority of Ezra over Nehemiah, Ulrich Kellermann found that only the rescript and the list of bullion brought to the temple by Ezra (Ezra 8:26–27) can be considered authentic. The rest of the Ezra narrative was worked up as a kind of midrash on the rescript, the end-result filled out by a *listenfreudig* scribe of the Hasmonaean period. The intent of the author, none other than the Chronicler, was to present the priest Ezra as a counterpart to Nehemiah the layman. The midrash idea was later taken up by In der Smitten, but has not enjoyed much success in the scholarly guild, and for good reason.[13] More recently, in a detailed analysis of the Ezra

---
11 Charles Cutler Torrey, *Ezra Studies* (New York: Ktav, 1970[1910]), 250–51.
12 Robert Pfeiffer, *Introduction to the Old Testament* (London: Adam & Charles Black, 1952), 825–27.
13 Ulrich Kellermann, "Erwägungen zum Problem der Esradatierung," *ZAW* 80 (1968): 55–87; also, more briefly, *Nehemia: Quellen, Überlieferung und Geschichte* (Berlin: Walter de Gruyter,

story, Reinhard Kratz whittled down Ezra 7–10 to an extremely small narrative core consisting in the rescript within the rescript, or more precisely the core of this rescript in Ezra 7:21–22 addressed to the treasurers in the Transeuphratene satrapy. The rest is legendary accretion paralleling the account of the building of the temple in Ezra 5–6 and the Nehemiah Memoir which the author or editor of the Ezra material had before him.[14] Kratz's attention to the detail of the account is commendable, but the choice of the decree to the satrapal treasurers as an irreducible authentic minimum seems far from inevitable, if not arbitrary. In the first place, this part of the rescript contains the same characteristically Jewish terminology as the rest, even in the two verses which Kratz assigns to the core. It also strains credulity that Artaxerxes would command the satrapal treasurers to hand over 100 talents of silver bullion (about three and a quarter tonnes) for a temple in a minor province of the empire, especially when we recall that the annual tribute from the entire satrapy, including the wealthy Phoenician cities, Cyprus and Syria amounted to no more than 350 silver talents (Her. III 91).

2 The rescript section by section, verse by verse

In his contributions to the discussion about the rescript, Grabbe has provided a fairly comprehensive list of objections to the thesis of authenticity. However, I think it possible to make out an even stronger case, though without entertaining any illusions about foreclosing debate. I noted earlier that, *pace* Meyer, the occasional Old Persian word, or an expression reflecting Achaemenid usage, does not necessarily indicate authenticity, much less suggest a translation from Old Persian into Aramaic.[15] That a Jewish author writing in the late Achaemenid or early Hellenistic period could make use of such expressions to give the work in hand a semblance of authenticity is evident from the Book of Esther. At any

---

1967), 56–60; Wilhelm In der Smitten, *Esra: Quellen, Überlieferung und Geschichte* (Assen: van Gorcum, 1973), 6–66.
14 Reinhard Kratz, *Die Komposition der erzählenden Bücher des Alten Testaments* (Göttingen: Vandenhoeck & Ruprecht, 2000), 53–91 = *The Composition of the Narrative Books of the Old Testament*, Transl. John Bowden (London: T. & T. Clark, 2005), 49–86, especially 73–76.
15 The words and expressions in question are *paršegen* (7:11; also 4:11,23; 5:6; Esth 3:14) > OP *pati-çagna*; *ništěvan* (7:11; also 4:7) > OP *ništ van*; *melek malkayy '* (7:12) cf. Akk. *šar šarr ni*, OP *xš yaθiya xš yaθiy*; *d t '* (7:12,14,25–26); *gĕmîr* (? 7:12); *'asparn '* (7:17; also 7:21; 5:8; 6:12–13) > OP *usprna*. The reference to the king's seven counselors (*šib'at y 'ăt hî*, 7:14–15; also Esth 1:14), which seemed to be confirmed by allusions to seven *dikastai* in Her 3,31,71,83–84 and to seven *aristoi* in Xenophon, *Anabasis* I 6.4–5 has been questioned by Pierre Briant, *Histoire de l'Empire Perse*, 140–42.

rate, the following notes on the rescript, verse by verse, are intended as no more than addenda to Professor Grabbe's observations. They deal exclusively with the language used in the edict.[16]

Presentation of the rescript (v 11)

This is a copy of the letter that King Artaxerxes gave to the priest Ezra, the scribe, a scholar of the text of the commandments of the Lord (Yahweh) and his statutes for Israel.

Use of traditional Jewish words for law in the combination *děbarîm, misvôt, huqqîm* rather than Persian *dātā'* (as in v 12) is implausible in an imperial edict; the combination of *misvôt* and *huqqîm* appears occasionally in Nehemiah (1:7; 9:13–14; 10:30) but is otherwise rare. This presentation of the document is probably from the editor, either the author of Chronicles or someone associated with him; for Ezra as law scribe see Ezra 7:6.

Address: sender and recipient (v 12)

Artaxerxes, king of kings, to the priest Ezra, the scribe of the law of the God of Heaven: Greetings!

The standard superscription to a letter: sender, recipient, greetings, which could also be from the Jewish editor or author, especially in view of Ezra's scribal character repeated here. The word *gĕmîr* defies translation.

Ezra's first commission (vv 13–14)

I decree that any of the people of Israel or their priests and Levites in my kingdom who freely offer to go to Jerusalem may go with you, since you are sent by the king

---

[16] See Sebastian Grätz, *Das Edikt des Artaxerxes: Eine Untersuchung zum religionspolitischen und historischen Umfeld von Esra 7,12–26* (Berlin: Walter de Gruyter, 2004), 63–214 for a recent detailed study of the language of the rescript. Grätz's placing of the rescript in the context of Hellenistic politics raises issues which cannot be taken up here; see also his "Esra 7 im Kontext hellenistischer Politik: Der königliche Euergetismus in hellenisticher Zeit als idealer Hintergrund von Esra 7,12–26," in *Die Griechen und das antike Israel: Interdisziplinäre Studien zur Religions- und Kulturgeschichte des Heiligen Landes*, ed. Stefan Alkier and Markus Witte (Fribourg: Academic Press; Göttingen: Vandenhoeck & Ruprecht, 2004), 131–54.

and his seven counsellors to make enquiry about Judah and Jerusalem according to the law of your God with which you are entrusted.

The threefold grouping of Israel-priests-Levites, and especially the technical use of "Israel" for laity, common in Chronicles (1 Chr 9:2; 2 Chr 7:6; 19:8; 35:18) and Ezra–Nehemiah (Ezra 9:1; 10:5,25; Neh 11:3) have no place in an imperial rescript.

mitnaddēb: the language of "volunteering" (also 7:15–16) is characteristic of and almost exclusive to Chronicles (1 Chr 29:5,6,9,14,17; 2 Chr 17:6) and Ezra–Nehemiah (Ezra 1:6; 2:68; 3:5; Neh 11:2); the only exceptions occur in the Song of Deborah (Judg 5:2,9).

The same can be said for "Judah and Jerusalem", characteristic of Chronicles (twenty-five times) and infrequent elsewhere.

Ezra's second commission (vv 15–16)

You are to convey the silver and gold that the king and his counselors have freely offered to the God of Israel whose dwelling is in Jerusalem, together with all the silver and gold that you may find in the entire Babylonian satrapy; also the freewill offerings of the people and the priests given willingly for the house of their God in Jerusalem.

The expression "the God of Israel" (*'ēl' yiśra'ēl*) is implausible; we would expect "the God of Heaven" or "the God who is in Jerusalem." In the Elephantine papyri the Jewish residents are *yĕhûdayyē'*, never *yiśra'ēl* or *bĕn yiśra'ēl*. This is an inner-Jewish self-designation. The language of making a freewill offering or volunteering (verb *hitnaddēb*, vv 13, 15, 16) occurs elsewhere exclusively in Chronicles and Ezra–Nehemiah (1 Chr 29:5–17; 2 Chr 17:16; Ezra 1:6; 2:68; 3:5; Neh 11:2).

What is to be done with the money (vv 17–18)

With this money you shall with all diligence buy bulls, rams, and lambs together with their grain offerings and drink offerings, and you shall offer them on the altar of the house of your God in Jerusalem. Whatever seems good to you and your colleagues to do with the rest of the silver and gold you may do, according to the will of your God.

The list of sacrificial animals to be purchased is identical with the list in the Darius rescript (Ezra 6:9) and is standard in Chronicles (1 Chr 29:21; 2 Chr

29:21,32; also Ezra 8:35). Especially significant is inclusion of their corresponding cereal and drink offerings, cf. Num 15:1–16.

"To you and to your colleagues (literally 'brothers')": a common designation among Jews but not expected when Jews are addressed in an imperial edict; cf. Elephantine texts AP 21:1–2,11, where the term *ah* ("brother") as here) is used only between Jews, with AP 30:1, 4, 18, 22 where the more official term *kĕnātā'* ("colleague") occurs in a letter to the governor of Judah with reference to the priest Jedoniah's associates.

The sacred vessels and other requirements for the temple (vv 19–20)

The vessels which have been given to you for the service of the house of your God you shall deliver before the God of Jerusalem. Whatever else is required for the house of your God which you may incur will be provided from the royal treasury.

The language here, including reference to "the God of Jerusalem" is unexceptionable. The return of the sacred vessels replicates a continuity theme from the edict of Cyrus (Ezra 1:7–11; 6:5), repeated in the report of the Jewish elders to Tattenai (5:14–16), and taken up again in the report of Ezra's return (8:26–30).[17]

The enclosed decree to the treasurers of the Transeuphratene province (vv 21–24)

I, King Artaxerxes, decree to all the treasurers in the Transeuphratene province: Whatever the priest Ezra, scribe of the law of the God of Heaven, requires of you, let it be done with all diligence: up to one hundred talents of silver, one hundred kor of wheat, one hundred bath of oil, and unlimited amounts of salt. All the commands of the God of Heaven are to be diligently fulfilled for the house of the God of Heaven, lest wrath come upon the realm of the king and his heirs. We also notify you that it is not lawful to impose tribute, poll tax or property tax on any of the priests, Levites, liturgical musicians, doorkeepers, temple servants or any other servants of this house of God.

---

17 Peter Ackroyd, "The Temple Vessels – A Continuity Theme," *VTSup* 23 (1972): 166–81.

As noted earlier, the language in the decree to the satrapal treasurers is not essentially different from the language used elsewhere in the rescript.[18] It runs parallel with the language of the reply of Darius to Tattenai in which the same commodities to be made available (wheat, oil, salt) are mentioned, with insistence that they be handed over "with all due diligence" (*'āsparnā'*). In both decrees temple liturgies are also for the benefit of the royal family in Susa. The reason given for subsidizing the cult, to deflect the wrath (*qeṣap*) of the God of Heaven (v 23), is reminiscent of the edict of Darius (Ezra 6:10) and reflects the Chronicler's theme of the divine wrath (*qeṣep*) incurred for cultic transgressions (2 Chr 19:2,10; 24:18; 29:8). As far as we can tell, general tax exemption for temple personnel was not inconsistent with Persian practice. A Greek inscription addressed by Darius[19] to "his slave Gadatas," perhaps a local satrap, reprimanding him for imposing tribute on the priests of Apollo serving at a sanctuary at Magnesia on the river Meander in Asia Minor, would be another example.[20]

Closing address to Ezra (vv 25–26)

As for you, Ezra, according to the wisdom of God with which you are entrusted,, appoint magistrates and judges to judge all the people in the Transeuphratene province who are acquainted with the laws of your God, and those who are not acquainted with them you must teach. Let judgement be strictly carried out on all those who refuse to obey the law of your God and the law of the king, whether it be death, banishment, confiscation of property, or imprisonment.

With "the wisdom of your God with which you are entrusted" compare."the law of your God with which you are entrusted", v 14, (literally "which is in your hand", *dî bîdāk*) which corresponds precisely to the Deuteronomic equivalence between law and wisdom (Deut 4:6). We would not expect to find this in an official imperial decree.

"The law of your God and the law of the king", probably to be understood as two distinct jurisdictions, invites comparison with David's appointment of officials to administer laws governing *děbar hā 'ĕlōhîm* and *děbar hammelek*, reli-

---

[18] *Pace* Wilhelm In der Smitten, *Esra*, 19; Reinhard Kratz, *The Composition of the Narrative Books*, 76–77.

[19] Since the date is uncertain, which of the three rulers named Darius is the addressee remains uncertain.

[20] For the text of the inscription and discussion see Russell Meiggs and David Lewis, *A Selection of Greek Historical Inscriptions to the End of the Fifth Century BC* (Oxford: Oxford University Press, 1980), n.16.

gious and civil law (1 Chr 26:32); compare the distinction between *děbar YHWH* and *děbar hammelek* during Jehoshaphat's reign (2 Chr 19:11).

The preponderance in the rescript of language peculiar to Jewish cultic and legal activites, including language of a technical nature, must be set alongside the implausibilities long familiar to students of the rescript; in particular, the extent of Ezra's jurisdiction and mandate and the improbably vast subsidies to the temple in particular (7:15 – 22; also 8:25 – 27). The conclusion is unavoidable that, if Ezra's mission is historical, and if it was officially authorized, which is entirely plausible, the authorization cannot very well have been issued in the terms used in the document before us. Meyer's objection that the edict was composed to reflect Ezra's request (7:6) cannot explain the extent to which the edict has been judaized. Moreover, it is simply incredible that a Persian monarch, with or without his seven counsellors, would have signed off on a rescript composed by a Jewish subject granting him powers equal or superior to those of a satrap, not to mention the disbursement of resources of such magnitude. With such a hypothesis we are in the fantasy world of the Book of Esther in which individual subjects can persuade a Persian monarch to write edicts, couched in the numerous languages in use throughout the empire, permitting the extermination of entire populations (Esth 3:12 – 15; 8:9 – 10).

3 Some provisional conclusions

In its narrative context in the Ezra story, the rescript has the fairly obvious purpose of authenticating and legitimating the account of Ezra's activities which follows. That Ezra was commissioned by Artaxerxes I to go to Judah in order to supervise temple worship and the observance of native ordinances, both means of preserving the *pax Persica* in a sensitive and strategically significant part of the western reaches of the empire, is entirely in keeping with imperial practice. Darius I sent the Egyptian Udjahorresnet on a mission to Egypt and Histiaeus of Miletus back to his own city on the occasion of an Athenian-backed local revolt.[21] If we concede this point, we must go on to ask to what extent the account of Ezra's activities in Ezra 8 – 10 corresponds to the scope of the commissioning in the rescript. What follows is no more than the outline of one way of addressing the issue. The story has three parts:

(1) Ezra's account of his relocation from Babylon to Judah, together with a group of co-religionists, in order to renew the temple cult (Ezra 7:1 – 8:36), con-

---

21 Herodotus, *Hist.* 5:23 – 24, 35 – 36, 105 – 7; 6:30.

sisting in a first-person account within a third-person introduction and conclusion (7:1–10; 7:27–8:34; 8:35–36). The introduction (7:1–10) is clearly not of a piece. The genealogical descent of Ezra as priest (7:1–5) has been taken from the official priestly genealogy in 1 Chr 5:27–41, necessitating a resumptive reference to "this Ezra" in v 6. The list of those who accompanied him, including Levites (7:6), must be a later insertion since it contradicts the notice that Levites were absent from Ezra's immigrant group (8:15–19). Ezra is presented first as priest, indeed as of the high-priestly line, and then as law scribe (7:6,10), indicating a conflation of the two goals of the mission according to the rescript. Ezra's prayer following the rescript, however, thanks God for the benevolence of the Persian monarchy towards the temple and for permission to go to Jerusalem, but says nothing about law enforcement (7:27–28).

(2) Ezra's participation in the public reading and explanation of the law, concluding with the celebration of Sukkoth, all in third-person narrative (Neh 7:72–8:18).

(3) The account of the intermarriage crisis, a conflation of first-person (Ezra 9:1–15) and third-person narrative (10:1–44).

As the principal actor, Ezra is described in the rescript as both priest and scribe (Ezra 7:11,12,21), elsewhere in the surrounding narrative as either one or the other. The dual function is therefore explicit only in the introduction (7:1–10) and the rescript. It seems that the narrative has been put together to combine two quite different and *mutually incompatible* functions. The mission to see to the administration and enforcement of the laws is of a kind assigned to one person of high rank, not to the leader of a miscellaneous group of emigrants; compare the parallel cases mentioned earlier: the mission of the Egyptian collaborator Udjahorresnet under Darius I, and that of the Milesian Histiaeus, Darius I's Ionian expert. In addition, there is no precedent for the function of priest-scribe. The *sôpēr* was either the humble scrivener with the tools of his trade (writing case, stylus, etc) familiar from Near Eastern iconography,[22] or a personal amanuensis, such as Baruch with Jeremiah (Jer 36:32), or a high-status state official, of a type attested throughout the history of Judah.[23] We hear of law scribes for the first time in Jeremiah's complaint about the false pen of the scribes who have turned the law into a lie, presumably by their legal interpretations (Jer 8:8), but they are clearly distinguished from priests. According to Deuteronomic theory, the law was the province of the levitical priests (Deut 17:18; 31:9–13) but

---

22 Ezek 9:2–3; 1 Chr 2:55 mentions guilds or "families" (*mišpĕḥôt*) of scribes.
23 2 Sam 8:17; 20:25; 1 Kgs 4:3; 2 Kgs 12:11, etc. Shaphan during the reign of Josiah is perhaps the best known (2 Kings 22; Jer 36:10).

they are never called scribes. According to the Chronicler (2 Chr 34:13), some Levites served as scribes during Josiah's reign, and we know that at a later time Levites were heavily involved in scribal activities. But, to repeat, Ezra as priest-scribe is a unique and improbable phenomenon.[24]

The conclusion suggests itself that the rescript, whether an entirely Jewish creation or a thoroughly rewritten imperial authorization for travel from Babylon to Judah, now no longer available, was intended to provide post-factum legitimacy for the activities of Ezra and his group as described in the Ezra story. These activities appear to have had two goals: first, control of the temple and its considerable assets, implying a considerable degree of civic control including *kārēt*, exclusion from the community and confiscation of property to the temple (Ezra 10:8); second, power to enforce the laws, in the case of the marriage crisis a restrictive and by no means self-evident interpretation of law.[25] The rescript could have been interpreted as legitimating both these goals, which in addition are encapsulated in the dual role of the principal beneficiary. Common to both goals, finally, was the objective of forming a ritually self-segregating, in effect sectarian community within the province of Judah, beginning with the attempted solution to the problem of intermarriage narrated in Ezra 9–10. We can be sure that no Persian monarch would have authorized such a measure, calculated as it was to alienate the lay and priestly aristocracy and stir up a hornet's nest in a sensitive part of the empire. This circumstance may help to explain why the Ezra story comes to a sudden, shuddering halt (Ezra 10:44) and had so little effect on later developments.

---

24 Hans Heinrich Schaeder argued that Ezra's title *sāpar* connoted his official position in the Persian bureaucracy, something like High Commissioner for Jewish Affairs in the Transeuphratene Satrapy, and k h n was the role acknowledged in the Jewish community, an opinion no longer in favour; see his *Esra der Schreiber: Beiträge zur Historischen Theologie*, Vol. 5 (Tübingen: Mohr/Siebeck, 1930), 48.

25 Shecaniah, a leader of the golah group, insisted that the policy of coercive divorce be implemented according to the law, but also according to the advice of Ezra and his supporters, those who trembled at God's command, which can be interpreted to mean according to their interpretation (Ezra 10:3)

IX. The Nehemiah Autobiographical Memoir

Source: *Language, Theology and the Bible: Essays in Honour of James Barr*, ed. by Samuel Balentine and John Barton, 199–212. Oxford: Clarendon, 1994.

1 Autobiography in antiquity

Towards the beginning of his massive *Geschichte der Autobiographie*, Georg Misch defined his topic as "the history of human self-awareness".[1] The definition, which no doubt owed a debt to the influence of his father-in-law Wilhelm Dilthey, would certainly apply to Augustine's *Confessions*, often taken to be the first example of the genre.[2] Yet in spite of his definition, Misch represented Augustine as more a terminus than a point of departure and, true to his word, reached him only on page 265 of his history. A search for Augustine's literary antecedents would no doubt take us back along several different tracks, some of them poorly signposted. We would have to take account of the genre of soliloquy or *pensées*, as in the writings of Seneca and Marcus Aurelius and perhaps here and there in the letters of Cicero. A suggestion of a different kind is that the *Confessions* may be read as a Christian version of the quest for transformation and salvation exemplified by Lucius in the *Metamorphoses* of Apuleius,[3] or as the interiorization of the journey narrative, precursor of the picaresque novel, adopted ironically in the *Satyricon* of Petronius. Other antecedents could be found in Xenophon and Scylax of Carianda and, much earlier, the autobiographical narrative of the Egyptian Wen-amon.

In contrast to the *Confessions*, however, first-person narratives from these early times are, for the most part, either propagandistic and apologetic or merely anecdotal. The former type attained its mature form in the *Bios* of Josephus, but the best-known examples are Mesopotamian royal inscriptions in the first person dealing with military campaigns, the building, rebuilding and dedicating of temples, and the like. Evidence for the anecdotal type can be extracted from Herodotus and the gossipy Ctesias, with emphasis on episodes about incidents

---

1 Georg Misch, *Geschichte der Autobiographie*, Vol. 1, *Das Altertum* (Leipzig & Berlin, 1907), 5 = *A History of Autobiography in Antiquity*, Vol. 1, Transl. Ernest Dickes (Cambridge/Mass: Harvard University Press, 1951), 18.
2 E.g. Roy Pascal, *Design and Truth in Autobiography* (London: Routledge & Kegan Paul, 1960), 21–24.
3 Robert Scholes and Robert Kellogg, *The Nature of Narrative* (Oxford: Oxford University Press, 1966), 73–79.

which, if not invented, must derive from the individuals featured in them.[4] Characteristic of all these, including the memoirs of Ezra and Nehemiah, is an almost total lack of those qualities of subjectivity, interiority, and self-awareness to which Misch attributed such importance.

Like other all-too-brief records from the first two centuries after the fall of Jerusalem, the Nehemiah memoir[5] must be read in the political and cultural context of the Persian empire to which the province of Judah (Yehud) belonged after 539 BC The material for reconstructing that context is not abundant, but some tentative observations are in order before we take a closer look at the text itself. Momigliano remarked on the striking fact that, in the Greek-speaking world, biography and historiography originated about the same time, in the fifth century BC and during the heyday of the Persian imperial system.[6] While there are few *direct* literary contacts between Jews and Greeks at this time, it is fair to assume that both peoples would have been stimulated, negatively or positively, by critical reaction to the Persian imperial regime. With few exceptions, the extant Jewish sources evince an attitude favorable to, or at least willing to accommodate to Persian rule. The mainland Greeks, on the other hand, were increasingly opposed to it, especially after the Ionian revolt under Darius I. Both nevertheless were engaged, in their own ways, in defining their ethnic and national identity over against the dominant power in the world at that time. To grasp the point, one has only to compare Nehemiah with his contemporary Pericles, founder of the Athenian empire, restorer of temples, and enforcer of the stringent law of citizenship enacted about the same time that Nehemiah arrived in Judah; or with his older contemporary Themistocles, restorer of the walls of Athens. It is therefore not surprising if the political situation at that time generated new literary expressions; if, for example, Greek political biography was stimulated by Persian biographical memoirs, or Jewish historiography began to incorporate archival documents cited verbatim, or if both began to show a certain partiality for novelistic elements. It is noteworthy that the lively biographical sketches in Herodotus are more often Eastern and specifically Persian or Egyptian rather than Greek in origin. From the Jewish side Esther, whatever date is assigned to it, reflects the same situation.

---

4 Examples in Arnaldo Momigliano, "Fattori Orientali della Storiografia Ebraica Post-Esilica e della Storiografia Greca," *Accademia Nazionale dei Lincei* 76 (1966): 137–46.
5 I will use the descriptive term "memoir" as a provisional way of referring to the Nehemiah text without prejudicing the attempt to determine its genre more precisely.
6 Arnaldo Momigliano, *The Development of Greek Biography* (2nd ed., Cambridge/Mass: Harvard University Press, 1993), 12.

Nehemiah was also a contemporary of Ion of Chios who wrote personal accounts of visits (*epidēmiai*) with prominent individuals like Pericles and Sophocles containing autobiographical notes. Like so much else from that century, his writings have survived only in fragments.[7] How much else of interest to our topic has not survived we do not know, but what there is suggests that Momigliano was correct in concluding that "autobiography was in the air in the Persian Empire of the early fifth century, and both Jews and Greeks may have been stimulated by Persian and other oriental models to create something of their own."[8]

2 The first-person Nehemiah narrative

The author of the Nehemiah memoir was wine steward or cupbearer to Artaxerxes I at the royal court in Susa. Like the court physician Democedes (Herodotus 3:125, 129–37), and perhaps also the Egyptian notable Udjahorresnet, of whom more will be said shortly, he used his position to obtain leave to return on important business to his homeland. Once there, Nehemiah succeeded in getting himself appointed governor of the province, and set about the work of consolidating the struggling Jewish immigrant community. The memoir tells the story of how he achieved this goal.

The Nehemiah narrative as a whole has the title *dibrê nĕhemyâ* (Neh 1:1), which should be translated "chronicle" rather than "words" or "sayings", since what follows is not a collection of sayings comparable to a prophetic book (e.g. Jer 1:1; Amos 1:1). The title may be compared with the several texts on which the author of Chronicles claims to draw for historical information, dealing with the *res gestae* (also *dĕbārîm*) of the kings of Judah. The Nehemiah story, like that of Ezra, combines first- and third-person narrative. It is basically a story about Nehemiah which has selectively incorporated autobiographical material. That the compiler or editor has excerpted passages from a no longer extant complete and independent first-person account is strongly suggested by its uneven distribution, almost exclusively in chapters 1–7 and chapter 13, and the abrupt opening (after the title), where we would expect the author to introduce himself.

The first-person narrative begins with Nehemiah in service at the imperial court in Susa where he receives news of the disastrous situation in Judah, is granted a leave of absence by Artaxerxes, arrives in Jerusalem, surveys the ruined city wall by night, and communicates his desire to rebuild it to certain

---

7 Felix Jacoby, *FGrHist*. IIIB, 276–83.
8 Arnaldo Momigliano, *The Development of Greek Biography*, 37.

supporters (1:1b–2:20). In this first section the prayer uttered by Nehemiah on hearing the bad news (1:5–11a) has probably been spliced into the memoir by an editor. In familiar psalmic language it speaks of prayer offered day and night (1:6), it does not refer to the sad news Nehemiah has just received, and it anticipates his request for a leave of absence (1:11). The list of work gangs and the sections of wall assigned to them is not in the first person and has probably also been added (3:1–32). The story then goes on to document the progress of the work punctuated by opposition from different quarters and the neutralization of the opponents by prayer and counter-measures (3:33–4:26; 6:1–7:5). The pattern is interrupted by an account of the removal of social abuses, reminiscent of Solon's first-person verse account of reforms preserved in Aristotle's *Constitution of Athens* a century and a half earlier (5:1–19).[9] The restoration of social order is also a standard topos in Egyptian biographical and autobiographical inscriptions, for example that of Djed-khons-ef-ankh from the twenty-second dynasty and Udjahorresnet from the time of Darius I.

The dedication service for the wall (12:27–43) would presumably have followed soon after the completion of the wall and repopulation of the city, but has been moved forward to serve as the finale to a long insert beginning and ending with lists (7:6–12:26). It introduces first-person discourse here and there (12:31,38,40), but since the narrative as a whole is in the third person, with no first person plural where we would expect it, it may be doubted whether this incident belonged originally to the memoir. Ezra also participates in the procession around the wall (12:33,36), and is therefore represented as a contemporary of Nehemiah, a strong pointer to a later stage in the formation of the book (cf. 12:26, "In the days of Nehemiah the governor and Ezra the priest and scribe"). Torrey argued many years ago that this incident is a pure invention of the author of Chronicles.[10] We should perhaps say, more cautiously, that it was composed by someone with an outlook similar to that of the author of Chronicles, or at any rate by some one living at least a century after the time of Nehemiah.[11]

---

9 Edwin Yamauchi, "Two Reformers Compared: Solon of Athens and Nehemiah of Jerusalem," in *The Bible World: Essays in Honor of Cyrus Gordon*, ed. Gary Rendsburg et al. (New York: Ktav, 1980), 269–92.
10 Charles Cutler Torrey, *The Composition and Historical Value of Ezra-Nehemiah* (Gießen: J. Ricker,1896), 43–44; *Ezra Studies* (New York: Ktav, 1970 [1910]), 248–49.
11 This can be deduced by comparing the seven-member linear genealogy of the Levitical precentor Zechariah (12:35) with that of the liturgical musician Mattaniah (11:17 cf. 1 Chr 9:15). The former is the great-grandson of the latter who is said to be living in Jerusalem at the time of Nehemiah. This would place the composition of this incident in the mid-fourth century BC.

Since the editor of the memoir, or of the book as a whole, writing no earlier than the fourth century BC, seems to have had no scruples about re-arranging his material, we cannot be sure that these excerpts are presented in chronological order. The position of Nehemiah's *apologia* in 5:14–19 is particularly subject to suspicion since it would fit much better at the end of the memoir. It recapitulates twelve years of governorship and ends with the "remember me" (*zokrâ-lî*) formula elsewhere restricted to the last chapter. It would certainly make a more fitting conclusion to the memoir than the rather inconsequential allusion to the wood offering with which the memoir, and the book, now end (13:31). This kind of self-justification is, of course, a standard feature of autobiographical writing both ancient and modern. It is interesting, and even somewhat amusing, to note the rabbinic tradition according to which Nehemiah wrote the entire book but was not given credit for it on account of his bad habit of disparaging his predecessors (*b. Sanh.* 93b).

The census in 7:5b–72a is introduced in the first person (7:5b) and is therefore often taken to belong to the memoir, but this repetition – in an otherwise succinct narrative – of the long list in Ezra 2:1–67 of "those who had come up at the beginning" (*hā'ôlîm bāri'šônâ*), or "those who had come up from the captivity of the diaspora" (*hā'ôlîm miššĕvî haggôlâ*), calls for an explanation which goes beyond the scope of the memoir. The place of the list at the conclusion of Nehemiah's work of securing the city, before the introduction of the Ezra material in chapters 7–8 (possibly 7–9), and its linking Nehemiah's achievement with the first return, suggests an editorial intent along the same lines as the festal letters in 2 Macc 1:1–2:18 which present Nehemiah as the real founder of the new Jewish commonwealth. Perhaps, then, the census list represents a kind of realized eschatology, the saved community consisting in those who had survived the exile with their faith intact. It was this community, "the penitents of Israel" (*šāvê yiśrā'ēl*) with which the Qumran sectarians claimed ideological continuity; see, for example, the list of the founding fathers (*hāri'šônîm*) referred to but not reproduced in the Damascus Document (CD 4:2–12).

The last section of the memoir consists in three fairly brief sections of unequal length, each beginning with a vague temporal phrase and concluding with the "remember me" (*zokrâ-lî*) formula (13:4–14, 15–22, 23–31). They deal, respectively, with reform of temple management, sabbath observance, and marriage practices. It is worth noting that the measures recorded here and in the account of Nehemiah's social reforms (5:1–19) correspond to the seven stipulations of the covenant in 10:1–40: avoidance of foreign marriages, prohibition of trading on the sabbath and holy days, sabbatical year and debt forgiveness (cf. 5:11–12, also confirmed by an oath), contributions for the upkeep of the temple, the wood offering, first-fruits, and tithing. Since this is hardly coincidental, it suggests that the covenant, from at least a century after the time of Nehemiah, was drawn up with Nehemiah's measures in mind.[12]

These surviving excerpts represent a very uneven coverage of an administration which lasted from the twentieth year of Artaxerxes I (445/444) to some time after the thirty-second year of the same ruler (Neh 13:6). The first and by far the longest excerpt covers only the fifty-two days it took to repair the wall (6:15), while the last records events in the final, possibly quite brief period of his administration. The most salient feature of the first section is the pattern of opposition from the evil trio of Sanballat, Tobiah and Geshem and the spirited reaction of Nehemiah. Beginning with Nehemiah's arrival in the province (2:9–10), the pattern is repeated seven times, as it describes a first stage in the work of reconstruction, how their activities came to the attention of Nehemiah's enemies ("when Sanballat *et alii* heard ..."), the hostile reaction to the news (anger, ridicule, threats, machinations), and Nehemiah's counter-measures (rebuttal, prayer, vigorous action). The seven stages are as follows: arrival in the province (2:9–10), decision to repair the wall (2:17–20), the work gets underway (3:33–37), the wall is half-finished (3:38–4:3), plots are frustrated (4:11), the work is completed apart from the gates (6:1–9), the work is finished (6:15–16). This seems to be a deliberate patterning device, with the notice that the wall was half-finished at the centre of the series where it belongs, and it suggests that the first-person narrative was put together with more care than we would expect from a simple journal entry.

Another patterning device in this first section draws on the traditional language of the "holy war". Our attention is drawn to it at the point where Nehemiah assures his followers that their God will fight for them (4:14), but it is quite pervasive. The sequence is somewhat as follows: enemies conspire together; the righteous, whose numbers and resources are limited, call on God for help; they form battle lines according to tribes; they are told not to fear for their God is with them; the evil devices of the enemy are thwarted by divine intervention and they are obliged to acknowledge the hand of God in what has transpired. This last item – "It seemed to them [the enemy] a truly astonishing achievement, and they realized that this work was our God's doing" (6:16) – can be compared

---

12 On the date of Nehemiah's covenant see Wilhelm Rudolph, *Esra und Nehemia samt 3. Esra* (Tübingen: Mohr Siebeck, 1949), 172–76; Joseph Blenkinsopp, *Ezra-Nehemia: A Commentary* (Philadelphia: Westminster, 1988), 308–19. Morton Smith, "The Dead Sea Sect in Relation to Ancient Judaism," *NTS* 7 (1960/1961): 347–60, and *Palestinian Parties and Politics that Shaped the Old Testament* (New York: Columbia University Press, 1971), 173–74, argued that the covenant derives from Levites in the mid-fourth century BC who attributed it to their hero Nehemiah.

with the exclamation "this is YHVH's doing, and it is marvellous in our eyes" (Ps 118:23).

3 The genre issue

The title of Nehemiah 1–13, *dibrê něhemyâ*, does not provide sure guidance on the issue of genre. Where this type of superscription introduces prophetic books (Jeremiah 1:1; Amos 1:1), or didactic collections (Prov 30:1; 31:1; Qoh 1:1) the reference is clearly to sayings, which would be inappropriate for Nehemiah 1–13 which is not a prophetic or sapiential book in any obvious sense of these terms. In the summary statements which punctuate the history in Chronicles, *děbārîm* can refer both to the deeds of the characters – David, Solomon and others – and to the writings of the putative author. Since Neh 1:1 introduces the book as a whole and not just the autobiographical parts, it would seem better to understand the title as a chronicle about Nehemiah, especially since the only other occurrence of this titular form in the book, in 12:23, has this meaning.

Bearing on the issue of genre is the suggestion that the Nehemiah first-person narrative was written up as a report to the Persian authorities, and specifically as a refutation of charges brought against him by opponents who play such a prominent part in his story. While it is probable that such reports were required of provincial governors, the literary character and content of the narrative do not support this conclusion. Not only is there much in the memoir that would be entirely out of place in such a report, the short invocations and imprecations scattered throughout the narrative suggest that it was directed to God not to the Persian king. Hugh Williamson argued that Nehemiah could have sent off a report to Susa about the wall shortly after the work was finished, therefore within a year of his arrival in the province, and could subsequently have expanded it to justify himself before the Judaean community. He bases this conclusion on the fact that, while the wall building takes up most of the space in the memoir, none of the invocations to be remembered by God occurs in it; which would suggest a two-phase composition.[13] The uneven distribution of the invocations is certainly an issue calling for an explanation, but the actual account of the rebuilding of the wall is not in the first person singular or plural, and it is doubtful that the opposition theme would have been considered appropriate matter for such a report.

---

13 Hugh Williamson, *Ezra, Nehemiah* (Waco/Texas: Word Books, 1985), xxvi–xxviii.

I noted earlier how in some respects the memoir follows the pattern of those psalms in which a wronged party pleads his cause with God. Among recent commentators, Kellermann has made the most of this analogy, arguing that this *Gebet des Angeklagten* ("prayer of the accused"), which appears also in Job and the "confessions" of Jeremiah, provides the only adequate explanation of the form in which the Nehemiah material is cast.[14] Taking over from earlier studies by H. Schmidt and H. J. Boeker,[15] Kellermann concluded that this kind of language is rooted in forensic procedures of the Judaean cult community. There may be echoes of judicial proceedings here and there, especially in the "remember me" prayer to God for a hearing, but there is much in the first-person narrative which does not fall into that particular pattern. In fact, there is nothing in the Israelite literary corpus comparable to the memoir, with the obvious exception of the Ezra first-person narrative which may have been influenced by its Nehemiah counterpart.

Other scholars have found the closest parallels in those Mesopotamian inscriptions commemorating the accomplishments, mostly military and architectural, of the rulers of cities and states. The most thorough investigation along these lines was that of Sigmund Mowinckel who returned to it several times.[16] These inscriptions are in the first person, the speaker generally identifies himself in the opening sentence, the favour of the deity is invoked and the piety and devotion of the devotee is emphasized. Various deeds are recorded, not necessarily in the order in which they took place, opponents are denounced as impious, and the speaker's predecessors are often disparaged. Since the purpose was to keep the speaker's memory alive with both the deity and posterity, an inscription of this kind would have been set up in a public place, generally a temple, thus assuring a lasting memorial.[17] Several of these texts also contain the invocation to

---

14 Ulrich Kellermann, *Nehemia: Quellen, Überlieferung und Geschichte* (Berlin: Walter de Gruyter, 1967), 84–88.
15 Hans Schmidt, *Das Gebet des Angeklagten im Alten Testament* (Berlin: Walter de Gruyter, 1928); Hans-Jochen Boecker, *Redeformen des Rechtslebens im Alten Testament* (Neukirchen-Vluyn: Neukirchener Verlag, 1964).
16 Sigmund Mowinckel, "Die vorderasiatischen Königs- und Fürsteninschriften," in *EYXAPIΣTHPION: Studien zur Religion und Literatur des Alten und Neuen Testaments. Festschrift für Hermann Gunkel*, Vol. 1, *Zur Religion und Literatur des Alten Testaments*, ed. by Hans Schmidt (Göttingen: Vandenhoeck & Ruprecht, 1923), 278–322; *Studien zu dem Buche Esra-Nehemia*, Vol. 2 (Oslo: Universitetsforlaget, 1964).
17 Cf. Isa 56:5 and 1 Macc 14:48–49. The inscription of Idrimi of Alalakh was discovered in a temple in that city; see *ANET* 557–58; Sydney Smith, *The Statue of Idri-mi* (London: British Institute of Archaeology in Ankara, 1945); John Van Seters, *In Search of History: Historiography in the Ancient World and the Origins of Biblical History* (New Haven: Yale University Press, 1983),

a deity to bear in mind (*zakāru*) the good deeds of the speaker or the evil deeds of his opponents. Nebuchadnezzar II, for example, prays as follows: "O Marduk, my lord, remember my deeds favourably for good; may these my good deeds be always before your mind".[18]

This type of text served as a model for commemorative inscriptions of different kinds throughout the Near East during well beyond the Achaemenid period. The call to be remembered "for good" by the deity, or posterity, or both, can still be found, for example, in Aramaic synagogue inscriptions from the Byzantine period.[19] The commemorative intent remains the same whether the petitioner is the ruler of an empire or a pious Jew putting up the money for a mosaic or column in the local synagogue. And, to come to what are undoubtedly the closest parallels to the Nehemiah text, this is also the case with Egyptian commemorative inscriptions from the Saitic period to the Ptolemies.

4 Egyptian commemorative inscriptions

Some of the parallels between these inscriptions and the Nehemiah material have been noted since the beginning of the last century,[20] but the first attempt at a systematic comparison was that of von Rad in an article published in 1964.[21] Von Rad noted that these Egyptian texts address the reader and the deity directly, catalogue the speaker's achievements on behalf of the state, especially the care of temples and restoration of a disturbed social order, emphasize religious motivation, and feature the *Gedächtnismotiv*, the appeal to be remembered "for good". Von Rad also identified a special point of contact in such expressions as "(the) god prompted me", "God put into my heart" (Neh 2:12; 7:5) which he took to be a borrowing from the Egyptian prototype.

The Egyptian commemorative texts preserve the same format as the type of monumental inscription from the tomb of Djed-khons-ef-ankh, twenty-second dynasty, to the tomb text of Petosiris, late fourth or early third century BC, and no doubt beyond. The most interesting of these for our purpose is the in-

---

60–68; Tremper Longman III, *Fictional Akkadian Autobiography: A Generic and Comparative Study* (Winona Lake/Indiana: Eisenbrauns, 1991), 60–77, 216–18.
18 *ANET* 307; other examples at 316, 317, 562–63. The *Gedächtnismotiv* is studied by Willy Schottroff, *'Gedenken' im Alten Orient und im Alten Testament* (Neukirchen-Vluyn: Neukirchener Verlag, 1967).
19 Willy Schottroff, *'Gedenken'*, 86–89.
20 Alfred Bertholet, *Die Bücher Esra und Nehemia* (Tübingen & Leipzig: Mohr Siebeck, 1902), 91.
21 Gerhard von Rad, "Die Nehemia-Denkschrift," *ZAW* 76 (1964): 176–87.

scription on the naophorous statue of the physician Udjahorresnet in the Vatican Museum, composed during the reign of Darius I.[22] It resembles the Nehemiah text in its overtly apologetic, intent, and like the Nehemiah memoir it records the role of the author in resolving a national crisis. The apologetic character of the Udjahorresnet text is understandable given the author's compromised position as a Persian collaborator during and after the conquest of Egypt by Cambyses. Nehemiah is apologetic in a different way, but he too was in basic sympathy with the imperial authorities while exploiting their benevolence for his own purposes. Both returned to their own countries at a time of crisis, restored the social order, reformed the cult, ejected foreigners from the principal sanctuary (respectively Jerusalem dedicated to Yahweh and Sais dedicated to the goddess Neith), and provided for its upkeep.

There are, of course, differences. While the Udjahorresnet inscription is a fairly substantial text of forty-seven lines of hieroglyphic, the Nehemiah *Denkschrift*, even in its excerpted form, is considerably longer. It was probably also written on papyrus and deposited in the temple archives (since it is addressed to the deity), whereas the Egyptian text had to fit on the open spaces of a green basalt statue only 70 cm. high. Kellermann also points out that the Nehemiah text deals primarily with one event while the Egyptian text contains a catalogue of good deeds.[23] This, however, would not necessarily be the case if, as suggested earlier, the final editor has preserved only selections from Nehemiah's first-person narrative.

The Udjahorresnet text opens with a list of royal offerings on behalf of the *ka* of the writer, followed by a brief prayer to Osiris, lord of eternity (lines 1–6). There follow eight sections of unequal length, each beginning with the speaker's titulary and a prefatory "he says" followed by first-person narrative. The sequence seems to be in rough chronological order: events under Cambyses, return to Egypt by order of Darius, and a summary. The content may be summarized briefly as follows: (1) his appointment as chief physician and master of protocol by Cambyses after the conquest of Egypt (lines 7–15); (2) the cleansing of the Sais sanctuary of foreign elements, restoration of its cult and cult personnel and their endowment (16–23); (3) Cambyses' visit to Sais with gifts for the sanctuary, for which the speaker takesn personal credit (24–27); (4) Cambyses offers libations and ex-votos for the sanctuary, again at the urging of Udjahorresnet (28–30); (5) the speaker himself endows the sanctuary and describes how he

---

22 For a more detailed description of the inscription see my "The Mission of Udjahorresnet and those of Ezra and Nehemiah," *JBL* 106 (1987): 409–21.
23 Kellermann, *Nehemia*, 80–82.

saved the people during the invasion, taking the side of the weak against the strong (31–36); (6) he goes on to describe how he advanced the cause of his family, especially his brothers (37–42); (7) he was sent by Darius back to Egypt on a mission to restore the "House of Life" whose activities included the study of medecine, theology, temple administration, and ritual (43–45); (8) he details the honours and privileges bestowed on him by Cambyses and Darius (46). The narrative is rounded off with the remembrance prayer:

> O great gods who are in Sais! Remember all the benefactions done by the chief physician Udjahorresnet. And may you do for him all benefactions! May you make his good name endure in this land for ever! (47).

The similarity with the Nehemiah text in both form and content is quite striking. Nehemiah also claims to have been sent – admittedly at his own prompting – to his homeland on an important mission, to have restored and endowed the cult, purged it of foreign elements, protected the weak against the strong, and furthered the careers of family members (Neh 5:14; 7:2). These similarities cannot be explained by direct borrowing, for which there is no evidence. It seems rather that the formal features of the ancient Near Eastern commemorative inscriptions continued to be reproduced, with local variations, in Egypt, Judah, and no doubt other parts of the Persian empire.

Perhaps the most striking formal element shared by the two texts is the prayer for remembrance, the *Gedächtnismotiv* with which, very probably in my opinion, the Nehemiah texts also ended: "Remember for my good, O my God, all that I have done for this people" (Neh 5:19). This is one of eight such invocations scattered throughout the text,[24] all but two of which (3:36–37; 6:9) begin with the "remember me" formula. Three of the invocations are directed against enemies, and are therefore really imprecations (3:36–37; 6:14; 13:29). It results that those in which Nehemiah prays that God may remember him occur only at the conclusion of his apologia (5:19) and in the last chapter. This final section consists in three statements about Nehemiah's activity in reforming the cult (13:4–14), enforcing the observance of sabbath (13:15–22) and taking action to exclude marriage with outsiders (13:31). Each of these ends with the remembrance formula. As I suggested earlier, the apologia (5:14–19) would fit better as a conclusion to the memoir. Only here and at the beginning of the last section does Nehemiah refer to the conclusion of his term of office in the thirty-second year of Artaxerxes (5:14; 13:6), which confirms the impression that, in some way, these two sections of the memoir formed part of the conclusion to the memoir in its original form.

---

24 Neh 3:36–37; 5:19; 6:9,14; 13:14,22,29,31).

Having said all of this, we would have to add that in several important respects the Nehemiah autobiographical material is quite different from the Udjahorresnet inscription. There is nothing in the latter comparable to the brief but vivid description of incidents – the night ride around the wall (2:12–16), Shemaiah's plot and its undoing (6:10–14), the confrontation with Tobiah (13:4–9) and the encounter with the foreign women (13:23–27). The Nehemiah narrative also makes frequent use of dialogue and allows the principal actor to express emotion, especially sadness and anger in reaction to different situations. Several of these features are no doubt traceable to the writer's native literary tradition. A close reading would no doubt come up with analogies with Moses in Deuteronomy and Jeremiah in the canonical book. But it seems that, in taking over and transforming the commemorative inscription in use at that time, the author of the Nehemiah memoir has come up with a new Israelite way of writing history, and for this too he should be remembered.

X. Ideology and Utopia in the book of Chronicles

Source: *What was Authoritative for Chronicles?*, ed. by Ehud Ben Zvi and Diana Edelman, 89–103. Winona Lake/Indiana: Eisenbrauns, 2011.

1 The Political Situation: A Troubled Time

My title, borrowed from Karl Mannheim's well-known study *Ideology and Utopia*,[1] will be misleading if it conjures up images such as Plato's *Atlantis*, Francis Bacon's *New Atlantis*, or. Thomas More's utopian commonwealth. But if we understand utopia in Mannheim's sense as the creation of an ideal counter-reality in reaction to incongruent present realities, a creation located in the distant past or future, it might help us to understand the impulse leading to the composition of the book of Chronicles, hence what was important and authoritative for the author.

The point of departure is therefore the situation in the international sphere and in the narrower world which the author inhabited and against which he reacted in constructing his utopian vision of the past. This starting point necessarily raises the question of the date of composition. As is well known, the task of coming up with even an approximate date is complicated by theories of multiple redactions or substantial additions spread over a considerable period of time, as well as the disputed issue of the relation of 1–2 Chronicles with Ezra-Nehemiah. These are weighty issues, but I take the view that it is possible to advance a hypothesis about 1–2 Chronicles as we have it, leaving to the commentaries discussion and evaluation of the many accounts of its origins which have been put forward since the eighteenth century and perhaps earlier. Since the more serious difficulties have been raised against the proponents of either a very early or a very late date,[2] I think it legitimate, for the purpose of presenting the following

---

[1] Karl Mannheim, *Ideologie und Utopie* (Frankfurt am Main: Vittorio Klostermann, 1995 [1929]) = *Ideology and Utopia*, Transl. Louis Worth and Edward Shils (New York: Harcourt, Brace, Jovanovich, 1936).

[2] Among the proponents of an early date for the work as a whole or the first and most important redactional strand in it are Adam Welch, *The Work of the Chronicler: Its Purpose and its Date* (London: British Academy, 1939): early post-exilic; David Noel Freedman, "The Chronicler's Purpose," *CBQ* 23 (1961): 436–42: ca. 515, with a later expansion; Frank Moore Cross, "A Reconstruction of the Judean Restoration," *JBL* 94 (1975): 4–18: similar to Freedman, three stages: ca. 520 ending with Ezra 3:13; ca. 450, 1 Chr 10–2 Chr 34 + the *Vorlage* of 1 Esdras; ca. 400, Chr 1–9 + 10:1–2 Chr 34 + Ezra-Nehemiah Hebrew; James Newsome, "Towards a New Understanding of the Chronicler and His Purpose," *JBL* 94 (1975): 201–17: 538–515, from the same milieu as Haggai-

hypothesis, to assume a date of composition in line with what I take to be the majority opinion today. I propose, therefore, to allow for a broad chronological span comprising the roughly three decades preceding and the three following the Macedonian conquest; beginning, therefore, with the accession of Artaxerxes III in 359 BC and ending shortly after the conquest of Palestine by Ptolemy I Soter in 301 BC. This generous time span allows for a definition of authorship in terms of a school sharing the same ideology and *Weltanschauung* active over more than one generation.

What, then, was the situation in the eastern Mediterranean region at that time, and how might it have influenced the Chronicler's work? It is unfortunately the case that, while we have a fairly clear picture of the sequence of events during those decades, we have practically no information bearing directly on their impact on Judah and its people. After his lengthy paraphrase of Esther, which he regarded as the last biblical book, Josephus ran out of biblical material (*Ant.* 11:302–5). None of the other historians of the period, principally Diodorus, Arrian, Curtius Rufus and Plutarch, so much as mention Judah and its Jewish population. But the convulsive events accompanying a major redistribution of political and military power, the endless series of military campaigns, the movement of mercenary armies back and forth between Egypt, Syria and the Phoenician cities, the prevailing sense of chaos and anomie, must have affected the province; and it would be unusual if they had made no impact on a major his-

---

Zechariah 1–8; David Petersen, *Late Israelite Prophecy: Studies in Deutero-Prophetic Literature and in Chronicles* (Missoula/Montana: Scholars, 1977), 57–60: ca. 515; Mark Throntveit, *When Kings Speak: Royal Speech and Royal Prayer in Chronicles* (Atlanta: Scholars, 1987), 97–101: 527–517; William Foxwell Albright, "The Date and Personality of the Chronicler," *JBL* 40 (1921): 104–24, held that it was authored by Ezra, while Joel Weinberg, *Der Chronist in seiner Mitwelt* (Berlin: Walter de Gruyter, 1996) dates it during Nehemiah's governorship. Several opt for the beginning of the fourth century, including Kurt Galling, *Die Bücher der Chronik, Esra, Nehemia* (Göttingen: Vandenhoeck & Ruprecht, 1954), 14–17; Wilhelm Rudolph, *Chronikbücher* (Tübingen: Mohr Siebeck, 1955), viii; John Myers, *I Chronicles* (Garden City/New York: Doubleday, 1965), lxxxvii–lxxxix. Proponents of a date later in the Hellenistic period include Charles Cutler Torrey, *Ezra Studies* (New York: Ktav, 1970 [1910]), 35–36 and *The Chronicler's History of Israel. Chronicles-Ezra-Nehemiah Restored to its Original Form* (New Haven: Yale, 1954), XIV–XV: 250 BCE or later; Edward Lewis Curtis and Albert Alonzo Madsen, *A Critical and Exegetical Commentary on the Books of Chronicles* (Edinburgh: T. & T. Clark, 1910), 5–6: ca. 300 or later; Robert Pfeiffer, *Introduction to the Old Testament* (London: Adam & Charles Black, 1952), 811–12: ca. 250. See the surveys in Thomas Willi, "Zwei Jahrzehnte Forschung an Chronik und Esra-Nehemia," *Theologische Rundschau* 67 (2002): 61–104; Isaac Kalimi, "The Date of the Book of Chronicles," in *God's Word for Our World: Theological and Cultural Studies in Honor of Simon John de Vries*, Vol. 1, ed. by Deborah Ellens et al. (London & New York: T. & T. Clark, 2004), 347–72.

toriographical work written at that time and in that place. The events in question begin with Artaxerxes III's initially unsuccessful attempts to reconquer Egypt, which helped to instigate revolt in the Phoenician cities supported by Nectanebo and opposed by the satrap of the Transeuphratene satrapy.[3] Artaxerxes finally brought Egypt back into the Persian empire, if only for little more than a decade (344/343). The Macedonian conquest involved further "disasters of war", with Parmenides advancing through Syria and Alexander moving down the coast to Egypt. The trail of death and destruction he left in his wake was certainly not confined to Tyre and Gaza which resisted him. Jerusalem must have yielded about this time, though its submission would not have involved Alexander visiting Jerusalem and consulting with the high priest Jaddua.[4] Samaria revolted while Alexander was in Egypt, resulting in its destruction and resettlement as a Macedonian military colony, events which have been confirmed by the finds from the Wadi Daliyeh in the Jordan Valley.[5] Other items of information, about the deportation of Jews to Hyrcania near the Caspian Sea and the destruction of Jericho, derive from late ecclesiastical authors and, while not implausible, lack independent confirmation.[6]

The situation would not have improved during the protracted power struggle among the diadochoi following on Alexander's death in 323. Ptolemy Soter finally annexed Palestine to his Egyptian empire, but only after three unsuccessful attempts spread over two decades (320–301), certainly not without a great deal of murder, mayhem, and wholesale destruction. Diodorus, for example, records how Ptolemy adopted a scorched-earth policy on retreating after his second invasion (*Diod.* 19:93. 3–7). The author of 1 Maccabees tells us that Alexand-

---

[3] On the account of the Tennes rebellion in Diod. 16:40–45 see Pierre Briant, *Histoire de l'Empire Perse de Cyrus à Alexandre*, Vol. 1 (Paris: Libraire Arthème Fayard, 1996), 1;701–4 = *From Cyrus to Alexander: A History of the Persian Empire*, Transl. Peter Daniels (Winona Lake/Indiana: Eisenbrauns, 2002), 68–85; Lester Grabbe, *Judaism from Cyrus to Hadrian*, Vol.1, *The Persian and Greek Periods* (Minneapolis: Fortress, 1992), 99–100, with a critical discussion of Dan Barag, "The Effects of the Tennes Rebellion on Palestine," *BASOR* 183 (1966): 6–12.

[4] The incident is thoroughly discussed in James VanderKam, *From Joshua to Caiphas: High Priests after the Exile* (Minneapolis: Fortress, 2004), 64–72 Older discussions in Viktor Tcherikover, *Hellenistic Civilization and the Jews* (New York: Atheneum, 1975), 42–47 and Robert Marcus, *Josephus: Jewish Antiquities Books IX–XI* (Cambridge/Mass: Harvard, 1937), 512–32.

[5] Documentation in Hanan Eshel, "The Governors of Samaria in the Fifth and Fourth Centuries BCE," in *Judah and the Judeans in the Fourthy Century BCE*, ed. Oded Lipschits, Gary Neil Knoppers and Rainer Albertz (Winona Lake/Indiana: Eisenbrauns, 2007), 223–24.

[6] For references to Eusebius, Jerome, Syncellus and Orosius see Emil Schürer, *The History of Jewish Palestine in the Age of Jesus Christ: A New English Edition*, Vol. 2, revised and ed. by Geza Vermes et al. (Edinburgh: T. & T. Clark, 1986), 6 and n.12.

er's successors "caused many evils on the earth" (1 Macc 1:9). Josephus adds that the cities of Syria, which included Palestine, lost much of their population during these prolonged wars, and suffered the reverse of what was indicated by Ptolemy's assumed title *Sōtēr* (*Ant.* 12:3). He goes on to record how, when finally successful, Ptolemy captured Jerusalem by guile by launching his attack on the sabbath. He then ruled his Jewish subjects harshly and deported many to Egypt (*Ant.* 12:3–7,138).[7]

As some commentators have suggested, aspects of the ruinous situation of those decades may be reflected in biblical texts datable to that time or shortly afterwards. Some commentators have been tempted to identify the unnamed "city of chaos" in Isaiah 24–27 with Samaria destroyed by Parmenides.[8] Others have connected the comminations against Tyre and Gaza in Zech 9:1–8 with the siege and capture of those cities by Alexander after the battle of Issus. Others again have viewed the denunciation of trade in Jewish slaves between the Phoenician cities and the Greeks in Joel 4:1–3,6 as fitting that period better than any other. An anonymous prophetic saying, probably more or less contemporary with Chronicles, speaks more directly:

> I will arouse your sons, O Zion,
> against your sons, you Greeks,
> and make you into a warrior's sword! (Zech 9:13)[9]

---

[7] Josephus took this information from the second century BC historian Agatharchides of Cnidus, but in *Against Apion* 1:186–189 he transmits from Hecataeus a more benign version of Ptolemy whose *philanthrōpia* led many Jews, including a leading priest named Ezechias, to accompany him to Egypt. On these traditions see Tcherikover, *Hellenistic Civilization and the Jews*, 55–57 and, for the text of Hecataeus Menahem Stern, *Greek and Latin Authors on Jews and Judaism*, Vol. 1, *From Herodotus to Plutarch* (Jerusalem: Israel Academy of Sciences, 1976), 35–38.

[8] Isa 24:10; 25:2; 26:5; 27:10. The identification is admittedly speculative, but no more so than Bernhard Duhm's proposal to refer these allusions to the destruction of Samaria by Hyrcanus in 107 BC, surely too late; see Bernhard Duhm, *Das Buch Jesaja* (4th ed., Göttingen: Vandenhoeck & Ruprecht, 1922), 179, and the account of the event in Josephus, *Ant.* 13:280. For the range of opinion on the date of this section and the identity of the "City of Chaos" see my *Isaiah 1–39: A New Translation with Introduction and Commentary* (New York: Doubleday, 2000), 347–48.

[9] A nationalistic reaction to Ptolemy I's seizure of power has been read into a recently discovered coin horde with what may be the head of Ptolemy I on one side and *yhdh* (Yehudah/Judah) in Paleo-Hebrew letters on the other. See Martin Hengel, *Jews, Greeks and Barbarians: Aspects of the Hellenization of Judaism in the Pre-Christian Period.* (Philadelphia: Fortress Press, 1980), 18, 144 n.28, and for the coinage in general Lester Grabbe, *Judaism from Cyrus to Herod*, Vol. 1, *The Persian and Greek Periods* (Minneapolis: Fortress Press, 1992), 70–72.

2 Holy war, holy warriors

To repeat, we have no information bearing *directly* on the impact of these events on life in the province of Judah. With regard to Chronicles, however, it might be worth while to explore the possibility that the experience of being helpless witnesses and victims of the incessant warfare going on at the time may have had some influence on one of the most salient features of the author's presentation of the past, the overwhelming military power at the disposal of Judean monarchs beginning with David. In Chronicles the people constitute a community both liturgical and military, organized in units of 1000 and 100. David had at his disposal an army of 1,570,000 not counting Levi and Benjamin who were exempt from the draft (1 Chr 21:5–6). There was a perhaps additional force of 24,000 on standby for each month of the year (1 Chr 27:1–15). The good king Jehoshaphat had an army of 1,160,000 not counting garrisons throughout the country (2 Chr 17:13–19; 20:1–23). We note how numbers are calibrated to the moral standing of the ruler in question. Rehoboam, a religiously ambiguous figure, can assemble only 180,000 against an invasion from the north (2 Chr 11:1). By the time of Asa, one of the good kings, Judah and Benjamin can muster only 580,000 against an Ethiopian army a million strong (2 Chr 14:8), which however turned out to be more than adequate. I suggest that these and other examples of the author's numerological exuberance should not be understood as an egregious display of naiveté. In adopting the practice of exaggerating numbers common in ancient historiography (e.g. Herodotus' estimate of Xerxes' army at 1,700,000; *Her.* 7:60), and pushing it to the limits, the author is signaling that his intention is not at all to write history as a simple record of the past. His purpose is rather to use the genre of historiography, re-editing his sources so as to exhibit a utopian situation existing in its pure state during the reigns of David and Solomon and residually thereafter. This is a durational rather than topographical utopia, in the sense in which Karl Mannheim understood utopia as a reaction against incongruent reality expressed in the creation of an ideal counter-reality.[10] In this instance the incongruence is the brutal reality of violence, war, violation of rights, being at the mercy of forces over which one has no control. The counter-reality is a land secured by a powerful native ruler who governs as God's viceroy and maintains the temple cult, the life and soul of the national life, in full vigor, free from violence and oppression from without and from corrupting influences from within.

---

[10] Karl Mannheim, *Ideology and Utopia*, 192–263.

It is not surprising, therefore, if some commentators have found evidence in Chronicles of the revival of the idea of holy warfare or "Yahweh's war" (cf. "The Book of Yahweh's Wars", Num 21:14). The pattern is familiar from von Rad's well-known monograph.[11] The ruler, a priest or a prophet consults the deity before action is engaged; assurance of victory is given, with an injunction to have faith and not to fear the enemy; the troops, usually vastly outnumbered by the enemy, are consecrated for battle; the blast of trumpets and the war cry inspire panic, often ending with the enemy destroying themselves; Yahweh himself, as a warrior (explicitly so described at Exod 15:3), has the decisive part in the action which concludes with the utter destruction of the enemy and the dismissal of the victorious army. It would not be difficult to put together a composite picture from Chronicles corresponding to this pattern: Abijah defeats Jeroboam by virtue of Judah's legitimate cult practice, and the *coup de grace* is delivered by the blast of the priests' trumpets on the battlefield (2 Chr 13:4–15). Asa seeks divine guidance before engaging with an Ethiopian army which outnumbers him two-to-one (2 Chr 14:11). The Levite Jahaziel gives assurance of success and tells Jehoshaphat and his men not to fear their Transjordanian foes (2 Chr 20:13–17). Yahweh does the fighting for Asa (2 Chr 14:12) and Jehoshaphat (2 Chr 20:17); the enemy, dispirited, end up destroying themselves, and not one is left alive (2 Chr 20:23–24).

All these examples of holy war episodes are taken from the time of the two kingdoms, but they are all intelligible only as dependent on the author's presentation of the "golden age", the utopian epoch, of the Davidic-Solomonic monarchy. Accounts of David's victories over neighbouring states are taken over with only minor modifications from his primary source,[12] and the booty goes to equip and embellish the future temple (1 Chr 18:8, 10–11). Military statistics for David's reign, already high in the source (2 Sam 24:9), are even higher in Chronicles (1 Chr 21:5). The Israelite *qāhāl* can assume the form of both the liturgical assembly and the military levy. The military is thoroughly "liturgized" from the outset; we might think of it as the military-liturgical complex. David consults with his military leaders even in liturgical matters (1 Chr 13:1–4), and together with them he appoints the temple musicians (1 Chr 25:1–8). One of the earliest examples of divinely-inspired speech is attributed to Amasai, commander of an elite military unit (1 Chr 12:16–19). The boundaries of the land in Chronicles

---

11 Gerhard von Rad, *Der heilige Krieg im alten Israel* (3rd ed., Zürich: Zollikon, 1958) = *Holy War in Ancient Israel*, Trans. Marva Dawn and John Howard Yoder (Grand Rapids: Eerdmans, 1991); also *Studies in Deuteronomy* (London: SCM, 1953), 45–59.
12 1 Chr 14:8–17 cf. 2 Sam 5:17–25; 1 Chr 18:1–13 cf. 2 Sam 8:1–14; 1 Chr 19:1–9 cf. 2 Sam 10:1–19.

reflect the Davidic imperial ideal, and in fact correspond rather closely to the boundaries of the Transeuphratene satrapy in the later Persian period ("From the Euphrates to the land of the Philistines and the border of Egypt", 2 Chr 9:26, cf. 1 Chr 13:5). Allusions to military equipment of different kinds may also be examples of contemporizing by the author.[13] To repeat a point made earlier: Chronicles was not written, and was not intended to be read, as a historical record comparable to the author's principle source, the so-called Deuteronomistic History. It was written to present, as counter-reality to the contemporary experience of the author and his fellow-Judeans, the ideal image of a people living under a powerful ruler who creates and maintains the conditions necessary for their life of worship centred on the temple. In this respect there is a correspondence between David at the beginning of the Chronicler's history of the nation and Cyrus at its close. Cyrus was inspired by Yahweh to prepare the way for rebuilding the temple as David had been inspired to prepare for its building in the first place (1 Chr 17:1–27; 2 Chr 36:22–23).

3 Priests and Levites

This last point brings us to the central concern in Chronicles, namely, the proper functioning of the temple cult. At the time of writing, the principal internal obstacle to achieving this ideal arose, paradoxically, from the temple priesthood. The problem is already apparent in Ezra-Nehemiah dealing, ostensibly, with the situation in Jerusalem in the mid-fifth century. Ezra's mission is described as a mandate to restore the temple cult; hence the abundant subventions, the new set of sacred vessels, and the need for priests and Levites (Ezra 7–8). In this respect, it is significant that we hear of no high priest waiting to welcome Ezra on his arrival in Jerusalem and take delivery of the gifts and vessels (Ezra 8:33–34). As governor, Nehemiah had to struggle to maintain control of the temple, its operations, and its considerable assets (Neh 13:4–9,28). In this struggle he recruited Levites whose interests had previously been neglected and who were therefore not surprisingly in short supply.[14] Tension between priests and

---

13 For example, Uzziah's equipment for sustaining a siege (2 Chr 26:9,26), on which see Francesco Bianchi and Gabriele Rossoni, "L'Armée d'Ozias (2 Ch 26,11–15) entre Fiction et Réalité: Une Esquise Philologique et Historique," *Transeuphratène* 13 (1997): 21–37. It has been suggested that the frequent allusion to shield and lance (1 Chr 12:9,25; 2 Chr 11:12; 14:7; 25:5) may have been inspired by the Greek phalanx; see, for example Martin Hengel, *Jews, Greeks and Barbarians*, 19.
14 Ezra 8:15; Neh 13:10–14. In the census list (Ezra 2:36–42 = Neh 7:39–45) priests outnumber Levites by about 12 to 1.

Levites, to which we shall return, suggest something approaching a class struggle going on among the temple personnel (Neh 12:44–47; 13:10–14,22). Priests were among the leading transgressors in the intermarriage crisis (Ezra 9:18–22; 10:5) and in the social unrest during Nehemiah's governorship (Neh 5:12). Nehemiah's accusation that the priests were defiling their office (Neh 13:29) is reminiscent of the vitriolic attack on the priesthood by the roughly contemporary prophet known as Malachi (Mal 1:6–7; 2:8).

In the period subsequent to Nehemiah's administration, the Persian governor Bagohi (Bagōsēs in Josephus) offered to secure the high priesthood for his friend Jeshua, brother of Johanan, the incumbent, no doubt on terms favourable to himself. The offer led to an altercation in the temple precincts which concluded with the murder of Jeshua by Johanan (*Ant*. 11:297–301, 304–305). The outcome was that the governor imposed a punitive tax of fifty drachmas on each lamb offered for the daily sacrifice over the next seven years (*Ant*. 11:297–301). This disedifying episode gives us some idea of the state of affairs in the operation of the temple at that time, and looks like an early stage in the politicization and commercialization of the high priesthood which reached its climax, or nadir, under Antiochus Epiphanes IV. This incident is followed in Josephus by another dispute in the high-priestly family occasioned by the marriage of Manasseh, brother of the high priest Jaddua, to the daughter of Sanballat, governor of Samaria. This one ended with the defection of Manasseh to Samaria lured by the promise of the high priesthood in a temple to be built for him on Mt Gerizim (*Ant*. 11:302–312). Leaving aside the long-standing debate about the historical character of Josephus' account and its chronological context, I note simply his observation that Manasseh's conduct was not untypical of the temple clergy at that time. Josephus states that "many priests and Levites were involved in such marriages" (*Ant*. 11:312), and adds that Manasseh's decision was not an isolated event:

> Whenever anyone was accused by the people of Jerusalem of eating unclean food or violating the Sabbath or committing any other sin, he would flee to the Shechemites, saying that he had been unjustly expelled. This, then, is the way things were with the people of Jerusalem at that time." (*Ant*. 11:346–347)

The indications are that the way things were then did not improve under Ptolemaic control, the high priesthood of Onias II, described by Josephus as "small-minded and passionately fond of money" (*Ant*. 12:158), and the ascendancy of the Tobiad Joseph and his son Hyrcanus who had close links of a pecuniary and commercial nature with the temple bureaucracy (*Ant*. 12:160–236).

The question now arises whether this less than flattering picture of the temple priesthood, or at least its more socially and economically prominent members, is reflected in any way in Chronicles. It is clear in the first place that the author venerates the institution of the priesthood established by Moses and Aaron. There is no overt and consistent polemic against priests. But it is equally clear that priests receive far less attention than Levites, especially Levitical musicians. After presenting the high-priestly line from Levi to the exiled Jehozadak (1 Chr 5:27–41 [Eng. 6:1–15] and 6:34–38 [Eng. 6:49–53]), the author goes into much more detail in providing genealogical legitimacy to the Levites down to David's reign (6:1–15 [Eng. 6:16–30]). It was David who organized the Levites and assigned them their permanent functions in the temple liturgy (1 Chr 6:16–23 [Eng. 6:31–48]; 23:6–24) so that they might "minister to Yahweh forever" (1 Chr 15:2). The Levitical function of ark-bearers was established by Moses for as long as it was necessary (1 Chr 15:15; 23:26), but it was David not Moses who assigned them a permanent place in the liturgical and civic life of the people (1 Chr 15:16–24; 16:4–36). This innovation was authorized by David, without reference to Moses, as liturgical prophet in his own right (1 Chr 25:1–3) and recipient of direct revelation with regard to the temple and cultic matters. The plan or blueprint (*tabnît*) for the future temple which David wrote at Yahweh's dictation, and which remained available as a sacred text for future generations (1 Chr 28:11–19; 2 Chr 35:4,15), put him on the same level as Moses, recipient of instructions for the wilderness sanctuary and its cult at Sinai/Horeb (Exod 24:15–18; 25:9,40).[15]

There is therefore no doubt about David's preferential option for Levites, especially Levitical liturgical singers and musicians, in Chronicles. We see it in the account of the transfer of the ark to Jerusalem in which both priests and Levites participate but only Levites are listed and addressed (1 Chr 15:14–15); and since God helped the Levites they were able, quite exceptionally, to offer sacrifices (15:25–29). Likewise, in preparing to designate Solomon as his successor David assembled lay leaders, priests and Levites, but addressed his words only to Levites, 38,000 of them (1 Chr 23:2–5).[16] Concern for Levitical legitimacy

---

[15] On this extraordinary claim see the remarks of Simon J. De Vries, "Moses and David as Cult Founders in Chronicles," *JBL* 107 (1988): 619–39. De Vries argues convincingly that the legitimation of Levites vis-à-vis the priests and in opposition to the condemnation of Levites in Ezek 44:10–31 (also part of a visionary revelation) was one of the principal concerns of the Chronicler.

[16] Contrast with this very high number the disparity in numbers between priests and Levites in Ezra-Nehemiah: in the census list 4289 priests and 341 (in the Nehemiah version 360) Levites, musicians and gatekeepers (Ezra 2:36–42; Neh 7:39–45). Ezra managed to recruit thirty-eight

together with a certain lack of enthusiasm for priests comes to even clearer expression in the author's account of Hezekiah's reign (2 Chr 29–32). Hezekiah, presented as a second David, reopened the temple and restored the cult to its pristine (that is, Davidic) condition after the apostasy of Ahaz, his predecessor. The initial event of the reign was a plenary assembly of priests and Levites in front of the temple at which, however, like David, Hezekiah addressed only the Levites (2 Chr 29:4–11). After self-purification, they were to cleanse the temple of pollution (*niddâ*) following on the desecration to which it had been subjected in the previous reign, certainly not without the acquiescence of the temple priesthood (2 Chr 29:3–11, cf. 28:22–25). The Levites carried out this assignment (29:12–19), the priests participating only to the extent of removing pollution from the inner sanctum which only priests were permitted to enter (29:16). Since it was found that many priests were ritually unclean and therefore unfit to take part in sacrificial ritual, Levites were called on to make up for their absence since they had been more conscientious in remaining in a state of ritual cleanness (29:34). The same substitution was called for in the great Passover which followed, following the rubrics for the delayed celebration set out in Num 9:9–13 (2 Chr 30:1–27); and for this the Levites received a special commendation from Hezekiah (30:22). This cultic restoration was legitimated and carried out on the prophetic authority of David himself and of Gad, Nathan and Asaph, his charismatic cabinet (2 Chr 29:25–30). The same point is made even more explicitly in the account of the reign of Josiah during which Levites were to follow the *written* instructions of David and Solomon (2 Chr 35:4), and Asaphite Levites were to perform their duties according to the prescriptions of David and the inspired founders of the guilds of liturgical musicians (2 Chr 35:15). We may suppose that these instructions were also available in written form.

4 The Chronicler's Emancipation from Tradition

If, then, we go on to ask on what basis the author legitimated his views about the role of Levites vis-à-vis priests and about the temple cult in general, we should begin by emphasizing the importance attributed throughout the work to authoritative written texts. This is obviously the case with the detailed genealogical lists

---

Levites from Casiphia after discovering there were none in his immigrant group (Ezra 8:15–20), and during Nehemiah's administration Levites had to abandon the temple due to lack of material support (Neh 13:10).

which so exasperated Wellhausen.[17] In compiling his lists of names, the author takes the occasion to remind the reader that the kinship units kept written genealogical records,[18] that these records are ancient (*haddĕbārîm 'attîqîm*, 1 Chr 4:22), and that they have been preserved for posterity in "The Book of the Kings of Israel" (1 Chr 9:1). From that point on, the history of Judah is covered by a text or texts variously described as "The Book of the Kings of Judah and Israel" (2 Chr 16:11; 25:26; 28:26), "The Book of the Kings of Israel and Judah" (2 Chr 27:7; 35:27; 36:8), "The Book of the Kings of Israel" (2 Chr 20:34; 33:18), and "The Commentary (*midraš*) on the Book of Kings" (2 Chr 24:27).[19] More authoritative, since inspired, are texts attributed to prophetic individuals. David's reign is covered by the records (*dĕbārîm*) of Samuel the seer, Nathan the prophet and Gad the visionary (1 Chr 29:29); that of Solomon by Ahijah the Shilonite prophet and Iddo the visionary in addition to Nathan (2 Chr 9:29). Other prophetic writings serve to document the reigns of later Judaean rulers, including those of Shemaiah (2 Chr 12:15), Iddo (12:15; 13:22), Jehu ben Hanani (20:34), and Isaiah ben Amoz (2 Chr 26:22; 32:32), but a very different Isaiah from the prophet of the canonical book.[20]

In asking and trying to answer the question about the authoritative sources for the Chronicler's work, what emerges as its most remarkable and perhaps least acknowledged feature is its emancipation from tradition.[21] The first and most obvious example is the author's radical rewriting of his principal source, especially the long section dealing with the David story, the ideal, utopian period. Everything even remotely detrimental to David's reputation is omitted, including his

---

17 See, for example, his remarks on 1 Chronicles 22–29 in Julius Wellhausen, *Prolegomena to the History of Ancient Israel*, Transl. William Robertson Smith (New York: Meridian Library, 1957), 181, and his rhetorical question on p. 361: "What sort of creative power is that which brings forth nothing but numbers and names?"
18 1 Chr 4:33,41; 5:1,7,17; 7:5,7,9,40.
19 The identity of this "Midrash of/on the Book of Kings" is uncertain, and rendered more so by the only other occurrence of the term with reference to a prophetic text, "the Midrash of the prophet Iddo" (2 Chr 13:22). Whether *midraš* as used in 2 Chr 24:27 is simply an alternative allusion to the author's one and only source, as Hugh Williamson, *1 and 2 Chronicles* (London: Marshall, Morgan & Scott, 1982), 18, 326, or to a source relating events in greater detail, as Sara Japhet, *I & II Chronicles* (Louisville: Westminster John Knox Press, 1993), 854, or "a reconstructed history of Israel embellished with marvellous tales of divine interposition and prophetic activity", as Edward Curtis and Albert Madsen, *A Critical and Exegetical Commentary on the Books of Chronicles*, 23, may for the present purpose be left undecided.
20 In MT 2 Chr 33:19 Manasseh's reign is covered by the records of Hozai (*hôzāy*), but it seems advisable to read *hôzîm* with LXX or *hôzāw*, "his seers".
21 See on this aspect of the work the illuminating remarks of Elias Bickerman, *From Ezra to the Last of the Maccabees* (New York: Schocken Books, 1962 [1949]), 20–3.

struggle for survival and ascendancy against Saul and his family (1 Samuel 16 – 30) and the entire history of the court intrigues eventuating in the accession of Solomon, the so-called *Thronfolgegeschichte* ("The History of the Succession to David's Throne", 2 Samuel 11– 20 + 1 Kings 1– 2). The rewriting does not neglect detail. David could not have had concubines, his sons could not have been priests, and Yahweh could not have incited him to take a census of his kingdom, so the requisite changes were made.[22] David is now not only a prophet but the mediator of new revelations with regard to worship, revelations dictated to him by Yahweh (1 Chr 28:11– 19). These new prescriptions, preserved in writing, serve as an extension, updating and completion of that part of the Torah dealing with worship, and are accepted centuries later as authoritative and sacred texts (2 Chr 29:25; 35:4,15).[23] To that extent the David of the Chronicler is placed on a par with Moses and his prescriptions on a par with the Mosaic ritual law.

The issue of authority and legitimation raises in an acute form the author's understanding of prophecy. Here, too, we note a remarkable freedom from traditional ways of thought and expression. The author follows, in part, his principal source in overlooking the so-called classical prophets (*nĕbî'îm 'aḥărōnîm*) with the exception of Isaiah and Jeremiah. However, the Isaiah of Chronicles has a quite different profile from the Isaiah of the canonical book. There are no discourses and certainly no condemnations of temple worship (as in Isa 1:10 – 17). During the Assyrian crisis Hezekiah and Isaiah pray together (2 Chr 32:20), the king recovers without the prophet's miraculous intervention (32:24– 26), and the Babylonian embassy is mentioned in passing without the prophet's reproach and prediction of future disaster (32:31). Isaiah, finally, is transformed into the historian of the reigns of Uzziah and Hezekiah (26:22; 32:32).[24] Apart from a passing allusion to his warnings neglected by the last Judean ruler (36:12), Jeremiah is named only as the author of a lament over the dead Josiah (35:25) and the prophet who foretold a seventy-year exile (36:21– 22).[25]

---

22 Respectively 2 Sam 5:13 – 16 cf. 1 Chr 14:3 – 7; 2 Sam 8:18 cf. 1 Chr 18:17; 2 Sam 14:1 cf. 1 Chr 21:1.
23 Note also the allusion in Neh 11:23 to a *miswat hammelek* concerning Levitical liturgical musicians which very probably refers to David, cf. other references to David's dispositions for worship in Neh 12:24, 45 and 13:5.
24 On the Isaiah of Chronicles see Peter Höffken, "Der Prophet Jesaja beim Chronisten," *BN* 81 (1996): 82–90; Joseph Blenkinsopp, *Opening the Sealed Book: Interpretations of the Book of Isaiah in Late Antiquity* (Grand Rapids: Eerdmans, 2006), 43 – 45.
25 On reasons for the absence of the classical prophets from Chronicles – many of which would apply equally to the Deuteronomistic History (the so-called *Prophetenschweigen* problem) see Christopher Begg, "The Classical Prophets in the Chronistic History," *BN* 32 (1988): 100 – 7. Also characteristic of the Chronicler's attitude to his sources is his mention of Elijah's letter to Jehoram predicting plague and disease (2 Chr 21:12 – 15).

Apart from and beyond this omission, which takes over and takes further a feature of the author's principal source, Chronicles exhibits throughout a greatly expanded semantic range for the standard terminology for prophetic mediation (*nābî', rō'eh, hōzeh, 'îš hā'ĕlōhîm*). Divine inspiration can come upon a priest (2 Chr 24:20–22), a Levite (2 Chr 20:14–17), a commander of an elite military unit (1 Chr 12:16–18), or even rank outsiders like Pharaoh Neco (2 Chr 35:20–24) and Cyrus (2 Chr 36:21–22). The range of prophetic activity can take in the writing of historical records, an expansion of the prophetic function which helps to explain the designation of the canonical histories as "Former Prophets" and will prove to be useful to Josephus in promoting his own writings.[26] But the most interesting and, for the author, clearly the most significant of these transformations is the redefinition of the composition and rendition of liturgical music as a prophetic activity. We can only speculate as to how the author arrived at this conclusion. It is in keeping with an ancient tradition which links poet and prophet under the rubric of inspiration of divine origin. More specifically, it must have drawn on traditions about David as inspired musician (1 Sam 16:18–23; 18:10–11; 19:8–10),[27] a tradition which would persevere into the Roman period and beyond and be reflected in the *lĕdāwid* of several psalm titles.[28] It was through their association with *this* David that the eponyms of the Levitical guilds of liturgical music, Asaph, Jeduthin and Heman, and by implication their successors, claimed, as liturgical poets (*mĕšōrĕrîm*) and trained singers (*mĕlummĕdê-šîr*), to be engaged in inspired prophetic activity (1 Chr 25:1–8).[29] One of the guild leaders, Chenaniah, is referred to as *śar halĕwiyyîm bĕmaśśā'* (1 Chr 15:22) or more simply *haśśar hammaśśā'* (15:27), usually translated "leader of the music" (NRSV), or "in charge of the song" (JPS), or "precentor" (REB) or something similar. Sigmund Mowinckel, however, translated it "master of the oracle", and indeed usage fa-

---

26 "With us (Jews) it is not open to everybody to write the records seeing that, on the contrary, the prophets alone had this privilege, obtaining their knowledge of the most remote and ancient history through the inspiration which they owed to God" (Josephus: *C. Ap.* 1:37). On Josephus as historian see Joseph Blenkinsopp, "Prophecy and Priesthood in Josephus," *JJS* 25 (1974): 239–62.
27 The last words of David, in verse, are introduced as a *nĕ'um*, as oracular therefore, and the poem begins with the statement that "Yahweh's spirit speaks through me" (2 Sam 23:1–7).
28 According to 11QPs[a] David composed 4,050 hymns by virtue of his *nĕbû'â*; see James Sanders, *Discoveries in the Judaean Desert of Jordan*, Vol. 4,. *The Psalms Scroll of Qumran Cave 11* (Oxford: Oxford University Press, 1965), 137–39. As composer of psalms, David was considered a prophetic figure in early Christianity (Acts 1:16; 2:25,31,34).
29 In his account of the Josian religious reform (2 Chr 34:30), the author has followed his source (2 Kgs 23:1–2) but has substituted "Levites" for "prophets", no doubt with reference to the prophetic gift of the Levitical singers and instrumentalists responsible for the temple liturgies.

vors the meaning "oracle" rather than "song" or "music" for *maśśā'*.³⁰ We can at any rate accept that it was among the Levitical guilds of liturgical musicians during the period of the Second Temple that this idea of a prophetic ministry of liturgical song originated and matured.³¹

5 The author and his circle

A final note. The remarkable prominence given throughout the work to Levitical temple musicians makes it difficult to resist the conclusion that the author belonged to their ranks and wrote in order to further their interests. The service of song in the temple did not rule out the acquisition of other skills and the performance of other functions. Membership in one or other of the Levitical guilds involved intellectual formation and the acquisition of scribal skills.³² We hear of a Levitical scribe compiling a list of priests (1 Chr 24:6), Levites were involved in intensive educational and judicial activities during the reign of Jehoshaphat (2

---

30 Sigmund Mowinckel, *The Psalms in Israel's Worship*, Vol. 2 (New York & Nashville: Abingdon, 1967), 56. Leaving aside the meaning "burden", "load", *maśśā'* occurs predominantly in prophetic contexts, not all by any means in verse.

31 On prophecy in Chronicles see Thomas Willi, *Die Chronik als Auslegung* (Göttingen: Vandenhoeck & Ruprecht, 1972), 216–41; David Petersen, *Late Israelite Prophecy: Studies in Deutero-Prophetic Literature and in Chronicles* (Missoula/Montana: Scholars Press, 1977), 55–96; Rosemarie Micheel, *Die Seher- und Propheten-Überlieferungen in der Chronik* (Frankfurt: Lang, 1983); Yairah Amit, "The Role of Prophecy and the Prophets in the Teaching of Chronicles," *BM* 28 (1982/1983): 113–33; William Bellinger Jr., *Psalmody and Prophecy* (Sheffield: JSOT, 1984); Simon de Vries, "The Forms of Prophetic Address in Chronicles," *HAR* 10 (1986): 15–36; Jürgen Kegler, "Prophetengestalten im Deuteronomistischen Geschichtswerk und in den Chronikbüchern: Ein Beitrag zur Kompositions- und Redaktionsgeschichte der Chronikbücher," *ZAW* 105 (1993): 481–97; William Schniedewind, *The Word of God in Transition: From Prophet to Exegete in the Second Temple Period* (Sheffield: Sheffield Academic Press, 1995), 163–208; Joseph Blenkinsopp, *A History of Prophecy in Israel* (2ⁿᵈ ed., Louisville: Westminster John Knox Press, 1996), 222–26; Ralph Klein, "Prophets and Prophecy in the Books of Chronicles," *TBT* 36 (1998): 227–32.

32 We are unfortunately not well informed on guild structure in Second Temple Judah. 1 Chr 2:55 refers to "the families of scribes dwelling at Jabez" where *mišpĕhôt* refers to guilds; on which see Samuel Klein, "Die Schreiberfamilien: 1 Chr 2:55," *Monatschrift für Geschichte und Wissenschaft des Judentums* 70 (1926): 410–16; Isaac Mendelsohn, "Guilds in Ancient Palestine," *BASOR* 80 (1940): 17–21. In Babylonia the scribal office was generally hereditary, and scribes took pride in preserving their family trees, and the indications are that in these respects Judaean Levitical scribalism was no different. On Babylonian guilds see Isaac Mendelsohn, "Guilds in Babylonia and Assyria," *JAOS* 60 (1940): 68–72; Adam Falkenstein, "Die babylonische Schule," *Saeculum* 4 (1953): 125–37; David Weisberg, *Guild Structure and Political Allegiance in Early Achaemenid Mesopotamia* (New Haven: Yale University Press, 1967).

Chr 17:7–9; 19:4–11), Levitical scribes were active also during Josiah's reign when, we are told, "they taught all Israel" (2 Chr 34:13; 35:3), and we hear of Levitical musicians multitasking as overseers (2 Chr 34:12–13). Irrespective of specialization, all Levites were expected to demonstrate a high level of skill both practical and intellectual; to be, in other words, *mēbîn* and *maśkîl*, a description which we may suppose would fit the author of 1–2 Chronicles.[33]

The importance of the authoritative claims made in 1–2 Chronicles on behalf of the Levitical guilds can be gauged by viewing them in the longer *durée* context of Second Temple history. The liturgical, educational and scribal roles of these Levites, taken together with the decline in prestige of the temple priesthood, detectable already in Chronicles, led to what Elias Bickerman referred to as the democratization of instruction in the law, previously the exclusive province of the priesthood (Jer 18:18; Ezek 7:26; Mal 2:7, etc).[34] In that respect, Chronicles stands at the beginning of a process which would confer on Judaism its character as a lay religion which it has maintained to the present.

---

[33] Chenaniah, a precentor, referred to earlier, is described as *mēbîn* (1 Chr 15:22), and the same epithet is used of this category in general in 1 Chr 25:7.

[34] "The democratization of the instruction in the law in the fourth century opened the way to the coming of the scribe, and imperceptibly compromised the supremacy of the priest", Elias Bickerman, *From Ezra to the Last of the Maccabees*, 17–18. See related comments in Joseph Blenkinsopp, "Sage, Scribe, and Scribalism in the Chronicler's Work," in *The Sage in Israel and the Ancient Near East*, ed. John Gammie and Leo Perdue (Winona Lake, Indiana: Eisenbrauns, 1990), 307–15.

XI. The social context of the "Outsider Woman" in Proverbs 1–9

Source: *Biblica* 72 (1991): 457–73.

1 The Date and Setting of Proverbs 1–9

The Book of Proverbs is a manual of didactic material containing nine compilations: two collections of aphorisms attributed to Solomon venerated as the paradigm and paragon of wisdom (1:10–22:16; 25:1–29:27); a collection of thirty sayings modelled on the Egyptian *Wisdom of Amen-em-ope* (22:17–24:22) to which an appendix has been attached under the title "Sayings of the Sages" (24:23–34); a series of numerical or counting proverbs, especially in the familiar two-three, three-four series (30:10–33); the sayings of Agur ben Jakeh, a sceptic in the manner of Qoheleth (30:1–9), and a rather platitudinous admonition addressed to a king called Lemuel, otherwise unknown, by the Queen Mother warning against the dangers of women and wine (31:1–9). This miscellaneous assemblage is rounded off with an acrostic poem on "the excellent woman," or "the woman of substance," or "the capable wife," depending on how one translates the Hebrew *'ēšet hayil* (31:10–31). This poem corresponds to wisdom (*hokmâ*) personified as a wise, learned and desirable woman, shadowed by the *'iššâ zārâ* or *hannokriyyâ*, the "Outsider Woman" (1–9), in the first and introductory section of the book (chapters 1–9), thus rounding off the work. We will be concerned in what follows primarily with this counter-image of *Hokmâ, Sophia*) to whom I have assigned the name "the Outsider Woman" which in due time will call for clarification and disambiguation.

It is agreed that these first nine chapters were composed some time in the Second Temple period as an introduction to the compilation as a whole, but unfortunately the text itself offers little help in coming up with a more precise date of composition. An early commentator, C. H. Toy, proposed a date in the mid-third century BC with some sections (6:1–19 and 9:7–12) even later.[1] One of the more recent commentators favours a date in the early Hellenistic period, though he agrees that an earlier date, in the mid to late Achaemenid period,

---

[1] Crawford Howell Toy, *A Critical and Exegetical Commentary on the Book of Proverbs* (Edinburgh: T. & T. Clark), xxx.

is possible.² Much depends on the identification and characterization of this antithesis to personified wisdom. The cosmopolitan background to these chapters, and to the book as a whole, cannot be urged in favor of a date in the Hellenistic period since Hellenistic influences were at work in Judah before the Macedonian conquest.³ Moreover, there are no clear indications in the book of Greek philosophy, leaving aside the possibility that the more philosophically sounding passages, such as the self-praise of Wisdom in 8:22–31, reminiscent of Sir 24:1–22 and the Isis aretalogies, may have been inserted subsequently. Additions were in any case almost certainly made to the core composition.

The case for the earlier date is reinforced by some interesting linguistic and thematic parallels with prophetic texts by most scholars assigned to the Achaemenid period. In the first place, there is wide agreement that where the Woman Wisdom speaks she does so in the guise of a prophetic figure, and her admonitions make use of prophetic types of discourse (1:20–33; 8:1–21).⁴ A close parallel can be drawn with respect to the invitation-response pattern in the first discourse in which Wisdom's offer falls on deaf ears:

> Because I called and you refused (to listen),
> stretched out my hand and no one took heed ... (Prov 1:24)

or

> Then they will call on me and I will not answer,
> they will seek me but will not find me (Prov 1:28)

This reaction of Wisdom can be compared with the following passages from the third segment of the book of Isaiah:

> Then when you call, Yahweh will answer;
> When you cry out, he will say, 'Here I am' (Isa 58:9)

---

2 Michael Fox, *Proverbs 1–9: A New Translation with Introduction and Commentary* (New York: Doubleday, 2000), 48–49.
3 Morton Smith, *Palestinian Parties and Politics that Shaped the Old Testament* (New York: Columbia University Press, 1971), 57–71. Even if *sôfiyyâ* , Prov 31:27, was intended to suggest *sophia*, wisdom, by assonance, as proposed by Al Wolters and accepted by others, this would not oblige us to date the final redaction of the book in the Hellenistic period. See Al Wolters, "*Sopiyyâ* [Prov 31:27] as Hymnic Participle and Play on Sophia," *JBL* 104 (1985): 577–87.
4 See, for example, Norman Whybray, *Wisdom in Proverbs* (London: SCM, 1965), 77. William McKane, *Proverbs: A New Approach* (Philadelphia: Westminster, 1970), 273, 276, prefers the analogy of a wise teacher, though the analogy does not make an easy fit with preaching in the streets, squares and crossroads (1:20–21).

> I was ready to be sought out, but they did not ask for me,
> I was ready to be found, but they did not seek me;
> I said, 'Here I am, here I am'
> to a nation that did not invoke my name.
> All day long I spread out my hands
> to a stubborn, rebellious people. (Isa 65:1–2a)
>
> When I called no one answered,
> I spoke, but no one listened;
> they did what was evil in my sight,
> choosing what was displeasing to me. (Isa 66:4)

A variation on the same pattern occurs in the invitation which Wisdom extends to the immature youths to participate in a banquet (Prov 9:1–6), recalling the invitation to eat and drink gratis at the conclusion of the second segment of Isaiah (55:1–2). An even closer, though contrasting, parallel is the image of the spread table and mixed wine prepared for the deities of good luck, Gad and Meni, in Isa 65:11, possibly a cultic meal of the *marzeah* type.

Similar echoes can be heard in the description of the gang of renegades in Prov 1:10–19, with its emphasis on civil disorder, violence and oppression. While the situation as described here is not confined to one place or one time, it tends to recur in prophetic texts generally assigned to the Achaemenid period (Isa 58:3–4; 59:1–15; Zech 8:10). The social and economic inequalities of Judaean society in the mid-fifth century, including profiteering (*besa'*, Isa 56:11b; Prov 1:19), called for drastic action during Nehemiah's governorship (Neh 5). The complaint that the feet of the renegades run to commit evil in Isa 59:7a is even reproduced verbatim in Prov 1:16.[5] Here, too, it seems much more likely that a discursive and didactic text like Proverbs 1–9 is drawing on prophetic material than the contrary. A final example is the description of the "Outsider Woman" forsaking "the partner of her youth" (*'allûp nĕ'ûrêhāh*) and forgetting the covenant of her God (*bĕrît 'ĕlohêhāh*, Prov 2:17), reminiscent of Malachi's indictment of the individual, perhaps a priest, who had "married the daughter of a foreign god," in the process forsaking the wife of his youth (*'ēšet nĕ'ûrêkā*) who is his covenanted wife (*'ēšet bĕrîtekā*, Mal 2:11,14–15; cf. Isa 54:6, *'ēšet nĕ'ûrîm*). Similar *attaches littéraires* will be noted as we proceed.[6]

---

[5] That Prov 1:16 is absent from the Old Greek version does not justify eliding it as a later insertion, simply on the grounds of it reproducing the Isaianic text. See Michael Fox, *Proverbs 1–9*, 88.
[6] Many of these are assembled by André Robert, "Les Attaches Littéraires Bibliques de Prov I–IX," *RB* 43 (1934): 42–68, 172–204, 374–84; *RB* 44 (1935): 344–65, 502–25.

This kind of didactic writing is far removed from the sphere of cult and ritual inhabited by temple personnel. It belongs to the world of the secular rather than the sacred, yet it is by no means detached from religious beliefs and traditions; witness the frequent appeal to "the fear of Yahweh" (1:29; 2:5; 8:13; 9:10) and to Yahweh as the source of wisdom (2:5–8). While elements of folk wisdom, at home in the ethos of clan and household, have been worked up and polished for inclusion in the collections of aphorisms elsewhere in the book, the intellectualist and urban matrix of these nine chapters is apparent throughout. The setting is the town, with its streets, open spaces and crossroads where Woman Wisdom has her pitch and finds her audience (1:20). It would make sense to think of such writing as the product of a literate and learned institutional setting of some kind, but unfortunately any conclusion reached must be based on inference in the absence of evidence. In spite of vigorous attempts to prove the existence of schools or academies of scholarship and learning in pre-Hellenistic Israel, the earliest clear indication we have of such an institution is from Jesus ben Sira who invites the under-educated to lodge in his "house of instruction" (Sir 51:23).[7] Having said this, it is safe to infer that there must have been some sort of school or academy associated with the temple for the training of cult personnel, and with the royal court for the training of government officials, judges and diplomats. The discourses or lectures in Proverbs 1–9 could have emanated, directly or indirectly, from such a school or academy for training young males, sons of socially and economically more prominent families, for a career in public office. The inference is eminently reasonable but, to repeat, the evidence to back it up is not forthcoming.[8]

2 Solomon, fictive author, and his problematic marriages

As the title, "Proverbs of Solomon, Son of David, King of Israel" indicates, the wisdom inculcated in Proverbs 1–9 and throughout the book (10:1; 25:1) is

---

[7] Michael Fox, *Proverbs 1–9*, 7, understands Ben Sira's *bêt midrāš* to refer metaphorically to his book, but it seems to me that an appeal to lodge in his book would be a little too *recherché* for this author.

[8] On educational institutions in Israel see Hans-Jürgen Hermisson, *Studien zur israelitischen Spruchweisheit* (Neukirchen-Vluyn: Neukirchener Verlag, 1968), 97–136; André Lemaire, *Les Écoles et la Formation de la Bible dans l'Ancien Israël* (Fribourg: Editions Universitaires, 1981); David Jamieson-Drake, *Scribes and Schools in Monarchic Judah* (Sheffield: Almond, 1991); James Crenshaw, *Education in Ancient Israel: Across the Deadening Silence* (Garden City/New York: Doubleday, 1998), 85–113. In view of the dearth of evidence, the subtitle of this last work, "Across the Deadening Silence," seems appropriate if a little too sensational.

royal wisdom, specifically the wisdom of Solomon. The narrative tradition about Solomon presents his wisdom as a quality divinely bestowed, one which conferred administrative and judicial skills, encyclopedic knowledge, and literary expertise (1 Kgs 3:5–14, 16–28; 5:9–14, 26), and of this we are reminded from time to time in these chapters (e.g. Prov 8:15–16). The same narrative tradition faults Solomon only in one respect, his addiction to foreign women (*nāšîm nokriyyôt*, 1 Kgs 11:1–8). The reproof complains that his attachment to them, whether as wives or harem women, was in violation of the law, and the outcome was that they "turned away his heart", and did so by inducing him to adopt the cults of their non-Israelite deities (1 Kgs 11:9–13). It is therefore not surprising that in a composition attributed to Solomon the foreign woman would present the greatest obstacle to the acquisition of wisdom, and would do so by virtue of her allegiance to non-Yahwistic cults.

An understanding of these nine chapters requires that we take seriously the author's conviction of Solomonic authorship, a tradition which he inherited and found no reason to reject. The sayings which it contains are examples of Solomon's divinely bestowed wisdom, meaning wisdom for living, encapsulated in the figure of the Woman Wisdom. The greatest obstacle to the acquisition of this wisdom is addiction to false worship, and for Solomon himself the occasion for adopting these cults, namely, idolatry, was his addiction to foreign women who "turned away his heart." This danger is therefore encapsulated in the figure of the "Outsider Woman."

In taking Solomon to task for this one aberration, the biblical historian cites what he takes to be a law forbidding intermarriage between Israelites and foreigners, the purpose of which was to avoid contaminating the cult of Yahweh by adopting alien cults. We find such a law, with the same rationale, in Deut 7:1–4, and it would be natural to assume that this is the law which the narrator had in mind. Though the wording is somewhat different, the general drift in 1 Kgs 11:2 is identical with the law in Deuteronomy, with one significant difference that the peoples supplying women to Solomon are foreigners (Egyptian, Moabite, Ammonite, Edomite, Sidonian, Hittite) while the seven nations listed in Deut 7:1 are indigenous to the land of Judah (Hittites, Girgashites, Amorites, Canaanites, Perizzites, Hivites, Jebusites). The only people common to both are the Hittites, who could presumably be considered either indigenous or foreign. Correspondingly, the reprehensible cults in question in 1 Kings 11 are those of foreign deities. Four are mentioned by name – the goddess Astarte, patroness of Sidon, Milcom and Molech of Ammon, and Chemosh of Moab (1 Kgs 11:5–8). The list is clearly intended to be illustrative rather than exhaustive.

Closer to the list of supplier nations in 1 Kings 11 is the law in Deut 23:2–9 which disqualifies certain categories from membership in the *qāhāl*, the Israelite assembly: Ammonites and Moabites in perpetuity, Edomites and Egyptians to the second generation.[9] These are the first four of the six (seven in LXX) nations in 1 Kgs 11:1. The citation of a law in 1 Kgs 11:2 forbidding marriage with women from the countries mentioned in the previous verse is therefore a paraphrase rather than a direct quote, and its purpose was to bring together (1) the general prohibition of exogamous marriage in Deut 7:1–4; (2) the law forbidden the king to accumulate women, that is, set up a harem, in Deut 17:17, a law which also speaks of the turning away of the heart; and especially (3) the disqualification law in Deut 23:2–9.[10]

The only other allusion to Solomon's foreign women – there is none in Chronicles – occurs towards the end of the Nehemiah memoir where he reports a brisk encounter with Judaeans who had married Ashdodite, Ammonite and Moabite women (Neh 13:23–27). Here, too, it seems that the reference to Ammonite and Moabite women is a later insertion.[11] The outcome was that, after roughing them up, Nehemiah imposed an oath on these men to foreswear marriage with foreign women, the prohibition to apply both to themselves and their children. But since they had already contracted such marriages, we would be led to believe that they were being coerced to divorce their wives, though we are not told this. The wording of the oath follows fairly closely that of the law in Deut 7:3:

> You shall not give your daughters to their sons in marriage, nor shall
> you take wives from among their daughters for your sons or for
> yourselves (Neh 13:25b)
>
> You shall not give your daughter to a son of theirs nor shall you take
> a daughter of theirs for your son (Deut 7:3)

---

9 A date for this law in the pre-monarchic period was proposed by Kurt Galling, "Das Gemeindegesetz in Deuteronomium 23" in *Festschrift Alfred Bertholet*, ed. by Walter Baumgartner, Otto Eissfeldt and Alfred Bertholet (Tübingen: Mohr Siebeck, 1950), 176–91, but it appears more likely that it is a Deuteronomistic attempt to control ethnic boundaries at a much later time.
10 The awkward syntax of 1 Kgs 11:1 suggests that the six nations mentioned, including all four excluded from membership in the assembly of Israel in Deut 23:2–9, has been inserted into the narrative at this point. Michael Fishbane, *Biblical Interpretation in Ancient Israel* (Oxford: Clarendon, 1985), 125–26, is therefore probably correct in postulating a post-exilic reformulation of the list of pre-Israelite nations in Deut 7:1 and elsewhere. On the different variations of the nations list see Tomoo Ishida, "The Structure and Historical Implications of the Lists of Pre-Israelite Nations," *Bib* 60 (1979): 461–90.
11 There is no conjunction before ʿammôniyyôt, the following verse (13:24) speaks only of Ashdod, and the final phrase, wĕkilĕšôn ʿam wāʿām, literally "according to the language of a people and a people") has been added to accommodate the insertion; on which see Joseph Blenkinsopp, *Ezra-Nehemiah: A Commentary* (Philadelphia: Westminster, 1988), 362.

Nehemiah goes on to supply a more specific illustration of the consequences of such marriages by citing the example of Solomon (13:26). The implication is that marriages of this kind can lead not just to the introduction of alien cults but also to the undermining of ethnic and national identity, in this instance indicated by the inability of the children to speak Hebrew – the kind of outcome familiar among immigrant communities today.

Marriage with foreign women was also an issue for Ezra, one indication of which is that reference to foreign women (*nāšîm nokriyyôt*), as in 1 Kgs 11:1, occurs seven times in the account of his campaign against exogamous marriage in Ezra 9–10. This passage probably represents a conflation of two versions of what happened. A shorter version reports the bad news brought to Ezra, his reaction, the support of "those who trembled at the word of the God of Israel," Ezra's fasting and praying, and the administration of the oath committing priests, Levites and laity to send away wives and offspring (9:1–15; 10:5). The alternative version gives a fuller account of Ezra's support group. It introduces the intervention of a certain Shecaniah together with the same *hărēdîm* "tremblers" as in the shorter version; Ezra fasts, mourns and keeps vigil in the temple – *after* the oath had been administered – a meeting is called to solve the problem, it is sent to committee, and the account ends with the list of the delinquents who were obliged to send away both wives and children (10:1–4,6,7–44). As it stands, the account opens with a report delivered to Ezra by the community leaders to the effect that the people, lay and clerical, had contracted marriage with "the peoples of the land" (*'ammê hā'ărāsôt*). The wording, taken from the blanket prohibition in Deut 7:1–4, is similar to the oath formula in Neh 13:25: "They have taken some of their womenfolk (literally "daughters") for themselves and their sons" (Ezra 9:2). The "peoples of the land" comprise Canaanites, Hittites, Perizzites, Jebusites, indigenous peoples in the standard list in Deut 7:1, but also Ammonites, Moabites, Egyptians, Edomites, the peoples excluded from the congregation in Deut 23:2–9; much the same situation, therefore, as with the women beloved by the uxorious monarch in 1 Kgs 11:1 whose women are of Moabite, Ammonite and Edomite origin, with one from Egypt. It would seem, then, that the plural "peoples of the land" was chosen deliberately to include elements both inside and outside the province of Judah, and that therefore the women to whom Ezra took such exception were outsiders with respect to the golah community (*běnê haggôlâ*), the social and religious elite of Judaeo-Babylonian origin to which Ezra himself belonged.

This last point calls for further elaboration. The marriage crisis encountered and probably instigated by Ezra is presented as a problem for this social entity, the *běnê haggôlāh*, rather than for the province as a whole. The transgression of the law takes place among its members (Ezra 9:4; 10:6), the assembly summoned to deal with the problem consists of the same members in plenary session (10:7), non-attendance carries the penalty of excommunication and forfeiture of property (10:8), and the measures decided on are carried out within the same group (10:16). On the assumption that Nehemiah followed Ezra,[12] by the time of Nehemiah's governorship (beginning 445 BC) the integration of the province had proceeded to the point where the chief danger was perceived to derive from outside influences, one example being Nehemiah's action against a member of the high priestly family who had married into the Sanballats of Samaria (Neh 13:28–29).[13] The attitude of Shecaniah, prominent among the supporters of these drastic measures, may be gauged by the fact that, as it seems, he turned in his own father Jeiel who is listed among the delinquents (Ezra 10:26). It was he, Shecaniah, who proposed that the measures to be taken should be "according to the law" and should conform to the decision of "those who tremble at the commandment of our God" (Ezra 10:3). Since, however, there is no law mandating coercive divorce from foreign women, what is implied is an interpretation of a law dictated by the legal rigorism of Ezra and his support group; and the law in question is clearly Deut 7:1–4 (not in any case a law), also referred to in Ezra's penitential prayer in the same narrative context (Ezra 9:10–12).

Before moving to the next stage of the argument, it should be added that this rejection of exogamous marriage is by no means unambiguously attested in the narrative and legal traditions of Israel. Abraham married two Arab women (Gen 16:1–6; 25:1–4). Moses married a Midianite, therefore an Arab woman (Exod 2:21–22), and was rebuked by Miriam and Aaron for a second marriage to a Cushite woman, a rebuke which was brushed aside (Num 12:1–9). David's numerous women included a Calebite, a Jezreelite, and a Geshurite, not to mention Bathsheba wife of a Hittite, and many others whose origin is not specified – all of these without negative comment.[14] The narrative traditions of Priestly origin, in general much more inclusive than Deuteronomy and related texts, are in this respect somewhat ambiguous. There is certainly a strong concern to preserve ethnic integrity, illustrated by the full integration of the *gēr* (resident alien) into the social and cultic life of the community.[15] Jacob must not marry a local woman

---

12 For a defense of this order see Joseph Blenkinsopp, *Ezra-Nehemiah*, 139–44.
13 Compare the similar story in Josephus, *Ant.* 11.302–12.
14 1 Sam 18:20–29; 25:39–42; 30:5; 2 Sam 3:3–5; 5:13; 2 Sam 11:26–27.
15 The native born (*'ezrah*) and the resident alien (*gēr*) celebrate passover (Exod 12:19,49; Num 9:14), sabbath (Lev 16:29), and other ceremonies and rituals (Lev17:8,10; 22:17–20; Num 15:29–30) and both are under obligation with respect to purity laws (Lev 17:15; 18:26; 24:22). There is one law for both native born and resident alien (Exod 12:49; Lev 24:22; Num 9:14; 15:29), and the Israelite is even told that he is to love the resident alien like himself. As Bickerman put it, an Athe-

(Gen 27:46 – 28:2,6), and one of the few paradigmatic narratives in Leviticus, the execution of the blasphemer, son of an Israelite mother and Egyptian father, appears to have been intended as a cautionary tale about the undesirable consequences of such "mixed" marriages (Lev 24:10 – 23). The Baal Peor incident, involving the Simeonite Zimri and the Midianite Cozbi (Num 25:6 – 18), was not a matter of fornication pure and simple, since it is clear that Zimri was introducing his newly-married Midianite wife to his family and the Israelite assembly when the proceedings were brought to a brutal halt by the zealous Phineas, grandson of Aaron, who slaughtered both of them in their tent. We should perhaps read this as illustrating only one attitude to the issue, at the extreme integrationist end of the spectrum of priestly opinion.[16] It is also apparent that the ideology of Ezra, Shecaniah and the *hărēdîm* did not pass uncontested during the Second Temple period. This is not the place for a thorough review of this issue, but we should at least mention the assurance addressed in Isa 56:1 – 8 to members of the Judaic community of foreign descent of their good standing, the law in Deut 23:2 – 9 notwithstanding. Later, there is Ruth the Moabitess who became the wife of Boaz the Israelite, and Achior the Ammonite who converted to Judaism, both in defiance of the same law (Judith 14:10).

3 The Identity of the "Outsider Woman"

We now need to take a closer look at the identity of the woman who is the antithesis of Wisdom in Proverbs 1 – 9 against this background. Finding an appropriate translation term for the Hebrew terms has not proved to be an easy task. Consider the following attempts: "strange, stranger" (KJV), "alien, forbidden" (JPS), "adulteress, loose" (REB, NRSV), "adulteress, wife of another" (NAB). The Hebrew terms are *'iššâ zārâ* (Prov 2:16; 7:5) or simply *zārâ* (5:3,20) and *nokriyyâ* (2:16; 5:20; 6:24; 7:5). Whether used as substantive or adjective both are negative, defining the person in question out of a normative category or group. They occur more often than not in parallelism (2:16; 5:10,20; 6:24; 7:5), though *zārâ* can have a broader range of connotation than *nokriyyâ*. It can indicate an outsider vis-à-vis a married couple (Ezek 16:12; Prov 5:17), or a kinship group (Deut 25:5; Prov 5:10), or the *zārâ* can be a foreign woman (Isa 1:7; Jer 3:13, etc) or a stranger, a person unknown (Prov 11:15; 14:10). In ritual texts the *zār* is the lay-

---

nian contemporary of Ezra would be astonished to hear that he has to love the metics: Elias Bickerman, *From Ezra to the Last of the Maccabees* (New York: Schocken Books, 1962 [1949]), 19.
16 Joseph Blenkinsopp, "The Baal Peor Episode Revisited," *Biblica* 93/1 (2012): 86 – 97.

man, the non-priest or non-Levite (Exod 30:33; Lev 22:10 – 13; Num 1:51, etc), and the *'ĕlohîm zārîm* are alien deities, deities other than Yahveh God of Israel (Deut 32:16; Ps 44:21; 81:10, etc).[17] The social status of the woman is therefore determined with reference to a particular social configuration to which society, a particular society, assigns a normative character. The most basic instantiation would be a prostitute or a married woman in search of sexual adventure outside of marriage; or, as McKane put it, "any woman outside of the conventions".[18] While the female personification is a composite of different images, the common representations of prostitute (6:26; 7:10) and unfaithful spouse are much in evidence and sometimes combined. In most of the passages dealing with the Outsider Woman she is represented as married, either explicitly (2:16 – 1; 7:19) or by implication, as in the contrast between consorting with the Outsider Woman and fidelity to one's wife (5:3 – 23), and in the warning about the same consequences which are likely to follow from sleeping with a neighbour's wife (6:29 – 35). The point is also made by presenting the Woman Wisdom as "more precious than pearls" (3:15), which seems to have been a conventional way of praising a wife's excellence (cf. 31:10). The avoidance of prostitutes and unattached women is, of course, a standard piece of advice to young males about to be launched on a career, often urged on basically prudential grounds. Take this example from ancient Mesopotamia:

> Do not marry a prostitute, whose husbands are legion,
> a temple harlot who is dedicated to a god,
> a courtesan whose favours are many.
> In your trouble she will not support you,
> in your dispute she will be a mocker.[19]

The same injunction is delivered by Ben Sirach, the Polonius of ancient Judaism, in terms no less pedestrian:

> Do not go near a loose woman, or you will fall into her snares.
> Do not dally with a singing girl, or you will be caught by her tricks.
> Do not look intently at a virgin, or you may stumble and suffer for it.
> Do not give yourself to prostitutes, or you may lose your inheritance.
> (Sir 9:2 – 6)

---

17 On these terms see Paul Humbert, "Les Adjectifs 'zar' et 'nokri' et la Femme Étrangère des Proverbes Bibliques," *Mélanges Syriens offerts à Monsieur René Dussaud* (Paris: 1939), Vol. 1, 259 – 66; Lambertus Arie Snijders, "The Meaning of *zar* in the Old Testament," *OTS* 10 (1954): 103 – 4; *TDOT* 4 (1980), 52 – 58.
18 William McKane, *Proverbs*, 286.
19 Wilfred Lambert, *Babylonian Wisdom Literature* (Oxford: Clarendon, 1960), 103.

In Proverbs 1–9, however, there is more to the *zārâ/nokriyyâ* than this kind of moralizing commonplace. In the didactic literature of the ancient Near East, especially the vast amount from Egypt, the influence of which on Israel is incontestable, the *femme fatale* is typically a foreigner, or at least an outsider with respect to the society or extended kinship group within which the recipient of the advice moves. An example may be taken from the often-quoted Egyptian *Wisdom of Ani*:

> Beware of a woman who is a stranger,
> One not known in her town;
> Don't stare at her when she goes by,
> Do not know her carnally.
> A deep water whose course is unknown,
> Such is a woman away from her husband.[20]

As for Israel, we have seen that Solomon provides the basic paradigm with respect to the unfortunate consequences of union with women who are strangers or outsiders, but the paradigm is often replicated. The ancestor Judah had nothing but trouble as a result of his marriage to a Canaanite woman (Genesis 38).[21] Then there were the Hittite wives of Esau, a source of general vexation according to the Priestly version of the Jacob saga (Gen 26:34–35; 27:46–28:1); or the Baal Peor incident, in which the Israelite Zimri was summarily despatched for marrying – not simply consorting with – a Midianite and therefore a foreign woman (Numbers 25). Often rehearsed as the "original sin" of Israel on the eve of the occupation of the land, since Peor was the last stop before entering Canaan,[22] it would have taken on new relevance with the return from Babylon and encounter with the diverse ethnic groups in and around Judah. In view of Solomonic authorship, it seems therefore necessary to go beyond the level of conventional moral admonition and emphasize the foreignness, the fascination of the unfamiliar, in the presentation of the Outsider Woman in Proverbs 1–9, a point which will become clearer as we go on to examine more closely the vivid, almost lurid, characterization of this woman and her activities.

---

20 Translation of Miriam Lichtheim, *Ancient Egyptian Literature*, Vol. 2, *The New Kingdom* (Berkeley & Los Angeles: University of California Press, 1976), 137.
21 In Gen 38:3 she is identified only as the daughter of a Canaanite named Shua, but in 1 Chr 2:3 the woman is Bathshua, perhaps not by coincidence identical with the name which the same author assigns to Bathsheba wife of Uriah the Hittite (1 Chr 3:5).
22 Num 31:16; Josh 22:17; 23:12; Judg 3:5–6; Hos 9:10; Ps 106:28–31.

4 The Outsider Woman as devotee of foreign cults

There is some precedent for this kind of descriptive prose in those prophetic passages, not among the most attractive for the sensitive modern reader, in which perceived feminine characteristics are the object of vituperation. If, however, we take seriously the attribution of Proverbs 1–9 to Solomon we will give due weight to the real concern of the historian of his reign at this point, which is that "when Solomon grew old, his women (wives) turned away his heart (to follow) after alien gods, so that his heart was not perfectly with Yahweh his god, as was the heart of David his father" (1 Kgs 11:4). This historian goes on to name the deities to whom he offered cult and built "high places," and the first named of these is a female deity, Astarte of the Phoenicians.[23] Goddess cults are well attested in Israel both before and after the exile, and were understandably of special interest to women. The Astarte worshiped by Solomon according to the Deuteronomistic historian (Dtr) was probably assimilated to the cult of other goddess figures, especially Anath, to judge by the iconography, but also Asherah. The worship of Asherah was promoted by Maacah the queen-mother during Asa's reign (1 Kgs 15:13), by the Phoenician Jezebel wife of Ahab (1 Kgs 18:19), and presumably also by Athaliah, the only Judaean queen (2 Kgs 8:18; 11:1–20). These and other literary attestations are abundantly confirmed by the relevant inscriptional and iconographic material, including important evidence from Kuntillet 'Ajrud and Khirbet el-Qôm which suggests a close association between the cult of Asherah and that of Yahveh. Proscribed by the reform party under Josiah (2 Kgs 23:4–7), the cult of this goddess persisted nevertheless after the deportations when her image was reinstated in the precincts of the temple during the last decade of its existence (Ezek 8:3,5).

Devotion to "the Queen of Heaven" appealed especially to women (Jer 44:15–19), and still had its devotees as late as the two centuries of Persian rule and, under changed forms, even later.[24] During the early years of the reign of Darius I, Zechariah (Zech 5:5–11) records a strange vision in which the prophet sees a woman – more likely a female figurine – seated in a basket who is transported

---

[23] MT 'aštōret is a dysphemism formed after the term bōšet, "a shameful object"); the real name is Astarte, a popular deity worshiped at Ugarit, in the Phoenician cities, Egypt, and Israel. See John Day, "Ashtoreth," in *ABD* 1, 491–94; Nicholas Wyatt, "Astarte," in *DDD²*, 109–14.

[24] The identity of "the Queen of Heaven", whether Asherah, Anath, Astarte-Ishtar, or a syncretic combination of one or more of these, is uncertain. There is a huge literature on the Asherah cult and other goddess cults in ancient Israel. See Nicholas Wyatt, "Asherah," in *DDD*, 99–105 and John Day, *Yahweh and the Gods and Goddesses of Canaan* (Sheffield: Sheffield Academic Press, 2000), both with extensive bibliographies.

through the air from Judah to Shinar (Babylon) by two winged females. Since she is to have a temple dedicated to her there, she is certainly a goddess. The seer's visionary interlocutor identifies the woman's name in cryptic fashion as "The Wickedness" (*hāriš'â*, 5:8), perhaps intended to suggest, by assonance, the name of the goddess *'ăšērâ* (Asherah). From that time, or a little later, date the denunciations of non-Yahvistic cults in the third and last segment of Isaiah. Two are of special interest. The first, which appears unexpectedly and out of context towards the end of Isaiah, denounces those who consecrate and purify themselves (to enter) the gardens, following the one in the middle, who partake of swine's flesh, unclean things, and rodents. Their deeds and their devices will together come to an end. (Isa 66:17)

The most intriguing aspect of this ritual is the reference to the hierophant as "the one in the middle". The Kethiv reads *'ehad*, masculine, but Qere *'ahat*, feminine, is supported by more than thirty Hebrew mss, both Qumran Isaiah scrolls, the Targum and Vulgate. LXX has a quite different translation at this point. It seems therefore legitimate to conclude that the hierophant was a female who presided over the ceremony in the sacred enclosure. The decidedly non-kosher meal was no doubt part of a sacrificial ritual, and the combination of a female leader and location in a garden suggests the presence of a sacred tree (cf. Isa 1:29), probably associated with the cult of the goddess Asherah.[25] Garden symbolism requires that a "tree of life" be situated in the centre of the garden, and the Asherah-tree is associated in the biblical texts with sacrifice, chthonic cults, and cults with an erotic content.[26]

Another passage of possible relevance in our attempt to contextualize Proverbs 1–9 is Isa 57:3–13. Not everything said about the sorceress in this text is clear, but the principal gravamen is participation in idolatrous and necromantic rites of a sexual nature. In several respects the description of the transgressive woman in Isaiah 57 runs parallel with the outsider woman in Proverbs 1–9. Both are accused of adultery and prostitution, and the sorcery practised by the one is reflected in the seductive behavior of the other. Both exploit their sexuality: the Sorceress engages in sexually explicit rituals while ritualized sexuality

---

25 Asherah was represented iconically as a tree, known as an *'ăšērâ*; see Exod 34:13; Deut 7:5; 12:3; Judg 6:25–26; 2 Kgs 18:4; 23:14–15; 2 Chr 14:2.
26 Sacrifice is associated with the Asherah-tree: Deut 16:21; Jer 17:2; 2 Chr 34:4,7; chthonic cults: 2 Kgs 16:4 = 2 Chr 28:4; an erotic element: 1 Kgs 14:23; Jer 2:20; 3:6,13. The stock phrase "under every tree in leaf" often designates a place where Asherah was worshipped (Deut 12:2; 1 Kgs 14:23; 2 Kgs 17:10; Jer 17:2). On Isa 66:17 see Joseph Blenkinsopp, "The One in the Middle," in *Reading from Right to Left: Essays on the Hebrew Bible in Honour of David Clines*, ed. Cheryl Exum and Hugh Williamson (Sheffield: Sheffield Academic Press, 2003), 63–75.

is part of the subtext of the Outsider Woman's activity, especially in Prov 7:6–27.[27] Both have their pitch on an elevated spot (Isa 57:7; Prov 9:14), and both have their own houses in which the most important piece of furniture is the bed (Isa 57:7a,8b; Prov 5:8; 7:16–17). Both sacrifice (Isa 57:6–7; Prov 7:14), and both are associated with the underworld, the shades and spirits of the dead (Isa 57:6a,9a; Prov 2:18–19; 5:5; 7:27; 9:14). Thematic affinity will help to contextualize the negative female imagery in Proverbs 1–9, and both Isaianic passages reinforce the sense that the Outsider Woman is the representative and embodied presence of a foreign deity, a goddess whose cult is addictive and at the same time destructive.

The negative characterization of the Outsider Woman is highlighted by contrast with the way the Woman Wisdom is described. Endowing this woman with a range of desirable personal traits is a natural corollary to the way in which the teacher, the Solomon of the title, speaks of his instruction as desirable, to be embraced, and so on (Prov 3:18; 4:13). The mere fact of personification is not in itself remarkable; it is one example of the kind of figurative language which the prologue leads us to expect (1:6). What rather deserves note is the deliberate strategy of juxtaposing the Woman Wisdom and the Outsider Woman as rivals for the student's attention. Both seek to influence their audience, the younger, male population, principally but not exclusively by seductive speech.[28] They both therefore go out in the public arena – the streets, suqs, the open plaza by the city gate, the acropolis – where the male population is likely to be found (1:20–21; 7:10–12; 8:1–3; 9:13–15). Both also provide entertainment, of a sharply contrasting nature, in their own houses (2:18; 5:8; 7:27; 9:1–6, 13–15). Both can be grasped and embraced (3:18; 4:8; 5:20), but while contact with one is life-enhancing, the other is death-dealing, a *femme fatale* in the literal sense. They both use much the same metaphorical language – water from your own well, stolen water – but the effect in the one case is salvific, in the other corrupting.

This being the situation, it seems much more likely that the figure of the Woman Wisdom was conceived as a counter to the Outsider Woman than the contrary. As the personification of the sage's teachings, Wisdom is the quality which opposes aberrant moral conduct which, for the author, stems ultimately from aberrant religious conduct, in a word, idolatry, which came to be known in Judaism as *'ăvôdâ zārāh*, alien or foreign worship. Furthermore, the connection between the allure of foreign deities and sexual seduction was well estab-

---

[27] On the sexual element in the description of the Sorceress, and the considerable amount of sexual *double entendre* in the passage see Joseph Blenkinsopp, *Isaiah 56–66: A New Translation with Introduction and Commentary* (New York: Doubleday, 2003), 162–66.
[28] Jean-Noel Aletti, "Seduction et Parole en Proverbes I–IX," *VT* 27 (1977): 129–44.

lished by the time of writing – witness the recurring metaphor "whoring after (foreign) gods" and the failure to identify an Israelite or Canaanite goddess of wisdom.[29] The Woman Wisdom is therefore in all essentials a reverse mirror image of the Outsider Woman.

The process by which the contrast is set up may be detected in Prov 7:4–5 where the pupil is invited to call Wisdom his sister (i.e. spouse) and Insight his intimate acquaintance, we might say his significant other; and he is to do this in order to insulate himself against the seduction of the Outsider Woman. But the clearest indication is Wisdom's invitation to a banquet in her house with seven columns, an invitation which has been closely modeled on that of the seductress which follows (9:13–18).[30] It has been pointed out that the young women sent out by Wisdom to issue the invitation are a pale reflection of the devotees of the goddess of love, except that, as McKane put it, "they invite young men not to bed but to school".[31] We may therefore conclude that the personification of Wisdom is a secondary elaboration, a reaction and response to the Outsider Woman, in the context of the endogamy-exogamy issue in Judah of the early Achaemenid period.

5 The social and economic consequences of marrying outside the group

Solomonic authorship makes the point that the Outsider Woman represents and embodies the danger that marriage or liaison with a woman outside the group – in the Second Temple context either the Israelite covenant or the dominant *gôlāh* assembly, the *běnê haggôlāh*, – can have the most serious consequences. Among the more immediate of these for the individual member could be expulsion from the group, loss of status, and even confiscation of property. The implications of succumbing to the wiles of the Outsider Woman are stated at some length in Prov 5:7–14. The sage begins with yet another admonition:

> Keep your way far from her,
> do not approach the entrance to her house (5:7)

---

29 See William Foxwell Albright, "The Goddess of Life and Wisdom," *AJSL* 36 (1919/20): 258–94; Richard Clifford, "Proverbs IX: A Suggested Ugaritic Parallel," *VT* 25 (1975): 298–306; Bernhard Lang, *Wisdom and the Book of Proverbs: An Israelite Goddess Redefined* (New York: Pilgrim, 1986).
30 The section Prov 9:7–12, or at least 9:7–10 + 12, is undoubtedly a later addition; see Michael Fox, *Proverbs 1–9*, 306–9, 317–18.
31 William McKane, *Proverbs*, 360.

Without having recourse to the house-body symbolic equivalence in psychoanalytic theory, we can detect a *double entendre* in this couplet, an exhortation to avoid sexual intercourse with the woman.[32] He goes on to predict that failure to follow this advice will result in loss of honour or status, surrendering one's wealth to outsiders (*zārîm*), and the fruits of one's labours to a foreign household. The net result will be that the young male addressed ends up in all kinds of trouble.

This admonition could be interpreted as a recital, exaggerated in keeping with the genre of moralising exhortation, of the sad effects of sexual indiscretions in general, but the specificity of the language used and the severity of the outcome justify a more specific explanation. At this point we recall that non-attendance at the plenary session of the golah assembly, the *qĕhal haggôlāh* convoked by Ezra to solve the problem of exogamous marriage, carried the penalty of expulsion from that body, and those who failed to attend were also threatened with confiscation of their property (Ezra 10:8). However this penalty is interpreted, it is difficult to see how any one expelled from this body, therefore deprived of civil status and excluded from the temple cult, could maintain property rights over inherited land holdings. According to Ezek 11:14–15, those left behind after the first deportation claimed possession of the land, and therefore of properties vacated by the deportees, on the grounds that the latter had been expelled from the Jerusalem cult community. This self-interested claim implied that social status and title to property depended in some way on one's good standing in the Judaean cult community. According to the sage's teaching in Proverbs 1–9, one of the advantages of resisting the wiles of the Outsider Woman is secure possession of land, while the penalty for succumbing is to be "cut off" from the land:

> The upright will abide in the land,
> the blameless will remain therein,
> while the wicked will be cut off from the land,[33]
> and the traitors will be rooted out from it. (Prov 2:21)

---

32 This would include use of the word *derek* ("way") which can carry a sexual connotation. In Jer 3:13 the accusation addressed to Israel is that "you have scattered your "ways" (i.e. sexual favors) among strangers under every green tree", and in Prov 31:3 Lemuel is advised "do not give your strength to women, and your "ways" to those who destroy kings" (Solomon, for example). The conclusion of the numerical proverb in Prov 30:18–19, *derek geber bĕ'almâ*, "the way of a man with a maiden", may also encode this other connotation. In this connection the female deity Derketo or Darkatu worshiped in Roman Ascalon may be mentioned. See Mitchell Dahood, "Ugaritic DRKT and Biblical DEREK," *TS* 15 (1954): 627–31 who defends this secondary sense, and Hans Zirker, "drk = potentia?," *BZ* 2 (1958): 291–94 who questions it.

33 "Will be cut off" (*yikkārētû*), cf. the excommunication formula in the P laws, e.g., Gen 17:14; Exod 12:15; 31:14; Lev 7:20; 17:4; Num 9:13; 15:30–31.

5 The social and economic consequences of marrying outside the group — 175

Concern to avoid the undesirable social and economic consequences of *zār* marriages, especially in those instances when the wife survived the husband, is reflected in several stipulations of law. The most obvious example is the levirate law (Deut 25:5–10). To prevent the alienation of family property, the law stipulates that the childless widow, the *yĕbāmāh*, must not marry an *'îš zār*, a man outside the family unit. The law served to mitigate somewhat the situation in which, exceptionally in the context of ancient Near Eastern law, the widow did not inherit the property of her deceased husband.[34] The ruling in favour of the daughters of Zelophahad had the same intent. It stipulated that the surviving daughter of a property-holder with no male heir could inherit in preference to a brother, uncle or other male relative of the deceased, but to this provision of law was added a codicil forbidding the female heir to marry outside her own tribe, a fortiori outside of the Israelite community (Num 27:1–11; 36:1–12, cf. Josh 17:3–6). Here, too, the purpose of the law was to prevent alienation of patrimonial domain as a result of marriage with an outsider to the kinship group.[35]

These legal issues concerning marriage and property loomed especially large during the first century of Persian rule with the resettlement of Judaeo-Babylonians in Judah and consequent disputes over title to property. One aspect of this situation is reflected in a brief homily or disputation in Mal 2:10–16, from around the middle of the fifth century BC. After accusing his fellow-Judaeans in general terms of betrayal of the ancestral covenant, the anonymous or pseudonymous author indicts them on the specific charge of marriage with "the daughter of a foreign god" and consequent profanation of the sanctuary. Much about this passage remains obscure, but the expression "daughter of a foreign god" (*bat-'ēl nēkār*) is best taken to refer to a foreign woman, devotee of a foreign deity, and therefore outside the circle of those claiming descent from the same ancestor and owing allegiance to the ancestral deity. This interpretation seems to be preferable to the alternative, according to which marriage to the daughter of a foreign god is metaphorical for adopting a foreign, that is, non-Yahvistic cult.[36] It becomes clear as we read on that the author is concerned with real

---

34 On which see Eryl Wynn Davies, "Inheritance Rights and the Hebrew Levirate Marriage," *VT* 31 (1981): 138–44, 257–68.
35 Ze'ev Wilhelm Falk, "The Rights of Inheritance of a Daughter in Bible and Talmud," *Tarbiz* 23 (1951/1952): 9–15.
36 Charles Cutler Torrey, "The Prophecy of Malachi," *JBL* 17 (1898): 4–5,9–10; Flemming Friis Hvidberg, *Weeping and Laughter in the Old Testament: A Study of Canaanite-Israelite Religion* (Leiden: Brill, 1962), 120–23; Gösta Werner Ahlström, *Joel and the Temple Cult of Jerusalem* (Leiden: Brill, 1971), 49–50. The issues are discussed by Ralph Smith, *Micah-Malachi* (Waco/Texas: Word Publications, 1984), 321–25; Beth Glazier-McDonald, *Malachi: The Divine Messenger* (Atlan-

not just metaphorical marriage. Exogamous marriage can also involve divorcing one's original wife, described as "the wife of your youth" and "your companion and covenanted wife" (2:14–15). The penalty for contracting such compromised marriages is expulsion from the community., In the marriage crisis addressed by Ezra and his supporters (Ezra 10:8); the guilty one is to be "cut off from the tents of Jacob" and refused access to the temple cult (2:12). Assuming a fifth century date, the most plausible setting for this indictment would be the situation of those Babylonian immigrants who abandoned the wives they brought with them for indigenous Judaean women, and one important reason for doing so would have been the acquisition or reacquisition of property deeded to the women in question.

That the same situation is envisaged in Proverbs 1–9 is suggested by the use of similar terminology about the Outsider Woman who "forsakes the partner of her youth and forgets her sacred covenant" (Prov 2:17 cf. Mal 2:14). It is also reflected in the almost lyrical praise of "the wife of your youth" addressed to the young male tempted to embrace the bosom of a foreign temptress (5:15–20, cf. Mal 2:14). The outcome of giving in to the temptation is also described in similar terms: "The wicked will be cut off from the land, and the unfaithful ones will be rooted out of it" (2:22), which mirrors the threat of being cut off from the tents of Jacob in Mal 2:12. The parallelism between the wicked (*rĕšā'îm*) and the unfaithful ones (*bōgĕdîm*) in Prov 2:22, finally, recalls the fivefold use of the same verbal stem (*bgd*) with reference to marital infidelity in Mal 2:10–16 (cf. Exod 21:8; Jer 3:20).

6 Some provisional conclusions

The upper-class origins and ethos of much of the didactic literature in the Hebrew Bible, including Proverbs 1–9, suggest that warnings against the Outsider Woman were directed primarily at members of the socially and economically dominant lay and priestly families, many of Judaeo-Babylonian origin, who formed the controlling elite in the Achaemenid province of Judah (Yehud). The report to Ezra states that the leaders of this section of the population were among the first to contract marriages with women outside of this originally diasporic community (Ezra 9:2). The list of offenders in Ezra 10 provides no insight into their social status and connections, but we hear elsewhere of intermarriage

---

ta: Scholars Press, 1987), 91–93 and "Intermarriage, Divorce, and the *Bat-'el Nēkār:* Insights into Mal 2:10–16," *JBL* 106 (1987): 603–11.

involving the Sanballat family in Samaria and the Ammonite Tobiads (Neh 6:18–19; 13:28–29). The main object of these *mariages de convenance* was doubtless the promotion of the political and economic interests of these leading families. In opposing them, Nehemiah seems to have enjoyed the backing of the Persian authorities, in spite of strenuous efforts to discredit him. This support appears to correspond to one aspect of Achaemenid imperial policy, which was to maintain or, where necessary, put in place in the different satrapies and provinces an elite group on which the court felt it could rely. The *gôlāh* collectivity to which Ezra and Nehemiah belonged was one such entity. It is represented as enjoying imperial support in the building of the temple, the control of the operations of which translated into a large measure of social control.

Achaemenid social custom also favored endogamy, including marriage with close relatives, in order to preserve intact the material patrimony of the family or phratry.[37] Insistence on endogamy, with a view to preserving the integrity of the dominant elite, would therefore presumably have been looked on with official favour, though the same benevolence may not have been extended either to Ezra's policy of coercive divorce or to the manner in which he carried it out.

The argument presented here, that the diatribe against the Outsider Woman in Proverbs 1–9 is to be read in the context of Achaemenid Judah, may incidentally mediate between the different meanings attached in the commentary tradition to the terms *zārāh* and *nokriyyāh*. For some, these terms refer to a foreign woman, while for others they allude to an Israelite woman who is either an adulteress or, in some way, on the margins of society and respectability. What is lacking is perhaps an appreciation of the complex realities of Judaean society during the two centuries of Iranian rule, especially the presence within it of a dominant elite of diasporic origin. The anxiety of this elite to preserve its distinct identity and its economic assets could therefore have been an important factor in generating the language in which the Outsider Woman in Proverbs 1–9 is described and her activities denounced.

---

37 Martin Schwartz, "The Old Eastern Iranian World View according to the Avesta," in*CHI* 2, 640–663 (655–56); Claude Herrenschmidt, "Notes sur la Parenté chez les Perses au Debut de l'Empire Achéménide," in *Achaemenid History*, Vol. 2, *The Greek Sources*, ed. Heleen Sancisi-Weerdenburg and Amélie Kuhrt (Leiden: Nederlands Instituut voor het Nabije Oosten, 1987), 53–67.

XII. Social Roles of Prophets in Early Achaemenid Judah

Source: *JSOT* 93 (2001): 39–58.

1 Reading and Writing in the Persian province of Judah

Since we have to rely exclusively on the pertinent biblical texts for information on prophecy in early Achaemenid Judah, we begin by asking questions about these texts which can be put under the category of the sociology of reading and writing: When, how, and by whom were they published? Who were the intended readers real or implicit? Who *could* read in sixth and fifth century BC Judah anyway? And among those who could read, who would have had the motivation to read these texts? Further, if sayings attributed to prophets were delivered orally, to what extent are the surviving texts transcripts of, or at least paraphrases of the spoken word? Do we have any information on the social situations which generated the performances or in which these readings took place? I doubt whether we will be able to address, much less answer, all of these questions, but it may help to have formulated them. And it hardly needs saying that biblical texts are not windows through which we get a clear, unobstructed view of social realities in this or any other period.

I therefore assume a shared awareness that there are gaps between biblical texts and social situations, that some of these gaps may be bridgeable and some not, and that the best we can hope for in any case is a pontoon not a suspension bridge. Our task is therefore to assemble enough pieces of the literary debris left to us to make possible an evocation or imagining of a world in which people who, for want of a better word, we call prophets, said and did the things, or something like the things that the texts say they said and did; in other words, to recompose the literary *disiecta membra* into some kind of coherent picture.

To begin with the question of literacy: the data necessary for forming an opinion on this subject are inadequate not least since papyrus, the preferred writing surface for texts of any length, had a hard time surviving the Palestinian winter; in fact, only one palaeo-Hebrew papyrus has survived from the biblical period (seventh century BC), a palimpsest discovered in the Wadi Murabbaʻat. We can nevertheless assume that, given that Judah was a predominantly agrarian society, and in the absence of the means for the wide dissemination of writings, literacy, understood as the ability to read and write, was for the most part confined to professional groups. These would include scribes, priests, and those artisans or merchants engaged in specialist activities. Nothing in the biblical record contradicts this assumption. Allusions to Moses, Joshua, Samuel, David *et alii* writing or reading[1] cannot be taken at face value, and other references to individuals reading and writing may simply mean that they had a specialist do their reading and writing for them. At a comparatively late date a courtier, Jehudi, had to read Jeremiah's prophecies to king Jehoiakim (Jer 36:21). We hear that Hezekiah read a letter sent to him by the Assyrian commander, but we are not told whether the latter could write Hebrew or the former could read Akkadian. Neither seems at all likely.

Understood as the ability to read and write, literacy, therefore, could not have been widespread. The ability to scratch a few letters of the Hebrew alphabet on pots, jar handles, seals, or the high priest's rosette (*qōdeš laYHWH*, "holy to Yahweh", Exod 39:30) hardly amounts to evidence for literacy. The conditions necessary for widespread literacy did not exist even in the great riverine cultures. For example, the extent of literacy in Egypt of the Old Kingdom has been calculated between 0.3 and 1.0 per cent of the population,[2] and even in Athens of the fifth to the fourth century it did not exceed ten per cent.[3] We therefore conclude that, in the absence of the means for reproducing and disseminating written material, and the absence of the ability and the motivation to read on the part of the great majority of the population, basically agrarian as it always had been, none of the prophetic writings from the early Achaemenid period was written for a mass audience.[4] The assumption that prophetic texts reproduce oral performance is, however, reasonable and in many cases probable, though we shall see that it will rarely be the case that the spoken word has been recorded and transmitted verbatim or free from later intrusion well-meaning or otherwise.

---

[1] E.g. Exod 24:4; Deut 31:9–13; Josh 1:8; 1 Sam 10:25; 2 Sam 11:14.
[2] John Baines, "Literacy, Ancient Near East," in *ABD* 4, 333–37.
[3] William Harris, *Ancient Literacy* (Cambridge/Mass: Harvard University Press, 1989), 114.
[4] The case for widespread literacy throughout the entire biblical period is argued strenuously by Alan Millard: "The Practice of Writing in Ancient Israel," *BA* 35 (1972): 98–112; "An Assessment of the Evidence for Writing in Ancient Israel," in *Biblical Archaeology Today*, ed. Avraham Biran (Jerusalem: Magnes Press, 1985), 301–12. A more recent contribution to the debate is that of Ian Young, "Israelite Literacy: Interpreting the Evidence. Part 1," *VT* 48 (1998): 239–53, whose estimates are more realistically low.

2 Labels and roles

Biblical texts assigned wholly or in part to the Achaemenid period testify to the belief that prophecy did not come to an end with the liquidation of the nation state. The rabbinic teaching on "the end of prophecy" is based not on evidence but on the ideological requirement of privileging law and cult as the basis of religious life, combined with an acute and not entirely unjustified sense of the unpredictability and dangers of institutionally unattached prophetic activity.[5] Haggai, Zechariah 1–8, Malachi, Joel, much of Isaiah 56–66, a good part of Isaiah 1–39, and a variably calculated percentage of the material in other prophetic books, depending on who is doing the calculating, are assigned to this period. Haggai and Zechariah are referred to as "prophets" (něbî'îm). One or two other names of individual prophets have come down to us. The Shemaiah ben Delaiah visited by Nehemiah is called a prophet (nābî') and his message to Nehemiah is called a prophecy (něbû'â). The episode involving this prophet is obscure. It is unclear what is meant by the prophet being "in seclusion" ('āsûr, Neh 6:10– 13);[6] he appears to have been recruited by Sanballat to counter the prophets allegedly in support of Nehemiah's pretensions to kingship (Neh 6:7), perhaps also to arrange for him to be assassinated. The Nehemiah memoir goes on to deprecate a female prophet Noadiah and other unnamed prophets who were active in the opposition party (Neh 6:14).

The designation nābî' ("prophet") is difficult to pin down since it underwent a semantic development in the post-destruction period, covering a wide range of activities and roles including preaching, the composition and rendition of liturgical music,[7] historiography, and the interpretation of earlier prophecy[8]. One result was that other terms or labels came into use to indicate activities and functions more closely associated with classical ideas about prophecy. We saw that Haggai is called a nābî' even though the pamphlet bearing his name has little in common with classical prophecy in spite of such traditional prophetic mark-

---

[5] Joseph Blenkinsopp, "'We pay no heed to heavenly voices': the 'End of Prophecy' and the Formation of the Canon," in *Biblical and Humane: Festschrift for John Priest*, ed. Linda Bennett Elder, David Barr and Elizabeth Struthers Malbon (Atlanta: Scholars Press, 1996), 19–31.
[6] For the range of possibilities see Hugh Williamson, *Ezra, Nehemiah* (Waco/Texas: Word Books, 1985), 249. He opts for "extremely worried" following a proposal of Ernst Kutsch, "Die Würzel עצר im Hebräischen," *VT* 2 (1952): 57–69.
[7] See Joseph Blenkinsopp, *A History of Prophecy in Israel* (2nd ed., Louisville: Westminster John Knox Press, 1996), 222–26.
[8] David Petersen, *The Roles of Israel's Prophets* (Sheffield: JSOT Press, 1981); Joseph Blenkinsopp, *A History of Prophecy*, 26–30, 194–245.

ers as "thus says Yahweh", "the word of Yahweh came to Haggai", and the like. But the editor also refers to him as "the messenger of Yahveh" (*mal'āk YHVH*) whose function is therefore to deliver a message (*mal'ăkût*, Hag 1:13). This term seems to have passed into general usage as a prophetic designation.[9] It is even transferred to the heavenly sphere in the nocturnal visions of Zechariah in which the *angelus interpres* performs the traditional prophetic functions of intercession (1:12–13) and issuing oracular statements introduced by the familiar prophetic rubrics (1:14,16,17; 2:9,10,14), as well as the less traditional role of interpreter of older prophecies (2:1–6). This last is one of several indications of the scribalization of prophecy in the post-destruction period, and the emergence of a second-order prophetic function, consisting in the interpretation of earlier prophecy, the transition from prophet to inspired exegete. The author of Chronicles uses all the standard terms for prophetic individuals and their productions – *nābî'*, *nĕbû'â*, *rō'eh* (seer), *hozeh* (visionary), etc, but also considers the composition and rendition of liturgical music and the composition of royal annals and midrash – whatever the word means in that context – as within the broad scope of prophecy.

Another perspective on social perceptions of prophets, and prophetic role performance, is available starting out from the diatribe against corrupt leaders in Isa 56:9–12. The writer invites wild animals to enter the sheepfold and devour the sheep since the watchmen are blind and the watchdogs are dumb. The metaphoric language in this passage, and in Jer 12:9–10 on which it appears to draw, has given rise to much discussion. Paul D. Hanson took the watchmen and nonbarking dogs to be Zadokite priests in keeping with his thesis of conflict between these priests and their prophetic opponents, though there is no allusion to anything priestly in the passage. Westermann argued that the text is pre-exilic, referring to community leaders in general, since only in the pre-exilic period was Judah threatened by external enemies, but even a cursory reading of Ezra-Nehemiah will suffice to show that this is not the case.[10] The designation *sōpeh*, "watchman", "sentinel") for "prophet," occurs also in Jeremiah (6:17) and Ezekiel (3:17; 33:2,6–7), hence both sentinels and guard dogs in Isa 56:9–12 are metaphors for prophets.[11]

---

[9] Hag 1:13; Zech 3:6; 4:1; Mal 1:1; 3:1.
[10] Claus Westermann, *Isaiah 40–66: A Commentary* (London: SCM, 1969).
[11] This interpretation will be strengthened if we read (*ḥōzîm*, "visionaries") with 1QIsa[a] for MT *hōzîm*) in Isa 56:10c. The latter is hapax, and none of the proposed meanings, reached on the basis of alleged cognates ("to pant in one's sleep", "to talk irrationally") is right for the context. See Joseph Blenkinsopp, *Isaiah 56–66: A New Translation with Introduction and Commentary* (Garden City/New York: Doubleday, 2003), 144.

In this passage the watchmen are condemned as inattentive to their task, greedy, and addicted to strong drink. The dogs also come in for severe criticism as greedy brutes who cannot be bothered to bark when danger threatens. Criticism of the *něbî'îm* was widespread in the post-destruction period. A Second Temple gloss on Isa 9:13, "Yahweh will cut off from Israel the head and the tail", identifies the head as the elder and the tail (of the dog?) as the prophet, the teacher of lies. The gloss suggests that many held prophets to be of low social status. The same impression is conveyed in Zech 13:2–6. The writer associates the prophet with pagan cults and an unclean spirit. The prophet who speaks lies in the name of Yahweh, is subject to the death penalty in keeping with Deuteronomic law (Deut 18:20), and therefore goes to great pains to avoid being identified as a prophet.

The label *sōpeh* ("watchman", "sentinel") for prophet was appropriate since the task of the sentinel posted on the city wall or the watchtower was to look out for danger approaching the city and warn those inside the walls in good time. The metaphor could therefore serve for the admonitory, and perhaps also the predictive role of the prophet in society. In Isa 52:8, Jerusalemite *sōpîm* lift up their voices and sing for joy when – presumably from their lookout posts – they see the Lord Yahweh returning to the city. If this appears to be too much of a theological abstraction, we might consider the *šōměrîm* ("guards", "watchmen") in Isa 62:6–7 who are posted on the walls of Jerusalem and who, unlike the non-barking dogs of Isa 56:9–12, refuse to keep silent. They are described as *mazkîrîm 'et-YHVH*), literally, "they who cause God to remember", they activate God's memory. Their task, more plainly stated, is round-the-clock prayer for the re-establishment of Jerusalem, thus fulfilling the traditional prophetic role of intercessory prayer. Even more firmly grounded in social reality is the lookout (*měsappeh*) keeping his watch (*mišmeret*) on the watchtower (*mispeh*) and waiting day and night for the news of the fall of Babylon, and who finally announces *năpělāh, năpělāh băbel!* ("fallen, fallen is Babylon!", Isa 21:6–9).

This example of prophetic watchmanship follows the reception of "a hard vision", which brings into play the psychological process involving in soliciting a visionary experience, a state of transformed consciousness.[12] Consider the language in Hab 2:1–2, probably from the Neo-Babylonian period: "On my watchtower I take my stand, on the rampart I take my station; I keep vigil to see what he will say to me and what he will reply to my complaint." He then hears the words, "Write down the vision; inscribe it on tablets so that it can

---

[12] For a range of examples from other cultures see Ioan Lewis, *Ecstatic Religion: A Study of Shamanism and Spirit Possession* (3rd ed., London & New York: Routledge, 2003).

be read on the run ..." In this instance the experience involves an extraordinary state of consciousness, but the experience is apparently auditory not visual. The book of Isaiah provides other examples. In Isa 21:11–12, the oracle against Dumah (Edom), we hear a brief exchange between the sentinel and a passer-by the meaning of which is somewhat opaque. A more colourful example in Isa 63:1–6 also involves question and answer beginning with the query: "Who is this coming from Edom, from Bozrah with his clothes stained red?" The poet and scholar Johann Gottfried Herder proposed an analogy to this situation in the border ballads where the warrior, returning from a foray, is questioned, generally by the women – as, for example: "Why is your sword so red with blood, Edward, Edward?". A more prosaic setting would be the sentinel's challenge and the reply. Here, the challenge is addressed to Yahweh himself as warrior returning from visiting vengeance on Edom, for many today, admittedly, an unpleasant and disturbing image. It appears to be a case of a visionary experience, if not the transcription of an actual vision or dream.

The sentinel metaphor, therefore, serves to present the prophet as a kind of antenna, an early warning system, for the community to which he is answerable. But irrespective of the question whether the texts correspond to the actual soliciting or inducing of messages in a state of transformed consciousness, which seems to me to be entirely plausible, we have the impression that the vision report is becoming more of a literary device, generally with arcane language and imagery, for communicating a political message. Ezekiel is appointed as a watchman (*sōpeh*) with a twofold responsibility: blowing the trumpet to warn his people against imminent attack by enemies; delivering moral exhortation, or commination, addressed to both the well-disposed and the reprobate (Ezek 3:16–21; 33:1–9). From the beginning, prophets have always been involved in politics. During the last days of Babylonian rule the prophets Zedekiah and Ahab were executed, some would say martyred, for stirring up trouble among the Judaean deportees in Babylon (Jer. 29:20–23). During the decades preceding the fall of Babylon, the anonymous prophet known as Deutero-Isaiah urged his Judaean contemporaries to accept Cyrus the Persian as the one divinely appointed to rule over them now that the Davidic dynasty had come to an end. During the critical months between 522 BC and 520 BC, when Darius, probably an usurper, was desperately establishing his hold on the empire founded by Cyrus, there was a flurry of prophetic activity aimed at restoring the national dynasty in the person of Zerubbabel, governor of the province. Then, seventy years after the rebuilding of the temple in Jerusalem and the disappearance of Zerubbabel from the scene

– note the significant number[13] – Nehemiah was accused of making a bid for kingship with prophetic backing even though not of Davidic descent. All of this is consistent with Weber's contention that Israelite prophets, whom he characterized at one place as demagogues and pamphleteers, were concerned in the first place with international politics since that was the primary sphere of their God's concern and activity.[14]

3 The prophet as preacher

Another prophetic role is preaching. This was not an innovation of the Achaemenid period since earlier prophets were preachers, as it were by default, since preaching was not then, as it is now, associated with priests. The closest term in Hebrew for preacher is *mattip* from the verbal stem *ntp*, meaning "to drip" which, as far as we know, did not then have the unfortunate connotation which it now has in the vernacular. Amaziah, head priest at the Bethel sanctuary, tells Amos not to prophecy and not to "drip" (Amos 7:16),[15] and the same combination of verbs occurs elsewhere in prophetic writings (Mic 2:6; Ezek 21:2, 7). Over a period of time we note a gradual transition from the relatively brief oracular prophetic saying to a longer type of discourse of a recognizably homiletic nature. The many examples in Jeremiah, Deuteronomy and Chronicles are well known,[16] but homiletic features can be found throughout the prophetic books. An example of the thematic homily from the late Neo-Babylonian or early Achaemenid period would be the homily on fasting in Isa 58:1–14 which can be compared with the more succinct sayings on the same theme in Zech 7:1–23. The pointedly disputatious character of this passage, making full use of the rhetorical question, is representative of much of the prophetic material from this period: Haggai, Zechariah 1–8, Joel, Deutero-Isaiah and especially Malachi.

People can of course write sermons for their own personal edification, but the genre was so prevalent during the Persian period that it cannot easily be understood without reference to an institutional infrastructure of some kind. In the

---

13 Cf. Jer 25:11–12; 29:10; Isa 23:15–17; Zech 1:12.
14 Max Weber, *Economy and Society: An Outline of Interpretative Sociology*, Vol. 1, Transl. Guenther Roth and Claus Wittich (Berkeley & Los Angeles: University of California Press, 1978), 444–46.
15 NEB translated "do not go drivelling on" at Amos 7:16, wisely omitted in REB.
16 See Gerhard von Rad, "The Levitical Sermon in I and II Chronicles," in *The Problem of the Hexateuch and Other Essays*, Transl. Trueman Dicken (Edinburgh & London: Oliver & Boyd, 1966), 267–80.

first place, an ecclesiastical location is the obvious setting for the sermon. The address of king Jehoshaphat faced with invasion from Judah's Transjordanian neighbors, followed by the stirring words of the Levitical prophet Jahaziel, both took place in the presence of the assembly and in the temple, accompanied with prayer, prostrations and hymn-singing (2 Chr 20:5–17). It has long been suspected that the prose sermons in the book of Jeremiah were composed for delivery in a synagogue or synagogue-like setting either in Judah or, more probably, in the diaspora.[17] The emphasis on sabbath, more than on circumcision, in texts from the early to mid-Persian period[18] would also, plausibly, be connected with the practice of meeting on the sabbath for reading Torah (as in Neh 7:73b–8:12), preaching, and communal prayer, and in these activities individuals recognized as prophets would have played a part.

4 The prophetic role of the liturgical musicians

For the prophetic role of the temple singers and instrumentalists (*měšōrěrîm*) we must rely exclusively on Chronicles, Ezra-Nehemiah, and what can be gleaned from a close reading of Psalms. An initial problem is their uncertain relation with the temple Levites. The author of Chronicles provides no clear solution. At one place he tells us that during David's reign there were 38,000 Levites of whom 4,000 were singers (1 Chr 23:2–5), while elsewhere the lead liturgical singers, Heman, Asaph and Ethan, and the members of their respective groups, are listed separately from Levites (1 Chr 6:16–23). They are also listed separately in the lists of repatriated diaspora Jews in Ezra 2:41 (also Neh 7:44; 1 Esd 5:27). This issue need not be settled here and now; it will suffice to note that the different views about their status vis-à-vis Levites at the time of David reflect their changing fortunes throughout the history, especially during the time of the second temple.

What should be retained is the statement about their prophetic and oracular character in 1 Chr 25:1–8 where we are told that, under the tutelage of the prophetically inspired king David, they "prophesied" with lyres, lutes, and cymbals. David himself is recognized as both musician and seer, often depicted in art as

---

17 Paul Volz, *Der Prophet Jeremia* (Leipzig: Deichert, 1928), 300; Enno Janssen, *Juda in der Exilzeit: Ein Beitrag zur Frage der Entstehung des Judentums* (Göttingen: Vandenhoeck & Ruprecht, 1956), 107–10; Wilhelm Rudolph, *Jeremia* (3rd ed., Tübingen: Mohr Siebeck, 1968), xvi, xviii; Ernest Nicholson, *Preaching to the Exiles: A Study of the Prose Tradition in the Book of Jeremiah* (Oxford: Blackwell, 1970), 134 and *passim*.
18 Isa 56:2, 4, 6; 58:13–14; 66:23; Neh 10:32; 13:15–22, cf. Jer 17:19–27.

the Hebrew Orpheus, whose playing on the lyre relieved Saul most of the time (1 Sam 16:14 – 23). His name appears among the introductory notes and rubrics to seventy-four psalms and, according to one count, he composed a grand total of 4050 psalms through the spirit of prophecy given him from on high.[19]

Three of the principal guild founders and eponyms are also said to be seers (*hōzîm*): Heman (1 Chr 25:5), Jeduthun (2 Chr 35:15), and Asaph (2 Chr 29:30). This dual function of prophecy and song has ancient roots: Orpheus son of Apollo whose singing charmed animals, plants and stones and even brought the dead in Hades back to life, or the god Pan in Arcadia with his syrinx who induced panic and ecstatic possession. Closer to home, Levi, ancestor of all temple personnel, is a specialist in divination by manipulating the Urim and Thummim (Deut 33:8), a function which was passed on to the priesthood.

The author of Chronicles provides a narrative example of this kind of prophecy in action in his account of the reign of Jehoshaphat of Judah (870 – 846 BC). Threatened by a powerful coalition of the kingdoms east of the Jordan, king and people gathered in the temple to seek divine assistance. In the course of this service the spirit of Yahweh fell upon an Asaphite Levite and musician named Jahaziel who, in an ecstatic state, assured the those present that all manner of things would be well, the victory would be theirs, they would not even have to fight, an assurance that was greeted with songs of praise and thanksgiving from a choir of Kohathite-Levitical musicians. The pattern was replicated the next day as they went out to meet the enemy: the king urged them to trust in the prophetic word, the singers and instrumentalists gave voice, and the enemy self-destructed. All, then, returned to Jerusalem, the king leading the way, accompanied by the Levitical singers and players on lutes, lyres and trumpets (2 Chr 20:13 – 30).

5 Prophecy and Politics: the case of Haggai, Zechariah, and Zerubbabel

No account of prophecy during the period of the second temple would be complete without a consideration of the prophets Haggai and Zechariah who were in good part responsible for the rebuilding of a temple in Jerusalem. Their role in getting this project underway is recorded in the Aramaic source in Ezra 4:8 – 6:18 where they are linked with Zerubbabel ben Shealtiel of the line of David and Jeshua ben Jozadak (Jehozadak) the high priest designate (Ezra

---

[19] See the note appended to the Qumran psalms (11Q5 col. XXVII).

5:1–2). The same source records how the task was completed with the help of their prophesying in the sixth regnal year of Darius I, therefore March 516 BC, though now Jewish elders have taken the place of Zerubbabel and Jeshua (Ezra 6:13–15). The entire section Ezra 1–6 forms a prologue to the story about Ezra. It has enough in common with Chronicles in both language and thematic to suggest that it was put together either by the author of Chronicles or someone in the Chronicler's milieu, making use of an extensive range of sources.[20] It concentrates heavily on opposition to the project and how it was overcome (Ezra 4:1–24), but is silent on the messianic expectations linked with the restoration of the temple cult in the prophecies of Haggai and Zechariah. It represents Zerubbabel and Jeshua (Joshua) the high-priest designate as active from the time of the first return in the reign of Cyrus, and they are even numbered among the leaders of the mass immigration together with Nehemiah (Ezra 2:2). This practice of foreshortening or retrojecting to a real or imaginary beginning is well attested and will reappear in the self-identification of the Damascus Document sectarians with the first to return from exile.[21]

The discourses and accounts of visions or dreams of Haggai and Zechariah (chapters 1–8) occupy a critical position during the first two years of Darius, very probably a usurper to the Persian throne, when he was engaged in suppressing a series of rebellions throughout the empire, including two in Babylon. They are not only unique in being dated not just to the year but to the month and the day, but they can be synchronized with the sequence of events in Darius' Behistun inscription.[22] The discourses of Haggai are presented as delivered orally within a period of less than four months, between the late summer and the winter of 520 BC, the second year of the reign of Darius I. Those of Zechariah cover a longer period from the late autumn of 520 to the early winter of 518, with the first vision, and perhaps the entire series of visions, dated to the late winter or early spring of 519. Synchronized with relevant events in the Behistun inscription the chronological sequence looks as follows:

---

20 On parallels between Ezra 1–6 and Chronicles see Joseph Blenkinsopp, *Ezra-Nehemiah: A Commentary* (Philadelphia: Westminster, 1988), 47–54 in response to Sara Japhet, "The Supposed Common Authorship of Chronicles and Ezra-Nehemiah Investigated Anew," *VT* 18 (1969): 330–371; Hugh Williamson, "The Composition of Ezra i–vi," *JTS* 34 (1983): 1–30; *Ezra, Nehemiah*, xxxiii–xxxv.
21 On these *ri'šonîm*, also *šābîm* ("penitents", also "those who returned") see CD I 4–5; III 10–11; IV 7–10, etc.
22 For the text of the inscription in Old Persian and an English translation see Ronald Kent, *Old Persian: Grammar, Texts, Lexicon* (New Haven: American Oriental Society, 1953), 116–35. Muhammad Dandamaev, *A Political History of the Achaemenid Empire* (Leiden: Brill, 1989), provides a convenient chronological table , pp. 331–34.

Oct–Dec 522	Babylonian revolt of Nidintu-bel (Nebuchadnezzar III)
Aug–Nov 521	Second Babylonian revolt of Arakha (Nebuchadnezzar IV)
Jan–Dec 520	Suppression of revolts in Elam
Aug 29, 520	First discourse of Haggai (1:1–11)
Sept 21, 520	Second discourse of Haggai (1:15a + 2:15–19)
Oct 17, 520	Third discourse of Haggai (1:15b–2:9)
Oct–Nov, 520	First discourse of Zechariah (Zech 1:1–6)
Dec 18, 520	Fourth discourse of Haggai (Haggai 2:10–14)
Dec 18, 520	Fifth discourse of Haggai (Haggai 2:20–23)
520–516	Building of the temple (or 519–515)
519	Darius' campaign against the Saka
Jan–Feb, 519	Zechariah's first vision (Zech 1:7–17)
518	Darius in Egypt; re-organization of the empire

Haggai's discourses are presented in an editorial framework which provides the date, the speaker, the recipients, and a narrative commentary recording the positive outcome of Haggai's preaching, the point of which was to persuade the two leaders and, if possible, the people that the time was right for rebuilding the temple. There is great concern to emphasize that the speaker is a *nābî'* (prophet; 1:1, 3, 12; 2:1, 10), at one point also a messenger with a message from God (*mal'āk*, 1:13), reinforced with a rather redundant repetition of traditional prophetic formulae, especially "Thus says Yahweh". The same kind of redactional arrangement is replicated in Zechariah 1–8 which also provides precise dates (Zech 1:1,7; 7:1) and prophetic-type formulae like those in Haggai attached to the sayings, including the sayings of messengers or angelic beings (*mal'ākîm*) in the interactive visions reported in this section.[23] The sayings of Haggai themselves, none of which takes more than a few seconds to read, implies that they must be telegrammatically brief synopses or abstracts of actual discourses delivered orally. It is equally clear that they are of a different kind from what is traditionally understood as prophetic. The injunction to consider, pay special attention (*sîmû lĕbabĕkem*, Haggai 1:5, 7; 2:15, 18), the frequent rhetorical questions (Haggai 1:4; 2:3, 16, 19), the alternation of reproof and reassurance, and the hortatory tone in general belong more to the language of the preacher or teacher than the prophet. The casual citation of Amos 4:9 in Haggai's second discourse (2:17) is also indicative of late prophetic or post-prophetic developments; compare Zechariah's allusion to "the former prophets" (1:4).

There seems to be little doubt that the same scribal hand has edited and prepared for "publication" the discourses of both Haggai and Zechariah together

---

[23] Prophetic speech patterns used by the *angelus interpres* in the visions are consistent with the term (*mal'āk*, "messenger") as a synonym for "prophet" (Hag 1:13; Mal 3:1).

with the vision narratives of the latter, consistent with the linking of both names in the Aramaic source in Ezra 5:1–2 and 6:14. There are other points of contact between this source and the collections of Haggai's and Zechariah's sayings, but the most obvious difference is the absence from the Ezra narrative of the political factor, namely, the linking of the rebuilding the temple and reactivating the temple cult with the restoration of the native dynasty. The first three discourses of Haggai are addressed, either directly or indirectly through Zerubbabel governor of Judah and Joshua high priest designate, to the people, perhaps assembled in a kind of proto-synagogal setting. In the fourth discourse someone not named is told to seek a ruling from the priests on a question of ritual purity. The question was in fact disingenuous since its purpose was to condemn offerings made at a sanctuary other than Jerusalem ("What they offer *there* is unclean", 2:14).[24] The fifth discourse is a quite different matter. It is dated December 520, in the second year of Darius I, and is addressed to Zerubbabel alone. It reads as follows:

> On the twenty-fourth day of the month the word of Yahweh came to Haggai a second time: "Give the following message to Zerubbabel, governor of Judah: 'I am about to shake the heavens and the earth. I shall overthrow the throne of kingdoms and destroy the power of the kingdoms of the nations. I shall overthrow chariots and their riders, and horses and their riders will fall by the sword of their comrades. On that day I will take you, Zerubbabel, son of Shealtiel, my servant, and wear you as my signet ring, for it is you that I have chosen. (Hag 2:20–23)

The message was no doubt delivered to Zerubbabel by the prophet in secret.

Disseminating prophecies about the collapse of the Persian empire and enthronement of a messianic king in the winter of the year 520 could have had decidedly unpleasant consequences for the speaker and his audience; suffice it to recall the fate of Darius' opponents described in unsparing detail in Darius' Behistun inscription. If carried out, this prophetic mandate would have led to the

---

24 We are not told who these priests were, and where the unclean offerings were being made. On the location indicated by the adverb šām, "there", the alternatives on offer in the commentaries are either a sanctuary frequented by the mixed population settled around Samaria, or the altar set up – by Jeshua the priest and Zerubbabel! – shortly after the arrival of the first immigrants at the beginning of the reign of Cyrus (Ezra 3:1–3). But since we know of no sanctuary in Samaria at that time, and the altar erected by Jeshua and Zerubbabel is historically implausible, I propose as a third alternative the sanctuary at Bethel attached to the administrative center of the province at Mizpah. I argue the case for this situation in the aftermath of the destruction of the Jerusalem temple in "Bethel in the Neo-Babylonian Period" in *Judah and the Judeans in the Neo-Babylonian Period*, ed. Oded Lipschits and Joseph Blenkinsopp (Winona Lake/Indiana: Eisenbrauns, 2003), 93–107.

third *dynastic* revolt from within the former Babylonian empire. Nidintu-bel's claim to a kingdom as Nebuchadnezzar III, successor to the ruler who destroyed Jerusalem, was put down less than two years earlier. Arakha, of unknown antecedents but perhaps Armenian, had laid claim to the title of Nebuchadnezzar IV in the city of Babylon itself, and his revolt had come to an end with his capture and execution late in the previous year; a circumstance which may explain the urgent call to expatriate Jews to leave Babylon without delay (Zech 2:10–11 [ET 2:6–7]).

The atmosphere of secrecy and concealment is felt throughout Zechariah 1–8. It is reflected in the use of the term *semah* ("Branch") for Zerubbabel as heir-apparent to the throne of David, a term familiar to Zechariah and his colleagues but not to the authorities in Susa.[25] There is another prophetic message for Zerubbabel, more cryptic that Haggai's (Zech 4:6–7); in fact, the vision series in Zech 1:7–6:8 expresses throughout in symbolic and arcane language the linked themes of the new temple and the restoration of the dynasty.

The climactic event in what is now evidently a clandestine nationalistic movement of independence from Darius, still fully engaged in putting down insurrections in Elam and on the furthest eastern reaches of the empire he inherited, is the secret coronation of Zerubbabel, carried out in reality or in symbolic form, in the house of Josiah ben Shephaniah, presumably in Jerusalem (Zech 6:9–15). Precisely because of the circumstances in which this event took place, the text is more than usually obscure. The action begins with the arrival of three wealthy Judaeo-Babylonians with rich gifts, presumably for the rebuilding of the temple. Following an inspired word from the prophet Zechariah, some of this silver and gold was redirected to making a crown.[26] As the text stands, this crown is to be placed on the head of the high priest Joshua ben Jehozadak, but this is contradicted by the oracle accompanying the symbolic act: "Here is a man whose name is *semah* (Branch) ... It is he who will rebuild Yahweh's temple, and it is he who will assume royal dignity, sit on his throne and rule." This is evidently the same person addressed in Haggai's fifth discourse and designated "my servant Branch" in Zech 3:8; a descendant of David bearing the same epithet prophetically foretold by Jeremiah (23:5–6; 33:15). This dissonance at the very centre of the event can be reconciled either on the supposition that the priest was

---

25 Zech 3:8; 6:12, cf. Jer 23:5; 33:15. The term *semah*, referring in its basic meaningto anything growing out of the ground, may have been seen to have a certain connaturality for Zerubbabel whose name derives from the Akkadan *zēr bābili*, "seed of Babylon", no doubt indicating his origins in the Babylonian diaspora.

26 MT has *'ătārôt*, "crowns" (6:11), but probably to be read *'ăteret*, singular, with some Greek mss, Syriac and Targum. Only one person is to wear a crown.

standing in for Zerubbabel or, as I consider more probable, that the name Joshua ben Jehozadak has replaced the name Zerubbabel ben Shealtiel, probably in reaction to the disconfirmation of the predictions of the two prophets. concerning Zerubbabel, or the fate of Zerubbabel himself about which, unfortunately, we can only speculate. According to the Aramaic source in Ezra 5:1–2 Zerubbabel and the priest Jeshua (Joshua) supported by prophets began the building of the temple, but when the buildng was completed in the sixth year of Darius, 516 BC, the work was under the direction of "the elders of the Jews" with no mention of Zerubbabel who therefore disappeared from the scene some time between 520 and 516. No episode involving prophets is recorded in biblical texts in such detail and with such chronological precision as this ultimately unsuccessful attempt to challenge the overwhelming political and military power of empire, but unfortunately we shall never know for certain what happened that day in the house of Josiah ben Zephaniah.[27]

---

[27] For further discussion and documentation on the episode see the chapter on Zerubbabel in Joseph Blenkinsopp, *David Remembered: Kingship and National Identity in Ancient Israel* (Grand Rapids: Eerdmans, 2013), 71–103.

XIII. The sectarian element in early Judaism

1 What is a sect and how can it be recognized as such?

According to the Oxford English Dictionary, the word "sect", from the Latin *secta* with the etymological sense of either something cut off (verb *secare*) or following a leader or a way of life (verb *sequi*), was first used in the Middle Ages to describe dissident Christian groups and even, in the writings of John Wyclif, religious orders like the Franciscans and Dominicans. This specifically contextualized usage goes back to the seminal study of Ernst Troeltsch on the social teaching of the Christian churches published in 1912. Troeltsch worked out a phenomenology of sect by contrasting it with church, meaning Western Christianity, the Roman Catholic Church as it existed in the Middle Ages. Where the church is conservative the sect is radical; where it is universalizing and open to the secular order, the sect renounces the world and its values in favour of asceticism and the spiritual perfection of the individual; where, above all, the church is overwhelmingly composed of those born into it, the sect is a voluntary association entry into and continuing membership in which depend on satisfying certain criteria and demonstrating possession of certain qualifications. On this basis, Troeltsch went on to identify and characterize a number of examples from the history of the Christian church in the Middle Ages including Cathars, Joachimites, Waldensians and Lollards.[1]

Troeltsch made an observation at the beginning of his chapter on church-sect typology which could provoke reflection on the subject of our study. His point was that from the very beginnings of the Christian church there existed a dualistic tendency or potentiality within Christian social teaching. On the one hand there was the ecclesiastical ethic which, because of its universalistic claims, called for a degree of compromise with the social and political order, while on the other hand there was the invitation and allure of adhering to the radical claims and demands of the gospel. Troeltsch argued that the latter option, once reinforced by an equally radical interpretation of the natural law and the primitive state of nature, would lead inevitably to the formation of sects.[2] It is possible to detect indications of a similar duality within emergent Judaism with the potential for developing into different ways of understanding Ju-

---

1 Ernst Troeltsch, *The Social Teaching of the Christian Churches*, Vol. 1, Transl. Olive Wyon (Louisville: Westminster John Knox Press, 1992), 328–69 = Die Sozialllehren der christlichen Kirchen und Gruppen (Stuttgart: Mohr Siebeck, 1994 [1912]).
2 Ernst Troeltsch, *The Social Teaching*, 329–30, 161–64.

daism and being Jewish, including the one which would eventuate in the overt sectarianism of the Graeco-Roman period. I would argue that the potentiality for the formation of sects was not only present from the very beginnings of both Judaism and Christianity, but in both cases was actualized in terms of social realities from the earliest times. In the present chapter we will try to get a clearer picture of how this actually worked out within the history of Second Temple Judaism.

In biblical scholarship the term "sect" evokes Josephus' triad of Sadducees, Pharisees and Essenes in speaking of whom he uses the terms *hairesis, hairetistai* ("sect", "sectarians").[3] The first Christians preferred other self-descriptions. Paul's accusers referred to him as a ringleader of the Nazarene *hairesis*, but Paul corrected them by declaring that he worshipped "according to the Way (*hodos*) which they call a sect (*hairesis*)" – they, not us, understood (Acts 24:5, 14). Yet Paul did not hesitate to apply the same term to the Pharisees, representatives of the Judaism which he himself had professed (Acts 26:5; cf. 15:5). This terminology (sect, sectarian, sectarianism) unfortunately still retains something of a negative aura about it, due to its original use to designate heterodox groups throughout the history of Christianity. In current usage, in the media and everyday speech, terms such as "sect" or "cult" tend to characterize a group or movement as narrow and extremist, perhaps dangerously so. It is important to set this prejudicial idea aside at the outset. The term is the one used in the sociological literature and there seems to be no acceptable alternative. Weber himself spoke of charisma and virtuosity in connection with sectarian movements over against mass religion. Belonging to a sect may be the only vehicle for pursuing certain ideals for living.[4] Each case must therefore be considered on its own terms and its own merits, without prejudice.

Writing in evident dependence on Troeltsch's distinction between church type and sect type, Max Weber sketched out in his great masterpiece *Wirtschaft und Gesellschaft (Economy and Society)* and in other writings his basic understanding of sectarianism, with special reference to the sectarian movements provoked by the Reformation (Anabaptists, Puritans and others)[5] Weber's contribution to the understanding of sectarianism is fundamental, but both his work and

---

[3] *War* II 119–166; *Ant.* XIII 171–173; XVIII 23–25.
[4] Max Weber, *Economy and Society: An Outline of Interpretative Sociology*, Vol. 1, Transl. and ed. Günther Roth and Claus Wittich (Berkeley: University of California Press, 1978), 206–7.
[5] Max Weber, *Economy and Society* 2:1204–11. Weber's many contributions to the subject are listed and discussed by David Chalcraft, "Max Weber on Sects and Voluntary Associations with Specific Reference to Second Temple Judaism," in *Sectarianism in Early Judaism: Sociological Advances*, ed. David Chalcraft (Oakville: Equinox, 2007), 26–111.

that of Troeltsch illustrate the dilemma that definition and description depend on and are circumscribed by the cases under consideration. Following the lead of these two great pioneers we can, however, hazard some generalizations:

(1) The sect is a voluntary association. To become a member of a sect one must satisfy criteria and qualifications dictated by the purpose of the group. Membership entails obligations freely undertaken, hence the difference between the dictated state law under the monarchy and the voluntary self-commitment to specific points of law in the covenants in Ezra-Nehemiah and in the rules of the Damascus community and the Qumran *yahad*.

(2) The sect is characterized by a strong sense of boundaries, of an insider-outsider differentiation; this sense will typically be embodied in practices with respect to some or all of the following: worship, purity rules, commensality and dress, connubium and sexual relation in general. The sect will use great vigilance in admitting postulants and will exercise the right to expel members who transgress its rules. Names of members will often be listed in an official document.

(3) The sect will either be introversionist and withdraw from "the world" outside as corrupt and corrupting or it will be reformist and undertake a mission to transform and save the world.

(4) Since we will be speaking about Jewish sects during the period of the Second Temple, we add that the sect will tend either to define itself with reference to the parent body from which it has dissociated itself or from which it has been forcibly dissociated, or it will stake an exclusive claim to be the authentic heir and possessor of the traditions cherished by the parent body. In other words, in early Judaism we witness the emergence of a type of sect which takes over the identity and the claims which it either believes the parent body has forfeited or to which it denies title to other claimants. It will see itself as the only representative of the Israel to which the traditions testify, with the result that the world outside its boundaries consists not only of Gentiles but of other Jews. To what extent the schism is complete and definitive will depend on the level of tolerance or intolerance on either side of the divide.

(5) In the nature of the case, a sect will generally arise and function at the margins of the society in which it is embedded, and will therefore be deprived of access to the sources of political and religious power in that society. But it can also happen that, as a result of specific circumstances, a sect can move temporarily into a position of influence and power. A case in point would be the Puritans after their establishment of a commonwealth in the New England colonies in the early seventeenth century.

In his *Das Antike Judentum*, published posthumously as volume three of his *Gesammelte Aufsätze zur Religionssoziologie*, Weber sketched out what he called the *Sektenreligiosität* ("sectarian religiosity") of the Pharisees and their antecedents the Hasideans (*asidaioi, hăsîdîm*) mentioned in 1–2 Maccabees.[6] Reflecting a point made by Troeltsch, Weber argued that this Pharisee sectarianism replicated certain basic features of Judaism present inchoately from the beginning. Its roots are to be sought in the transition from nation state to confessional community (*Bekenntnisgemeinde*) at the time of the Babylonian exile and the emergence, in Judah, of a ritually segregated community. The principal aim of Weber's study of ancient Judaism was to explain how the loss of statehood led to the emergence of Judaism as a *Pariavolk* ("pariah people") in the post-exilic period, that is, a social group characterized by ritually based prohibitions against commensality and intermarriage with those outside it.[7] For Weber, however, the emergent Judaism of the *běnê haggôlāh* was not sectarian since, in his view, sectarianism properly so called appeared only much later with the Pharisee *hăvûrôt* ("fellowship groups"). Yet his account of the golah group in the early post-exilic period corresponds closely in several important respects to his theoretical account of sectarianism in *Economy and Society*, a point to which we shall return.

While acknowledging the fundamental importance of the contribution of Troeltsch and Weber, it is important to keep in mind that both worked to a greater or lesser extent within the context of the Christian church in the west, leaving us with the task of looking further afield for other frames of reference and other kinds of comparative material. In presenting his three Jewish haireseis to an educated Greek-reading public, Josephus compared them to philosophical schools, matching Pharisees with Stoics (*Life* 1 2), Essenes with Pythagoreans (*Ant.* XV 371) and, by implication, Sadducees with Epicureans (*Ant.* XIII 171–173). Josephus even adds Judas the Galilean, a guerilla warlord, to the list of founders of sects (*War* II 118), this one identified as the fourth philosophy (*Ant.* XVIII

---

6 Max Weber, *Ancient Judaism*, Transl. and ed. Hans Gerth and Don Martindale (New York: The Free Press, 1952), 385–404. A new translation has long been overdue. When the time comes, it will presumably be based on the recent edition *Max Weber. Die Wirtschaftsethik der Weltreligionen: Das Antike Judentum. Schriften und Reden 1911–1920*, Max Weber Gesamtaufgabe I/21.2, ed. Eckart Otto, (Tübingen: Mohr Siebeck, 2005), 777–848. See further *Max Webers Studie über das Antike Judentum: Interpretation und Kritik*, ed. Wolfgang Schluchter (Frankfurt am Main: Suhrkamp, 1981).

7 In view of the pejorative associations of this term, it should be noted that for Weber it had a technical sense not restricted to Judaism; for Weber and others, in fact, it applied more directly to the study of the caste system in Buddhism than to early Judaism. In *Economy and Society* Weber defined it as follows: "A distinctive, hereditary social group lacking autonomous political organization, and characterized by internal prohibitions against commensality and intermarriage, originally founded upon magical, tabooistic and ritual injunctions" (Vol. 1, 493). See also Max Weber, *Ancient Judaism*, 336–55.

23). Philosophical schools do in fact have some features in common with sects as generally understood. The Latin term *secta* occurs in Cicero, Livy and Tacitus with the meaning of a party or philosophical school. In the laws of Solon in Athens philosophical schools were granted legal status as religious associations. The Stoic school of the third century BC has been compared to a church. Pythagoreans practised community of property, and some schools expelled members who deviated from accepted teachings. But we would probably not feel comfortable describing the Damascus community or the Qumran *yahad* as philosophical schools. Something along the same lines could be said about the many associations (*thiasoi, collegia*) attested in inscriptions and papyri from the Hellenistic period, including clubs, burial societies and guilds under the patronage of a popular deity such as Herakles, Asklepios or Dionysos. There would be some form of initiation ceremony including sprinkling with or immersion in water, new members would be required to take oaths (e.g. Lucius before initiation into the Isis cult in *Metamorphoses* XIX 15,30), and in several cases the name of the new entrant would be entered in a list.[8]

To go further back in time in search of parallels, the biblical record attests to the existence of distinctive sub-groups in northern Palestine from at least the ninth century BC. There were the "sons of the prophets", ecstatic conventicles established in connection with sanctuaries. They lived a cenobitic but not celibate existence in segregated settlements, and were recognizable by their attire and other distinctive features including self-lacerations (1 Kgs 20:35–41; 2 Kgs 1:8, 13). With the help of music, percussion and perhaps also psychotropic drugs they attained states of collective mental dissociation under the direction of a master-*nābî'*, somewhat like the Sufi Dervish *tawaf* under the direction of its sheik. While preserving their own distinctive way of life, these conventicles were involved in political activities, often as a force to be reckoned with. There were the Rechabites, an order of the strict observance whose members eschewed intoxicants and other amenities of urban existence, including living in houses.[9]

---

[8] Moshe Weinfeld, *Normative and Sectarian Judaism in the Second Temple Period* (London & New York: T. & T. Clark, 2005), 235–36, gives the example of an edict of Ptolemy IV requiring all devotees of the Dionysos cult in Alexandria to provide written proof of their status. He compares this with the census list in Ezra 2 = Nehemiah 7 and 1QS V 25, XIV 3–6. On these associations see *Voluntary Associations in the Graeco-Roman World*, ed. John Kloppenborg and Stephen Wilson (New York: Routledge, 1996); Philip Harland, *Associations. Synagogues, and Congregations* (Minneapolis: Fortress Press, 2003).
[9] The hypothesis of Matthew Black, *The Scrolls and Christian Origins: Studies in the Jewish Background of the New Testament* (New York: Scribner's, 1961), 15–16, that the origins of the Essenes can be traced ultimately to the nomadic lifestyle of the Rechabites and Kenites is vitiated by an outdated understanding of the supposed nomadic origins of early Israel. See Chris Knights, "The

The Nazirites, dedicated warriors had rules excluded strong drink, contact with the dead and shaving the hair, and there were no doubt other such groups which might seem to qualify as sectarian.

We know very little about the organization and internal affairs of these conventicles, but they acknowledged the leadership of an individual whose miraculous charisma called for acknowledgment by the members. Thus, the "sons of the prophets" at Jericho witnessed Elisha working a miracle with the mantle of his master Elijah after the latter had been taken up in the fiery chariot, and this led them to acknowledge his leadership: "The spirit of Elijah (now) rests on Elisha." They then approached him and prostrated themselves before him (2 Kgs 2:15). Such a leader, addressed as "father,"[10] presided over such a nebiistic assembly.[11] Like the sects of the Hasmonean and Roman periods, these assemblies deviated from accepted societal norms, some shared common space, and they had a marked affinity with states of mental dissociation reinforced by group solidarity, whether solicited or spontaneous. They would fit comfortably into several of the sect types listed by contemporary sociologists: they could be revolutionary and manipulationist, some were thaumaturgical and all were, to different degrees, conversionist.[12] Nevertheless we do not call them sects, and it would be instructive to ask why not. I suggest that the answer lies in the relation of the sub-group to the parent body to which it belongs. All of the sub-groups mentioned to a greater or lesser extent rejected contemporary societal and cultural values and opposed the political status quo, but none would have thought of their status as Israelites as in any way problematic, nor would they have questioned the status of fellow-Israelites. The Damascus community, the Qumran *yahad* and the early Christian community, on the contrary, took over the identity and claims of the parent body which, on their view, it had forfeited. In other words, they claimed to be what the parent body claimed to be but, again on their view, had ceased to be.

Rechabites of Jeremiah 35: Forerunners of the Essenes?," in *Qumran Questions*, ed. James Charlesworth (Sheffield: Sheffield Academic Press, 1995), 86–91.
10 *'āb*, 2 Kgs 2:12; 13:14; Jer 35:6 , Jonadab "father" of the Rechabites.
11 1 Kgs 4:28; 6:1; 9:1.
12 Bryan Wilson's typology of sects is well known. See his *Sects and Society* (Berkeley: University of California Press, 1961); "A Typology of Sects in a Dynamic and Comparative Perspective," *Archives de Sociologie de Religion* 16 (1963): 49–63; *Patterns of Sectarianism: Organization and Ideology in Social and Religious Movements* (London: Heinemann, 1967); *The Social Dimensions of Sectarianism: Sects and New Religious Movements in Contemporary Society* (Oxford: Clarendon, 1990). Somewhat different criteria in Rodney Stark and William Sims Bainbridge, *The Future of Religion: Secularization, Revival and Cult Formation* (Berkeley & Los Angeles: University of California, 1985).

We appreciate therefore that much can be learned from the comparative study of sect formation and maintenance in different cultures and epochs, but in the last analysis each case must be studied on its own terms and without unnecessary preconceptions. With this in mind, we now turn to the phenomenon of sectarianism during the time of the Second Temple.

2 Aspects of sectarianism in Ezra-Nehemiah and Persian period prophetic texts

It is testimony to the vigor and cogency of Weber's thought that, in spite of the fact that he was not a specialist in the literature of the period, and notwithstanding the criticism to which his ideas have been subjected, his writings can still serve as a point of departure for discussion of the issue of the earliest Jewish sectarianism. We recall once again Weber's argument that loss of political autonomy led to the emergence of a confessional, that is, a voluntary community. The transition from political institution to community (*Gemeinde*) resulted in a social entity which was depoliticized, demilitarized and deterritorialized. That is how Weber understood Wellhausen's dictum that Judaism came into existence from Israel ("aus Israel wird das Judentum"). The community which emerged from the disaster sought to maintain its identity by means of ritual self-segregation (circumcision, dietary rules, sabbath), strictly enforced endogamy, prohibition of commensality with non-members, full incorporation of resident aliens (*gērîm*), and the enforcement of the physical and ethnic disqualifications for membership specified in Deut 23:2–9 which Weber dated to the exilic period. The struggle to achieve this goal began in the Babylonian diaspora and was complete by the time of Ezra and Nehemiah. Both leaders belonged to the socially and economically dominant Judaeo-Babylonian party in Judah which kept itself apart from the local population. Since most of the latter belonged to the rural poor, their daily occupations made it practically impossible for them to observe dietary restrictions or the sabbath rest, which widened the gap between the immigrant golah group and the indigenous population. By Weber's own definition, the golah looks like a sect, though he maintained that sectarianism properly so called arose only with Pharisaism. The reason for his hesitation to date sectarianism any earlier may be that the golah became the dominant party in the province, whereas for both Troeltsch and Weber sectarian movements tend to arise among the socially and economically marginal elements of society.[13] It remains to be seen whether that is always and everywhere the case.

After the passage of so many years (the papers which went into *Antike Judentum* appeared in 1917–1918), and the discovery of so much archaeological and epigraphic material since that time, it would be remarkable if Weber's description of the situation following on the dissolution of the Judaean state were to have survived intact. One criticism focuses on Weber's use of the term "community" ("Gemeinde") which, when referred to the province of Judah during the Neo-Babylonian and early Persian periods, tended to underestimate its specifically political status as the province of an empire under the rule of a governor. The terms "theocracy" or "hierocracy" can be equally misleading since the high priesthood achieved political dominance only in the early Hellenistic period. Another criticism is that Weber overestimated the place of ritual prescriptions within the law, sometimes practically implying that the law was essentially about ritual. In short, the social and religious situation in the province was much more complex than is suggested by Weber's schematic description.[14]

A more positive engagement with Weber's study of early Judaism was published by Shemaryahu Talmon in German in the same collection of papers as Crüsemann's article (see n.14) and in English the following year.[15] He began with the observation, often repeated, that Weber's strength lay in the description of overall processes, in highlighting the typical, rather than in the careful and detailed study of specific situations. This is surely the case, if not necessarily a negative criticism. In dealing with the early Second Temple period Weber did not have the rich database at his disposal as in his studies of sectarian movements at the time of the Reformation, and what he did have was rather less than what we have today almost a century later. We should also bear in mind that his work on ancient Judaism remained unfinished at his death in 1920. On the "Aus Israel wird das Judentum" issue, Talmon pointed to two fundamental changes

---

13 Max Weber, *Economy and Society*, Vol. 1, 492–500; Vol. 2, 1204–10; *Ancient Judaism*, 356–64, 385–91.
14 Frank Crüsemann, "Israel in der Perserzeit: Eine Skizze in Auseinandersetzung mit Max Weber," in *Max Webers Sicht des antiken Christentums: Interpretation und Kritik*, ed. Wolfgang Schluchter (Frankfurt am Main: Suhrkamp, 1985), 205–32.
15 Shemaryahu Talmon, "Jüdische Sektenbildung in der Frühzeit der Periode des Zweiten Tempels: Ein Nachtrag zu Max Webers Studie über das antike Judentum," in *Max Webers Sicht des antiken Christentums*, 233; "The Emergence of Jewish Sectarianism in the Early Second Temple Period," in *King, Cult and Calendar in Ancient Israel: Collected Studies* (Jerusalem: Magnes, 1986), 165–201, practically identical with "The Internal Diversification of Judaism in the Early Second Temple Period," in *Jewish Civilization in the Hellenistic-Roman Period*, ed. Shemaryahu Talmon (Philadelphia: Trinity Press, 1991), 16–43.

resulting from the dissolution of the Judaean state and its institutions. The first was a loss of equilibrium and stability formerly maintained by a kind of balance of power involving king, priest, and prophet. The disappearance of the native dynasty, together with the transformations undergone by prophecy, left room for centrifugal forces to pull in different directions: local hieratic control contingent on the restoration of the cult on the one hand with, on the other hand, utopian and eschatological speculations calculated to undermine the will to accept and come to terms with historical realities. The other development Talmon named was a change from monocentrism to pluricentrism. In the first and most obvious instance this implied the Babylonian and Egyptian diasporas as distinct and distinctive centers of Jewish life and thought. Less obviously, after the resettlement of expatriates in Judah the in-group out-group mentality which originated in the diaspora situation assumed the form of a distinctive, segregated golah group within a Jewish ethnos itself segregated, in theory at least, from foreigners. It will be seen that Talmon's pluricentricity is actually not so different from Weber's analysis in *Ancient Judaism*.

One of the first biblical scholars to comment explicitly on the sectarian character of the golah as profiled in Ezra-Nehemiah was none other than William Foxwell Albright who was certainly aware of Weber's potential relevance for biblical scholarship.[16] In a co-authored article on the Qumran Essenes he remarked that "the Babylonian exile, often described as the great watershed of Israel's history, may well have seen the first stirrings of classical Jewish sectarianism, and of this we get hints in the memoirs of Ezra and Nehemiah".[17] Albright's statement provides us with the cue for testing this hypothesis against the characterization proposed above. We are dealing in the first place with those referred to in Ezra-Nehemiah as *haggôlāh* or *běnê-haggôlāh* (*běnê-gālûtâ* Aramaic), a Judaeo-Babylonian group which voluntarily relocated in Judah and, at least in theory, segregated itself from the indigenous population. It had its own assemblies (Ezra 10:8,14), maintained control over its members, and exercised the right to excommunicate deviants including those who failed to take part in its assemblies (Ezra 10:8; Neh 13:3). It was prepared to go to extreme lengths, beyond any explicit statement of law, to exclude marriage with outsiders. It reinforced its corporate identity and bound its members to it by covenants which, rather

---

[16] In his *From the Stone Age to Christianity: Monotheism and the Historical Process* (2nd ed., Garden City/New York: Doubleday, 1957 [1940]), 95, 283, William Foxwell Albright noted Weber's influence on Albrecht Alt's description of the Judges as charismatic warlords.

[17] William Foxwell Albright and Christopher Stephen Mann, "Qumran and the Essenes: Geography, Chronology, and the Identification of the Sect," in *The Scrolls and the New Testament*, ed. Matthew Black (London: SPCK, 1969), 16.

than enjoining commitment to the law in general terms as in the standard Deuteronomic formulations, featured stipulations relating to the golah group's own specific commitments confirmed by an oath to which the participants appended their names.[18] These sworn commitments can be viewed as transitional between the Deuteronomic covenant and the covenant in the land of Damascus of the Damascus document (CD).

The golah therefore corresponds to the introversionist type of sect by virtue of its self-segregation not only from the Gentile world but also from other Jews who did not share its theology and agenda. Its claim to be the exclusive embodiment of the Israel of the pre-disaster period is exhibited in the language in which it describes itself. It is "the holy seed" (Ezra 9:2), "the seed of Israel" (Neh 9:2), "the remnant of Israel"[19] or "Israel" *tout court*.[20] It can also express its appropriation of the traditions of twelve-tribal Israel by duodecimal symbolism.[21] It is sectarian not in breaking away from the parent body, as with the sects studied by Troeltsch and Weber, but in claiming the right to constitute Israel to the exclusion of other claimants. On its own view, it is the only surviving representative of the Israel to which the traditions testify.

In the account of the intermarriage crisis the solution and its legal justification are left in the hands of Ezra and "those who tremble at the commandment of our God" (Ezra 10:2–4). The designation of this core group of Ezra's supporters, *ḥărēdîm* ("tremblers"), is less than a title such as "Pharisees" or "Essenes" but more than simply a way of referring to devout Israelites. Shecaniah, who plays an important but rather mysterious role in the proceedings, refers to them as a distinct group with a special relationship to Ezra and a commitment to observe and apply the law according to their own interpretation. What is especially noteworthy about the designation *ḥārēd, ḥărēdîm* is that its only other occurrence is in Isaiah 66:1–5. In Isa 66:2 Yahveh looks with favour on the poor, the afflicted in spirit, and those who tremble at his word and, to judge by the verses immediately preceding and following, this favorable regard is contrasted with the temple personnel or at least with the current priesthood. Then a prophetic utterance is addressed to the same group of those who tremble at God's word:

---

18 Ezra 10:3–5; Neh 10:1–40; 13:23–27. There are also lists of those who accompanied Ezra (Ezra 8:1–14) and those who had married local women (10:18–44), cf. the list of the founders of the Damascus sect referred to but not appended in CD IV 2–12.
19 Neh 1:2–3; 7:71; 10:29; 11:1,20.
20 Ezra 2:59 = Neh 7:61; Ezra 3:1; 7:28; 10:2; Neh 8:17; 9:1; 13:3,18.
21 Ezra 2:2 = Neh 7:7 (12 leaders of the immigrant community); Ezra 8:3–14 (12 agnatic units in Ezra's caravan); Ezra 8:24 (12 priests charged with transporting the sacred vessels); Ezra 6:17; 8:35 (12 sacrificial animals).

> Hear the word of Yahweh, you who tremble at his word!
> Your brethren who hate you,
> who cast you out for my name's sake have said,
> "May Yahweh reveal his glory that we may witness your joy!"
> – but it is they who will be put to shame. (Isa 66:5)

Here, too, the designation has the qualifying phrase, "who tremble at his word", but those addressed are distinctive enough to be excommunicated or shunned as a socially visible collectivity.[22] They are addressed as a prophetic group by an anonymous seer, and their eschatological beliefs have something to do with their expulsion. Moreover, their attitude to the "brethren" who have cast them out, who in the nature of the situation must include the chief priests, is expressed in the typically sectarian form of eschatological reversal as expressed elsewhere in this last section of Isaiah (cf. Isa 65:13–14).

There is, of course, the difference between the *hărēdîm* of Ezra 9–10 and those of Isaiah 66:1–5 that the former are attached to a leader wielding apparently unlimited power in Judah and the latter have been expelled from the civic and cultic community and are, in consequence, among the poor and the defeated.[23] Yet this difference must be weighed against the consideration that both are dealing with the same opponents, namely, the priestly aristocracy in Jerusalem. The priests were prominent among the offenders (Ezra 9:2), were coerced into swearing the oath (10:5), and seventeen of them are listed among the transgressors as against six Levites (10:18–23). In his capacity as governor Nehemiah had to contend with unacceptable marriage alliances involving the high priestly family (Neh 13:4–9, 28), and the chief priests continued as leaders of the assimilationist party after the time of Nehemiah.[24] It is clear, moreover, that Ezra's policy was

---

[22] The verbal form *mĕnaddêkem* from *niddāh* occurs only here and Amos 6:3 where it means something like exorcize, neutralize by magical means. In rabbinic texts, however, it is a standard formula for excommunication from the synagogue (b. Ber. 19a; b.Pes. 52a). The formula in the Priestly texts in the Pentateuch is different (e.g Lev 7:20; 17:4). The verb "hate" (*śānē'*) implies active dissociation as in the divorce formula "I hate my wife", "I hate my husband"; see, for example, AP 15:23; 18:1, see Abraham Cowley, *Aramaic Papyri of the Fifth Century BC* (Osnabrück: Otto Zeller, 1967 [1923], 45, 55.

[23] The economic consequences of excommunication are apparent in the threat directed at those who failed to attend the assembly convoked to solve the marriage crisis (Ezra 10:8).

[24] On the interpretation of Isa 66:1–2 as an attack on temple priests engaged in syncretic cults see Alexander Rofé, "Isaiah 66:1–4: Judean Sects in the Persian Period as Viewed by Trito-Isaiah," in *Biblical and Related Studies Presented to Samuel Iwry*, ed. Ann Kort and Scott Morschauser (Winona Lake/Indiana: Eisenbrauns, 1985), 205–17 and Joseph Blenkinsopp, *Isaiah 56–66: A New Translation with Introduction and Commentary* (New York: Doubleday, 2003), 294–98.

not an unqualified success, and that the temple clergy quickly recovered their freedom to conduct business, including marital business, without interference. This would have been bad news for Ezra's supporters, leaving them exposed as a marginalized and shunned minority, thus explaining their situation as it appears in Isa 66:1–5. This is admittedly hypothetical, but a not implausible scenario in the light of the totally inadequate data at our disposal.. We may therefore be viewing basically the same social phenomenon from different perspectives and at different points in its historical development.[25]

Another text suggestive of early Second Temple sectarianism or quasi-sectarianism occurs near the end of the pseudonymous prophet Malachi (3:13–21). Malachi is the last of three originally anonymous units in the Book of the Twelve, all roughly equal in length and all certainly post-exilic. A more precise determination of the date of this last segment of the Twelve depends on allusions in the text itself and the political and social situation which it reflects. Historical indications include hostility towards Edomites and encroachment on their territory by Kedarite Arabs (1:2–5), a passing allusion to a governor unfortunately not identified by name (1:8), neglect of the temple cult and particularly vitriolic diatribe directed against the temple priesthood (1:6–2:9; 3:6–12) and, finally, in Mal 3:13–21, religious skepticism perhaps induced by disappointed hopes following on the building of the temple.[26] Malachi does not refer, directly at any rate, to either Ezra or Nehemiah, certainly not on the basis of an arbitrary emendation of *mal'āk* ("messenger") to *melek* ("king") in Mal 3:1b, understood to refer to Nehemiah as messianic figure.[27] But the polemical note about divorce associated with violence in Mal 3:16, often taken to be an interpolation, could be construed, whether interpolated or not, as an attack on Ezra's policy of coercive separation from wives and children. The suggestion that Malachi was written after Ezra but before or during Nehemiah's administration finds some support from complaints about non-payment of tithes and neglect of temple maintenance.[28] Allusions to

---

25 The designation *hărēdîm* itself suggests the emotionalism associated with certain types of prophecy, and the suggestion is somewhat confirmed by Ezra's reaction to the bad news about intermarriage, especially his lying on the ground in a catatonic state (*měšômēm*), cf. Ezek 3:15 *mašmîm* and Dan 8:27 *'eštômēm*. The eschatological element is explicit in Mal 3:13–18 (see below), and it is also possible that Ezra and his supporters were motivated by eschatological considerations as argued by Klaus Koch, "Ezra and the Origins of Judaism," *JSS* 19 (1974): 173–97.
26 See, for example, Hag 2:17; 3:13–15.
27 Argued by Aage Bentzen, "Priesterschaft und Laien in der jüdischen Gemeinde des fünften Jahrhunderts," *AfO* 6 (1930/1931): 282–83 and Ulrich Kellermann, *Nehemia: Quellen, Überlieferung und Geschichte* (Berlin: Walter de Gruyter, 1967), 2–3.
28 Mal 3:6–12, cf. Neh 13:10–14,31.

social injustice (3:5 cf. Neh 5:1–13), appeal to ethnic solidarity (2:10 cf. Neh 5:5), and emphasis on the levitical covenant (2:4–9 cf. Neh 13:29) could point in the same direction.[29] The situation is not nearly as clear as we would wish it to be (but when is that the case?), but it is clear enough to permit a probable conclusion that Malachi was composed not long after the marriage crisis episode described in Ezra 9–10.

Couched in the disputation form characteristic of this author,[30] the last section of Malachi records the complaint that God makes no distinction between the devout and the godless (3:13–18: my translation):

> "You have used strong speech against me", says Yahweh, and you reply, "How have we spoken against you?" "What you have said is, 'Serving God is futile. What profit is there in our observing his commandments and leading a penitential life in the presence of Yahweh of Hosts? So now we reckon the irreligious to be the ones who are blessed; evildoers not only flourish, but when they put God to the test they escape punishment." Then those who feared God conferred together, and Yahweh took heed and listened. A book of remembrance was inscribed in his presence with the names of those who feared Yahweh and thought on his name. Then, "They shall be mine,", said Yahweh, "my special possession, on the day when I act. I shall deal kindly with them as parents deal kindly with children who respect them. Then you will see the distinction between the righteous and the reprobate, those who fear God and those who do not."

The complaint is followed by the God-fearers conferring together, and this action elicits a positive response from Yahweh. A document is written containing the names of those who fear God and esteem his name. They will be his special possession on the day of his decisive intervention in human affairs, when the distinction between the righteous and the reprobate will be as clearly manifest to all as it is apparent to those so reassured (3:16–18). The passage concludes with the statement that on judgement day the reprobate will be destroyed, while those who revere Yahweh's name will triumph and rejoice (3:19–21).

There can be no doubt that those addressed in 3:13–15, who are giving strong expression to their doubts about the providence and justice of God, are

---

29 John Merlin Powis Smith, *A Critical and Exegetical Commentary on Haggai, Zechariah, Malachi and Jonah* (Edinburgh: T. & T. Clark, 1912), 7, even claimed that "the Book of Malachi fits the situation amid which Nehemiah worked as snugly as a bone fits its socket".
30 Mal 1:2–5, 6–8, 13; 2:10, 13–15; 3:7–8. See Egon Pfeiffer, "Die Disputationsworte im Buche Maleachi," *EvTh* 19 (1959): 546–68; Gerhard Wallis, "Wesen und Struktur der Botschaft Maleachis," *Das Ferne und Nahe Wort: Festschrift Leonhard Rost*, ed. Fritz Maass (Berlin: Töpelmann, 1967), 229–37; James Fischer, "Notes on the Literary Form and Message of Malachi," *CBQ* 34 (1972): 315–20.

identical with the God-fearers who are reassured in the following verses.³¹ The two paragraphs are therefore related as problem and solution. After all, the ones addressed in the first paragraph distinguish themselves from the irreligious, they have obeyed God and led a penitential life in spite of their doubts, and their complaints are no stronger than reproaches and laments uttered frequently in Psalms, not to mention Job. It is also possible, in view of the solution offered to their complaint, that this crisis of faith was precipitated by delay in the anticipated divine intervention in their affairs which many thought would follow on the building of the temple. The solution, at any rate, is eschatological. The distinction between the devout and the reprobates in the Jewish community is already established in principle and will be manifest for all to see on judgment day. The principle of eschatological discrimination, a common sectarian theme which appears in the gospels (Matt 13:37–43; 25:31–46), draws an invisible line through the community, separating the true Israel from those who are Israel only in name. Pointing in the same direction is the weighty theological term *sĕgullâ* ("special possession") used especially by the Deuteronomists to characterize Israel in contrast to the nations,³² but here designating a pietistic group in contrast to the rest of Israel.

The way in which those addressed are described suggests a connection of some kind with the Servants of the Lord in the last segment of Isaiah (Isa 65:8–9, 13–16) and those who tremble at God's word in Ezra 9:4; 10:3 and Isaiah 66:1–5. They are God-fearers;³³ God-servers, servants of God;³⁴ they esteem the name of God³⁵ and mourn in the present age in anticipation of rejoicing in the age to come.³⁶ They confer together, which suggests that they are entering into a pact or covenant constituting themselves as the true Israel, Yahweh's special

---

31 The problem for several commentators is with the adverb *'āz* ("then") with which the following paragraph begins, and therefore with continuity between vv 13–15 and 16–18. Wilhelm Rudolph, *Haggai, Sacharja 1–8, Sacharja 9–14, Maleachi* (Gütersloh: Gerd Mohn, 1976), 286–87, probably correctly translated "damals" indicating temporal succession. We can in any case agree with Julius Wellhausen, *Die Kleinen Propheten übersetzt, mit Noten* (Berlin: Reimer, 1893), 203: "Es sind die Frommen welche murren; und sie werden im Folgenden nicht gestraft sondern getröstet".
32 Exod 19:5–6; Deut 7:6; 14:2; 26:18–19; Ps 135:4.
33 Mal 1:6,14; 2:5; 3:5; cf. Isa 50:10; 63:17.
34 Mal 3:14,17,18; cf. Isa 65:8–9,13–16; 66:14.
35 Mal 3:16; cf. Isa 59:19; 65:15–16.
36 Mal 3:14, *hālaknû qĕdorannît*: the adverb is hapax, derived from the verbal stem *qdr* attested with the meaning "to be dark", "to lament or mourn"; compare the allusions to mourners (*'ăbēlîm, mit' abbĕlîm*) in Isa 57:18; 61:2–3; 66:10.

possession, language elsewhere associated with covenant-making.³⁷ The *sēper zikkārôn*, literally "a book of remembrance", is by some understood to be an inventory written by Yahveh in which are recorded either the names of the righteous³⁸ or good and evil deeds (e.g., Isa 65:6; Neh 13:14). But we are not told that this book was written by Yahweh, and other references to a document in the form of a *zikkārôn* refer to human records.³⁹ We are therefore entitled to read Mal 3:16–18 as divine authentication of the parties to a covenant whose names are recorded in writing, as were the names of the signatories to Nehemiah's covenant. The assembly of these God-fearers, therefore, anticipates the different prefigurations of the eschatological Israel in the sectarian movements of the late Second Temple period.

---

37 Moshe Weinfeld, "The Covenant of Grant in the Old Testament and Ancient Near East," *JAOS* 90 (1970): 184–203 (195), refers to the Akkadian cognate *sikiltum* used in treaty contexts.
38 Exod 32:32–33; Ps 69:29; 87:6.
39 Exod 17:14; Esth 6:1.

XIV. Jewish Sectarianism from Ezra to the Hasidim

Source: an expanded form of "The Development of Jewish Sectarianism from Nehemiah to the Hasidim." In *Judah and the Judeans in the Fourth Century BCE*, ed. by Oded Lipschits, Gary Neil Knoppers and Rainer Albertz, 385–404. Winona Lake/Indiana: Eisebnrauns, 2007.

A historian does not roam about at random through the past, like a ragman in search of bric-a-brac; rather he sets out with a specific plan in mind, a problem to solve, a working hypothesis to test ... To describe what one sees is one thing; but to see that which must be described, that is the hard part.[1]

1 The sources for the centuries before and after the Macedonian conquest

For the century from Ezra and Nehemiah to the Macedonian conquest and the century following, our sources of information about Jewish communities in Judah/Judaea and the diaspora are few and far between. We suspect that there are connections between the religious ideology of Ezra at the beginning and the well-known sectarian movements of the Graeco-Roman period at the end, but their existence is not easy to demonstrate. The best we can do is construct a hypothesis working forward from the situation in the mid-fifth century and backwards from the time of Daniel and the Hasidaeans (*ḥăsîdîm*) while looking for lines of continuity. To define the period somewhat more precisely: Ezra arrived in Jerusalem in the seventh year of Artaxerxes, probably Artaxerxes I, therefore 458 BC and Nehemiah began his tenure of office as governor of the province in the twentieth year of the same Artaxerxes, therefore 445/444 (Neh 1:2). After serving for twelve years he was recalled to the Persian court in the thirty-second year of the reign, therefore 433/432 (Neh 5:14), and returned to Judah where he continued to serve, for how long we are not told but certainly not beyond 424/423, the last year of Artaxerxes. As for a *terminus ad quem*, Josephus (*Ant.* XIII 171–173) introduces the brief account of his three "schools of thought" (*haireseis*) into the narrative of the activities of Jonathan Maccabee (160–142 BC), which might suggest that he took this to be the time when they originated. But if we

---

1 Lucien Febvre, "Leçon d'Ouverture au Collège de France, 13 Décembre 1933". I owe the quotation to Carlo Ginzburg, *The Judge and the Historian: Marginal Notes on a Late-Twentieth-Century Miscarriage of Justice*, Transl. Antony Shugaar (London & New York: Verso,1999), 35–36.

can agree at a minimum that the *asidaioi*, pietist conventicles of the devout of the type mentioned in 1 Maccabees (2:42; 7:12–17), represented a movement with a history reaching back some time before the reign of Antiochus IV, we can take this "Hasidic" phenomenon as it existed in the early Hellenistic period, as a convenient terminus for our discussion, initially at any rate.

What information is available from sources other than biblical for this obscure period? Josephus, our principal source external to the Bible, is not well informed on the Persian period, and he makes matters worse by conflating the four rulers named Artaxerxes and the three named Darius, thus drastically telescoping the two centuries of Persian rule. After his lengthy paraphrase of the book of Esther according to the expanded Greek version (*Ant.* XI 184–296), which he regarded as the last biblical book, he seems to have run out of biblical source material. He appears nevertheless to have had some independent information on the Jerusalemite high priests, but his account of the circumstances leading to the establishment of the Samaritan sanctuary during the Macedonian takeover, the most important event he records for this period (*Ant.* XI 302–305), is justifiably considered suspect.[2] He reports that Alexander granted permission for the construction of a sanctuary on Mount Gerizim, the one later destroyed by John Hyrcanus in 128 BC (*Ant.* XI 322–334), but no confirmation is available from the Samaritan Chronicle. However, one conclusion we can draw from what he does tell us is that the politicization and commercialization of the official priesthood, a significant factor in sect formation in the Seleucid and Hasmonaean periods, was already underway in the fourth century. One example: during the reign of Artaxerxes II (404–359) the Persian general Bagohi (Bagōsēs in Josephus) promised the high priesthood to Jeshua the brother of the current incum-

---

2 The *mariage de convenance* between Manasseh, brother of the high priest Jaddua, and Nikaso, daughter of Sanballat governor of Samaria, leading to the construction of a temple for Manasseh by Sanballat, is suspiciously similar to the incident recorded in Neh 13:28–29, on which see Joseph Blenkinsopp, *Ezra-Nehemiah: A Commentary* (Philadelphia: Westminster, 1988), 365. Furthermore, the Samaritan chronicles know of no Samaritan high priest called Manasseh. Josephus is presumed to have confused this Sanballat with the opponent of Nehemiah who bore the same name (*Ant.* XI 302). The occurrence in the Samaria papyri of a Sanballat, father of the mid-fourth century governor of Samaria, removes or at least alleviates this problem but does not necessarily authenticate Josephus' account. For the older interpretation of this incident, prior to the discovery of the Samaria papyri, see Victor Tcherikover, *Hellenistic Civilization and the Jews* (New York: Atheneum, 1975), 44–45, 419–20, and for an updated discussion Emil Schürer, *The History of the Jewish People in the Age of Jesus Christ (175 BC–AD 135): A New English Version*, Vol. 2, ed. Geza Vermes, Fergus Millar and Matthew Black (Edinburgh: T. & T. Clark, 1979), 17–19 and James VanderKam, *From Joshua to Caiphas: High Priests after the Exile* (Minneapolis: Fortress Press, 2004), 63–85.

1 The sources for the centuries before and after the Macedonian conquest — 209

bent, leading to an altercation in the temple between the brothers which ended with the murder of Jeshua and resulted in seven years oppression by the Persian authorities (*Ant.* XI 27–301).

The Greek historians who cover the period, principally Diodorus, Xenophon (to 362) and Ctesias (to 382), are concerned primarily with Greek-Persian relations and the Western Mediterranean region. None of them so much as mentions the Jews or Judah. At the same time, we can hardly suppose that Judah was unaffected by the constant military activity in the region, given its position on the main routes from Egypt to the eastern Mediterranean and the Persian heartland. An Egyptian revolt was already underway before Artaxerxes II came to the throne and disturbances from that quarter continued intermittently throughout the reign. Revolts also broke out in Cyprus (389–380) and the Phoenician cities (385–383). The failure of the Persians to subdue their erstwhile satrapy of Mudriya (Egypt) left the entire Transeuphratene satrapy, Judah included, open to Egyptian influence. Egyptian support for the so-called "Revolt of the Satraps" in the 360s, including Phoenicia, entailed another march from Egypt through Palestine-Syria with Greek mercenaries. The attempt to subdue Egypt continued under Artaxerxes III Ochus (359–338), at first unsuccessfully, but at length ending with Egypt being brought back into the Persian fold if only for the last decade of the empire's existence. The failure of Artaxerxes' initial campaign against Egypt (351–350) inspired another Phoenician revolt masterminded by Tennes ruler of Sidon, supported by Egypt under Nectanebo, and opposed by Belesys, satrap of the Transeuphrates region (Diodorus XVI 42), perhaps identical with a Belšunu mentioned in cuneiform texts.[3]

There is no evidence that Judah was directly involved in the revolt instigated by Tennes, but the involvement of Nectanebo and Belysis on opposite sides could hardly have left it unaffected. The archaeological indications of destructions alleged to have happened about this time – Hazor stratum II, Megiddo stratum I, Tel Qasile VI and others – are badly in need of further study and clarification.[4] The notice that many Jews were deported to Hyrcania, and perhaps also to Babylon, and that Jericho was destroyed about the same time, derive from late ecclesiastical writers who are not well informed on the Persian period.[5] At any

---

[3] See Pierre Briant, *Histoire de l'Empire Perse de Cyrus à Alexandre*, Vol. 1 (Paris: Libraire Arthème Fayard, 1996), 618–19 =*From Cyrus to Alexander: A History of the Persian Empire*, Transl. Peter Daniels (Winona Lake, Indiana: Eisenbrauns, 2002), 601–2.

[4] Listed by Dan Barag, "The Effects of the Tennes Rebellion on Palestine," *BASOR* 183 (1966): 6–12.

[5] On these notices from Eusebius, Jerome, Orosius, Syncellus and Solinus see Emil Schürer, *The History of Jewish Palestine*, Vol. 3/1, ed. Geza Vermes, Fergus Millar and Martin Goodman (Edin-

rate, the revolt was eventually put down and Tennēs executed in 345. This endless series of "the disasters of war" continued throughout the reign of Artaxerxes III and into those of his successors Arses and Darius III. Then, following on the Macedonian conquest, Josephus records the sufferings inflicted on the inhabitants of Judah during the interminable hostilities between the *diadochoi*. The country, he tells us, was devastated, Jerusalem was occupied more than once and was destroyed during the conquest of the country by Antiochus III (*Ant.* XII 138), and many Judaean Jews were deported to Egypt (*Ant.* XII 1–10).

Any assessment of the internal affairs of the province, its parties, politics and sects, must surely take this endemic state of warfare, the passing back and forth of armies living off the land, and the consequent social and economic disruption, into account. Such conditions are compatible with the frequent complaints of inequality, poverty, and social abuses of different kinds in late biblical sources – for example in Job (22:1–11; 24:1–25), Qoheleth (4:1–8) and psalms of lamentation.[6] There would also be support from archaeological evidence if the destruction levels identified at several sites could be dated precisely enough, or even approximately enough, to correlate them with the known facts of political and military history. The careers of the vastly wealthy Transjordanian Tobiads, descendants of the Tobiah who caused problems for Nehemiah, reveal the existence of a Jewish lay aristocracy not greatly concerned with either the Law or the Prophets (*Ant.* XII 160–236). Joseph and Hyrcanus, distinguished members of that family, went about their business as tycoons and tax collectors during the late third and early second century BC, but the conditions which made their careers possible existed already during the last century of Persian rule. These conditions were calculated to encourage discontent, opposition to policies pursued by the assimilationist ruling classes, and the creation of dissident groups, not necessarily confined to the poorest strata of the population.

Coming now to the biblical texts: the few usually located in the late Persian or early Hellenistic period reveal a broad range of religious practice and opinion. There is no polemic against intermarriage in the book of Esther where we might expect to find it. Like the tales in Daniel 1–6, the story in the book of Tobit un-

---

burgh: T. & T. Clark, 1986), 6 n.12. Several scholars have read the book of Judith against the backdrop of these events during the reign of Artaxerxes III, on which see Emil Schürer, Vol. 3/1, 217–18.

6 A continuation of the situation in the mid-fifth century reflected in Nehemiah 5 and Isaiah 58; but I doubt that the situation in fourth century Judah was any less severe than the "social crisis of the fifth century" postulated by Rainer Albertz, *A History of Israelite Religion in the Old Testament Period*, Vol. 2, *From the Exile to the Maccabees* (Louisville: Westminster John Knox Press, 1992.), 495–97.

folds against a background of at times uneasy co-existence in the diaspora. Both Tobit and Tobias are in all respects exemplary Jews living in a Gentile environment, solicitous in prayer (3:1–6; 12:8), almsgiving (1:16–17; 4:7–11), fasting (12:8), dietary regulations (1:10–11), and care for the dead (1:17–20; 2:3–8). Tobit marries a woman from his own clan (1:9) and warns his son against marriage with a woman outside of the extended kinship network (4:12–13), but this admonition is simply in keeping with the immemorial custom of clan-endogamous marriage, not for reasons of ritual purity.[7] Judith is almost ostentatiously scrupulous in such matters as dietary laws (Jud 11:12; 12:1–4, 19), fasting (8:6), ritual washing (12:7–8), and tithing (11:13–15), and she remains a widow after the death of her husband (16:22). The author presents her as the female ideal of piety and strict adherence to the law, yet permits Achior to be circumcised and admitted to the household of Israel in defiance of the Deuteronomic law (Jud 14:10; Deut 23:4–7). The Moabite woman Ruth is also accepted into the Israelite people notwithstanding the same exclusionary law: "Your people shall be my people, your God shall be my God" she says to her mother-in-law (Ruth 1:16).

Jewish writings from the later Hellenistic and Graeco-Roman periods with a strong apologetic intent, including 4 Maccabees, Baruch, Wisdom of Solomon and the Letter of Aristeas aim to present Judaism as a philosophy in accord with reason, and therefore tend to emphasize the more expansive and accommodating rather than the more integralist aspects of legal interpretation bearing on the realities of everyday life. The Jewish law, therefore, serves to promote the practice of virtue (4 Macc 5:22–24; Wisd 8:7), the dietary laws serve to inculcate self-control (4 Macc 1:14; 5:2), self-segregation is necessary in order to avoid the temptations of idolatry (Aristeas 139), yet the same author is prepared to concede that Jews worship the same deity as the Greeks, but under a different name (Aristeas 15).

On the basis of our brief survey we would have to conclude that, at least during the late Persian and early Hellenistic periods, there are few signs that the forms of ritualized self-segregation introduced by Ezra into the province of Judah had any great effect. This is most clearly evident with rules for marriage and divorce imposed by Ezra, Shecaniah and the *běnê haggôlāh* (Ezra 9–10). The abrupt ending to the Ezra story (Ezra 10:44) might in fact suggest that the disruptive results of their attempt to implement these measures brought Ezra's career to an equally abrupt terminus, with his recall by the imperial overlord.

---

7 The *'iššâ zārāh* is therefore a woman who does not belong to their clan (Tob 1:9; 4:12–13). The preservation of patrimonial domain has much to do with this form of endogamous marriage (Tob 7:12–13, cf. Num 36:5–9).

2 Reading history backwards

The dearth of information from the period as defined for the social and religious history of Judaism obliges the historian to fall back on inference based on information available for the time immediately preceding and following that period. In other words, we have to fall back on the *faute de mieux* of reading history forwards and backwards in the hope of presenting a plausible account of developments in between. Following this plan, we will begin by reading backwards from the symbolic histories in Daniel, Jubilees, the Enochian Apocalypse of Weeks and the Animal Apocalypse, the Testament of Levi, 4QPseudo-Moses (4Q390) and, most importantly, the Damascus Document. The intent will be to detect some historical, connective links underlying the sectarian ideology inscribed in these accounts. We may then be in a position to read forward from the book Ezra-Nehemiah and late prophetic texts, especially Isaiah and the Twelve, with a view to testing, and perhaps confirming conclusions already obtained.

I therefore propose to begin with the retrospective view from the perspective of one section of the late Second Temple period. A feature common to many texts from that time is the concern to link the present moment with the Babylonian exile and, in so doing, to airbrush out the intervening centuries. In writings from that time, the eastern diaspora appears to have been considered the most fitting location for edifying and didactic narrative and the period of the exile the most fitting time for visions and revelations. Didactic narratives and novellas like the diaspora stories in Daniel 1–6, Tobit, Esther in the expanded Greek version, Susanna, Bel and the Serpent, are set in that place and at that time, and the Qumran *Apocryphon of Joseph* (4Q371–373) even puts the Joseph story in an exilic setting following on the fall of Jerusalem. The vision reports in Daniel and 4 Ezra are likewise backdated to the time immediately following the exile. The diaspora tales in Daniel 1–6 represent Daniel (Belteshazzar) and his companions at the Babylonian court as a small-scale model or prototype for the pietist group in which and for which the book of Daniel was written long after the Neo-Babylonian period. In these stories Daniel's status vis-à-vis his companions corresponds to the status of the Danielic *maśkîl* vis-à-vis the *rabbîm*.[8] The Daniel of chapters 2, 4 and 5 also engaged in the same kind of pesher-like interpretation as the visionary Daniel of chapters 7–12 and, for that matter, the Qumran sectarians.

---

[8] The term *rabbîm* is used for members of the Danielic sect at least in Dan 12:3 and was later adopted as a technical term for the rank and file in the Qumran rule book (1QS).

The Danielic reading of Jeremiah's seventy years (Dan 9:1–2, 24–27), which eventuates in a sevenfold extension of the period of exile and punishment, is a typical example of this kind of reappraisal of the post-exilic period. This drastic reinterpretation is not confined to the book of Daniel. For the author of Jubilees (32:14–31) the exile was the time when God hid his face from Israel. It was followed by a long period of neglect of the law and corrupt temple worship which came to an end only when God raised up a "plant of righteousness", no doubt with reference to the pietist group from which the book derives. The pattern is reproduced in the Enochian "Animal Apocalypse" (1En 89:68–90:5) according to which worship in the temple of Zerubbabel was polluted from the beginning and the entire age was one of spiritual blindness (1En 89:72–90:5). In the final period, corresponding to the rule of the Seleucids, the devout who opposed the prevalent corruption are represented as lambs and – according to a common opinion – the slain lamb refers to the murder of the high priest Onias III at the instigation of Menelaus in or about 170 BC (1En 90:6–12). The "Apocalypse of Weeks" (1En 93:1–10 + 91:12–17) uses the same symbolic-chronological system as the book of Daniel. According to both these texts the entire period from the exile to the time of writing is a time of religious infidelity; in short, a failed history.

Like the "Apocalypse of Weeks," the Testament of Levi also organizes the religious history of Israel in weeks of years or jubilees. During the fifth week the exiles are repatriated and the temple rebuilt, and the seventh and last week witnesses, once again, the corruption of the priesthood. The sixth week, corresponding to the entire Second Temple period down to the time of writing, is, once again, passed over in silence. A final example: the fragmentary Qumran text 4Q Pseudo-Moses (4Q390) presents Moses, presumably *in articulo mortis*, predicting the course of history, again in jubilees. At the time of the exile the only ones to escape condemnation are "those who were the first to go up from the land of their captivity to build the temple." In the seventh and final jubilee evil will be triumphant, God will hide his face, but some few survivors will escape annihilation.

The consistency with which this symbolic historiography is reproduced in writings from the second and first centuries BC points to the existence of a common tradition , perhaps, as Philip Davies suggests, from the broader Essene movement in its pre-Qumran phase.[9] The politicization of the official priesthood, the assimilationist policies it pursued, and the consequent alienation of the

---

9 Philip Davies, *Behind the Essenes: History and Ideology in the Dead Sea Scrolls* (Atlanta: Scholars Press, 1987), 107–34.

more traditional elements from the temple as the principal focus of religious life, must have encouraged the formation of dissident groups long before the Seleucid epoch.

The theme of the exile as the great divide in the national and ethnic history, and the rite of passage which had to be traversed in order to belong to the gathered community of the new age, is most clearly and forcefully expressed in the Damascus Document. In the first section of the Admonition (CD I 3–II 1) the exile is the time when God hid his face from Israel and its sanctuary, the time of wrath.[10] At this point we come across the much-debated problem of the gap of 390 years between the "return to Zion" and the emergence of the Damascus sect. Some commentators hold that this gap, deriving from Ezekiel's sign-act indicating a period of punishment for Israel (Ezek 4:4–5), is an insertion which breaks up the narrative logic and perhaps also the prosodic regularity of the text. This may be so, but since the historical survey goes on to speak of the origins or immediate prehistory of the sect – the twenty years of disorientation (groping) with the appearance on the scene of the Teacher and his opponents – the insertion hypothesis could be justified only as part of a thorough rewrite of the survey.[11] What at any rate is clear is the intent to associate the Damascus sect with those few who survived the exile with their faith intact and returned to Judah where they constituted the prophetic remnant and the nucleus of a new community.

The same point is made later in the Admonition: God made a covenant with the remnant, those who left the land of Judah, went into exile, and eventually returned. There followed a long period when Israel was under the dominion of Belial, a period which lasted "until the number of those years was complete," that is, until the founding of the sect (III 12–IV 19). The connection with the exilic generation is made once again towards the end of the Admonition (V 20–VII 21). At the time of the destruction of the land, there came into existence a group composed of priests and lay members who left Judah and lived in "Damascus," that

---

10 For the expression *histîr pānîm* ("hiding the face") with explicit reference to the exile see Isa 54:8. It also occurs in Jub I 13; 4Q387a 3 III 4; 4Q390: 1 I 9–10.
11 Philip Davies, *The Damascus Covenant: An Interpretation of the "Damascus Document"* (Sheffield: JSOT, 1983), 61–72, 233–35, argues for an extensive rewrite of the entire section including the 390 years. Michael Knibb, "Exile in the Damascus Document," *JSOT* 25 (1983): 99–117 (112), agrees somewhat reluctantly but reads the additions as an early expansion of the account of sectarian origins. For an earlier form of the argument see Isaac Rabinowitz, "A Reconsideration of 'Damascus' and '390 Years' in the 'Damascus' ('Zadokite') Fragments," *JBL* 73 (1954): 11–35 (12–15).

is, the land of exile,[12] where they entered into a covenant and dedicated themselves to the study of the law under a leader known as "the Interpreter of the Law" (*dōrēš hattôrâ*).

The symbolic historiography of the Damascus Document raises the question as to its possible correspondence to history in real time or, alternatively, whether it is possible to detect historical and social continuities behind these symbolic and ideological constructions. There was certainly continuity during the fourth century, "the "lost century" as far as our information on Jewish history is concerned, at the level of the interpretation of texts deemed to be authoritative. And since interpretation is not a disembodied activity but is carried forward by specific individuals and groups it can count, in some form, as continuity at the level of social realities as well. Theological constructs, for example, the idea that the exile continued down to the emergence of the Damascus sect,[13] need not be dissociated from an awareness of real, historical situations and continuities. The question therefore arises as to whether the text provides any clues as to the origins of the sect. As far as I know, Albright was the first to propose a Babylonian origin for the Essenes, the putative addressees of the Damascus Document. This Judaeo-Babylonian sect migrated to Judah either inspired by the victories of the Maccabee brothers or to escape the Parthian invasion of Babylon some two decades later in or about the year 140 BC.[14] Not all the arguments presented by Albright have survived scrutiny. For example, an interest in astronomy and divination is not peculiar to Babylon and frequent lustrations would have been as hygienically necessary in Palestine as in Babylon. On the other

---

12 Since the interpretation of "the land of Damascus" continues to be discussed it would be out of place for me to be too apodictic. However, it seems arguable in the present state of the discussion that, in the texts referred to, leaving the land of Judah and dwelling in the land of Damascus means going into exile, and that therefore "the land of Damascus" is the land of exile, hence Babylon. This conclusion seems to be implied in the midrash on Amos 5:26–27 in which Damascus, or somewhere beyond Damascus, is a place of exile (CD VII 13–19), and it is worth noting that Stephen's citation of the same text in Acts 7:43 substitutes "Babylon" for "Damascus." The case for Damascus = Babylon has been argued in several publications by Jerome Murphy-O'Connor, most recently in "Damascus," in *EDSS* 1, 165–66 and criticized by Michael Knibb, "Exile in the Damascus Document". See also the summary of the CD history in Philip Davies, *Behind the Essenes*, 47–49.
13 Michael Knibb, "The Exile in the Literature of the Intertestamental Period," *HeyJ* 17 (1976): 253–72; "Exile in the Damascus Document," *JSOT* 25 (1983): 99–117 and "Exile," in *EDSS* 1, 276–77.
14 William Foxwell Albright, *From the Stone Age to Christianity: Monotheism and the Historical Process* (2nd ed., Garden City/New York: Doubleday, 1957 [1940])), 3, 21–22, 376; Albright and Christopher Stephen Mann, "Qumran and the Essenes: Geography, Chronology, and the Identification of the Sect," in *The Scrolls and Christianity*, ed. Matthew Black (London: SPCK, 1969), 19.

side of the ledger, the laws in the Damascus Document for those living in "camps" (VII 6) would seem to suggest a Gentile and therefore, plausibly, a diasporic environment.[15]

For this reason and others, not least the repeated insistence on continuity with the "remnant" of the Babylonian exile, the Babylonian origins of the sect has emerged as a serious though not undisputed alternative to the hypothesis of Palestinian origin and continuity with the Hasidim (asidaioi) of 1–2 Maccabees.[16] Jerome Murphy-O'Connor, one of the principal proponents of Babylonian origin, followed Albright in positing a return to Palestine in the mid to late second century BC, adding that the eschatological beliefs of the Judaeo-Babylonian group may have motivated them to return.[17] This is plausible if unprovable in the absence of relevant information on the eastern diaspora from the fourth to the second century BC. The first to return to Judah during the early Persian period, the "founding fathers" (*hāri'šōnîm*, CD IV 6,8) who constituted the original "plant root" (CD I 7), and who established themselves in Judah during the early Persian period as a self-segregating society, may represent only the first stage of a process, the first of several missions to Judah from the self-segregating Judaeo-Babylonian parent body. The process may have been going on throughout the Persian and early Hellenistic period, eventuating in the sectarianism clearly attested in the second century BC. Continuity of this kind over several centuries is not implausible. Sects – the Karaites for example – can continue in existence for centuries and preserve their essential tenets while making adjustments to new situations as they arise. Communication between Judah and the eastern diaspora must have been frequent throughout the period of the Second Temple. Josephus tells us that the Israelites as a whole remained in Babylon after Ezra's mission (*Ant.* XI 133). He quotes Hecataeus to the effect that many Jews were deported to Babylon by the Persians (*Against Apion* I 194), and notes that Jews were repatriated from Babylon during the reign of Antiochus III (*Ant.* XII 138). So the idea of sectarian activity in Judah throughout the late Per-

---

15 PhilippDavies, *The Damascus Covenant*, 202–4.
16 Isaac Rabinowitz, "A Reconsideration of 'Damascus'"; Samuel Iwry, "Was there a Migration to Damascus? The Problem of שבי ישראל," *Eretz Israel* 9 (1969): 80–88; Jerome Murphy-O'Connor, "An Essene Missionary Document? CD II,14–VI,1," *RB* 77 (1970): 201–29; "A Literary Analysis of Damascus Document VI,2–VIII,3," *RB* 78 (1971): 210–32; "A Literary Analysis of Damascus Document XIX,33–XX,34," *RB* 79 (1972): 544–64; "The Essenes and their History," *RB* 81 (1974): 215–44; "The Damascus Document Revisited," *RB* 92 (1985): 223–46. Philip Davies, *The Damascus Covenant*, 202–4, concluded that there is nothing to contradict an origin in the eastern diaspora for both the Damascus document and the community from which it came.
17 Jerome Murphy-O'Connor, "An Essene Missionary Document?," 214–15; "The Damascus Document Revisited," 224–30.

sian and early Hellenistic period which originated among Babylonian Jews and retained its association with them is hardly far-fetched. In the following two sections I will try to add substance to the hypothesis of *historical* linkage between the Damascus sect and the self-segregating diaspora community of the early Persian period with reference to Ezra-Nehemiah, Chronicles, and late prophetic texts.

3 Ezra-Nehemiah and Ezra and Nehemiah

First, the issue of dating. In his memoir Nehemiah dates his governorship from the twentieth year of Artaxerxes (Neh 1:1; 2:1), probably Artaxerxes I nicknamed Long Hand therefore 445/444, to the thirty-second year of the same ruler, therefore 433/432. After his recall and return to the province he continued in the same capacity for some time, but no later than the last year of Artaxerxes, therefore 425/424. . Ezra's mission to the province is dated to the seventh year of Artaxerxes (Ezra 7:1,8), either Artaxerxes Long Hand, therefore 458 or Artaxerxes nicknamed Memory Man, therefore 398, most probably the former. If we accept these data, we would have to add that the book Ezra-Nehemiah itself is the product of a considerably later time. The initial section, Ezra 1–6, the account of the first foundations of the new commonwealth, has enough in common with Chronicles to justify deriving it from the circle of the Chronicler. The lists of temple personnel in Nehemiah 12 take us well beyond the lifetime of Nehemiah himself, beginning with the list of high priests which ends with Jaddua, incumbent at the time of the Macedonian conquest.[18] The list of Levites looks back to "the time of Nehemiah the governor and Ezra the priest and scribe" as to a not too recent past (Neh 12:22–26). Practically all commentators agree that Nehemiah's covenant must be later than Nehemiah himself.[19] Morton Smith proposed that this *'ămānâ* (covenant) is the work of Levites in the early Hellenistic period who, as opponents of the dominant assimilationist party, especially its riestly component, attributed it to Nehemiah, their hero; as such, it can be described as "the first example of Jewish sectarianism".[20]

Nehemiah's covenant signatories form a self-segregating group, "all those who had separated themselves from the local population" (Neh 10:29). It exclud-

---

[18] Neh 12:10–11, cf. *Ant.* 11:325–29; 346–47.
[19] Wilhelm Rudolph, *Ezra und Nehemia samt 3. Esra* (Tübingen: Mohr Siebeck, 1949), 172–6. Rudolph held that Ezra-Nehemiah formed the *Schlussteil* (conclusion) to Chronicles from the early fourth century BC.
[20] Morton Smith, "The Dea Sea Sect in Relation to Ancient Judaism," *NTS* 7 (1960/61): 347–60.

ed those of mixed descent (Neh 13:3) and, like Ezra's *běnê haggôlāh*, it exercized the right to excommunicate (cf. Ezra 10:8). It constituted and maintained itself as a distinct *qāhāl* by covenanting together, as Ezra did in the marriage crisis, a crisis precipitated by his own arrival on the scene (Ezra 10:2). The prohibition of marrying outside the group was an essential feature for both the layman and the priest (Neh 10:30; Ezra 9–10). A close parallel can be found in Mal 3:16–18 where the God-fearers, who pact together and whose names are recorded in a *sēper zikkārôn*, are assured that they will be among the saved in the Day of Yahweh soon to come. Like the new covenant in the land of Damascus, the covenants in Ezra-Nehemiah and Malachi committed the signatories to a strict observance of self-segregating rules.[21]

For the Damascus covenanters, the real founders of the group are "the pioneers" (*hārišōnîm*), "the ones from Israel who returned from exile", also "the penitents of Israel" (*ha-šābîm*), a no doubt deliberate ambiguity.[22] Philip Davies pointed out that the way the contents of the list in the Damascus document are described confers on it an eschatological and predestinarian character.[23] We might juxtapose this passage with Nehemiah's detailed record of "the first to return" (Neh 7:5). This list, which corresponds to Ezra 2:1–67 and is deliberately repeated, marks the founding of a new commonwealth and encodes a kind of realized eschatology, a profile of the saved community. Both the Nehemiah list and the omitted or suppressed list in the Damascus Document illustrate the common practice of collapsing later stages or developments into the point of origin, the founding events. The Damascus list refers to the founders and those who came after them. The Nehemiah list, certainly not confined to the first batch of immigrants, may suggest that, during the period from the mid-fifth century onward, the principal source of recruits for the self-segregating golah group in Judah was the self-segregating home group in Babylonia. This view of the matter would fit very well with the hypothesis of Babylonian origins for the Essenes which, if demonstrated, would imply another return from the land of exile some time in the second century BC.

---

[21] CD VI 19; VIII 21; XIX 34. The list of signatories to the new covenant in the land of Damascus is referred to but not given in CD IV 2–6.
[22] The verb *šûb* means "return" or "do penance for sin".
[23] Philip Davies, *The Damascus Covenant*, 95–96.

4 Ezra and Nehemiah as emblematic of contrasting ideologies

There are some indications, admittedly obscure, that Ezra and Nehemiah served as contrasting points of reference in the parties and politics of Judah and the diaspora during the late Persian and Hellenistic periods. Sirach omits Ezra, certainly not by oversight, and applauds Nehemiah as rebuilder of the ruined city and co-founder of the new commonwealth together with Zerubbabel and Jeshua (Sir 49:11–13). Nehemiah was adopted as patron and intrepid defender of the Jewish people by the Hasmonaean family which traced its lineage back to the exile. It therefore comes as no surprise that the pro-Hasmonaean festal letters in 2 Maccabees (1:1–2:18) also backdates Nehemiah to the first return from exile.[24] He and not Zerubbabel and Jeshua set up the altar and rebuilt the temple (1:18), and he and not Ezra preserved the sacred books (2:13).

The canonization of Nehemiah by the Hasmonaeans would presumably have made him *persona non grata* with their sectarian opponents, including Pharisees, which in its turn would help to explain Nehemiah's low profile in rabbinic writings. A quite different reception was accorded Ezra. He was elevated to the high priesthood, founded the first yeshiva, presided over "the Men of the Great Assembly," authored the Targum, and compiled the Mishnah. He was above all the restorer of the law, so that if Moses had not preceded him he would have received it directly from God (b. Sanh. 21b, etc). The Ezra Apocalypse has, however, transmitted a somewhat different profile of Ezra as primarily prophet and apocalyptic seer. Under divine inspiration, and fortified by a fiery liquid, he rewrote the sacred books destroyed during the sack of Jerusalem, the exoteric twenty-four destined for the worthy and unworthy and the esoteric (presumably apocalyptic) seventy for "the wise among your people" (2 Esdras 14:19–48), an allusion to the *maśkîlîm* of the book of Daniel (2 Esd 14:19–48).

To find an explanation for this alternate image of Ezra we return once more to the account of the marriage crisis which arose, or was deliberately provoked, after Ezra's arrival from Babylon (Ezra 9–10). We learn that his principal supporters were "those who trembled at the word of the God of Israel" (9:4; 10:3). The term itself, *hărēdîm*, indicates the kind of intense religious emotion associated with prophetic and apocalyptic groups, and in the only other biblical allusion to *hărēdîm*, in Trito-Isaiah (Isa 66:1–5), they are a persecuted minority expelled from the Judaean cult community on account of their eschatological

---

[24] Nehemiah is identified with Zerubbabel in b.Sanh. 38a, based no doubt on the fiction that Zerubbabel was his Babylonian name.

beliefs (v.5). What is less obvious is that Ezra himself is presented as a prophetic figure, and we are perhaps being told that he himself was a *hārēd* who combined the heightened prophetic emotional state insinuated by that title with a rigorist interpretation of the laws – a combination by no means unusual, and familiar from the Qumran texts. Moreover, Ezra is described as moving in an atmosphere of fasting, mourning and penitential prayer not unlike the spiritual environment of the book of Daniel. Like Ezekiel he sits on the ground in a catatonic state (Ezra 9:3 cf. Ezek 3:15), and we are told that "the hand of YHVH was upon him" (Ezra 7:6,28 cf. Ezek 1:3), a familiar metaphor for prophetic possession.

We have seen that, like Nehemiah, Ezra is backdated in later tradition to the early Persian period,[25] a transposition which, however, contradicts the information that he and his supporters were Babylonian Jews who arrived in the province in 458 BC, almost a century after the first return. They came with a missionary agenda based on the legal and prophetic traditions of the Babylonian community to which they belonged. This might lead us to suspect that the mission of Ezra and his "Tremblers" was one moment, certainly a significant moment, in a process which has its place in the prehistory of the Damascus community. If this is plausible, we may be permitted a further suggestion. If the Damascus group understood itself to be the continuation of the "founding fathers" Ezra could have served as a model, perhaps not the only one, for the Teacher of Righteousness. Like many proposals with respect to the Qumran Teacher proof is beyond our grasp, but both are presented as Zadokite priests,[26] teachers, scribes, and prophetic figures,[27] and both espoused a rigorist interpretation of the laws. Above all, both were seen, and apparently saw themselves, as the founders of a new community.

---

[25] According to the genealogy in Ezra 7:1–5 he was the son of Seraiah, the last pre-exilic high priest executed by the Babylonians (2 Kgs 25:18–21). He is also high priest (*archiereus*) in 1 Esdras 9:39–40 cf. Josephus: *Ant.* XI 121 (*protos hiereus*), and in 2 Esdras he lived thirty years in Babylon before coming to Judah after the fall of Jerusalem.
[26] Ezra 7:1–5; Neh 8:9; 12:26; 4QpPs^a III 15.
[27] For the Teacher see, for example, 1QpHab VII 4.

XV. A Case of Benign Imperial Neglect and its Consequences: An Exercize in Virtual History

Source: *Virtual History and the Bible*, ed. by Cheryl Exum, 129–36. Leiden: Brill, 2000.

If Jerusalem had not been part of a Gentile empire, the nomads would have driven the Jews into the sea or swallowed up Palestine, and the rock of Zion would have been the foundation of an Arabian sanctuary a thousand years before Omar's mosque.[1]

1

In 586 BC the Babylonians finally extinguished the Judaean state, destroyed Jerusalem, and deported members of the ruling and professional class. The administrative centre of the province was set up several miles north of Jerusalem at Mizpah (Tell en-Nasbeh) under Gedaliah, scion of a prominent Judaean family, one of those opposing Zedekiah's ill-advised revolt. Gedaliah's rule as a puppet king did not last long, however, for he was assassinated in the course of a short-lived nationalistic uprising in 582 BC. This act of foolish bravado led predictably to further repressive measures including another deportation. Destruction inflicted on other Judaean sites during the Babylonian conquest, though severe, was selective, but the province itself was considerably reduced in size, especially to the south. According to immemorial tradition reinforced by myth, danger could be expected to come from the north; but the fate of the rump province of Judah was to be decided from the opposite point of the compass. Edomites had been settled in the Judaean Negev since the heyday of the Assyrians in the seventh century, and we may suppose that their relations with the local population (including closely related Kenites, Kenizzites and Jerahmeelites) were not invariably hostile. But during the western revolt against the Babylonian superpower, which ended with the successful siege of Jerusalem and the unsuccessful siege of Tyre, the Edomites stayed on the sidelines, and as a result were able to infiltrate even further into Judah. As long as some form of effective imperial administration remained in place in the Babylonian province of Yehud they were restricted more or less to the eastern Judaean Negev. But once the local admin-

---

[1] Elias Bickerman, *From Ezra to the Last of the Maccabees: Foundations of Post-Biblical Judaism* (New York: Schocken Books, 1962 [1949]), 10.

istration collapsed with the fall of Babylon in 539, organized resistance to their colonization more or less disintegrated.

What happened then can be pieced together in the light of what little we know of the transition period to Achaemenid rule and with prudent recourse to the archaeological record, incomplete and always subject to revision as it is. A close reading on and between the lines of the relevant biblical texts will also be called for.

The policy of the early Achaemenid rulers towards the former Babylonian province of Judah, to the extent that there was a policy, was determined by three factors: (1) control of the Mediterranean north-south coastal route, the route taken by both Cambyses in 525 and Alexander in 332 as they advanced on Egypt without feeling the need to move inland; (2) control of the east-west trade route from the Arabian peninsula and the Red Sea to the Mediterranean; (3) friendship with the Arab peoples whose co-operation was crucial for keeping open the trade routes through the Arava, Sinai and Negev, and was to prove invaluable during Cambyses' conquest of Egypt in 525 BC. It is hard to see what stake the Achaemenid rulers would have had in the region apart from these considerations. Quite the contrary, Cyrus II, Cambyses and Darius I would have had absolutely no interest in re-establishing Jerusalem, that "rebellious city hurtful to kings and provinces" (Ezra 4:15), or in financing the rebuilding of its temple, whose personnel had provided the requisite religious justification for the disastrous rebellion of Zedekiah, or in encouraging Judaeo-Babylonians resident in and around Nippur to resettle in the ancestral homeland, if indeed there were any disposed to do so. The conditions for Edomite colonization were therefore in place, and the motivation was supplied by steady infiltration of Kedarite Arabs into the Edomite homeland east and south of the Salt Sea, not to mention the prospect of better land for grazing and growing crops in Cisjordania.

Even before the sack of Jerusalem, Edomites were well established in the eastern Negev. Their hostile presence in the Arad region is attested on ostracon number 24, and Edomite names on other ostraca from Arad together with Edomite pottery from the site suggest that they were at that time or shortly afterwards in possession of this important centre. A well-constructed Edomite cult center on the Wadi Qatamat (Horvat Qitmit) some fifteen kilometres south of Arad dedicated to their supreme deity Qaus (Qôs), one of whose priests is represented on a stone seal discovered there, strongly suggests that they meant business, that they were there to stay. The entire region is dotted with Edomite sites: Tell el-Milh (Tel Malhata), Khirbet Ghara (Tel Ira), Khirbet el-Mashash (Tel Masos), Horvat Radum, Tel Aroer, Khirbet Ghazza (Horvat 'Uzza). We even have a letter addressed to the Edomite commander at this last location, situated about twelve kilometers south-east of Arad, telling him to deliver some foodstuffs to some one and blessing him in the name of Qôs.

Once it became clear that the Persian imperial authorities were not about to intervene, the pace of Edomite colonization quickened. Judaean forts in the eastern Negev (e.g. at Horvat 'Anim, Horvat Tov) and in the Hebron hills were soon overwhelmed or bypassed. Cities whose defenses had been dismantled as a result of the Babylonian conquest and never rebuilt (En-Gedi, Hebron, Tell el-Hesi, Mareshah, Lachish) were occupied, though it is not always clear whether the occupants were Edomites, Kedarites, or related Arab peoples. As Cambyses, with the assistance of the contiguous Arab peoples, was marshalling his forces along the coastal area for the conquest of Egypt in 525 BC, Edomite bands were passing through Ramat Rahel on their way to an undefended and thinly populated Jerusalem. By the time Cambyses died five years later under mysterious circumstances, a modest sanctuary to the supreme deity Qôs had been erected on the site of the Judaean temple burnt by the Babylonian Nebuzaradan more than six decades earlier.

Far from being in any way extraordinary, the situation resulting from Edomite, Kedarite and, later, Nabataean encroachment at the southern end of the Syro-Palestinian corridor fits the overall settlement pattern throughout the region. After existing for a few centuries, the monarchies of Edom, Moab, and Ammon had also been extinguished by the Neo-Babylonian period, or the early Achaemenid period at the latest, and the entire region was gradually taken over and occupied by Arabian tribes and eventually incorporated into the Nabataean kingdom. Thus, by the first century A.D., Josephus could refer to Moabites quite simply as Arabs (*Ant.* 13:374,382).

2

We have precious little information on the situation of Judah (Yehud) under Achaemenid rule (6th to 4th century BC). It formed a small and relatively unimportant part of the fifth satrapy (Babili-Ebirnari) governed initially by one Ushtani (for the Greeks, Hystanes). The administrator of the western section of the satrapy, initially Tattenai, resided in Damascus, and the oversight of the southern end of Palestine was confided to the Sanballat dynasty in Samaria. Mizpah retained its status as administrative center with a small palace used by the provincial governor on occasional visits. The Edomite-Arabs meanwhile continued to consolidate their settlement in the Northern Negev, the Shephelah, the Hebron highlands, the Judaean highlands and the Judaean wilderness. Their penetration extended roughly to a line running from Tel Miqne (Ekron?), through Beth-Shemesh and Jerusalem to Jericho. No doubt admonished by the authorities in Samaria, their forward movement stopped just north of Jerusalem. The territorial ambitions of the Kedarite Arabs under their ruler Gashm were likewise held in check, at least for the time being.

The mixed population in southern Palestine included $y^ehûdîm$, descendants of the original inhabitants of the Judaean kingdom, but as time passed intermarriage inevitably blurred ethnic lines. By this time most Jews lived elsewhere – in Samaria, the Galilee, the Transjordanian region, the Phoenician cities. The principal concentrations, however, were in Babylonia and Egypt, but there were Jewish settlements as far afield as Sardis to the north and the island of Jeb at the first cataract of the Nile to the south. In the territory of the former tribe of Judah the age-old pattern of subsistence farming continued. Life was never easy for most of the population, and was made worse by Achaemenid fiscal policy and the heavy taxation required to put down incessant revolts and finance campaigns of conquest and reconquest. Ethnic mingling brought with it syncretic cults involving a wide range of deities – Qôs, Yahu, Milkom, Anath, Han'ilat and no doubt others.

Decisive for the course of the future was the fact that, as a result of this situation, the descendants of those deported to southern Mesopotamia in 597, 586 and 582 were unable to return to the former kingdom of Judah. In this respect the situation was similar to what happened to the deportees from Samaria after the incorporation of the kingdom of Israel into the Assyrian empire in 722 BC. In keeping with their usual practice, the Assyrians replaced the 27,290 deportees mentioned in Sargon II's inscriptions with a mixed population from northern Syria and southern Mesopotamia who, as a matter of prudence, worshipped Yahweh whose writ had formerly run in that region, alongside their own deities – Nergal, Ashima, Adrammelek and no doubt others. Unable therefore to return, the deportees were assimilated into the Mesopotamian melting pot and disappeared. If it is true that the Assyrians over the course of three centuries deported four and a half million people, as has been alleged, the situation of the Samarians must have been replicated many times.

The impossibility of a Judaean repatriation for somewhat different reasons meant the loss of a fixed point of reference, an emblem of common identity, for the many "hyphenated" Judaeans scattered over the Near East and beyond. That the major centres of settlement in southern Mesopotamia and elsewhere in the Neo-Babylonian empire nevertheless survived was due in the first instance to a contingent factor of state policy. The Babylonians found it more cost-effective to settle deported ethnic groups as tenant farmers rather than as slaves, and to use the additional labour force on sites due for redevelopment, especially in the Nippur region. To facilitate administrative supervision and the collection of taxes they also permitted, indeed obliged them to maintain their own organization. The same policy continued into the Achaemenid period. Each enclave developed its own mix of ethnically distinctive and local traditions, customs, laws, and practices. Some built their own temples – Shechem, Elephantine, Leontopolis, perhaps Casiphia (Ezra 8:15–20) – but with the phasing out of animal sacrifice the trend was inevitably towards lay organization. Some concentrated more exclusively on the old, national deity while others hedged their religious bets by offering cult to the local gods and goddesses. Customary law, for example regarding marriage and divorce, generally involved accommodation with local practice. This at least was the case with the Jewish military colony on the island of Elephantine on the southern border of Egypt, and it was probably not significantly different in other Jewish settlements.

The impossibility for the descendants of the deportees to return to the traditional homeland was therefore the norm rather than the exception. It meant that, like immigrants everywhere and in every age, they had no realistic option but to seek the welfare of the cities to which they were sent, following Jeremiah's advice (Jer. 29:7). At the same time, this necessity increased the probability of assimilation to the local culture. Judaean enclaves seem, however, to have been more successful than most in preserving a distinctive identity. Though there was no one prescriptive code of law and no central authority to enforce it, a tradition of ritual self-segregation developed, for example with respect to dietary practices and rituals of avoidance, together with commemorative rites that could be carried out without priests or other religious specialists – Sabbath and Passover in particular. Traditions of national origins about warrior kings, sages and holy men and women continued to be recited, no doubt with advantages, and in the Hellenistic period tracts and histories were written comparing Israelite wisdom favourably with the wisdom of the Greeks. Clearchus, for example, reports an encounter between Aristotle and a philosophical Jew from Coele-Syria who not only spoke Greek but had the soul of a Greek.

Another unforeseen long-term effect of Persian neglect of this small (about 1,000 square miles) corner of their vast empire, and the consequent loss of a Judaean homeland, was that the descendants of the original deportees were spared the turmoil of nationalistic politics and the apocalyptic *Schwärmerei* so often inseparable from defence of national turf. In the early years of Persian rule "messianic" movements in Babylonia precipitated by political crisis – the revolts of Nidintu-bel and Arakha against Darius and Bel-shimani against Xerxes, all three claiming descent from the great Nebuchadnezzar II – must have ignited similar aspirations among some of the expatriates – perhaps the prophecies about national and dynastic restoration were to be fulfilled after all. But these aspirations faded with the collapse of the revolts and, as far as we know, Jewish settlers throughout the Middle East, though occasionally the object of local hostility – for example, their temple in Elephantine was burnt down during a riot in 411 BC – took no further part in uprisings against the Persians or their imperial successors. Meanwhile, the Nabataeans consolidated their control on both sides of the Jordan, first as a fully independent kingdom, then as a client of Rome, until the entire region was annexed by Rome in 106 BC. At this point an entirely new chapter in the history of the far-scattered Jewish communities begins.

Abbreviations

ABD. *Anchor Bible Dictionary.* 6 Volumes, ed. by David Noel Freedman. New Haven & London: Yale University Press, 1992.

ANET. *Ancient Near Eastern Texts Relating to the Old Testament*, ed. by James Pritchard. 3rd ed., Princeton/New Jersey: Princeton University Press, 1969.

CAH². The Cambridge Ancient History. 14 Volumes. 2nd ed., Cambridge: Cambridge University Press, 1970–2005; Vol. 4, Persia, Greece and the Western Mediterranean (c.525 to 479 BC), ed. by John Boardman, Nicholas Geoffrey Lemprière Hammond, David Malcolm Lewis and Martin Ostwald, 1988.

CHI. *The Cambridge History of Iran.* 7 Volumes. Cambridge: Cambridge University Press, 1968–1990; Vol. 2, *The Median and Achaemenian Periods*, ed. by Martin Schwartz and Ilya Gershevitch, 1985.

CHJ. The Cambridge History of Judaism. 4 Volumes. Cambridge: Cambridge University Press, 1984–2006; Vol. 1, Introduction, The Persian Period, ed. by William David Davies and Louis Finkelstein, 1984.

DDD. *Dictionary of Deities and Demons in the Bible*, ed. by. Karel van der Toorn, Bob Becking and Pieter Willem van der Horst. 1st ed., Leiden: Brill, 1995; 2nd ed., Grand Rapids: Eerdmans, 1999.

EAEHL. *Encyclopedia of Archaeological Excavations in the Holy Land.* 4 Volumes, ed. by Michael Avi-Yonah. Upper Saddle River/New Jersey: Prentice Hall Trade, 1975–1978.

EDSS. *Encyclopedia of the Dead Sea Scrolls.* 2 Volumes, ed. Lawrence Schiffman and James VanderKam. Oxford & New York: Oxford University Press, 2000.

NEAEHL. New *Encyclopedia of Archaeological Excavations in the Holy Land.* 4 Volumes, ed. by Ephraim Stern, 'Ayelet Levinzon-Gilboʻa and Joseph Aviram. Jerusalem: Carta Jerusalem, 1993.

OEANE. *The Oxford Encyclopedia of Archaeology in the Near East.* 5 Volumes, ed. by Eric Meyers. Oxford: Oxford University Press, 1997.

TAD. *Textbook of Aramaic Documents from Ancient Egypt.* 4 Volumes, ed. by Berkeley Porten and Ada Yardeni. Jerusalem, 1986–1999.

TDOT. *Theological Dictionary of the Old Testament.* 15 Volumes, ed. by Johannes Botterweck, Helmer Ringgren and Heinz-Josef Fabry. Grand Rapids: Eerdmans, 1975–2015.

Bibliography

Ackroyd, Peter. *Exile and Restoration: A Study of Hebrew Thought of the Sixth Century BC*. Philadelphia: Westminster, 1968.
—, "The Temple Vessels: A Continuity Theme." *VTSup* 23 (1972): 166–81.
—, "The Chronicler as Exegete." *JSOT* 2 (1977): 2–32.
Adams, Robert McCormick. *The Uruk Countryside*. Chicago: University of Chicago Press, 1972.
—, *Heartland of Cities: Surveys of Ancient Settlement and Land Use on the Central Floodplain of the Euphrates*. Chicago: University of Chicago Press, 1981.
Ahlström, Gösta Werner. *Joel and the Temple Cult of Jerusalem*. Leiden: Brill, 1971.
Albertz, Rainer. *A History of Israelite Religion in the Old Testament Period*. Vol. 2, *From the Exile to the Maccabees*. Louisville: Westminster John Knox Press, 1992.
Albright, William Foxwell. "The Goddess of Life and Wisdom." *AJSL* 36 (1919/20): 258–94.
—, "The Date and Personality of the Chronicler." *JBL* 40 (1921): 104–24.
—, "The Kyle Memorial Excavations at Bethel." *BASOR* 56 (1934): 2–15.
—, *From the Stone Age to Christianity: Monotheism and the Historical Process*. 2nd ed., Garden City/New York: Doubleday, 1957 [1940].
—, *The Biblical Period from Abraham to Ezra: An Historical Survey*. New York: Harper Torchbooks, 1963.
—, and Christopher Stephen Mann. "Qumran and the Essenes: Geography, Chronology, and the Identification of the Sect." In *The Scrolls and Christianity: Historical and Theological Significance*, ed. by Matthew Black, 11–25. London: SPCK, 1969.
Aletti, Jean-Noel. "Seduction et Parole en Proverbes I–IX." *VT* 27 (1977): 129–44.
Alt, Albrecht. *Kleine Schriften zur Geschichte des Volkes Israel*. Vol. 1. Munich: Beck, 1964 [1929].
—, "Die Rolle Samarias bei der Entstehung des Judentums." In *Kleine Schriften zur Geschichte des Volkes Israel*. Vol. 2, 316–337. Munich: Beck, 1953.
Amit, Yairah. "The Role of Prophecy and the Prophets in the Teaching of Chronicles." *BM* 28 (1982/1983): 113–33.
Andrews, D. K.. "Yahweh the God of the Heavens." In *The Seed of Wisdom: Essays in Honor of Theophile James Meek*, ed. by Warren Sturgis McCullough, 45–57. Toronto: University of Toronto Press, 1964.
Auscher, Dominique. "Les Relations entre la Grèce et la Palestine avant la Conquête d'Alexandre." *VT* 17 (1967): 8–30.
Avigad, Nahman. *Bullae and Seals from a Post-exilic Judaean Archive*. Jerusalem: Hebrew University, 1976.
Baines, John. "Literacy, Ancient Near East." *ABD* 4 (1992): 333–37.
Baltzer, Klaus. *Deutero-Isaiah: A Commentary*. Minneapolis: Fortress Press, 2001.
Barag, Dan. "The Effects of the Tennes Rebellion on Palestine." *BASOR* 183 (1966): 6–12.
Barr, James. "The Question of Religious Influence: The Case of Zoroastrianism, Judaism, and Christianity." *JAAR* 53/2 (1985): 201–35.
Barstad, Hans Magnus. *The Babylonian Captivity of the Book of Isaiah: "Exilic" Judah and the Provenance of Isaiah 40–55*. Oslo: Novus Forlag, 1997.
Bauer, Georg Lorenz. *Theology of the Old Testament: A Biblical Sketch of the Religious Opinions of the Ancient Hebrews from the Earliest Times to the Commencement of the Christian Era*. London: Charles Fox, 1838 [1796].

Beaulieu, Paul-Alain. *The Reign of Nabonidus King of Babylon 556–539 BC.* New Haven & London: Yale University Press, 1989.
Bedford, Peter Ross. *Temple Restoration in Early Achaemenid Judah.* Leiden: Brill, 2001.
Begg, Christopher. "The Classical Prophets in the Chronistic History." *BN* 32 (1988): 100–7.
Bellinger Jr., William. *Psalmody and Prophecy.* Sheffield: JSOT, 1984.
Bengtson, Hermann. *The Greeks and the Persians: From the Sixth to the Fourth Centuries.* New York: Delacorte Press, 1968.
Bentzen, Aage. "Priesterschaft und Laien in der jüdischen Gemeinde des fünften Jahrhunderts." *AfO* 6 (1930/31): 282–83.
Berger, Paul-Richard. "Das Neujahrsfest nach den Königsinschriften des ausgehenden babylonischen Reiches." In *Actes de la XVIIe Rencontre Assyriologique Internationale*, ed. by André Finet, 155–159. Brussels: Université Libre de Bruxelles, 1970.
—, "Zu den Namen ššbsr und šn'sr." *ZAW* 83 (1971): 98–100.
Berges, Ulrich. *Das Buch Jesaja: Komposition und Endgestalt.* Freiburg: Herder, 1998.
Bertholet, Alfred. *Die Bücher Esra und Nehemia.* Tübingen & Leipzig: Mohr Siebeck, 1902.
Beuken, Willem. "Isa. 55.3–5: The Restoration of David." *Bijdragen* 35 (1974): 49–64.
Bianchi, Francesco and Gabriele Rossoni. "L'Armée d'Ozias (2 Ch 26,11–15) entre Fiction et Réalité: Une Esquise Philologique et Historique." *Transeuphratène* 13 (1997): 21–37.
Bickerman, Elias. "The Edict of Cyrus in Ezra 1." *JBL* 65 (1946): 249–75.
—, *From Ezra to the Last of the Maccabees.* New York: Schocken Books, 1962 [1949].
—, "The Babylonian Captivity." In *CHJ* 1, 342–358.
—, *The Jews in the Greek Age.* Cambridge/Mass: Harvard University Press, 1988.
Black, Jeremy. "The New Year Ceremonies in Ancient Babylon." *Religion* 11 (1981): 39–59.
Black, Matthew. *The Scrolls and Christian Origins: Studies in the Jewish Background of the New Testament.* New York: Scribner's, 1961.
Blenkinsopp, Joseph. "Prophecy and Priesthood in Josephus." *JJS* 25 (1974): 239–62.
—, "The Structure of P." *CBQ* 38 (1976): 275–92.
—, "The Mission of Udjahorresnet and Those of Ezra and Nehemiah." *JBL* 106 (1987): 409–21.
—, *Ezra-Nehemiah: A Commentary.* Philadelphia: Westminster, 1988.
—, "Sage, Scribe, and Scribalism in the Chronicler's Work." In *The Sage in Israel and the Ancient Near East*, ed. by John Gammie and Leo Perdue, 307–15. Winona Lake/Indiana: Eisenbrauns, 1990.
—, "Temple and Society in Achaemenid Judah." In *Second Temple Studies.* Vol. 1, *Persian Period*, ed. by Philip Davies, 22–53. Shefflield: Sheffield Academic Press, 1991.
—, *The Pentateuch: An Introduction to the First Five Books of the Bible.* New York: Doubleday, 1992.
—, *Sage, Priest, Prophet: Religious and Intellectual Leadership in Ancient Israel.* Louisville: Westminster John Knox Press, 1995.
—, *A History of Prophecy in Israel.* 2nd ed., Louisville: Westminster John Knox Press, 1996.
—, "'We pay no heed to heavenly voices': the 'End of Prophecy' and the Formation of the Canon." In *Biblical and Humane: Festschrift for John Priest*, ed. by Linda Bennett Elder, David Barr and Elizabeth Struthers Malbon, 19–31. Atlanta: Scholars Press, 1996.
—, "The Judaean Priesthood during the Neo-Babylonian and Achaemenid Periods: A Hypothetical Reconstruction." *CBQ* 60 (1998): 25–43.
—, *Isaiah 1–39: A New Translation with Introduction and Commentary.* Garden City/New York: Doubleday, 2000.

—, *Isaiah 40–55: A New Translation with Introduction and Commentary*. Garden City/New York: Doubleday, 2002.
—, *Isaiah 56–66: A New Translation with Introduction and Commentary*. Garden City/New York: Doubleday, 2003.
—, "The One in the Middle." In *Reading from Right to Left: Essays on the Hebrew Bible in Honour of David Clines*, ed. by Cheryl Exum and Hugh Williamson, 63–75. Sheffield: Sheffield Academic Press, 2003.
—, "Bethel in the Neo-Babylonian Period." In *Judah and the Judeans in the Neo-Babylonian Period*, ed. by Oded Lipschits and Joseph Blenkinsopp, 93–107. Winona Lake/Indiana: Eisenbrauns, 2003.
—, *Opening the Sealed Book: Interpretations of the Book of Isaiah in Late Antiquity*. Grand Rapids: Eerdmans, 2006.
—, "The Midianite-Kenite Hypothesis and the Origins of Judah." *JSOT* 33 (2008): 131–53.
—, "The Mystery of the Missing 'Sons of Aaron'." In *Exile and Restoration Revisited*, ed. by Gary Neil Knoppers and Lester Grabbe, 65–77. London & New York: T. & T. Clark, 2009.
—, "Abraham as Paradigm in the Priestly History in Genesis." *JBL* 128/2 (2009): 225–41.
—, "The Cosmological and Protological Language of Deutero-Isaiah." *CBQ* 73 (2011): 493–510.
—, "The Baal Peor Episode Revisited." *Biblica* 93/1 (2012): 86–97.
—, *David Remembered: Kingship and National Identity in Ancient Israel*. Grand Rapids: Eerdmans, 2013.
Blidstein, Gerald. "Atimia: A Greek Parallel to Ezra X 8 and to Post-biblical Exclusion from the Community." *VT* 24 (1974): 357–60.
Blum, Erhard. *Studien zur Komposition des Pentateuch*. Berlin: Walter de Gruyter, 1990.
Boardman, John. *Persia and the West*. London: Thames & Hudson, 2000.
Boecker, Hans-Jochen. *Redeformen des Rechtslebens im Alten Testament*. Neukirchen-Vluyn: Neukirchener Verlag, 1964.
Bogaert, Raymond. *Les Origines Antiques de la Banque de Dépôt*. Leiden: Brill, 1966.
Bordreuil, Pierre. "Les 'Grâces de David' et I Maccabee ii 57." *VT* 31 (1981): 73–76.
Borger, Riekele. *Handbuch der Keilschriftliteratur*. Vol. 3. Berlin: Walter de Gruyter, 1975.
Boyce, Mary. *A History of Zoroastrianism*. Vol. 2, *Under the Achaemenians*. Leiden: Brill, 1982.
—, *Textual Sources for the Study of Zoroastrianism*. Chicago: Chicago University Press, 1984.
—, "The Religion of Cyrus the Great." In *Achaemenid History*. Vol. 3, *Method and Theory*, ed. by Amélie Kuhrt and Heleen Sancisi-Weerdenburg, 5–21. Leiden: Nederlands Instituut voor het Nabije Oosten, 1988.
—, *Zoroastrians: Their Religious Beliefs and Practices*. 2nd ed., London & New York: Routledge, 2001.
Brettler, Marc Zvi. "Judaism in the Hebrew Bible? The Transition from Ancient Israelite Religion to Juduaism." *CBQ* 61 (1999): 429–47.
Briant, Pierre. *Histoire de l'Empire Perse de Cyrus à Alexandre*. Vol. 1. Paris: Libraire Arthème Fayard, 1996 = *From Cyrus to Alexander. A History of the Persian Empire*, transl. by Peter Daniels. Winona Lake/Indiana: Eisenbrauns, 2002.
—, "Histoire et Archéologie d'un Texte: La Lettre de Darius Gadatas entre Perses, Grecs et Romains." In *Licia e Lidia Prima dell'Ellenizzazione: Atti del Convegno Internazionale, Roma 11–12 Ottobre 1999*, ed. by Mauro Giorgieri, Mario Salvini, Marie-Claude

Trémouille and Pietro Vannicelli, 107–44. Rome: Consiglio Nazionale delle Ricerche, 2003.
Browne, Laurence. "A Jewish Sanctuary in Babylonia." *JTS* 17 (1916): 400–1.
Burkert, Walter. "The Meaning and Function of the Temple in Classical Greece." In *Temple in Society*, ed. by Michael Fox, 27–48. Winona Lake/Indiana: Eisenbrauns, 1988.
Cardascia, Guillaume. *Les Archives des Murašû: Une Famille d'Hommes d'Affaires Babyloniens à l'Époque Perse (455–403 av. J.C.)*. Paris: Imprimerie nationale, 1951.
Carr, David. *Reading the Fractures of Genesis*. Louisville: Westminster John Knox Press, 1996.
Carter, Charles. *The Emergence of Yehud in the Persian Period: A Social and Demographic Study*. Sheffield: JSOT, 1999.
Carter, George William. *Zoroastrianism and Judaism*. New York: AMS Press, 1918.
Caquot, André. "Les 'Grâces de David': A Propos d'Isaïe 55,3b." *Sem* 15 (1965): 45–59.
Causse, Antonin. *Les Dispersés d'Israël: Les Origines De La Diaspora et Son Rôle Dans La Formation Du Judaïsme*. Paris: Alcan 1929.
Chalcraft, David. "Max Weber on Sects and Voluntary Associations with Specific Reference to Second Temple Judaism." In *Sectarianism in Early Judaism: Sociological Advances*, ed. by David Chalcraft, 26–111. Oakville: Equinox, 2007.
Chaumont, Marie-Louise. "Un Nouveau Gouverneur de Sardes à l'Époque Achéménide d'après une Inscription Récemment Découverte," *Syria* 67 (1990): 579–608.
Childs, Brevard. *Isaiah: A Commentary*. Louisville: Westminster John Knox Press, 2001.
Clay, Albert Tobias. *Neo-Babylonian Letters from Erech*. New Haven: Yale University Press, 1919.
Clifford, Richard. "Proverbs IX: A Suggested Ugaritic Parallel." *VT* 25 (1975): 298–306.
Clines, David. "Nehemiah 10 as an Example of Early Jewish Biblical Exegesis." *JSOT* 21 (1981): 111–17.
Cocquerillat, Denise. *Palmeraies et Cultures de l'Eanna d'Uruk (559–520): Ausgrabungen der deutschen Forschungsgemeinschaft in Uruk-Warka VIII*. Berlin: Deutsche Forschungsgemeinschaft, 1968.
Cogan, Mordechai and Hayim Tadmor. *II Kings: A New Translation with Introduction and Commentary*. Garden City/New York: Doubleday, 1988.
Cohen, Shaye. *The Beginnings of Jewishness: Boundaries, Varieties, Uncertainties*. Berkeley & Los Angeles: University of California, 1999.
Coogan, Michael David. *West Semitic Personal Names in the Murasu Documents*. Missoula/Montana: Society of Biblical Literature, 1976.
Cook, John Manuel. *The Persian Empire*. London: Dent, 1983.
Cornill, Carl Heinrich. *Einleitung in das Alte Testament*. Freiburg im Breisgau, 1892.
Cowley, Abraham. *Aramaic Papyri of the Fifth Century BC*. Oxford: Clarendon, 1923; reprint Osnabrück: Otto Zeller, 1967.
Crenshaw, James. *Education in Ancient Israel: Across the Deadening Silence*. Garden City/New York: Doubleday, 1998.
Cross, Frank Moore. *Canaanite Myth and Hebrew Epic: Essays in the History of the Religion of Israel*. Cambridge/Mass: Harvard University Press, 1973.
—, "A Reconstruction of the Judean Restoration." *JBL* 94 (1975): 4–18.
Crüsemann, Frank. "Israel in der Perserzeit: Eine Skizze in Auseinandersetzung mit Max Weber." In *Max Webers Sicht des antiken Christentums: Interpretation und Kritik*, ed. by Wolfgang Schluchter, 205–32. Frankfurt am Main: Suhrkamp, 1985.

—, "Le Pentateuque, une Tora: Prolègoménes à l'Interprétation de sa Forme Finale." In *Le Pentateuque en Question*, ed. by Albert de Pury, 345–54. Geneva: Labor et Fides, 1989.

—, *Die Torah: Theologie und Sozialgeschichte des alttestamentlichen Gesetzes*. Munich: Kaiser, 1992. = *The Torah: Theology and Social History of Old Testament Law*, transl. by Allan Mahnke. Minneapolis: Fortress Press, 1996.

Curtis, Edward Lewis and Albert Alonzo Madsen. *A Critical and Exegetical Commentary on the Books of Chronicles*. Edinburgh: T. & T. Clark, 1910.

Dahood, Mitchell. "Ugaritic DRKT and Biblical DEREK." *TS* 15 (1954): 627–31.

Dalglish, Edward. "Bethel (Deity)." *ABD* 1 (1992): 706–10.

Dandamaev, Muhammad. "Achaemenid Babylonia." In *Ancient Mesopotamia: Socio-Economic History. A Collection of Studies by Soviet Scholars*, ed. by Igor Diakonoff, 296–311. Moscow: Nauka, 1969.

—, "Der Tempelzehnte in Babylonien während des 6.–4. Jh. v.u.Z." In *Beiträge zur Alten Geschichte und deren Nachleben: Festschrift für Franz Altheim*, ed. by Ruth Stiel, 82–89. Berlin: Walter de Gruyter, 1969.

—, "Politische und wirtschaftliche Geschichte." In *Historia: Beiträge zur Achämenidengeschichte*, ed. by Walther Hinz and Gerold Walser, 15–58. Wiesbaden: Steiner, 1972.

—, "Social Stratification in Babylonia (7th–4th Centuries BC)." *AcAnt* 22 (1974): 433–44.

—, *Persien unter den ersten Achämeniden (6. Jahrhundert v. Chr.)*. Wiesbaden: Dr. Ludwig Reichert Verlag, 1976.

—, "Babylonia in the Persian Age." In *CHJ* 1, 326–42.

—, *Slavery in Babylon from Nabopolassar to Alexander the Great*. De Kalb/Illinois: Illinois University Press, 1984.

—, *A Political History of the Achaemenid Empire*. Leiden: Brill, 1989.

—, and Vladimir Lukonin. *The Culture and Social Institutions of Ancient Iran*. Cambridge: Cambridge University Press, 1989.

Davidson, Samuel. *An Introduction to the Old Testament: Critical, Historical, and Theological*. Vol. 3. London: Williams & Norgate, 1863.

Davies, Eryl Wynn. "Inheritance Rights and the Hebrew Levirate Marriage." *VT* 31 (1981): 138–144.257–268.

Davies, John Kenyon. "Religion and the State." In *CAH²* 4, 368–388.

Davies, Philip. *The Damascus Covenant: An Interpretation of the "Damascus Document"*. Sheffield: JSOT, 1983.

—, *Behind the Essenes: History and Ideology in the Dead Sea Scrolls*. Atlanta: Scholars Press, 1987.

Day, John. "Ashtoreth." In *ABD* 1, 491–94.

—, *Yahweh and the Gods and Goddesses of Canaan*. Sheffield: Sheffield Academic Press, 2000.

De Pury, Albert and Thomas Römer. *Israël Construit son Histoire: L'Historiographie Deutéronomiste la Lumière des Recherches Récentes*. Geneva: Labor et Fides, 1996.

De Vaux, Roland. *The Bible and the Ancient Near East*, transl. by Damian McHugh. Garden City/New York: Doubleday, 1971.

De Vries, Simon. "The Forms of Prophetic Address in Chronicles." *HAR* 10 (1986): 15–36.

—, "Moses and David as Cult Founders in Chronicles." *JBL* 107 (1988): 619–39.

Descat, Raymond. "Darius, le roi kapēlos." In *Continuity and Change: Proceedings of the Last Achaemenid History Workshop April 6–8, 1990*, ed. by Amélie Kuhrt, Margaret Cool Root

and Heleen Sancisi-Weerdenburg, 161–66. Leiden: Nederlands Instituut voor het Nabije Oosten, 1994.
Dever, William. "Archaeological Methods and Results: A Review of Two Recent Publications." *Orientalia* 40 (1971): 459–71.
—, "Bethel." In *OEANE* 1, 300–1.
Dougherty, Raymond Philip. *The Shirkûtu of Babylonian Deities*. New Haven: Yale University Press, 1923.
Driver, Samuel Rolles and George Buchanan Gray. *A Critical and Exegetical Commentary on the Book of Job*. Edinburgh: T. & T. Clark, 1921.
Duhm, Bernhard. *Das Buch Jesaja*. 4th ed., Göttingen: Vandenhoeck & Ruprecht, 1922.
Eissfeldt, Otto. *Einleitung in das Alte Testament*. 2nd ed., Tübingen: Mohr Siebeck, 1956. = *The Old Testament. An Introduction*, transl. by Peter Ackroyd. Oxford: Blackwell, 1956.
Elliger, Karl. *Deuterojesaja 40,1–45,7*. Neukirchen-Vluyn: Neukirchener Verlag, 1978.
Eph'al, Israel "The Western Minorities in Babylonia in the 6th–5th Centuries BC: Maintenance and Cohesion." *Orientalia* 47 (1978): 74–90.
Eshel, Hanan. "The Governors of Samaria in the Fifth and Fourth Centuries BCE." In *Judah and the Judeans in the Fourthy Century BCE*, ed. by Oded Lipschits, Gary Neil Knoppers and Rainer Albertz, 223–34. Winona Lake/Indiana: Eisenbrauns, 2007.
Falk, Ze'ev Wilhelm. "The Rights of Inheritance of a Daughter in Bible and Talmud." *Tarbiz* 23 (1951/52): 9–15.
Falkenstein, Adam. *Archaische Texte aus Uruk: Ausgrabungen der deutschen Forschungsgemeinschaft in Uruk-Warka II*. Berlin: Deutsche Forschungsgemeinschaft, 1936.
—, "Die babylonische Schule." *Saeculum* 4 (1953): 125–37.
—, "Zu den Inschriften der Grabung in Uruk-Warka 1960–1961." *Baghdader Mitteilungen* 2 (1963): 1–82.
Fensham, Frank Charles. "Mĕdînâ in Ezra and Nehemiah." *VT* 25 (1975): 795–97.
Fischer, James. "Notes on the Literary Form and Message of Malachi." *CBQ* 34 (1972): 315–20.
Fishbane, Michael. *Biblical Interpretation in Ancient Israel*. Oxford: Clarendon, 1985.
Fohrer, Georg. *Einleitung in das Alte Testament*. Heidelberg: Quelle & Meyer, 1965 = *Introduction to the Old Testament*, transl. by David Green. Nashville, New York: Abingdon, 1968.
Forschner, Maximilian. *Die Stoische Ethik: Über den Zusammenhang von Natur-, Sprach- und Moralphilosophie im altstoischen System*. Stuttgart: Klett-Cotta, 1981.
Fox, Michael (ed.). *Temple in Society*. Winona Lake/Indiana: Eisenbrauns, 1988.
—, *Proverbs 1–9: A New Translation with Introduction and Commentary*. Garden City/New York: Doubleday, 2000.
Freedman, David Noel. "The Chronicler's Purpose." *CBQ* 23 (1961): 436–42.
Frei, Peter. "Persian Imperial Authorization: A Summary." In *Persia and Torah: The Theory of Imperial Authorization of the Pentateuch*, ed. by James Watts, 5–40. Atlanta: Society of Bblical Literature, 2001.
—, and Klaus Koch. *Reichsidee und Reichsorganisation im Perserreich*. 2nd ed., Fribourg: Universitätsverlag; Göttingen: Vandenhoeck & Ruprecht, 1996.
Frye, Richard Nelson. *The History of Ancient Iran*. Munich: Beck, 1984.
—, *The Heritage of Persia*. Costa Mesa/California: Mazda Publications, 1993.

Galling, Kurt. "Denkmäler zur Geschichte Syriens und Palästinas unter der Herrschaft der Perser." *PJ* 34 (1938): 59–79.
—, "Das Gemeindegesetz in Deuteronomium 23." In *Festschrift Alfred Bertholet*, ed. by Walter Baumgartner and Otto Eissfeldt, 176–91. Tübingen: Mohr Siebeck, 1950.
—, *Die Bücher der Chronik, Esra, Nehemia*. Göttingen: Vandenhoeck & Ruprecht, 1954.
—, *Studien zur Geschichte Israels im persischer Zeitalter*. Tübingen: Mohr Siebeck, 1964.
Gardiner, Alan. "The House of Life." *JEA* 24 (1938): 157–79.
Garrison, Mark and Margaret Cool Root (eds.). *Seals on the Persepolis Fortification Tablets*. Vol 1, *Images of Heroic Encounter*. Chicago: Chicago University Press, 2001.
Getty, Robert John. "Isis." In *The Oxford Classical Dictionary*. ed. by Simon Hornblower and Antony Spawforth, 768–69. 3rd ed., Oxford: Oxford University Press, 1999.
Ginzburg, Carlo. *The Judge and the Historian: Marginal Notes on a Late-Twentieth-Century Miscarriage of Justice*, transl. by Antony Shugaar. London & New York: Verso, 1999.
Glazier-McDonald, Beth. *Malachi: The Divine Messenger*. Atlanta: Scholars Press, 1987.
—, "Intermarriage, Divorce, and the *Bat-'el Nēkār:* Insights into Mal 2:10–16." *JBL* 106 (1987): 603–11.
Goldingay, John and David Payne. *Isaiah 40–55: A Critical and Exegetical Commentary*. Vol. 2. London: T. & T. Clark, 2006.
Grabbe, Lester. "Reconstructing History from the Book of Ezra." In *Studies in the Persian Period*, ed. by Philip Davies, 98–106. Sheffield: JSOT Press, 1991.
—, *Judaism from Cyrus to Herod*. Vol. 1, *The Persian and Greek Periods*. Minneapolis: Fortress Press, 1992.
—, "What was Ezra's mission?" In *Second Temple Studies*. Vol. 2, *Temple and Community in the Persian Period*, ed. by Tamara Cohn Eskenazi and Kent Harold Richards, 286–99. Sheffield: JSOT, 1994.
—, "The 'Persian Documents' in the Book of Ezra: Are they Authentic?" In *Judah and the Judeans in the Persian Period*, ed. by Oded Lipschits and Manfred Oeming, 531–70. Winona Lake/Indiana: Eisenbrauns, 2006.
Grätz, Sebastian. *Das Edikt des Artaxerxes: Eine Untersuchung zum religionspolitischen und historischen Umfeld von Esra 7,12–26*. Berlin: Walter de Gruyter, 2004.
—, "Esra 7 im Kontext hellenistischer Politik: Der königliche Euergetismus in hellenisticher Zeit als idealer Hintergrund von Esra 7,12–26." In *Die Griechen und das antike Israel: Interdisziplinäre Studien zur Religions- und Kulturgeschichte des Heiligen Landes*, ed. by Stefan Alkier and Markus Witte, 131–54. Fribourg: Academic Press; Göttingen: Vandenhoeck & Ruprecht, 2004.
Gray, John. *Joshua, Judges and Ruth*. London: Nelson, 1967.
Greenberg, Moshe. *Yehezkel Kaufmann: The Religion of Israel from its Beginnings to the Babylonian Exile*. New York: Schocken Books, 1960.
Greenfield, Jonas. "The Aramaic Legal Texts from the Achaemenian Period." *Transeuph* 3 (1990): 85–92.
Haller, Max. "Die Kyros-Lieder Deuterojesajas." In *ΕΥΧΑΡΙΣΤΗΡΙΟΝ: Studien zur Religion und Literatur des Alten und Neuen Testaments. Festschrift für Hermann Gunkel*. Vol. 1, *Zur Religion und Literatur des Alten Testaments*, ed. by Hans Schmidt, 261–77. Göttingen: Vandenhoeck & Ruprecht, 1923.
Hallock, Richard. *Persepolis Fortification Tablets*. Chicago: Chicago University Press, 1948.
—, "The Evidence of the Persepolis Tablets." In *CHI* 2, 588–609.

Harland, Philip. *Associations, Synagogues, and Congregations.* Minneapolis: Fortress Press, 2003.
Harris, William. *Ancient Literacy.* Cambridge/Mass: Harvard University Press, 1989.
Heicksen, Martin. "Archaeological Light on Population Problems." *Bulletin of the Near Eastern Archaeological Society* 6 (1975): 31–39.
Heidel, Alexander. *The Babylonian Genesis: The Story of Creation.* 2nd ed., Chicago: Chicago University Press, 1951.
Hengel, Martin. *Judaism and Hellenism: Studies in their Encounter in Palestine during the Early Hellenistic Period.* Vol. 1 and 2 [in one vol.]. Philadelphia: Fortress Press, 1974.
——, *Jews, Greeks and Barbarians: Aspects of the Hellenization of Judaism in the Pre-Christian Period.* Philadelphia: Fortress Press, 1980.
Hermisson, Hans-Jürgen. *Studien zur israelitischen Spruchweisheit.* Neukirchen-Vluyn: Neukirchener Verlag, 1968.
——, "Einheit und Komplexität Deuterojesajas: Probleme der Redaktionsgeschichte von Jes 40–55." In *The Book of Isaiah. Le Livre d'Isaïe: Les Oracles et leurs Relectures,* ed. by Jacques Vermeylen, 286–312. Leuven: University Press/Peeters, 1989.
Herrenschmidt, Claude. "La Religion des Achéménides: État de la Question." *Studia Iranica* 9/2 (1980): 324–39.
——, "Notes sur la Parenté chez les Perses au Debut de l'Empire Achéménide." In *Achaemenid History.* Vol. 2, *The Greek Sources,* ed. by Heleen Sancisi-Weerdenburg and Amélie Kuhrt. 53–67. Leiden: Nederlands Instituut voor het Nabije Oosten, 1987.
Höffken, Peter. "Der Prophet Jesaja beim Chronisten." *BN* 81 (1996): 82–90.
Humbach, Helmut. *The Gāthās of Zarathushtra and the other Old Avestan Texts.* Vol. 1. Heidelberg: Universitätsverlag Winter, 1991.
Humbert, Paul. "Les Adjectifs 'zar' et 'nokri' et la Femme Étrangère des Proverbes Bibliques." In *Mélanges Syriens offerts à Monsieur René Dussaud.* Vol. 1, 259–66. Paris: Paul Geuthner, 1939.
Hussey, Edward. *The Presocratics.* New York: Charles Scribner's Sons, 1972.
Hutchinson, John and Anthony Smith (eds.). *Ethnicity.* Oxford: Oxford University Press, 1996.
Hvidberg, Flemming Friis. *Weeping and Laughter in the Old Testament: A Study of Canaanite-Israelite Religion.* Leiden: Brill, 1962.
In der Smitten, Wilhelm. *Esra: Quellen, Überlieferung und Geschichte.* Assen: van Gorcum, 1973.
Irwin, William Andrew. "Prometheus and Job." *Journal of Religion* 30 (1950): 90–108.
Ishida, Tomoo. "The Structure and Historical Implications of the Lists of Pre-Israelite Nations." *Bib* 60 (1979): 461–90.
Iwry, Samuel. "Was there a Migration to Damascus? The Problem of "שבי ישראל."" *Eretz Israel* 9 (1969): 80–88.
Jacobsen, Thorkild. "Mesopotamia." In *Before Philosophy: The Intellectual Adventure of Ancient Man,* ed. by Henri Frankfort, Henriette Antonia Groenewegen-Frankfort, John Wilson and Thorkild Jacobsen, 125–222. Baltimore: Penguin Books, 1949.
Jacoby, Felix: *Die Fragmente der griechischen Historiker* [FgrHist.], 3 Volumes. Leiden: Brill; Berlin: Weidmann 1923–1958.
Jamieson-Drake, David. *Scribes and Schools in Monarchic Judah.* Sheffield: Almond, 1991.
Janssen, Enno. *Juda in der Exilzeit: Ein Beitrag zur Frage der Entstehung des Judentums.* Göttingen: Vandenhoeck & Ruprecht, 1956.

Japhet, Sara. "The Supposed Common Authorship of Chronicles and Ezra-Nehemiah Investigated Anew." *VT* 18 (1969): 330–71.
—, *I & II Chronicles: A Commentary*. Louisville: Westminster John Knox Press, 1993.
Jones, Douglas. "The Cessation of Sacrifice after the Destruction of the Temple in 586 BC." *JTS* 14 (1963): 12–31.
Judge, H. G. "Aaron, Zadok and Abiathar." *JTS* 7 (1956): 70–74.
Kaiser, Walter. "The Unfailing Kindnesses Promised to David: Isaiah 55:3." *JSOT* 45 (1989): 41–98.
Kalimi, Isaac. "The Date of the Book of Chronicles." In *God's Word for Our World: Theological and Cultural Studies in Honor of Simon John de Vries*. Vol. 1, ed. by Deborah Ellens, Simon John de Vries, Harold Ellens, Rolf Knierim and Isaac Kalimi, 347–72. London & New York: T. & T. Clark, 2004.
Kaufmann, Yehezkel. *History of the Religion of Israel*. Vol. 4, *The Babylonian Captivity and Deutero-Isaiah:*, transl. Clarence Efroymson. New York: Union of American Hebrew Congregations, 1970.
Kegler, Jürgen. "Prophetengestalten im Deuteronomistischen Geschichtswerk und in den Chronikbüchern: Ein Beitrag zur Kompositions- und Redaktionsgeschichte der Chronikbücher." *ZAW* 105 (1993): 481–97.
Kellermann, Ulrich. *Nehemia: Quellen, Überlieferung und Geschichte*. Berlin: Walter de Gruyter, 1967.
—, "Erwägungen zum Problem der Esradatierung." *ZAW* 80 (1968): 55–87.
—, "Erwägungen zum Esragesetz." *ZAW* 80 (1968): 373–85.
Kelso, James. *The Excavation of Bethel (1934–1960)*. Cambridge/Mass: ASOR, 1968.
—, "Bethel." In *EAEHL* 1, 190–93.
—, "Bethel." In *NEAEHL* 1, 192–94.
Kent, John Harvey. "The Temple Estates of Delos, Rheneia and Mykonos." *Hesperia* 17 (1948): 243–338.
Kent, Roland. "The Oldest Old Persian Inscriptions." *JAOS* 66 (1946): 306–12.
—, *Old Persian: Grammar, Texts, Lexicon*. 2nd ed., New Haven: American Oriental Society, 1953.
Kidd, Ian. "Moral Actions and Rules in Stoic Ethics." In *The Stoics*, ed. by John Rist, 247–58. Berkeley & Los Angeles: University of California Press, 1978.
Kittel, Rudolph. "Cyrus und Deuterojesaja." *ZAW* 18 (1898): 149–62.
Klein, Jacob. "Akitu." In *ABD* 1, 138–40.
Klein, Ralph. "Prophets and Prophecy in the Books of Chronicles." *TBT* 36 (1998): 227–32.
Klein, Samuel. "Die Schreiberfamilien: 1 Chr 2:55." *Monatsschrift für Geschichte und Wissenschaft des Judentums* 70 (1926): 410–16.
Kloppenborg, John and Stephen Wilson (eds.). *Voluntary Associations in the Graeco-Roman World*. New York: Routledge, 1996.
Knauf, Ernst Axel. *Die Umwelt des Alten Testaments*. Stuttgart: Katholisches Bibelwerk, 1994.
Knibb, Michael. "Exile in the Damascus Document." *JSOT* 25 (1983): 99–117.
—, "The Exile in the Literature of the Intertestamental Period." *HeyJ* 17 (1976): 253–72.
—, "Exile." In *EDSS* 1, 276–77.
Knights, Chris. "The Rechabites of Jeremiah 35: Forerunners of the Essenes?" In *Qumran Questions*, ed. by James Charlesworth, 86–91. Sheffield: Sheffield Academic Press, 1995.
Koch, Klaus. "Ezra and the Origins of Judaism." *JSS* 19 (1974): 173–97.

Kratz, Reinhard. *Kyros im Deuterojesaja-Buch: Redaktionsgeschichtliche Untersuchungen zu Entstehung und Theologie von Jes 40–55.* Tübingen: Mohr Siebeck, 1991.
—, *Die Komposition der erzählenden Bücher des Alten Testaments.* Göttingen: Vandenhoeck & Ruprecht, 2000. = *The Composition of the Narrative Books of the Old Testament,* transl. by John Bowden. London: T. & T. Clark, 2005.
Kraus, Hans-Joachim. *Geschichte der historisch-kritischen Erforschung des Alten Testaments.* Neukirchen: Verlag der Buchhandlung des Erziehungsvereins, 1956.
Kreissig, Heinz. *Die Sozialökonomische Situation in Juda zur Achämenidenzeit.* Berlin: Akademie Verlag, 1973.
Kuhrt, Amélie. "The Cyrus Cylinder and Achaemenid Imperial Policy." *JSOT* 25 (1983): 83–97.
—, "Babylonia from Cyrus to Xerxes." In *CAH*² 4, 112–38.
—, *The Persian Empire: A Corpus of Sources from the Achaemenid Period.* Vol. 1. London & New York: Routledge, 2007.
—, and Heleen Sancisi-Weerdenburg (eds.). *Achaemenid History.* Vol. 3, *Method and Theory.* Leiden: Nederlands Instituut voor het Nabije Oosten, 1988.
Kutsch, Ernst. "Die Wurzel עצר im Hebräischen." *VT* 2 (1952): 57–69.
Lambert, Wilfred. "The Great Battle of the Mesopotamian Religious Year: The Conflict in the Akitu House." *Iraq* 25 (1963): 189–90.
—, *Babylonian Wisdom Literature.* Oxford: Clarendon, 1960.
Lang, Bernhard. *Wisdom and the Book of Proverbs: An Israelite Goddess Redefined.* New York: Pilgrim, 1986.
Le Déaut, Roger und Jacques Robert. *Targum des Chroniques.* Vol. 1, *Introduction et Traduction.* Rome: Pontifical Biblical Institute, 1971.
Lemaire, André. *Les Écoles et la Formation de la Bible dans l'Ancien Israël.* Fribourg: Editions Universitaires, 1981.
Lessing, Gotthold Ephraim. "The Education of the Human Race [1780]". In *Lessing's Theological Writings: Selections in Translation,* transl. by Henry Chadwick. London: Adam and Charles Black, 1956.
Leuze, Oscar. *Die Satrapieneinteilung in Syrien und im Zweistromlande von 520 bis 320.* Halle: Max Niemeyer Verlag, 1935.
Levine, Baruch."The Netînîm." *JBL* 82 (1963): 207–12.
Lewis, Ioan. *Ecstatic Religion: A Study of Shamanism and Spirit Possession.* 3rd ed., London & New York: Routledge, 2003.
Lichtheim, Miriam. *Ancient Egyptian Literature.* Vol. 2, *The New Kingdom.* Berkeley & Los Angeles: University of California Press, 1976.
Lindenberger, James. *The Aramaic Proverbs of Ahiqar.* Baltimore: Johns Hopkins University Press, 1983.
Lipiński, Edward (ed.). *State and Temple Economy in the Ancient Near East.* Vol. 1. Leuven: Department of Orientalistiek, 1979.
—, "Marriage and Divorce in the Judaism of the Persian Period." *Transeuph* 4 (1991): 63–71.
—, " "קָנָהIn *TDOT* 13 (2004), 58–65.
Lipschits, Oded. "The History of the Benjamin Region under Babylonian Rule." *Tel Aviv* 26 (1999): 155–90.
—, *The Fall and Rise of Jerusalem: Judah Under Babylonian Rule.* Winona Lake/Indiana: Eisenbrauns, 2005.

Liverani, Mario. *Oltre la Bibbia: Storia Antica di Israele.* 2nd ed., Rome & Bari: Editori Laterza, 2004.
Lloyd, Alan. "The Inscription of Udjahorresnet: A Collaborator's Testament." *JEA* 68 (1982): 166–80.
Lohfink, Norbert. "Die Priesterschrift in der Geschichte." *VTSup* 29 (1978): 189–225.
Long, Anthony Arthur. *Hellenistic Philosophy: Stoics, Epicureans, Sceptics.* 2nd ed., Berkeley & Los Angeles: University of California Press, 1986.
Longman III., Tremper. *Fictional Akkadian Autobiography: A Generic and Comparative Study.* Winona Lake/Indiana: Eisenbrauns, 1991.
MacIntyre, Alasdair. *A Short History of Ethics: A History of Moral Philosophy from the Homeric Age to the Twentieth Century.* New York: Macmillan, 1966.
Malamat, Abraham. "The Last Wars of the Kingdom of Judah." *JNES* 9 (1950): 218–27.
Mannheim, Karl. *Ideologie und Utopie.* Frankfurt am Main: Vittorio Klostermann, 1995 [1929] = *Ideology and Utopia*, transl. by Louis Worth and Edward Shils. New York: Harcourt, Brace, Jovanovich, 1936.
Marcus, Robert. *Josephus: Jewish Antiquities Books IX-XI.* Cambridge/Mass: Harvard, 1937.
Mason, Steve. "Jews, Judaeans, Judaizing, Judaism: Problems of Categorization in Ancient History." *JSJ* 38 (2007): 457–512.
McEvenue, Sean. "The Political Structure of Judah from Cyrus to Nehemiah." *CBQ* 43 (1981): 353–64.
McEwan, Gilbert. *Priest and Temple in Hellenistic Babylonia.* Wiesbaden: Franz Steiner Verlag, 1981.
McKane, William. *Proverbs: A New Approach.* Philadelphia: Westminster, 1970.
Meek, Theophile James. "Aaronites and Zadokites." *AJSLL* 45 (1929): 149–66.
Meiggs, Russell and David Lewis (ed.). *A Selection of Greek Historical Inscriptions to the End of the Fifth Century BC.* Oxford: Oxford University Press, 1980.
Meinhold, Arndt. "Die Gattung der Josephsgeschichte und des Estherbuches: Diasporanovellen II." *ZAW* 88 (1976): 72–93.
Mendelsohn, Isaac. "Guilds in Ancient Palestine." *BASOR* 80 (1940): 1–21.
—, "Guilds in Babylon and Assyria." *JAOS* 60 (1940): 68–72.
Menes, Abram. "Tempel und Synagoge." *ZAW* 50 (1932): 268–76.
Meyer, Eduard. *Die Entstehung des Judentums: Eine historische Untersuchung.* Tübingen: Niemeyer, 1896; reprint: Hildesheim: Georg Olms, 1965.
Micheel, Rosemarie. *Die Seher- und Propheten-Überlieferungen in der Chronik.* Frankfurt am Main: Lang, 1983.
Millard, Alan. "The Practice of Writing in Ancient Israel." *BA* 35 (1972): 98–112.
—, "An Assessment of the Evidence for Writing in Ancient Israel." In *Biblical Archaeology Today*, ed. by Avraham Biran, 301–12. Jerusalem: Magnes Press, 1985.
Miller, Maxwell and John Hayes. *Ancient Israel: A New History of Israelite Society.* Sheffield: Sheffield Academic Press, 1986.
Misch, Georg. *Geschichte der Autobiographie.* Vol. 1, *Das Altertum.* Leipzig & Berlin, 1907 = *A History of Autobiography in Antiquity.* Vol. 1, transl. by Ernest Dickes. Cambridge/Mass: Harvard University Press, 1951.
Momigliano, Arnaldo. "Fattori Orientali della Storiografia Ebraica Post-Esilica e della Storiografia Greca." *Accademia Nazionale dei Lincei* 76 (1966): 137–46.
—, *The Development of Greek Biography.* 2nd ed., Cambridge/Mass: Harvard University Press, 1993.

Moore, George Foot. *A Critical and Exegetical Commentary on Judges.* Edinburgh: T. & T. Clark, 1895.
Moulton, James. *Early Zoroastrianism: The Origins, the Prophet, the Magi.* Amsterdam: Philo Press, 1972 [1913].
Mowinckel, Sigmund. "Die vorderasiatischen Königs- und Fürsteninschriften." In *EYXAPIΣTHPION: Studien zur Religion und Literatur des Alten und Neuen Testaments. Festschrift für Hermann Gunkel.* Vol.1, *Zur Religion und Literatur des Alten Testaments,* ed. by Hans Schmidt, 278–322. Göttingen: Vandenhoeck & Ruprecht, 1923.
—, *He That Cometh: The Messiah Concept in the Old Testament and Later Judaism.* Oxford: Blackwell, 1959.
—, *Studien zu dem Buche Esra-Nehemia.* Vol. 2. Oslo: Universitetsforlaget, 1964.
—, *The Psalms in Israel's Worship.* Vol. 2. New York & Nashville: Abingdon, 1967.
Murphy-O'Connor, Jerome. "An Essene Missionary Document? CD II,14–VI,1." *RB* 77 (1970): 201–29.
—, "A Literary Analysis of Damascus Document VI,2–VIII,3." *RB* 78 (1971): 210–32.
—, "A Literary Analysis of Damascus Document XIX,33–XX,34." *RB* 79 (1972): 544–64.
—, "The Essenes and their History." *RB* 81 (1974): 215–44.
—, "The Damascus Document Revisited." *RB* 92 (1985): 223–46.
—, "Damascus" In *EDSS* 1, 165–66.
Myers, Jacob. *I Chronicles: A New Translation with Introduction and Commentary.* Garden City/New York: Doubleday, 1965.
Newsome, James. "Towards a New Understanding of the Chronicler and His Purpose." *JBL* 94 (1975): 201–17.
Nicholson, Ernest. *Preaching to the Exiles: A Study of the Prose Tradition in the Book of Jeremiah.* Oxford: Blackwell, 1970.
Niemeier, Wolf-Dietrich. "Archaic Greeks in the Orient: Textual and Archaeological Evidence." *BASOR* 322 (2001): 11–32.
Nilsen, Tina Dykesteen. "The Creation of Darkness and Evil (Isaiah 45:6C–7)." *RB* 115 (2008): 5–25.
North, Francis Sprarling. "Aaron's Rise in Prestige." *ZAW* 66 (1954): 191–99.
Noth, Martin. *The History of Israel.* London: A. & C. Black, 1960.
—, *Gesammelte Studien zum Alten Testament.* $2^{nd.}$ed., Munich: Kaiser, 1960 = *The Laws in the Pentateuch and Other Essays,* tranl. by Norman Porteous. Edinburgh & London: Oliver & Boyd, 1968.
O'Connor, David. "The Social and Economic Organization of Ancient Egyptian Temples." In *Civilizations of the Ancient Near East.* Vol. 1, ed. by Jack Sasson, 319–329. New York: Charles Scribner's Sons, 1995.
Oelsner, Joachim. "Zwischen Xerxes und Alexander: Babylonische Rechtsurkunden und Wirtschaftstexte aus der späten Achämenidenzeit." *Die Welt des Orients* 8 (1976): 310–18.
Olmstead, Albert. "Darius as Lawgiver." *AJSL* 51 (1934/1935): 247–49.
—, *A History of the Persian Empire.* Chicago: University Press, 1940.
Oppenheim, Leo. *Ancient Mesopotamia: Portrait of a Dead Civilization.* Chicago: University of Chicago Press, 1964.
—, "The Babylonian Evidence of Achaemenian Rule in Mesopotamia." In *CHI* 2, 529–87.
Pascal, Roy. *Design and Truth in Autobiography.* London: Routledge & Kegan Paul, 1960.

Pearce, Laurie. "New Evidence for Judeans in Babylonia." In *Judah and the Judeans in the Persian Period*, ed. by Oded Lipschits and Manfred Oeming, 399–411. Winona Lake/Indiana: Eisenbrauns, 2006.
——, "'Judean': A Special Status in Neo-Babylonian and Achemenid Babylonia?" In *Judah and the Judeans in the Achaemenid Period*, ed. by Oded Lipschits, Gary Neil Knoppers, Manfred Oeming, 267–77. Winona Lake/Indiana: Eisenbrauns, 2011.
Petersen, David. *Late Israelite Prophecy: Studies in Deutero-Prophetic Literature and in Chronicles*. Missoula/Montana: Scholars Press, 1977.
——, *The Roles of Israel's Prophets*. Sheffield: JSOT Press, 1981.
Pfeiffer, Egon. "Die Disputationsworte im Buche Maleachi." *EvTh* 19 (1959): 546–68.
Pfeiffer, Robert. *Introduction to the Old Testament*. London: Adam & Charles Black, 1952.
Pongratz-Leisten, Beate. *Ina šulmi īrub: Die Kulttopographie und ideologische Programmatik der akītu-Prozession in Babylonien und Assyrien im 1. Jahrtausend v. Chr.* Mainz: Phillip von Zabern Verlag, 1994.
Porten, Berkeley. *Archives from Elephantine: The Life of an Ancient Jewish Military Colony*. Berkeley & Los Angeles: University of California Press, 1968.
——, "The Religion of the Jews of Elephantine in Light of the Hermopolis Papyri." *JNES* 28 (1969): 116–21.
——, and Ada Yardeni, *Textbook of Aramaic Documents from Ancient Egypt. Vol 2, Contracts*. Jerusalem: Israel Academy of Sciences and Humanities, 1989.
Posener, George. *La Première Domination Perse en Egypte*. Cairo: IFAO, 1936.
Postgate, Nicholas. "The Role of the Temple in the Mesopotamian Secular Community." In *Man, Settlement and Urbanism*, ed. by Peter Ucko, Ruth Tringham and Geoffrey Dimbleby, 811–25. London: Duckworth, 1972.
Rabinowitz, Isaac. "A Reconsideration of 'Damascus' and '390 Years' in the 'Damascus' ('Zadokite') Fragments." *JBL* 73 (1954): 11–35.
Rappaport, Uriel. "Numismatics." In *CHJ* 1, 25–29.
Redford, Donald. *A Study of the Biblical Story of Joseph (Genesis 37–50)*. Leiden: Brill, 1970.
Reich, Nathaniel. "The Codification of the Egyptian Laws by Darius and the Origin of the 'Demotic Chronicle'." *Mizraim* 1 (1933): 178–85.
Renan, Ernest. *Vie de Jésus*. 13th ed., Paris: Calmann-Lévy, 1862. = *The Life of Jesus*, Transl. unknown. London: Watts & Co., 1935.
——, *Histoire du Peuple d'Israël*. Paris: Calman-Lévy, 1893.
Rendtorff, Rolf. "Esra und das Gesetz." *ZAW* 96 (1984): 165–84.
Rist, John Michael. *Stoic Philosophy*. Cambridge: Cambridge University Press, 1969.
Robert, André. "Les Attaches Littéraires Bbibliques de Prov I-IX." *RB* 43 (1934): 42–68.172–204.374–384; *RB* 44 (1935): 344–435.502–525.
Robert, Louis. "Une Nouvelle Inscription Grecque de Sardes: Réglement de l'Autorité Perse Relativ à un Culte de Zeus." *CRAI* (1976): 303–31.
Robertson, John. "The Social and Economic Organization of Mesopotamian Temples." In *Civilizations of the Ancient Near East*. Vol. 1, ed. by Jack Sasson, 443–54. New York: Charles Scribner's Sons, 1995.
Robinson, James. "'Logoi Sophon': On the Gattung of Q." In *Trajectories through Early Christianity*, ed. by James Robinson and Helmut Koester, 71–113. Philadelphia: Fortress Press, 1971.

Rofé, Alexander. "Isaiah 66:1–4: Judean Sects in the Persian Period as Viewed by Trito-Isaiah." In *Biblical and Related Studies Presented to Samuel Iwry*, ed. by Ann Kort and Scott Morschauser, 205–17. Winona Lake/Indiana: Eisenbrauns, 1985.
Rogerson, John. *Old Testament Criticism in the Nineteenth Century: England and Germany.* London: SPCK, 1984.
Röllig, Wolfgang. "Bethel." In *DDD²*, 173–75.
Römer, Thomas. *La Première Histoire d'Israël: L'Ecole Deutéronomiste.* Fribourg: Labor et Fides, 2006.
Roth, Martha. *Law Collections from Mesopotamia and Asia Minor.* Atlanta: Scholars Press, 1995.
Rudolph, Wilhelm. *Esra und Nehemia samt 3. Esra.* Tübingen: Mohr Siebeck, 1949.
—, *Chronikbücher.* Tübingen: Mohr Siebeck, 1955.
—, *Jeremia.* 3rd ed., Tübingen: Mohr Siebeck, 1968.
—, *Haggai, Sacharja 1–8, Sacharja 9–14, Maleachi.* Gütersloh: Gerd Mohn, 1976.
San Nicolò, Mariano. *Beiträge zu einer Prosopographie neubabylonischer Beamten der Zivil- und Tempelverwaltung.* Munich: Bayerische Akademie der Wissenschaften, 1941.
Sancisi-Weerdenburg, Heleen. "Darius I and the Persian Empire" In *Civilizations of the Ancient Near East.* Vol. 2, ed. by Jack Sasson, 1035–50. New York: Charles Scribner's Sons, 1995.
Sanders, James. *Discoveries in the Judaean Desert of Jordan.* Vol. 4, *The Psalms Scroll of Qumran Cave 11 (11QPs^a).* Oxford: Oxford University Press, 1965.
Sarkisian, Gagik. "City Land in Seleucid Babylonia." In *Ancient Mesopotamia: Socio-Economic History. A Collection of Studies by Soviet Scholars*, ed. by Igor Diakonoff, 312–31. Moscow: Nauka, 1969.
Schaeder, Hans Heinrich. *Esra der Schreiber: Beiträge zur Historischen Theologie.* Vol. 5. Tübingen: Mohr Siebeck, 1930.
Schluchter, Wolfgang (ed.). *Max Webers Studie über das Antike Judentum: Interpretation und Kritik.* Frankfurt am Main: Suhrkamp, 1981.
Schmidt, Hans. *Das Gebet des Angeklagten im Alten Testament.* Berlin: Walter de Gruyter, 1928.
Schniedewind, William. *The Word of God in Transition: From Prophet to Exegete in the Second Temple Period.* Sheffield: Sheffield Academic Press, 1995.
Scholes, Robert and Robert Kellogg. *The Nature of Narrative.* Oxford: Oxford University Press, 1966.
Schottroff, Willy: *"Gedenken" im Alten Orient und im Alten Testament.* Neukirchen-Vluyn: Neukirchener Verlag, 1964.
Schürer, Emil. *The History of Jewish Palestine in the Age of Jesus Christ (175 BC–AD 135): A New English Version.* Vol. 2 and 3/1, revised and ed. by Geza Vermes, Fergus Millar, Matthew Black and Martin Goodman Edinburgh: T. & T. Clark, 1986.
Schwartz, Martin. "The Old Eastern Iranian World View according to the Avesta." In *CHI* 2, 640–663.
—, "The Religion of Achaemenian Iran." In *CHI* 2, 664–97.
Schwiderski, Dirk. *Handbuch des nordwestsemitischen Briefformulars: Ein Beitrag zur Eichtheitsfrage der aramäischen Briefe des Esrabuches.* Berlin: Walter de Gruyter, 2000.
Shiloh, Yigal. "The Population of Iron Age Palestine in the Light of a Sample Analysis of Urban Plans, Areas, and Population Density." *BASOR* 239 (1980): 25–35.

Sinclair, Lawrence. "Bethel Pottery of the Sixth Century BC." In *The Excavation at Bethel (1934–1960)*, ed. by James Kelso, 70–76. Cambridge/Mass: ASOR, 1968.
Ska, Jean-Louis. "Un nouveau Wellhausen?" *Bib* 72 (1991): 261–62.
Smart, James. *History and Theology in Second Isaiah*. Philadelphia: Westminster, 1965.
Smith, John Merlin Powis. *A Critical and Exegetical Commentary on Haggai, Zechariah, Malachi and Jonah*. Edinburgh: T. & T. Clark, 1912.
Smith, Morton. "The Dead Sea Sect in Relation to Ancient Judaism." *NTS* 7 (1960/61): 347–60.
—, "II Isaiah and the Persians." *JAOS* 83 (1963): 415–21.
—, *Palestinian Parties and Politics that Shaped the Old Testament*. New York: Columbia University Press, 1971.
—, "Jewish Religious Life in the Persian Period." In *CHJ* 1, 230–33.
Smith, Ralph. *Micah-Malachi*. Waco/Texas: Word Publications, 1984.
Smith, Sydney. *Isaiah Chapters XL–LV: Literary Criticism and History*. London: Humphrey Milford; Oxford: Oxford University Press, 1944.
—, *The Statue of Idri-mi*. London: British Institute of Archaeology in Ankara, 1945.
Snijders, Lambertus Arie. "The Meaning of *zar* in the Old Testament." *OTS* 10 (1954): 103–4.
—, " "זָר/זוּר In *TDOT* 4 (1981), 52–58.
Soggin, Jan Alberto. *Introduction to the Old Testament from its Origins to the Closing of the Alexandrian Canon*. Philadelphia: Westminster, 1976.
—, *Judges: A Commentary*. Philadelphia: Westminster, 1981.
Sokolowski, Franciszek. *Lois Sacrées d'Asie Mineure*. Paris: Editions de Boccard, 1955.
Sommer, Benjamin. "The Babylonian Akitu Festival: Rectifying the King or Renewing the Cosmos?" *JANES* 27 (2000): 81–95.
Speiser, Ephraim Avigdor. "Unrecognized Dedication." *IEJ* 13 (1963): 69–73.
Spiegelberg, Wilhelm. *Die sogenannte demotische Chronik des pap. 215 der Bibliotèque Nationale zu Paris*. Leipzig: Hinrichs, 1914.
Stager, Lawrence. "The Archaeology of the Family." *BASOR* 260 (1985): 1–35.
Stark, Rodney and William Sims Bainbridge. *The Future of Religion: Secularization, Revival and Cult Formation*. Berkeley & Los Angeles: University of California, 1985.
Stausberg, Michael. *Die Religion Zarathusthras: Geschichte – Gegenwart – Rituale*. Vol. 1. Stuttgart: Kohlhammer, 2002.
Steck, Odil Hannes. "Israel und Zion: Zum Problem konzeptioneller Einheit und literarischer Schichtung in Deuterojesaja." In *Gottesknecht und Zion: Gesammelte Aufsätze zu Deuterojesaja*, 173–207. Tübingen: Mohr Siebeck, 1992.
Stern, Ephraim. *Archaeology of the Land of the Bible*. Vol. 2, *The Assyrian, Babylonian, and Persian Periods (732–332 B.C.E.)*. Garden City/New York: Doubleday, 2001.
—, *Material Culture of the Land of the Bible in the Persian Period*. Warminster: Aris & Philips, 1982.
—, "The Archaeology of Persian Palestine." In *CHJ* 1, 88–114.
Stern, Menahem. *Greek and Latin Authors on Jews and Judaism*. Vol. 1, *From Herodotus to Plutarch*. Jerusalem: The Israel Academy of Sciences and Humanities, 1976.
Stolper, Matthew. *Entrepreneurs and Empire: The Murašû Archive, the Murašû Firm and Persian Rule in Babylon*. Istanbul: Nederlands Historisch-Archaeologisch Instituut te Istanbul, 1985.
—, "The Governor of Across-the-River in 486 BC." *JNES* 48 (1985): 283–305.

Tal, Oren. "Negotiating Identity in an International Context under Achaemenid Rule: The Indigenous Coinages of Persian-Period Palestine as an Allegory." In *Judah and the Judeans in the Achaemenid Period*, ed. by Oded Lipschits, Gary Neil Knoppers and Manfred Oeming, 445–59. Winona Lake/Indiana: Eisenbrauns, 2011.

Talmon, Shemaryahu. "Jüdische Sektenbildung in der Frühzeit der Periode des Zweiten Tempels: Ein Nachtrag zu Max Webers Studie über das antike Judentum." In *Max Webers Sicht des antiken Christentums: Interpretation und Kritik*, ed. by Wolfgang Schluchter, 233–280. Frankfurt am Main: Suhrkamp, 1985.

—, "The Emergence of Jewish Sectarianism in the Early Second Temple Period." In *King, Cult and Calendar in Ancient Israel: Collected Studies*, 165–201. Jerusalem: Magnes, 1986.

—, "The Internal Diversification of Judaism in the Early Second Temple Period." In *Jewish Civilization in the Hellenistic-Roman Period*, ed. by Shemaryahu Talmon, 16–43. Philadelphia: Trinity Press, 1991.

Talon, Philippe (ed.). *The Standard Babylonian Creation Myth Enûma Eliš*. Helsinki: Helsinki University Press, 2005.

Tcherikover, Viktor. *Hellenistic Civilization and the Jews*. New York: Atheneum, 1975.

Throntveit, Mark. *When Kings Speak: Royal Speech and Royal Prayer in Chronicles*. Atlanta: Scholars Press, 1987.

Torrey, Charles Cutler. *The Composition and Historical Value of Ezra-Nehemiah*. Gießen: J. Ricker, 1896.

—, "The Prophecy of Malachi." *JBL* 17 (1898): 1–15.

—, *Ezra Studies*. New York: Ktav, 1970 [1910].

—, *The Second Isaiah: A New Interpretation*. New York: Charles Scribner's Sons, 1928.

—, *The Chronicler's History of Israel: Chronicles-Ezra-Nehemiah Restored to its Original Form*. New Haven: Yale, 1954.

Toy, Crawford Howell. *A Critical and Exegetical Commentary on the Book of Proverbs*. Edinburgh: T. & T. Clark, 1899.

Troeltsch, Ernst. *Die Soziallehren der christlichen Kirchen und Gruppen*. Stuttgart: Mohr Siebeck, 1994 [1912] = *The Social Teaching of the Christian Churches*. Vol. 1, transl. by Olive Wyon. Louisville: Westminster John Knox Press, 1992.

VanderKam, James. "Ahiqar, Book of." In *ABD* 1, 119–20. Garden City/New York: Doubleday, 1992.

—, *From Joshua to Caiphas: High Priests after the Exile*. Minneapolis: Fortress Press, 2004.

Van der Spek, Robartus Johannes. "Did Cyrus the Great Introduce a New Policy towards Subdued Nations?" *Persica* 10 (1982): 278–83.

Van der Toorn, Karel. "The Babylonian New Year Festival." *VTSup* 43 (1991): 333–44.

—, *Scribal Culture and the Making of the Hebrew Bible*. Cambridge/Mass: Harvard University Press, 2008.

Van Seters, John. *In Search of History: Historiography in the Ancient World and the Origins of Biblical History*. New Haven: Yale University Press, 1993.

Vatke, Wilhelm. *Die Religion des Alten Testament nach den kanonischen Büchern*. Berlin: G. Bethge,1885.

Vincent, Jean. *Studien zur literarischen Eigenart und zur geistigen Heimat von Jesaja Kap. 40–55*. Frankfurt am Main: Peter Lang, 1977.

Vink, Jacobus Gerhardus. "The Date and Origin of the Priestly Code in the Old Testament." *OTS* 15 (1969): 1–144.

Volz, Paul. *Der Prophet Jeremia*. Leipzig: Deichert, 1928.
Von Rad, Gerhard. *Studies in Deuteronomy*. London: SCM, 1953.
—, *Theologie des Alten Testaments*. Vol.1. Munich: Kaiser, 1957. = *Old Testament Theology*. Vol. 1, transl. by David Muir Gibson Stalker. New York: Harper & Row, 1962.
—, "Die levitische Predigt in den Büchern der Chronik." In *Gesammelte Studien zum Alten Testament*, 248–61. Munich: Kaiser, 1961. = "The Levitical Sermon in I and II Chronicles." In *The Problem of the Hexateuch and Other Essays*, transl. by Trueman Dicken, 267–80. Edinburgh & London: Oliver & Boyd, 1966.
—, "Die Nehemia-Denkschrift." *ZAW* 76 (1964): 176–87.
—, *Der heilige Krieg im alten Israel*. 3rd ed., Zürich: Zollikon, 1958. = *Holy War in Ancient Israel*, transl. by Marva Dawn and John Howard Yoder. Grand Rapids: Eerdmans, 1991.
Walker, Christopher. "A Recently Identified Fragment of the Cyrus Cylinder." *Iran* 10 (1972): 158–159.
Wallis, Gerhard. "Wesen und Struktur der Botschaft Maleachis." In *Das Ferne und Nahe Wort: Festschrift Leonhard Rost*, ed. by Fritz Maass, 229–37. Berlin: Töpelmann, 1967.
Walser, Gerold: "Beiträge zur Achämenidengeschichte." In *Beiträge zur Achämenidengeschichte*, ed. by Walther Hinz und Gerold Walser, 5–14. Wiesbaden: Steiner, 1972.
Weber, Max. *Die Wirtschaftsethik der Weltreligionen: Das Antike Judentum. Schriften und Reden 1911–1920*, Max Weber Gesamtausgabe I/21.2, ed. by Eckart Otto. Tübingen: Mohr Siebeck, 2005.
—, *Economy and Society: An Outline of Interpretative Sociology*. 2 Vol., transl. and ed. by Guenther Roth and Claus Wittich. Berkeley & Los Angeles: University of California Press, 1978.
—, *Ancient Judaism*, transl. and ed. by Hans Gerth and Don Martindale. New York: The Free Press, 1952.
Weinberg, Joel. "Demographische Notizen zur Geschichte der nachexilischen Gemeinde in Juda." *Klio* 34 (1972): 45–59.
—, "Probleme der sozialökonomischen Struktur Judäas vom 6. Jahrhundert v.u.Z. bis zum 1. Jahrhundert u.Z.: Zu einigen wirtschaftshistorischen Untersuchungen von Heinz Kreissig." *Jahrbuch für Wirtschaftsgeschichte* 1 (1973): 237–51.
—, "Das BÊIT ĀBÔT im 6.–4. Jh. v.u.Z." *VT* 23 (1973): 400–14.
—, "Der ʻam hāʼāres des 6.–4. Jh. v.u.Z." *Klio* 56 (1974): 235–335.
—, "Raby i drugije kategorii zavisimych ljudej v palestinskoj graždansko-chramovoj obščine VI–IV vv.do n.e. [Die Sklaven und anderen Kategorien abhängiger Leute in der palästinischen Bürger-Tempel-Gemeinde des 6.–4. Jh. v.u.Z.]." *Palestinskij Sbornik* 25 (1974): 63–66.
—, "Netînîm und ʻSöhne der Sklaven Salomos im 6. -4. Jh. v.u.Z." *ZAW* 87 (1975): 355–71.
—, "Die Agrarverhältnisse in der Bürger-Tempel-Gemeinde der Achämenidenzeit." In *Wirtschaft und Gesellschaft im alten Vorderasien*, ed. by János Harmatta and György Komoróczy, 473–86. Budapest: Akadémiai Kiadó, 1976.
—, "Bemerkungen zum Problem ʻder Vorhellenismus im Vorderen Orientʼ." *Klio* 58 (1976): 5–20.
—, "Zentral- und Partikulargewalt im achämenidischen Reich." *Klio* 59 (1977): 25–43.
—, *Der Chronist in seiner Mitwelt*. Berlin: Walter de Gruyter, 1996.
Weinfeld, Moshe. *Normative and Sectarian Judaism in the Second Temple Period*. London & New York: T. & T. Clark, 2005.

—, "The Covenant of Grant in the Old Testament and Ancient Near East." *JAOS* 90 (1970): 184–203.
Weisberg. David. *Guild Structure and Political Allegiance in Early Achaemenid Mesopotamia*. New Haven: Yale University Press, 1967.
—, *Texts from the Time of Nebuchadnezzar*. New Haven: Yale University Press, 1980.
Welch, Adam. *The Work of the Chronicler: Its Purpose and its Date*. London: British Academy, 1939.
Wellhausen, Julius. "Israel." *Encyclopedia Britannica* 13 (9th ed., 1881): 396–431.
—, *Die Kleinen Propheten übersetzt, mit Noten*. Berlin: Reimer, 1893.
—, Rezension zu Eduard Meyer "Die Entstehung des Judentums." *Göttingische Gelehrte Anzeigen* 159 (1897): 89–97 = reprint in *Das Judentum im Zeitalter des Zweiten Tempels*, ed. by Reinhard Kratz, 6–22. Tübingen: Mohr Siebeck, 2004.
—, *Prolegomena zur Geschichte Israels*. Berlin: Reimer, 1878 = *Prolegomena to the History of Ancient Judaism*, transl. William Robertson Smith. New York: Meridian Library, 1957.
Wenning, Robert. "Attische Keramik in Palästina: Ein Zwischenbericht." *Transeuphratène* 2 (1990): 157–67.
Westermann, Claus. *Isaiah 40–66: A Commentary*. Philadelphia: Westminster, 1969.
—, *Genesis 1–11: A Commentary*, transl. by John Scullion. Minneapolis: Augsburg Fortress, 1984.
—, *Genesis 12–36: A Commentary*, transl. by John Scullion. Minneapolis: Augsburg Fortress, 1985.
Whybray, Norman. *Wisdom in Proverbs*. London: SCM, 1965.
—, *Isaiah 40–66*. London: Oliphants, 1975.
—, "The Joseph Story and Pentateuchal Criticism." *VT* 18 (1968): 522–28.
Wiesehöfer, Josef. "The Question of Religious Influence: The Case of Zoroastrianism, Judaism, and Christianity." *JAAR* 53/2 (1985): 201–35.
—, *Ancient Persia from 550 BC to 650 AD*. London & New York: I. B. Tauris, 1996.
Willi, Thomas. "Zwei Jahrzehnte Forschung an Chronik und Esra-Nehemia." *Theologische Rundschau* 67 (2002), 61–104.
—, *Die Chronik als Auslegung*. Göttingen: Vandenhoeck & Ruprecht, 1972.
Williamson, Hugh. "'The Sure Mercies of David': Subjective or Objective Genitive?" *JSS* 23 (1978): 31–49.
—, *1 and 2 Chronicles*. London: Marshall, Morgan & Scott, 1982.
—, "The Composition of Ezra i-vi." *JTS* 34 (1983): 1–30.
—, *Ezra, Nehemiah*. Waco/Texas: Word Books, 1985.
—, "Judah and the Jews." In *Achaemenid History XI: Studies in Persian History, Essays in Memory of David Lewis*, ed. by Maria Brosius and Amélie Kuhrt, 145–63. Leiden: Nederlands Instituut voor het Nabije Oosten, 1998.
Wilson, Bryan. *Sects and Society*. Berkeley: University of California Press, 1961.
—, "A Typology of Sects in a Dynamic and Comparative Perspective." *Archives de Sociologie de Religion* 16 (1963): 49–63.
—, *Patterns of Sectarianism: Organization and Ideology in Social and Religious Movements*. London: Heinemann, 1967.
—, *The Social Dimensions of Sectarianism: Sects and New Religious Movements in Contemporary Society*. Oxford: Clarendon, 1990.
Winston, David. "The Iranian Component in the Bible, Apocrypha, and Qumran: A Review of the Evidence" *HR* 5 (1966): 187–89.

Wiseman, Donald. *Chronicles of Chaldean Kings (626–556 BC)*. London: The British Museum, 1961.
Wolters, Al. "Sopiyyâ (Prov 31:27) as Hymnic Participle and Play on Sophia." *JBL* 104 (1985): 577–87.
Woolley, Leonard and Max Mallowan. *Ur Excavations IX: The Neo-Babylonian and Persian Periods*. London: British Museum; Philadelphia: University Museum, 1962.
Wyatt, Nicholas. "Astarte." In DDD^2, 109–14.
—, "Asherah." In *DDD*, 99–105.
Yamauchi, Edwin. "Two Reformers Compared: Solon of Athens and Nehemiah of Jerusalem." In *The Bible World: Essays in Honor of Cyrus Gordon*, ed. by Gary Rendsburg, Ruth Adler, Milton Arfa and Nathan Winter, 269–92. New York: Ktav, 1980.
—, *Persia and the Bible*. Grand Rapids: Baker Book House, 1990.
Young, Ian. "Israelite Literacy: Interpreting the Evidence. Part 1." *VT* 48 (1998): 239–53.
Younger, Lawson. "The Deportations of the Israelites." *JBL* 117 (1988): 201–27.
Zadok, Ran. *The Jews in Babylonia during the Chaldean and Achaemenid Periods*. Haifa: The University Press, 1979.
—, *The Pre-Hellenistic Israelite Anthroponomy and Prosopography*. Leuven: Peeters, 1988.
Zimmerli, Walther. *1 Moses 12–25: Abraham*. Zürich: Theologischer Verlag, 1976.
Zirker, Hans. "drk = potentia?" *BZ* 2 (1958): 291–94.
Zorn, Jeffrey. "Estimating the Population Size of Ancient Settlements: Methods, Problems, Solutions, and a Case Study." *BASOR* 295 (1994): 31–48.

Author Index

Ackroyd, P.   17, 32, 45, 127
Adams, R. M.   83
Ahlström, G. W.   175
Albertz, R.   146, 210
Albright, W. F.   48, 51, 77, 145, 173, 200–201, 215
Aletti, J-N.   172
Alt, A.   56, 71
Amusin, J. D.   64
Andrews, D. K.   65
Auscher, D.   90
Avigad, N.   72
Bainbridge, W. S.   197
Baines, J.   179
Baltzer, K.   12
Barag, D.   209
Barr, J.   25
Barstad, H. M.   15
Bauer, G. L.   22
Beaulieu, P-A   11, 26, 42
Bedford, P. R.   81
Begg, C.   155
Bellinger Jr., W.   157
Bengtston, H.   69, 70
Bentzen, A.   203
Berger, P-R.   25, 70
Berges, U.   6
Bertholet, A.   140
Beuken, W.   4
Bianchi, F.   150
Bickerman, E.   38, 63, 68, 72, 82, 89, 91, 154, 158, 166–167, 221
Black, J.   25
Black, M.   196
Blenkinsopp, J.   4–5, 9, 10, 12, 14, 18, 27, 38, 60, 73, 81, 99, 108, 111, 117, 137, 141, 147, 155–156, 157, 158, 166–167, 171–172, 180, 189, 191, 202, 209
Blidstein, H.   69
Blum, E.   18, 116
Boardman, J.   90
Boeker, H. J.   139
Bogaert, R.   62
Bordreuil, P.   4

Borger, R.   66
Boyce, M.   22, 24
Brettler, M. Z.   37
Briant, P.   20, 26, 63, 103, 105, 106, 107, 122, 124, 146, 209
Browne, L.   83
Burkert, W.   64
Caquot, A.   4
Cardascia, G.   82
Carr, D.   117
Carter, C.   38, 81
Carter, G. W.   22
Causse, A.   83
Chalcraft, D.   193
Chaumont, M-L.   106
Childs, B.   4
Clifford, R.   173
Clines, D.   115
Cocquerillat, D.   67
Cogan, M.   42
Cohen, S.   36–37
Coogan, M. D.   50
Cook, J. M.   108
Cornill, C. H.   16
Cowley, A.   34, 36, 63, 79, 98, 109–110
Crenshaw, J.   162
Cross, F. M.   16, 144
Crüsemann, F.   116, 199
Curtis, E. L.   145, 154
Dalglish, E.   50
Dandamaev, M.   13, 14, 20, 21, 25, 26, 62, 63, 67–68, 70, 82, 83, 103, 187
Davidson, S.   15–16
Davies, E. W.   175
Davies, J. K.   88
Davies, P.   214, 215–216, 218
Day, J.   170
de Pury, A.   8
Descat, R.   102
de Vaux, R.   63, 106
Dever, W.   48
DeVries, S. J.   152, 157
Diakonoff, I.   64
Dougherty, R. P.   68

Driver, S. R.   97
Duhm, B.   147
Eissfeldt, O.   17–18
Elliger, K.   12
Eph'al, I.   82
Eshel, H.   146
Falk, W.   175
Falkenstein, A.   67, 157
Fensham, F. C.   71
Fishbane, M.   115, 164
Fischer, J.   204
Fohrer, G.   17
Forschner, M.   94
Fox, M.   95, 160, 161–162
Frankfort, H.   28
Freedman, D. N.   144
Frei, P.   63, 103, 105, 106–107, 112
Frye, R. N.   25, 103
Galling, K.   69, 70, 71, 111, 145, 164
Gardiner, A.   109
Garrison, M.   24
Getty, R. J.   96
Glazier-McDonald, B.   175–176
Goldingay, J.   5, 12
Grabbe, L.   34, 120–121, 146, 147
Grätz, S.   125
Gray, G. B.   97
Gray, J.   58,
Greenberg, M.   31
Greenfield, J.   102
Haller, M.   9
Hallock, R.   24
Hallowan, M.   63
Hambert, P.   168
Harland, P.   196
Harris, W.   179
Hayes, J.   52
Heicksen, M.   38
Heidel, A.   28
Hengel, M.   95, 147, 150
Hermisson, H-J.   6, 162
Herrenschmidt, C.   22, 177
Hinz, W.   66
Höffken, P.   155
Humbach, H.   24
Hussey, E.   97
Hutchinson, J.   32

Hvidberg, F. F.   175
In der Smitten, W.   124, 128
Irwin, W. A.   97
Ishida, T.   164
Jacobsen, T.   28
Jacoby, F.   134
Jamieson-Drake, D.   162
Japhet, S.   32, 154, 187
Jones, D.   55
Judge, H. G.   55
Kaiser, W.   6
Kalimi, I.   145
Kaufmann, Y.   31
Kegler, J.   157
Kellermann, U.   114, 120, 123, 139, 141, 203
Kellogg, R.   132
Kelso, J.   48, 49, 50, 91
Kent, J. H.   66,
Kent, R.   20, 21, 102, 187
Kittel, R.   12, 23
Klein, J.   25
Klein, R.   157
Klein, S.   157
Kloppenberg, J.   196
Knibb, M.   214, 215
Knoppers, G.   34, 146
Koch, K.   63, 103, 106–107, 112, 114, 203
Knauf, E. A.   117
Kratz, R. G.   6, 122, 124, 128
Kraus, H.-J.   30
Kuhrt, A.   10, 13–14, 19, 22, 26, 103
Lambert, W.   25, 168
LeDéaut, R.   86
Lemaire, A.   162
Leuze, O.   71
Levine, B.   68
Lewis, D.   106, 128
Lewis, I.   182–183
Lichtheim, M.   169
Lindenberger, J.   98
Lipiński, E.   17, 46, 62
Lipschits, O.   38, 52, 53, 73
Liverani, M.   18, 44
Lloyd, A.   108
Lohfink, N.   18
Long, A. A.   87
Lukonin, V.   20, 25, 63, 68, 103

McKane, W.   160, 168, 173
MacIntyre, A.   87, 95
Madsen, A. A.   145, 154
Malamat, A.   52
Mannheim, K.   144, 148
Marcus, R.   146
Mason, S.   37
McEvenue, S.   71
McEwan, G.   67, 68
Meek, T. J.   55
Meiggs, R.   106, 128
Meinhold, A.   98
Mendelsohn, I.   80, 157
Menes, A.   83
Meyer, E.   111, 122
Micheel, R   157
Millard, A.   179
Miller, M.   52
Misch, G.   132
Momigliano, A.   37, 133–134
Moore, G. F.   58
Moulton, J.   22, 24
Mowinckel, S.   9
Murphy-O'Connor, J.   215–216
Myers, J.   145
Newsome, J.   144–145
Nicholson, E.   185
Niemeier, W-D.   90
Nilsen, T. D.   20
North, F. S.   55
Noth, M.   120
Oelsner, J.   66
Olmstead, A.   101
Oppenheim, L.   68, 102
Pascal, R.   132
Payne, D.   5, 12
Pearce, L.   82
Petersen, D.   145, 157, 180
Pfeiffer, E.   204
Pfeiffer, R.   123, 145
Pongratz-Leisten, B.   25–26
Porten, B.   46, 51
Posener, G.   107
Postgate, N.   62
Rabinowitz, I.   214, 216
Redford, D.   98
Renan, E.   23, 121

Rendtorff, R.   113–114
Rist, J. M.   87, 94
Robert, A.   161
Robert, J.   86
Robertson, J.   62
Robinson, J.   98
Rofé, A.   202
Rogerson, J.   30
Röllig, W.   50
Römer, T.   8
Root, M. C.   24
Rossoni, G.   150
Roth, M.   46
Rudolph, W.   137, 145, 205, 217
Sancisi-Weerdenburg, H.   22, 24–25
Sanders, J.   156
San Nicolo, M.   67
Sarkisian, G.   64
Schaeder, H. H.   113, 131
Schmidt, H.   139
Schniedewind, W.   157
Scholes, R.   132
Schottroff, W.   140
Schürer, E.   146, 208
Schwartz, M   20, 25, 177
Scullion, J.   16
Shiloh, Y.   38
Sinclair, L.   51
Ska, J-L.   118
Smart, J.   12
Smith, A.   32
Smith, M.   12, 23, 71, 83, 110, 115, 117, 137,
    160, 217
Smith, R.   175
Smith, S.   9, 10, 139
Smith, W. R.   31
Snijders, L. A.   168
Soggin, A.   18, 58
Sokolowski, F.   65, 107
Sommer, B.   26
Spiegelberg, W.   107, 113
Stager, L.   38
Stark, R.   197
Steck, O. H.   6
Stern, E.   60, 90
Stern, M.   61, 96, 147
Stolper, M.   66, 71

Tadmor, H.   42
Tal, O.   91
Talmon, S.   199–200
Talon, P.   28
Tcherikover, V.   146–147, 208
Throntveit, M.   145
Torrey, C. C.   12, 123, 135, 145, 175
Toy, C. H.   159
Troeltsch, E.   192
VanderKam, J.   98, 146, 208
van der Spek, R.   9–10
van der Toorn, K.   25, 99
Van Seters, J.   89, 139
Vatke, W.   30
Vermeylen, J.   6
Vermes, G.   209–210
Vincent, J.   6
Vink, J. G.   18
Volz, P.   185
von Rad, G.   31, 86, 140, 149, 184
Walker, C.   63
Wallis, G.   204
Weber, M.   1, 31, 41–42, 85, 116, 184, 193–196, 198–199

Weinberg, J.   66, 75–76, 77, 79–80, 145
Weinfeld, M.   196, 206
Weisberg, D.   66, 80, 157
Wellhausen, J.   60, 84, 114, 122, 154, 205
Wenning, R.   90
Westermann, C.   12, 16, 89, 181
Whybray, N.   4, 98, 160
Wiesehöfer, J.   25
Willi, T.   145, 157
Williamson, H. G. M.   4, 81, 138, 154, 180
Wilson, B.   197
Wilson, S.   196
Winston, D.   22
Wiseman, D.   33
Woolley, L.   63
Wolters, A.   91–92, 160
Wyatt, N.   170
Yamauchi, E.   82, 135
Yardeni, A.   25, 46
Young, I.   179
Younger, L.   42
Zadok, R.   38, 82
Zimmerli, W.   18

Biblical Index

Genesis

1–11   16
1:1–2:3   17
2:4–3:24   16
11:27–25:11   42
12:2   41
12:8   48
13:3   48
13:11–12   43
13:16   41
14:18–24   16
15:18   42
16:15–16   45
17:6, 16   18, 33
17:8   43
17:23, 26   43

23:1–20   43
23:3   42
23:4–6   43
26: 34–35   169
27:46–28:1   169
28:10–22   48
31:13   50
35:6   49
35:11   18, 33
37–50   98
38:1–2   45
39:2   98
41:33   98
41:39   98
41:45   45

Exodus

2:21–22   45
6:8   40
12:1–6   114
15:3   149
15:16   17
21:8   176
24:4   179
25–27   18

28:42   116
29   114
29:38–42   114
30:11–16   115
30:33   168
32:25–29   58
38:25–26   115
39:28   115

Leviticus

8   114
16:29   115
17:15   166
18:11–13   45
18:26   166

22:10–13   168
23:5–6   114
23:27–32   115
24:10–23   167
24:22   166

Numbers

1:51   168
4:3, 23, 30   115
8:24   115
9:3–5   114
9:6–14   114
9:9–13   153
12:1–9   166
12:1   45

15:38   36
18:20   182
21:14   149
25   169
25; 6–18   167
27:1–11   175
36:1–12   175
36:5–9   211

Deuteronomy

4:1–40   16
4:6   92
4:32   16
7:1–6   59
7:1–4   45, 164, 166
7:3   114, 164
9:15–21   59
12:1–4   59
12:29–31   59
17:17   164
17:18   130
23:2–9   163, 165, 198

23:3–4   114
23:4–7   211
23:4–6   45
25:5–10   175
25:5   167
27:5   17
27:6–7   114
29:28   92
30:11–14   92
31:9–13   130, 179
33:25–26   41

Joshua

1:8   179
1:16   35
7:2   48, 49
8:1–29   49
11:21   35
12:9   49
14:1   58
16:1–2   48

17:3–6   175
17:4   58
18:1   18
18:12–13   48–49
18:27–31   58
18:30   58
19:51   58, 59
21:1   58, 59

Judges

1:22–26   49
19–21   55
20–21   56

20:1   54
20:28   59

1 Samuel

2:27–36   59
7:5–10   54
10:3   49
10:17–25   54
10:25   179
16–30   155

16:18–22   156
18:10–11   156
18:20–29   166
19:8–10   156
25:39–42   166
27:10   35

2 Samuel

3:3–5   166
3:18   11
5:13   166
7:8–17   5
11:14   179

11–20   155
11:26–27   166
19:22   11
23:5   5
24:18–25   74

1 Kings

1–2   155
3:5–14   163
3:16–28   163
4:29–34   85
5:9–14   163
5:15–32   74
6:2   74
7:51   74
8:24   11
9:10–14   74
11:1   165

11:2   164
11:4   170
11:5–8   163
11:9–13   163
12:28–33   49
12:31   58
13:1–10   59
15:13   170
15:16–17   49
18:19   170
20:35–41   196

2 Kings

1:8   196
1:13   196
2:2–3:23   49
2:12   197
2:15   197
8:18   170
11:1–20   170
13:14   197
15:19–20   75

17:6   42
17:24–28   50
17:27–28   54
18:11   42
19:34   11
19:37   57
21:24   8
22:3–10   35
22:3   34

23   50
23:1–14   35
23:4–7   170
23:15–20   52
24:1   53
24:14–16   75–76, 77
24:17   53
25:7   5, 7

25:11–12   76
25:2   83
25:13–17   32
25:18–21   220
25:18   54
25:22–26   8, 34, 53
25:25   53
25:27–30   7

Isaiah

1:7   167
9:13   182
11:11   17
21:6–9   182
21:11–12   183
23:15–17   184
24–27   147
24:10   147
25:2   147
26:5   147
27:10   147
37:38   57
40–66   4
40–55   15
40–48   5, 9, 10, 15, 16, 17, 19, 22, 23, 25, 26
40–45   1, 12
40:13–14   28
40:22   19
41:1–5, 25–29   9
41:22–23   10
41:25–29   10
42:1–7   9
42:1–4   11, 12, 15
42:5   21
42:18–25   11
43:3, 14   26
44:7–8   10
44:26, 28   18
44:27   19
44:28–45:4   72
44:28   9
45:1   18
45:2–3   26

45:7   19–20, 29
45:13   9
45:18   21
45:20–21   27
46:1   27
47:1, 2–3   29
47:8–9   29
47:13   28
48:14–16   26
49–55   9, 15
50:4   10
51:9–11   15
52:8   182
55:1–5   4, 5, 12
56:9–12   181, 182
56:11   161
57:3–13   171
58:1–14   184
58:3–4   87
58:9   160
58:13–14   185
59:7   161
59:9–15   87
62:6–7   182
63:1–6   183
65:1–2   161
65:6   206
65:13–14   202
65:17–18   16
66:1–5   205
66:4   161
66:5   202
66:17   171
66:23   185

Jeremiah

1:1   134, 138
3:13   167
3:20   176
6:17   181
17:19–27   185
17:24–25   6
18:18   158
22:1–4   6
22:26   7
23:1–8   33
23:5–6   6, 190
25:11–12   184
27:5, 6   17
28:1–4   2
29:1–28   35
29:1   79
29:3   35
29:5–6   39
29:7   225
29:21–23   2, 183
30:8–9   6

32:6–15   52
33:15   190
35:6   197
36:32   130
37:11–16   52
39:10   83
40–48   5
40:7–12   34
40:7–8   53
40:13–16   53
41:1   7, 53
41:4–8   54
41:4–5   57
43:9   35
44:1   35
44:16–18   3, 33
49:28   44
52:16   83
52:28–30   77
52:29   77

Lamentations

1:4   54
2:6   54

4:20   11

Ezekiel

3:15   82
3:16–21   183
3:17   181
4:4–5   214
5:5–11   170
7:26   158
8:1   79
8:3, 5   170
10:18–19   41
11:14–21   83
11:14–15   174
11:16   40–41
11:22–25   41

16:12   167
20:1   79, 83
20:32   83
21:2, 7   184
27:7   89
27:13   89
28:13, 15   16
32:26   89
33:1–9   181
33:6–7   181
33:23–29   40, 41
33:24   40
34:23–24   6, 33

36:1–5   40
37:24–28   6
38:2–3   89
38:6   89
39:6   89

40:45–46   59
43:19   59
44:1–9   39
44:15   59
48:11   59–60

Joel

4:1–3, 6   147

Amos

1:1   134, 138
4:13   16
5:8–9   16
5:26–27   215
7:13   74

7:16   184
8:5   115
9:5–6   16
9:11–12   6, 33

Micah

5:1–4   6

2:6   184

Habakkuk

2:1–2   182

Haggai

1:1, 3   188
1:1, 12   59
1:6   87
1:8–11   87
1:12–14   73
1:13   181

1:14   71
2:1   188
2:3   74, 188
2:10–14   57, 189
2:20–23   189

Zechariah

1–8   184, 187, 188

1:12–13   181

1:12   184
1:14   181
1:16   181
1:17   181
2:9   181
2:10–11   190
2:10   70
2:14   181
3:1–10   59
3:8   190
4:6–7   190

4:9   73
6:8–14   59
6:9–14   73, 190
6:12–13   73, 190
7:1–23   184
7:1–7   56, 57
8:10   87
8:23   36
9:1–8   147
13:2–6   182

Malachi

1:2–5   203
1:6–2:9   203
1:6–7   151
1:8   203
2:4–9   204
2:7   158
2:8   151
2:10–16   176
2:10   16, 204

2:11, 14–15   161
2:12   176
2:13–16   87
2:14   176
3:1   203
3:5   204
3:13–21   203
3:13–15   204
3:16–18   204, 206

Psalms

42:4   4
44:21   168
74:1–7   54
74:2   17
78:54   17
81:10   168
89:13, 48   16

89:27–37   5
89:39   3, 5
104:30   16
115:2   4
121   3
148:5   16

Job

22:1–11   210
22:14   19
24:1–25   210

26:10   19
28:28   85
38–41   97

Proverbs

1–9   162, 167, 169, 171, 172, 176, 177
1:6   98
1:9   159
1:10–22:16   159
1:20–33   160
1:20   95, 171
1:24   160
1:28   160
1:29   162
2:5–8   162
2:5   162
2:14–15   176
2:16   167
2:17   176
2:18–19   171
2:21   173
2:22   176
3:18   171
4:13   171
5:3   167
5:7–14   173
5:8   171
5:15–20   176
5:17   167
5:20   167
6:1–19   159
6:22   168
6:24   167
6:29–35   168
7:4–5   173
7:5   167
7:6–27   171
7:10–12   172
7:10   168
7:16–17   171
7:19   168
8:1–21   160
8:13   162
8:15–16   163
8:22–31   95, 96, 160
8:22   17
8:27   19
9:7–12   159
9:10   162
9:13–18   173
9:14   171
11:15   167
14:10   167
22:17–24:22   159
22:17   98
22:10:22–23:11   97
24:23–34   159
30:1–9   159
30:10–33   159
30:1–6   98
30:1   138
31:1   138
31:10–31   95, 159
31:27   91

Ruth

1:16   211

Qoheleth

1:1   138
4:1–8   210
12:11   98
12:12–13   85

Esther

1:13, 15, 19   104
1:14   124
2:8, 12   104
3:12–15   104
3:14   124
4:3, 8   104
8:17   36

Daniel

1–6   210, 212
2:9   103
2:13, 15   103
3:2   103
6:9   104
7–12   212
9:1–2   213
9:24–27   213

Ezra

1–3   120
1:4, 6   75
1–6   74, 217
1:7–11   32
1:8   70
2:1–67   52, 218
2:1   71
2:2–19   39
2:41   185
2:20–35   52
2:43–58   68
2:59   82
2:64   39, 78
2:68–69   75
2:70   32
3:1–3   73
3:2   114
3:3   57
3:7–11   73
3:8   115
4:1–5   73, 75, 81
4:1–4   57
4:7–16   72
4:8–6:18   36, 186
4:11   124
4:12, 23   36
4:15   7
5:1–2   189
5:1, 5, 14   36
5:3–5   72
5:6   124
5:8   71, 74
5:14–15   32
5:14   70, 71, 207
6:1–12   104
6:1–5   72
6:4   74
6:5   32
6:7–8:14   36
6:7   79
6:8–10   74
6:13–15   187
6:14   189
6:19–22   81
6:20   71
7:1   217
7:8   217
7–10   120
7:1–10   130
7:1–8:36   129
7:1–5   130
7:6   113, 123
7:8   90
7:11–26   111, 119, 124–129
7:11   124
7:12   113

7:14   94, 111, 113
7:16   71, 75
7:17   124
7:19   32
7:21–22   124
7:25–26   111, 123
7:25   111, 113
7:26   103, 112, 113
7:27–28   130
8–10   120
8:3–14   39
8:15–20   225
8:15–19   130
8:15   82
8:24–30, 33–34   32
8:26–27   123
8:32–34   72, 150
8:35   81

9–10   44, 131, 202, 202, 211, 218, 219
9:1–2   57
9:2   202
9:1–15   165
9:2   46, 201, 202
9:3   220
9:4   165, 205, 219
9:11–12   114
10:1–44   130, 165
10:2–4   201
10:2   57
10:3   205, 219
10:3–5   201
10:6   165
10:8   55, 131, 166, 176, 200, 218
10:16   166
10:44   131, 211

Nehemiah

1–7   134
1:1   134, 217
1:1b-2:20   135
1:2   207
1:1–4   52
1:2   79
1:3   71
1:5–11a   135
1:6   135
1:11   135
2:1   217
2:5–8   105
2:9–10   137
2:9   72
2:12–16   143
2:12   140
2:16   36
2:17–20   137
2:19   44
3:1–32   135
3:9   72
3:12   72
3:14–18   72
3:33–4:26   135

3:33–37   137
3:34   36
3:36–37   142
3:38–4:3   137
4:6   79
4:11   137
5:1–19   135
5:1, 17   36, 79, 100
5:12   151
5:14–19   136, 142
5:14   142, 207
5:15   71
5:19   142
6:1–9   137
6:1–2   44
6:7   180
6:9   142
6:10–14   143, 180
6:14   180
6:15–16   137
6:15   137
6:18–19   177
7:2   142
7:5   140, 218

7:6–68   52, 136
7:6   71
7:7–24   39
7:44   185
7:46–60   68
7:66   39, 78
8   112
9:2   201
10:1–40   201
10:29   201, 217
10:30   218
10:31–32   57
10:31   114
10:32   115, 185
10:33–34   115
10:32   115
10:35   115
10:39   80
11:1   201
11:7   34
11:22–23   110
11:23   80
11:24   80, 110
11:25–36   78
11:30   78
12:10–11   217

12:22–26   217
12:26   135
12:27–43   135
12:44–47   151
12:44   80
13   134
13:3   200, 218
13:4–14   136, 142
13:4–9   46, 80, 150, 202
13:6   137
13:10–14   151
13:10–12   80
13:13   80
13:14   206
13:15–22   115, 136, 142, 185
13:17–19   80
13:22   80
13:23–31   136
13:23–27   143, 201
13:23   164
13:25   114, 165
13:28–29   177, 202, 208
13:29   151
13:31   142
13:35   115

1 Chronicles

4:22   154
4:33   154
4:41   154
5:1   154
5:26   42
5:27–41   60, 152
6:1–15   152
6:16–23   152, 185
6:34–38   152
7:5   154
7:28   48
8:17   34
9:1   154
9:7–8   34
12:16–19   149, 156
13:5   150
13:1–14   148

15:2   152
15:14–15   152
15:15   152
15:16–24   152
15:22   156
15:27   156
16:4–36   152
18:8   149
18:10–11   149
21:5   149
21:18–22:1   73
21:5–6   148
22:12–13   93
22–29   84
23:2–5   152, 185
23:6–24   152
23:24–27   115

23:26   152
24:6   157
25:1–3   152
25:1–8   149, 156, 185
25:5   186, 186

26:32   113
27:1–15   148
28:11–19   152, 155
29:29   98, 154

2 Chronicles

6:42   4
9:26   150
9:29   98, 154
11:1   148
12:15   98, 99, 154
13:4–15   149
13:22   99, 154
14:8   148
14:11   148
14:12   148
16:11   154
17:7–9   158
17:13–19   148
19:4–11   158
19:8–11   112
19:10   113
20:1–23   148
13:30   186
20:14–17   156
20:17   148
20:23–24   148
20:34   99, 154
24:20–22   156
24:27   154
25:26   154
26:22   99, 154, 155
27:7   154

28:22–25   153
28:26   154
29–32   153
29:3–11   153
29:25–30   153
29:25   155
29:30   186, 186
29:34   153
30:1–27   153
30:22   153
32:20   155
32:24–26   155
32:31   155
32:32   99, 154, 155
34:13   131, 158
35:3   158
35:4   153, 155
35:15   153, 155, 186
35:20–24   156
35:20–27   7
35:25   155
35:27   154
36:8   154
36:12   155
36:20–21   32, 156
36:21–23   8, 82
36:22–23   150